peter l. gluck and partners
the modern impulse

peter l. gluck and partners
the modern impulse

edited by oscar riera ojeda
introduction by peter l. gluck
and joseph giovannini

ORO *editions*

contents

introduction

acknowledgments   by peter gluck

Architecture begins with clients who have the courage to "take the leap." Since we have never attempted to develop a particular look or identifiable style, our clients embark together with us in a design process without knowing where precisely it will lead. Since there are surely fewer good clients than good architects, we have been lucky to have found so many. You know who you are and we thank you.

Consultants, in particular mechanical and structural engineers, provide expertise that enhances both the conceptual and the technical quality of the buildings. We thank them for following our often complicated path from the earliest phases of the design process to the completion of construction, and beyond.

There are always those special craftsmen, tradesmen, and contractors for whom our projects become more than a job. Every successful building depends on these talented people, who put their heart and soul into the task of translating a design into three-dimensional form.

The entire process rests in large part on the shoulders of young architects. The continuous endeavor of creating, evaluating, remaking, and reevaluating goes on around the clock. It is their optimism, strength, and intellectual toughness that deserves ultimate credit for the work represented here.

OVERLAPPING SETS OF ATTRIBUTES

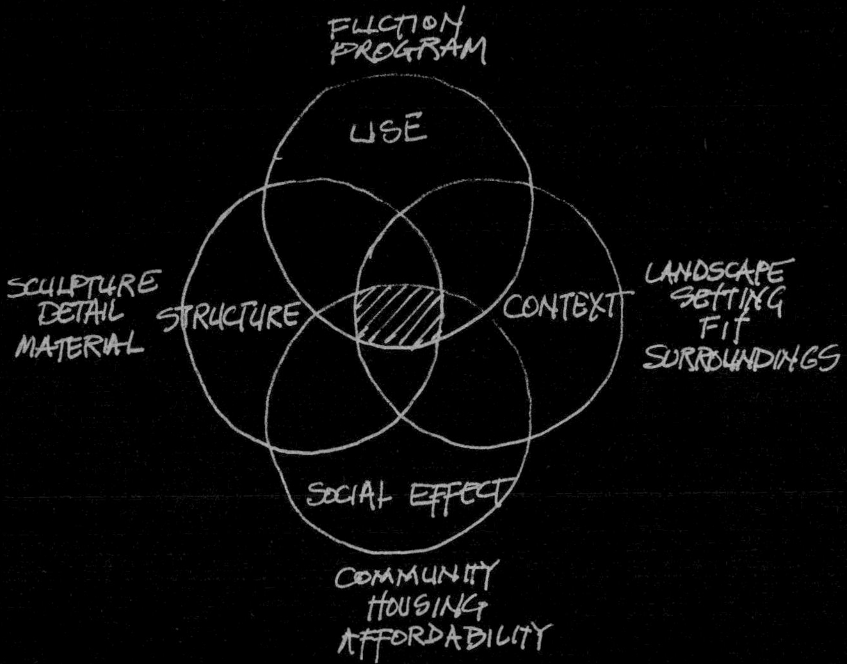

THE PERFECT DIAGRAM

MAXIMUM OVERLAP

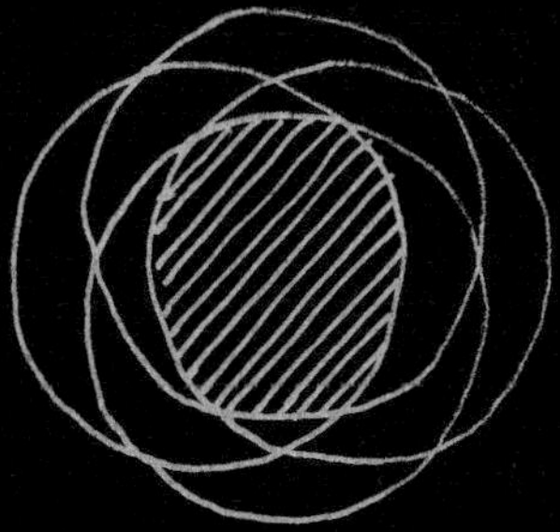

THE IDEAL
"THE MODERN PROJECT"
HEROIC
BUT - ARROGANT
FAILURE IMPLICIT
BUT STILL . . .

TENDENCIES

MINIMUM OVERLAP

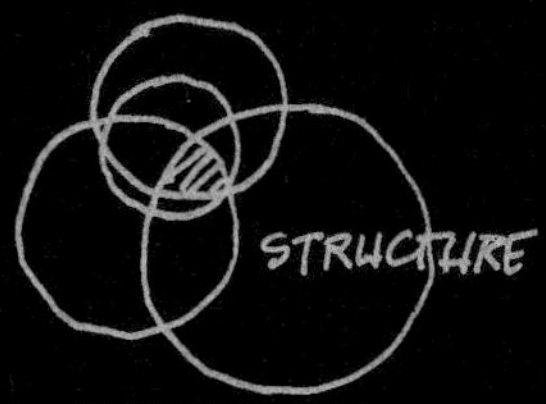

STRUCTURAL
EXPRESSIONISM

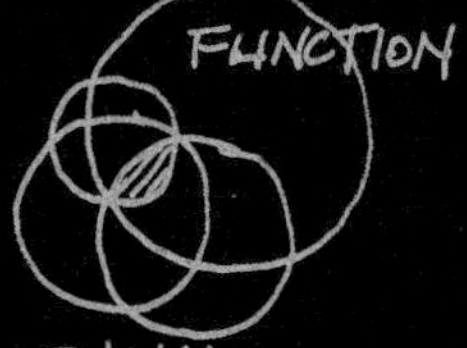

BANAL
CHEAP BUILDING
"RESPONSIBLE"

NOSTALGIA
SENTIMENT
CARTOON
THEMED

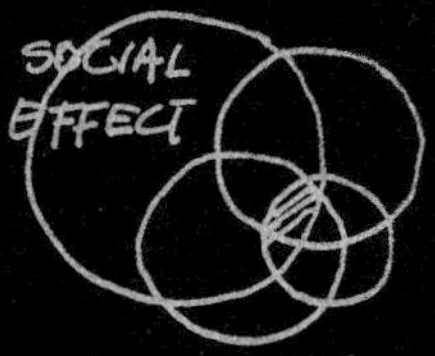

ORDINARY
REPETITIVE
"RESPONSIBLE"

the modern impulse by peter l. gluck

This is a book about architecture, which is to say, a book about buildings: in particular, buildings conceived and constructed from a perspective that I call "the modern impulse." By the modern impulse, I mean a set of principles that has animated the long history of architectural modernism and continues to inform the best buildings of our time. Although we may fail to realize them in practice, these principles represent the design imperatives appropriate to the age we live in and are therefore worth striving to fulfill.

A further contention here is that theoretical and aesthetic claims can best be evaluated when they are embodied in real buildings, which make demands on architecture that paper and computer schemes do not. It follows that the deeper the architect's engagement in the entire process – from the earliest phases of conceptualization to the final details of construction – the greater the chances for the realization of a design and the emergence of a good building. This book presents one architect's effort to embody the principles of the modern impulse in a variety of built forms, each with its own specificity of use and demand, constraint, and opportunity.

a very short history of modern architecture Modern architecture is one expression of the social, cultural, and technological temper of modernity, and like modernity, it has by now a long history of stirring manifestos, biting self-critiques, and widely varying forms. If Louis Sullivan, the Vienna Secession, and Catalan *modernismo* were avatars of the modern at the end of the 19th century; if Le Corbusier and the Bauhaus represented high modernism in the interwar years of the 20th century; if Mies van der Rohe and Louis Kahn were each differently modern during the booming postwar decades; if the postmodernism of the 1980s was in fact not *after* the modern but yet another critique *of* the modern; and if designers like Rem Koolhaas and Herzog and de Meuron heralded "new modernisms" at the turn of the millennium, then what possibly could the term "modern architecture" mean as it is applied to all these architects, and many more as well?

Obviously there is no such thing as a single modern style, or a singular manifestation of modernism as an architectural doctrine. But there are commonalities of consciousness that characterize the modern impulse over time. The most general is the commitment to newness, the conscious break with the past that virtually defines the modern temper. Unlike the Renaissance, which was named only later by critics of a subsequent age, modernity self-consciously announced itself as new, "modern," even revolutionary, from the moment of its inception. So the 19th-century moderns rejected the formulaic conventions of Beaux Arts classicism, and interwar high modernism abandoned ornament and tradition in favor of new technologies and social ideas. The aesthetic and technical achievements of postwar modernism were exemplified by projects like The Case Study Houses and the Seagram's Building. But when these gave way to the ossified vernacular of the much criticized International Style, along came the postmodernists to counter what they saw as the orthodoxies of canonical modernism. And after postmodernism met the same fate in the repetitive dilution of its pastiche in urban high-rises and suburban sprawl, innovative architects of the 1990s reached for a new vocabulary, new technologies, and new conceptions of the art and experience of the built environment. In this way, modern architecture always defined itself through a critique of the past and a leap toward a new and better future.

In making this leap, modern architecture, like modern society, did not jettison the past entirely but instead reworked parts of it dialectically to meet the demands of the present. Nor did the best architects strive for novelty for its own sake or in pursuit of a new or avant-garde style. Instead most were seeking solutions to the problems posed by their time, for which the existing practices no longer seemed adequate. But in another sense, one can say the best of modern architecture did favor the new, in that the effort to be *responsive* and *responsible* to the times meant that each project had to be conceived as if starting from zero. No formulas, typologies, or ready-made styles would suffice for the specificity of each context, budget, structure, and poetic opportunity. Indeed, whenever such formulaic or stylistic imposition occurred, it generally marked the banalization that provoked yet another critique and assertion of a different and better way of designing the modern.

the modern impulse The artistic inspiration and resolution of the modern impulse rests on four analytic attributes: use, structure, context, and social effect. Simpler to state than to realize, these criteria constitute the core of responsive and successfully realized design.

I begin with use, because above all a building has to work. The program – or function – has both a logic and a psychology to it, which is not so much a given as a challenge to the architect to interpret, together with the client, the possibilities that neither might have imagined based on the bare facts of the project (number of bedrooms, administrative offices, etc.). These imaginative horizons include the experiential sequencing of space, conceptual aspects such as separation between public and private functions, long-term considerations like maintenance, evolving needs, flexible use, and the rest. While it is no longer true that "form follows function" to the exclusion of other attributes, a building's use guides the form and is expressed by it, the more symbiotically the better.

Structure, the second attribute, includes materials, sculptural form, light, spatial organization, systems of construction – all the aspects that constitute the materiality of a building. The guiding words here are coherence and integrity, for even as form expresses function and the logic of construction, its inner imperative is to be true to itself. It is not an ad hoc solution to a series of design problems but a resolution of the analytic attributes in a way that makes aesthetic and experiential sense of their often conflicting demands.

Context is the third attribute, which does not mean that it comes after use and structure in order of importance or in the process of design. On the contrary, the challenge is to consider the attributes together like interlocking pieces in an artistic puzzle whose solution will not seem to favor any one part over another. Context refers to the site, the landscape or cityscape around it – not in terms of literal replication or mimicry but of sensitivity to scale, materials, and appropriateness. Context also includes more abstract considerations like the conceptual link to the larger fabric of American cities or even the context of modern architecture itself, which while dedicated to newness, now has a tradition of its own to which buildings may refer or defer but will in some way relate. No building stands alone; to pretend so is to let one attribute – often the sculptural form or the structure – run away with the design and violate the principle of appropriateness.

The fourth attribute, social effect or effectiveness, encompasses everything from cost and economy of means to the potential impact not only on the people who use the buildings but on the wider society as well. In earlier 20th-century modernism, architecture frequently sought to solve social problems, often based on visionary and utopian notions about urban planning, workers' housing, "machines for living," and other sometimes aggressively ideological schemes for improving (or "rationalizing") the way people lived and worked. More recently, architects have sought less to manipulate than to enable or facilitate socially positive effects of their buildings. Well-designed space, I think, can do something *for* people without narrowing their choices to a single approved use or prescribed organization for a particular room or space. The architect's social responsibility is to manage this challenge with acute attention to budget and to an economy of means that extends from inner city schools, which can provide spatial generosity at low cost, to expensive houses, whose opulence is no license for a gigantism that takes over the landscape. In urban designs the architect ought to respect the social uses and organization of city life so that the building both responds to and also improves the social fabric of which it is a part.

the perfect diagram Use, structure, context, social effect – ideally these attributes of the modern impulse would mutually determine and interact with one another throughout the design process and overlap, each aligned with the other, in the completed building. And they would be equally in evidence three, thirty, or even three hundred years later, long after the newness of the building had vanished. In fact, of course, this idealized alignment characterizes most of the great architecture of any period, from antiquity to the present, in different settings and cultures. It is the very definition of a "classic" that it be true to its time and place, which for us is modernity in its different cultural inflections.

The building's form would be both the inspiration and the resolution of the contending attributes, each of which would be legible because expressed by the form, its aesthetic integral to function, structure, context, and social meaning. Design legibility would correspond to the qualitative experience of living, working, or learning in the building. Conceived from and for a specific situation, the architecture would do more than meet its needs: it would enhance human experience and raise the threshold of aesthetic and social imagination.

It would, that is, if reality did not intervene, making it impossible for the attributes to overlap and align except in an imperfect and partial way.

But architects can at least make the effort to resolve the demands and opportunities of the different attributes, trying to integrate them and keep any one of them from dominating the whole. Whether formalism, functionalism, contextualism, or social utopianism, any attribute that becomes a doctrine rather than a response can destroy the alignment – and the building. That is why "style" is so often the enemy of good design.

Yet good design does not emerge merely from aligning the attributes, any more than a haiku is aesthetically moving because it follows the rule of 7-5-7 syllables per line. Architecture is a poetic as well as an analytic endeavor, and like most architects, I begin with form – sketching and re-sketching the sculptural forms of elevation and the schematic forms of section to see the way a building feels in its mass, shape, and proportion. But as the process continues, the attributes make their demands on the design, producing a constant back and forth between poetry and analysis in order to resolve the contradictions that arise every step of the way. When it works, the result is a design that is integral to itself and like nothing else but itself. In short, every building ought to look and also *be* different, precisely because it solves the problems posed by its particular needs. Following a set of principles like those embodied in the modern impulse produces not a recognizable "brand," but a distinctive artistic resolution that transcends the rules it follows.

Architecture has often been likened to frozen music. If so, the construction of a building is the equivalent of a musical performance, which is in fact the only thing that makes it real. To realize a design, in my view, the architect ought to be not only the composer but also the conductor, the more so because with a building there is only one performance. The best way to maintain whatever balance the architect has managed to achieve during the design phase is to direct the architectural process from initial conception to final construction. This makes it possible for the constant interaction among the various attributes to continue until the building is completed, so that issues of cost, technique, and construction help to inform the design and insure its integrity rather than impede its realization, as is so often the case when conventional construction methods clash with innovative design. The responsibility for the alignment of attributes in the completed building lies with the architect. And the goal of this complex process is the building it produces – a building that resolves the overlapping attributes in so strong and elegant a manner that experience of it is all the explanation it needs.

Described in this way, modern architecture (or architectural modernism) is a heroic enterprise seeking a poetic realization of an ideal alignment – the perfect diagram – that is doomed to fail. But the best buildings are the ones that try to achieve this balance, and in this they are a mirror of modern times and also of the human condition more generally. For even in their failure there is an authenticity, or truth, that emerges from the struggle. Good architecture is always of its time; anything less is anachronism. And since our times are still modern, our architecture must do its best to fulfill the aesthetic and social promise of the modern impulse in ways suitable to the 21st century to which, if successful, architecture has much to contribute.

modern continuities by joseph giovannini

Throughout his career, Peter Gluck has both attended to and practiced the principles of modernism even as his work changed in response to the opportunities of the times. He was graduated from the Yale School of Architecture in 1965, where he studied under Paul Rudolph and Louis Kahn, absorbing lessons of abstract space and sculptural form that would inspire his own designs. As the most progressive school of the period, Yale also encouraged him to seek alternative ways of understanding buildings, to look in unexpected places outside the official canon.

While still in school and over the next few years, Gluck designed a series of houses that in their directness, clarity, and elegance were recognized as significant by American and European architectural journals. This early work represented an evolving exploration of sculptural form, structure, and construction. The small size and simple program of these projects enabled him to focus on the development of a single architectural concept, whether manipulating space within a grid of columns, raising a platform seemingly untethered to the landscape, or producing form by eroding a solid mass.

After completing this series of houses by the age of 30, Gluck spent two years working as an architect in Japan, where he experienced firsthand the lessons of the temples and pavilions that have pervaded modernist architectural consciousness since the late 19th century. Gluck also found inspiration in urban environments almost too large to see – perceiving, for example, that Shinjuku, a mass-transit interchange and megastructure where one million commuters per day enter and leave Tokyo, is phenomenal in the philosophical sense of the term. The reality the commuters encounter is based on how they choose to experience a physically amorphous underground environment that is determined by the shifting behavior of consumers in a context of continuous change. Unlike the projects Gluck was exposed to during his formal training in architecture school, the laissez-faire context does not offer a fixed plan and aesthetic so much as it does a process of urban becoming where users experience options within a state of perpetual environmental flux.

The results of his research were exhibited at a show in 1975 at New York's Museum of Modern Art, which ran concurrently with the famous Beaux Arts show organized by Arthur Drexler. The two exhibitions juxtaposed two utterly different worlds. Sublime Beaux Arts renderings showed hyper-ordinated visions where axes, symmetries, and deliberate architectural massing and detail ordered space, dictating in no small measure how people walk and see. Gluck's analysis and exposition of "Shinjuku: The Phenomenal City" drew a different conclusion about this apparently chaotic environment. Created with Henry Smith, a historian of Japan, and Koji Taki, a Japanese architecture critic, Gluck's show represented the helter-skelter environment underground at Shinjuku. Like the indeterminate space of traditional Japanese buildings organized by walls of sliding shoji screens, the space in Shinjuku was permissive and even interactive, allowing several realities, structured not by a singular plan but by people and symbols.

It seems a leap from Shinjuku and traditional Japanese architecture to the suburban shores of Lake Michigan, outside Chicago, where Gluck designed an 11,000-square-foot house for a couple whose activities range from sunrise breakfasts to large benefits. But Gluck's Japanese epiphanies roll quietly, almost subconsciously, through his subsequent work, including this apparently placid house. As in the MoMA show, a process of phenomenological logic underlies his thought and practice.

Gluck conquered the requisite bulk of the house by dividing it into two linked buildings placed side by side: the front is a two-story structure curving around an encircled lawn, and the second, an orthogonal three-story structure in the rear. Between the two blocks, the architect inserted a wedge-shaped corridor with an adjacent staircase that leads from the more public rooms on the ground floor to the bedrooms and study on the second and third stories. With a palette of blond woods and softly colored stones, along with a well-tempered Euclidean geometry, the design imparts the sense of understatement usually associated with traditional European villas. But the unmistakable quiet and even poise of the bicameral house is deceptive. A subversive spatial ideology lies within the house's organization.

Most conventional houses on this site would present a formal front façade to the street and a more relaxed back façade to the lake, with a central corridor (and staircase) allowing a long view to the lawn and water beyond. Gluck, instead, has devised an interpretative plan based on experiential space. "I never think in terms of elevations but spatial movement — as a function of how you move through sculptural forms," says Gluck, speaking as the modernist he was trained to be. As an expert in Japanese spatial experience, he adds, "But space in Japan is a remembered sequence, a sequence of different paths that will be recalled through very personal constructions of memory and movement." The Japanese spatial experience, then, is a build-up of such recollections: "It's one thing at three o'clock, another at five. You don't analyze it as an abstract piece without thinking of movement and change. There's one route, and something happens, then another. You make your routes."

As in Frost's poem, two paths diverge in the front yard of the Lake Michigan house, one leading right on a steel-plate path crossing a checkerboard of moss and stone embraced by the concave façade, and the other, past the convex back of the semi-circular building, to what amounts to another front door at the wide end of the wedge. More pathways follow inside. The corridor in the wedge gives access to the front and back structures. Crossing the corridor from one building to the other is like passing through the Equator. Visitors are leaving one hemisphere for another, from the rings of a focusing concentric space to the openness of plate glass walls feasting on the panorama. The light, views, and geometries shift as one moves through the space.

The house sets up a multiple-choice format in the front yard that continues throughout the house, so that occupants determine their own path free of prescriptive geometries embedded in the plan. A curving wall with a half-dozen openings separates the two parts of the building and creates a porosity that allows people to "dial" their next space, depending on which passage they walk through: the opening could lead to the large living room, the formal dining room, or to the more intimate kitchen area, with a breakfast area breaking the dominant geometry and swinging east in the direction of the sunrise. The stairs, which curve within the ring separating the two halves, lead to more passages and more choices, and to deeply different spaces, depending on whether they are in the circular or rectangular wing. Different windows are designed to frame the lake in different ways – big and expansive, small and edited, wide and panoramic – each offering varying experiences related to the function of its respective room.

Unlike most Colonial central hall plans (or an overdetermined Haussmanian city plan), Gluck's domestic world is indeterminate and participatory, subject to the interpretations of the user.

"You can walk up, through, and around the passages to get to six or eight or nine different places, each with a different character," he says. The destructured circulation pattern is episodic and even playful: occupants make the house their own by using it. The interactive itinerary, along with overlaps and underlaps and even redundancies of program, creates a collage of space that determines itself through use rather than design fiat. Space for Gluck is a composite of sets and subsets.

The corollary to this treatment of space is his collagist approach to materials and forms, a design strategy that gives him great flexibility. Though his forms are planar and crisp and infused with a modernist sensibility, their sensuous richness draws on post-modernism. Trained as a modernist, Gluck still kept his mind open to the arguments of the opposition, and learned to introduce an enriched palette of materials that warmed modernism's cool, abstract forms.

On Lake Michigan, it was, in fact, the sun that broke down the usual geometry of a box-like house presiding over the property. Noting that plantings had not prospered on the street side of the original house, Gluck determined to create a heliotropic house whose geometry turned toward the sun, capturing its warmth and protecting the immediate yard from prevalent winds. He left the back façade frontal, facing the water. Streetside, he used the rotational capacity of the circle to turn the house south, forming an entrance court cupped by a curving façade. The convex side of the circle, with garage entries, faces north, toward the driveway. The house no longer just sits passively on the land, but shapes it into differentiated spaces.

Just as Gluck creates multivalent spaces inside, he differentiates outdoor space. Nowhere does his differentiated landscape yield more diversified experience than his own vacation house in upstate New York, where he used the house as a spade to cultivate the grounds. As in several of his additions to old farmhouses, Gluck left the original building intact along the road, and worked back into the property from the front. He had discovered while adding to historic houses that long, deep additions give lateral views, especially desirable where old farmhouses hugging the road are easily unsettled by traffic.

Building what is essentially a weekend camp capable of accommodating many guests, Gluck started the "addition" with a detached cubic structure placed at the end of a clearing in the wood behind the original farmhouse. The cube transfigures into a tall, simple Monopoly-shaped house, creating an irregular interior volume that accommodates living and dining areas and an open kitchen, along with a billiard space and library. The lofty interior houses a staircase that leads dramatically to a long, linear dormitory raised above the ground plane on steel pipe columns. To avoid removing trees, Gluck conceived a house with limbs that could easily dodge the existing trees. An elevated bridge takes visitors to the top of an escarpment out back, delivering them to an otherwise inaccessible part of the site.

The house, then, separates the landscape into different zones that are differently experienced. The clearing, where lawn sports are played, is the most public space, while the area between the dormitory and elevated walk is overgrown, dense, and private, a space of rumination. Tailings from a quarry spill into the third zone, next to the bridge that leads to the elevated portion of the site, which has an exploratory character.

The tentacular organization leading to a common room of several levels in overlapping forms allows guests the choice of keeping apart or coming together. The generously large common room itself is a space of possibility, defined by the many ways in which it can be used. The dining table, with an edge attached to a two-story column, epitomizes the socializing intent of a house that encourages variable configurations of people in dynamic groupings. Spatially, the house collects people, and its unstable configuration on several levels keeps bringing them together in unexpected ways.

From his first houses, and even a Vermont condominium completed in 1968, Gluck often raised his buildings above ground on pilotis in an effort to save the landscape he was building on. More recently he has burrowed parts of his structures into the earth to create a reciprocal relationship in which the house and landscape work as an integrated spatial and formal unit, the one explaining and contextualizing the other.

In a recent residence in Connecticut, Gluck tunneled a telescoping corridor leading from the entry (adjacent to the two-story cylinder) to the far side of the house. From the higher part of the site, the Double House appears to be made of two separate one-story structures, cubic and cylindrical volumes, but visitors walking through the door discover the two pieces are connected beneath a landscape that falls away on the far, down-slope side. The "crate" and "barrel" each have a floor at grade whose sliding doors open to a sloping vista overlooking a pond. From the pond, the house appears to be made up of two separate two-story buildings.

Again, different ways of perceiving the environment yield different ways of understanding it. "I don't like things totally resolved, or things that appear to be resolved," says Gluck. From the top of the site, two geometric single-story objects preside over the terrain. The view from the lake reveals that the two volumes have two stories, and an entirely different, more open character: the forms open generously at grade through expansive window walls. The volumes retain the hillsides that they carve. The indeterminacy in his plans and massing encourages occupants to form their own variable perceptions. There is no predetermined Gluck aesthetic that forecloses understandings that others may take from his projects. Gluck's approach is to invite users into perceptual interaction with the buildings.

That his buildings are open to interpretation reflects the ideological openness of his practice. Even during the difficult period of post-modernism, when it seemed apostate for modernists to even glance in that direction, Gluck admitted its more salutary aspects into his lexicon. For Gluck, the post-modernist critique of machine culture and aesthetic self-sufficiency encouraged him to expand his palette of construction materials, and to encourage context as an influence in design. In several projects, he developed collage as a strategy that compositionally allowed new additions to graft successfully onto older buildings. The palette could be adjusted to assure material transitions between old and new, and between components within the new. The collagist approach was integrative.

In 1984 and again in 1989, when Gluck was asked to add onto one of the few houses Mies van der Rohe had built in America, he had reservoirs of literacy to draw on. In the two additions, Gluck reinforced Mies's Japanese sensibility, while looking beyond modernism to Japan itself.

The additions actually improve on both the Miesian and Japanese originals with a steel structure whose walls of glass slide back to form vitreous stacks, its icy depths backed by the moiré effect of doubled screens. He has completely dissolved the boundary between outside and inside in a way never really achieved in either traditional Japanese architecture or Mies's pavilions. Gluck marks the distinction between outside and inside simply by raising the level of the interior floors and dropping the ceiling a few inches. The architect distilled an essence so pure in the two additions that he could hardly push it any further. He had to cultivate other directions for further professional growth. The near nothingness was complete.

In the early years of his practice, he did large projects, a huge hotel in Key West and a country resort in California, which are especially remarkable for their sensitivity to the landscape. The ecological emphasis signals from the beginning a strong social and moral concern that continues today in a dense New York context, where he is currently building in the Bronx and Upper Manhattan schools and social institutions in need of architectural care. The award-winning Social Services Center in East Harlem occupies a colorful five-story building designed to be convertible into condominiums, should rising real estate values make it desirable to realize earnings from the building to finance further growth in other locations. The volumetrically powerful Community Center in the Bronx, now in the design phase, will be an iconic landmark in its neighborhood. The Charter School in the South Bronx demonstrates that an architect's strong commitment can overcome the often defeating regulations and expectations of the bureaucratic mindset surrounding public school construction in the city. Spirit here survives the grind. In the Business School at Columbia University, Gluck performed a major act of remedial architecture by inserting in the forecourt of a particularly misguided 1960s tower a three-story limestone foreground piece that masks the offending building.

The limestone wall, strong in primary and secondary rhythms, defines one wall of a long plaza and completes McKim, Mead & White's original intentions for the north end of their campus plan.

Houses have provided Gluck with his greatest opportunity to experiment. In a recently completed large house overlooking Austin, Texas, Gluck develops the notions introduced at the Double House, where the earth and building carve into each other in a reciprocal spatial relationship. From the street, at a distance, a single, serene pavilion appears through a magnificent grove of live oak. The ground level of the two-story structure, housing the living room, is completely transparent, and the glass walls support a paneled box containing the master bedroom suite. Gluck posits a design that at first glance would seem to be, after his collagist period, a reprise of his interpretation of Mies. But enter the Texas house, and two wide swaths of lawn, projecting from either end of the two-story rectangle toward the distant view, are actually the roofs of parallel wings that border the long sides of a sunken court. The far end of the court ramps up to a berm occupied by a trapezoidal swimming pool.

House and landform weave in a three-dimensional matrix that unfolds on a promenade whose complexity prevents any direct understanding of the whole. Each wing and berm is, in itself, simple, but together, they achieve a complexity that is beguilingly counter-intuitive. Here Gluck is migrating from a collagist strategy to a more simplified expression that seems purist. The simplicity, however, is not reductive but takes place within the context of carved landforms. While his first buildings were lifted off the land, here he investigates notions of sculpting and occupying the earth. The design results in a pellucid architectural clarity embedded within the elusive opacity of the sculpted landscape.

Whether in his earlier projects or the more recent work, the designs are intense from a constructional point of view: the aesthetic crispness demands excellence in materials and craftsmanship. But instead of casting his designs into the contentious Bermuda triangle between contractor, client, and architect, Gluck has developed a way of protecting his work. Working as the construction manager in what has become a design-build practice, he stewards the designs. In recent projects in Aspen, Colorado, he has even emerged as developer.

In the spirit of Shinjuku, Gluck has proliferated paths within his practice so that there are several routes to creating extraordinary houses on ordinary budgets. A conventional architectural practice usually means a linear building process that starts with a phone call. But Gluck's firm, structurally, now resembles the floor plan of the Lake Michigan house, with alternative passages from design to completion. It is an interpretative practice that defines itself in the doing.

Gluck's operation consists of three interdependent entities, Peter L. Gluck and Partners, Architects, AR/CS, Architectural Construction Services, Inc., and the development company Aspen GK, Inc., which allow Gluck to take and maintain considerable initiative in the building process. Instead of accepting the increasing marginalization of the architect, one that puts architects on the defensive vis-à-vis contractors keen on blaming the drawings, Gluck has empowered his practice.

His own personal empowerment started early when, as an architecture student, he built the house he designed for his parents with his own labor. "Things happen when you begin to build yourself," says Gluck. "Buttresses, for instance, turned out to be perfect storage spaces for the window shutters; from regular working drawings, this would not have been obvious." Acting as contractor, an architect can take advantage of unexpected opportunities and insights. He can also avoid compromises that too often arise from competitive interests often raging in construction sites, where the owner's contracts with the architect and contractor usually place both in a confrontational, if not antagonistic, relationship. Too often the integrity of a design is at the mercy of contractors, or even clients, and by diversifying his company, Gluck effectively ensures the realization of his designs.

As construction manager, Gluck sends a representative from his office, usually the architect who has worked on the project, to set up a field office that identifies local subcontractors. The project architect collects the bids, awards contracts, and organizes the construction schedule. The architect runs the job on a day-to-day basis, including the detailed bookkeeping and overall financial management.

The purpose of the endeavor, says Gluck, is to build at the least possible cost for the owner, and the owner pockets the savings in the form of an enhanced house – the savings are spent within the project. Characteristically, the architect acting as construction manager saves some 40 percent.

Besides the cost savings, Gluck enumerates three reasons for acting as construction manager. First, the craft. "When we control the way it's built, we get much better craftsmanship from the subcontractors, who are forced to work together with us." he says.

Second, knowledge. "With this experience, you tend to have a better understanding of how things are built, and the increased knowledge increases our effectiveness on site and in the office."

Third, partnering. "When architects act as construction managers, they get together with the client early in the process, focusing on where to put the resources. Architects don't only consider their design ideas, but as contractors and architects, they also develop the program, budget, and site analysis with the client as partner. Partnering fosters cooperation and produces a better building."

Gluck maintains that the architects now in his firm who have worked as construction managers return changed, practiced in the bidding process, and conversant in the scope of work for each subcontractor, especially at the gray interface between the trades. He says they draw differently when they come back, with a more logical and detailed knowledge of building. Characteristically, in the office, the architects submit time sheets indicating, say, 12 hours working for Peter L. Gluck Architects, and 14 for AR/CS. Rather than doing just a single set of working drawings, applicable to all the trades on a job, they also do what are effectively shop drawings that isolate the work to be done by a subcontractor, clarifying both the task itself and the scope. Usually construction fees fall. Doing the shop drawings forces the architects to understand in greater detail the work actually done by subcontractors. For example, the excavation drawing for the foundations on the Austin house, done in axonometric, made the proposed work far more intelligible to the foundation contractor, and less expensive. The advantage of taking the four or five weeks necessary to draw the steel armature in a building is that the architects learn how it is built, and they gain experience in how to expose and express the structure in ways that engineers are generally not trained to consider.

In Aspen, Gluck took the idea of controlling a design one step further by developing three projects, the first two are houses, and the third a complex of affordable housing. Both houses are modernist compositions that capitalize on long views of the surrounding mountainscape, and edited views into the neighborhood. The houses make no ingratiating concessions intended to charm the market, but simply address issues of form, light, function, and space with classic directness.

Assuming the role of developer, Gluck found that he also enters the realm of development politics. In Aspen, where the entire built environment is themed by developers – Victorian, log cabin, Arts and Crafts – Gluck has been able to make a strong case for modernism by building it beautifully. The three projects to date provoked considerable discussion, much of it in the local newspapers. Gluck has refused to pander to a market determined by the lowest common denominator, but prefers instead to build sophisticated designs for a demand that the sales have confirmed. "Development gives us the opportunity to make conceptual points that will affect the environment," he says. By developing a project that includes affordable housing – and proving a profit can be made – the firm has been asked by the community to do more such housing. Gluck is performing a demographic and social service.

There are several dangers that lurk in Gluck's flexible process of conducting a practice, especially when he acts as a developer. Other architects following this route have been co-opted by the potential profits: the money saved finds its way to the bank rather than into the design itself. In the Double House, for example, the barrel itself was especially difficult to build, and the savings made through the design-build arrangement went into construction. This reinvestment saved the concept of two opposed forms anchored in the land. But the two houses in Aspen, though intelligent, handsome, and beautifully crafted, do stray to the more conservative side of modernism. Developing their own buildings, the architects confronted different risks from those that characterize the projects in which they served only as architect and contractor.

Still, these houses and housing have an integrity from drawing board to faucet rare even in high-end architect-designed buildings. Gluck is not interested in the business of contracting and development per se, but in facilitating the construction of designs as conceived. He never works solely as a construction manager; nor does he work only as a developer, building or developing projects designed by other architects. He remains first and foremost an architect. The other related endeavors simply improve the architecture in a more supportive process.

Gluck has been in practice now for 40 years, and the experience shows in work that is not only consistently mature but broad in its scope. Over the decades each project has carved out its points of intellectual and aesthetic expansion, and cumulatively the portfolio gives his practice a rare intuitive and practical depth. Never are the designs forced or contrived; they flow from a practice confident that there is always another project, and no need to display all the wares in a single work. Lessons from the previous projects have not been forgotten, and implementing the designs with construction management, Gluck is able to construct buildings remarkably faithful to their conceptual and aesthetic premises.

Gluck always attempts to invent something new from many elements mastered over time – structure, materiality, space, program – and never to bank on the foregone conclusions of established building typologies. In this rich, cumulative practice, the vector of his ideology is not toward reductiveness but completeness, tending to more rather than less, to complex buildings rather than narrowly defined, highly specialized ones. In synthesizing something new from his broad experience, Gluck has not only built an intellectual framework for his designs, but the practical framework of an office highly capable of bringing the designs to fruition. The urge to protect designs from defeat by budgets and the construction process, however, has not resulted in triumphs of over-design that dictate terms of everyday life. Gluck buildings may be intellectually provocative, but they are also temperamentally relaxed, easy-to-live-with structures based on the final wisdom of enabling occupants to determine their own experience.

JOSEPH GIOVANNINI is an author, critic, and the principal of Giovannini Associates, a New York City design firm. A Pulitzer Prize nominee, he has written as an architecture critic for The Los Angeles Herald Examiner and The New York Times, and has contributed to The New Yorker, Esquire, Vanity Fair, Progressive Architecture, Architectural Record, and Architectural Digest, among other publications. Mr. Giovannini has received numerous writing awards and has lectured widely. He earned his B.A. in English Literature at Yale, M.A. in French Language and Literature through studies at the Sorbonne, and M.Arch at the Graduate School of Design at Harvard University. He has taught at Harvard University, Columbia University, and at the University of Southern California School of Architecture.

history

history At Yale School of Art and Architecture in the 1960s, different viewpoints came together in a dynamic debate about the direction of modern design. Teachers as varied as Louis Kahn, Joseph Albers, James Stirling, Henning Larsen, Ralph Erskine, Shadrach Woods of Team Ten, Philip Johnson, Robert Venturi, and the dean of the school, Paul Rudolph, provided an ecumenical education in design that was comparatively free of the constraints of a particular orthodoxy. The economic and social optimism of the times offered architects the opportunity to build and the challenge to contribute to society, a combination that resembled the promise of modernism during the early part of the twentieth century.

There I began my engagement with the principles of what I now call the modern impulse, in which the form derived directly from the site and program rather than from any preconceived formal paradigm and was consciously expressed in both the form and the construction of the building.

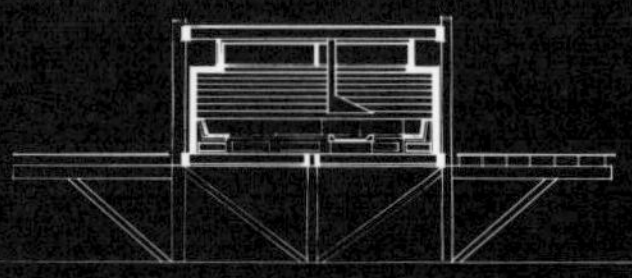

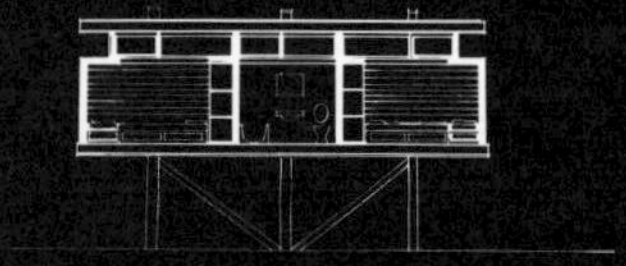

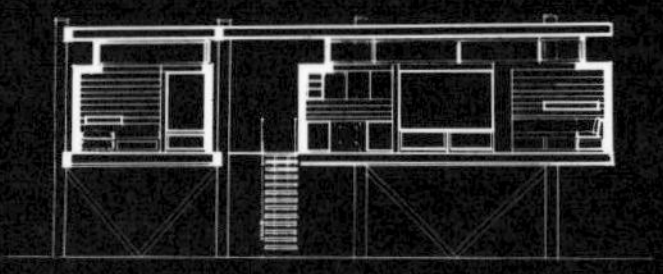

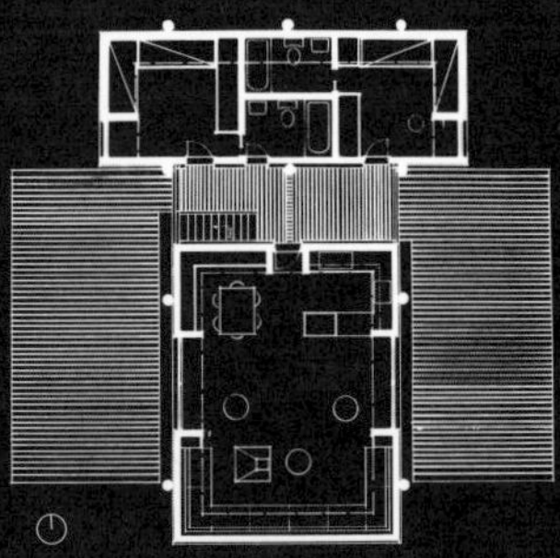

1965

beach house 1

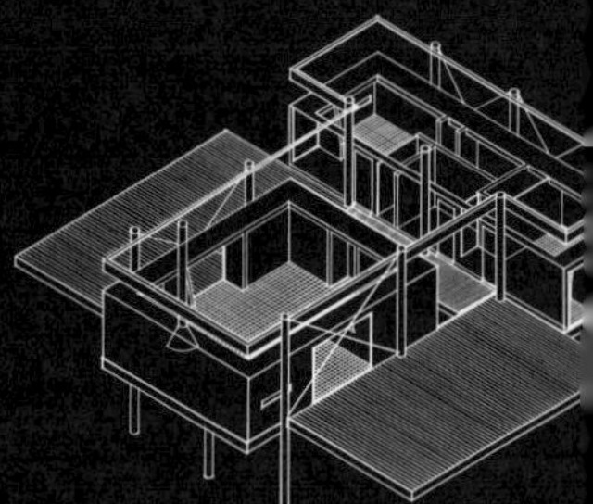

6

Beach House 1 The first of a series of inexpensive vacation houses published in *Progressive Architecture* in 1967 was built on sand dunes by the ocean and designed to withstand powerful North Atlantic hurricanes. The raised house is hung between a series of creosoted wood pilings that support the floor and roof. Cross-braced tension rods stabilize the building so that it would stand like a table even if the sand dunes were washed out from under it. • For privacy, the two small bedrooms were

7

11

section looking south
section looking north
section looking east
plan
axonometric
view from north east
piles
construction of roof girder
client at work
view from beach
living room looking north east
living room looking towards kitchen

8

10

12

separated from the living area by a covered breezeway. Kitchen cabinets, living room seating, and closets were built into the walls as if on a ship, leaving the living spaces unencumbered and open to the ocean views. This dialogue between mass and void provided a simultaneous sense of shelter and exposure. A free-standing sculptural fireplace set in a low coffee table in front of the couches had a steel hood that slid up into the ceiling during the summer.

1
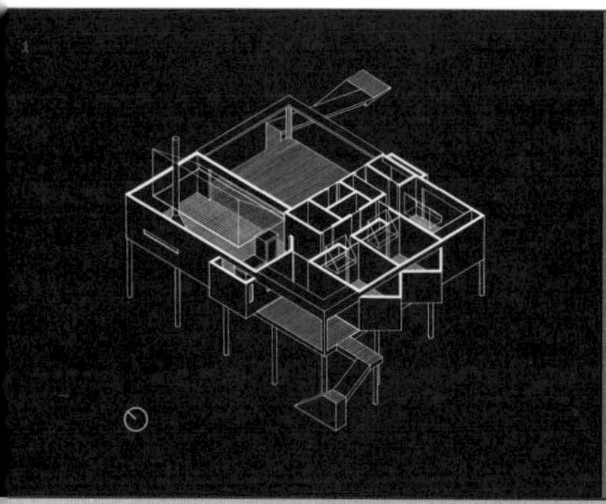

1966

beach house 2

2

5

3
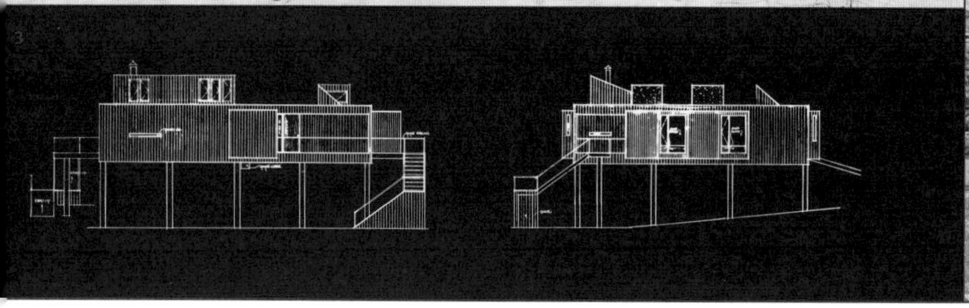

Beach House 2 A second house on a similar ocean-front site developed the idea of a form that responded to the effects of wind and weather and also separated private and public spaces. Influenced by Le Corbusier's Villa Savoie, the house is a rectangle with a large open deck cut out of it. The simple shape is punctuated by skylights projecting above the roof line and similar projections beyond the wall plane that capture the ocean views in the bedrooms. • Sliding wood panels around the deck complete

6

1 axonometric
2 view from ocean
3 north and west elevations
4 view to ocean
5 cover of *Progressive Architecture* 1967
6 view looking south east
7 view looking north east
8 section looking west
9 east elevation
10 north elevation

7

8

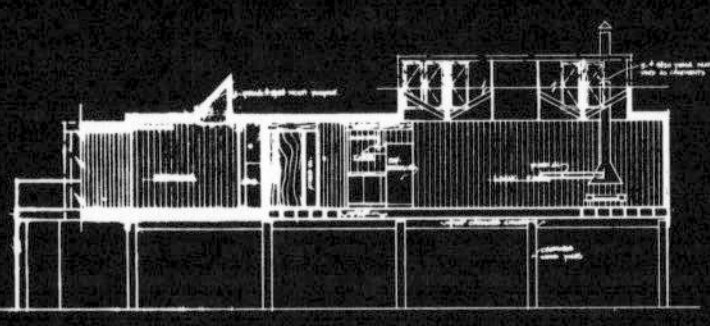

9

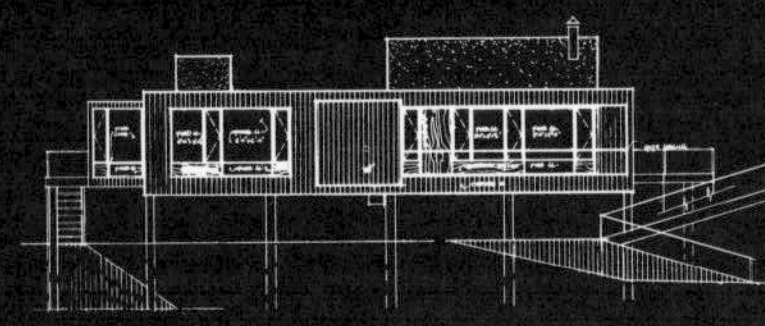

10

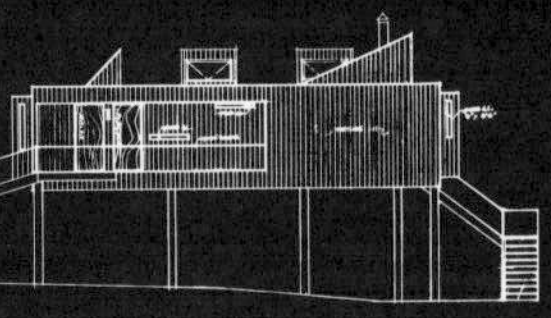

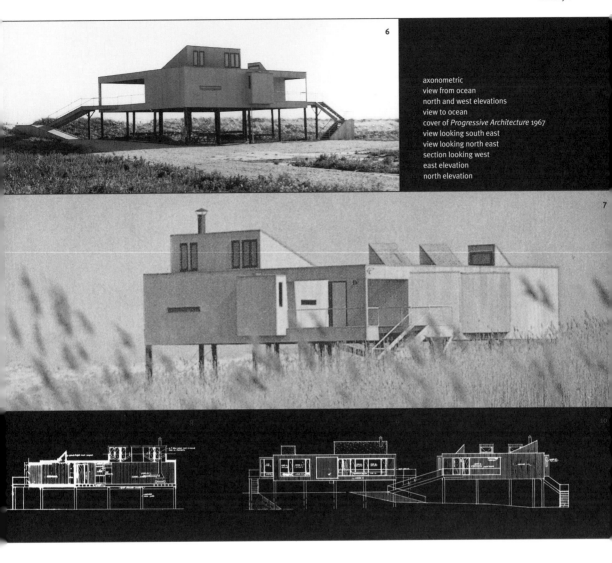

the rectangle, shielding the space from the strong, shifting winds and rolling in front of the window wall to protect it during the off season. The bedrooms are separated from the living spaces by a central mechanical core containing the kitchen and bathrooms, a device that lowered the cost and limited the area requiring winter heating. Costs were further reduced by using lumber and plywood in full standard sizes without cuts and waste.

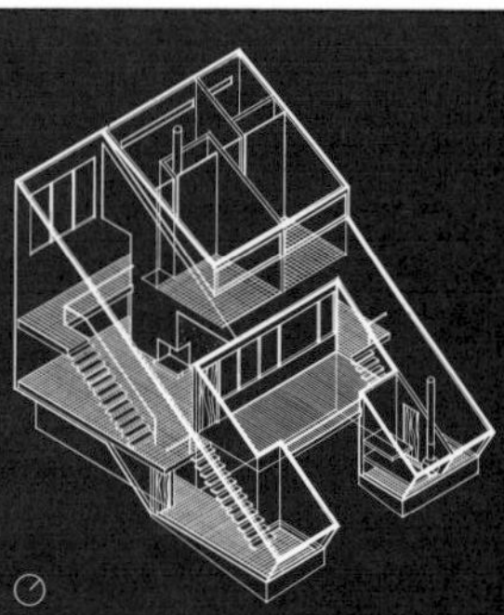

1966

sheltered house

4

2

3

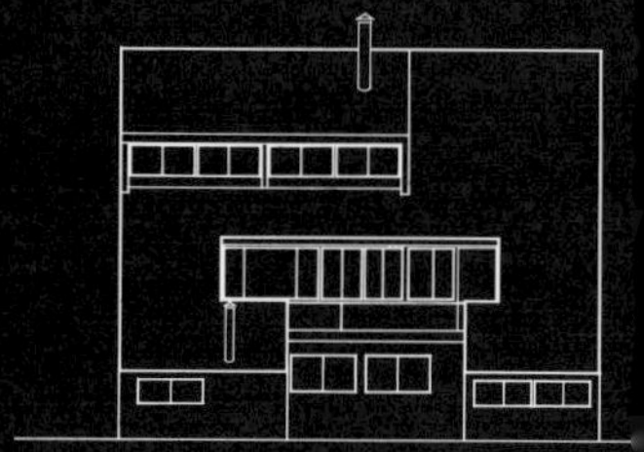

1 axonometric
2 view looking north
3 view looking west
4 view from bay
5 east elevation

Sheltered House A vacation house overlooking Newfoundland Bay in a severe winter climate demanded an emphasis on mass, not void, and shelter rather than exposure. The deck is notched into the form, fully protected on three sides, while the steeply pitched roof sheds snow and deflects the wind from the bay. The strength of the angular form completes the sweep of the slope from the sea in an echo of the harsh northern landscape.

Centered House Inspired by the geometric forms of Louis Kahn, this suburban house on a sloping wooded site addresses several themes of our later work. These include minimizing the building's impact on the landscape, reducing energy needs in a building buoyant with light, and above all, the combination of formal logic, sculptural interplay of shapes, and an experiential poetics based on the way the house would be used and felt by its occupants.

1

1967

faceted house

3

1 interpenetrating roofs
2 view from garden
3 view from street
4 sheltered decks
5 view toward ocean
6 side elevation
7 corner detail

4

Faceted House This project concludes a series of buildings that consciously reflected the influence of the three architects most important in my early thinking: Le Corbusier, Louis Kahn, and Alvar Aalto. Inspired by Aalto's sensitivity to human scale, in this house I used single-pitched roofs and a triple-stepped plan to break down the building's mass into smaller facets. And in the manner of Aalto's additive approach to design, the facets interpenetrate one another and at the same time clearly identify

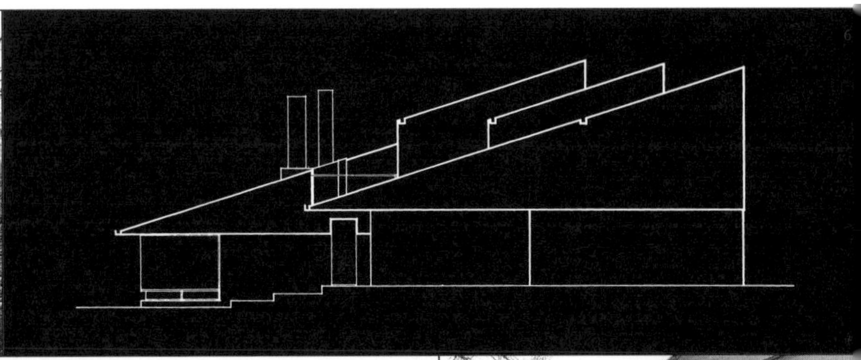

6

5

7

their function as bedrooms or public spaces. • The house sits on a hill just off a busy highway facing a landscape of sea pines, a sheltered bay, and the Atlantic Ocean. The wedge-shaped house has its tall two-story back to the street, its scale in keeping with the highway, automobile entry, and the garage. In contrast, the ocean-facing front of the house reads as a one-story elevation scaled to family activities and opening onto a sand-and-pebble garden. • The largest facet contains the main public space,

8

10

11

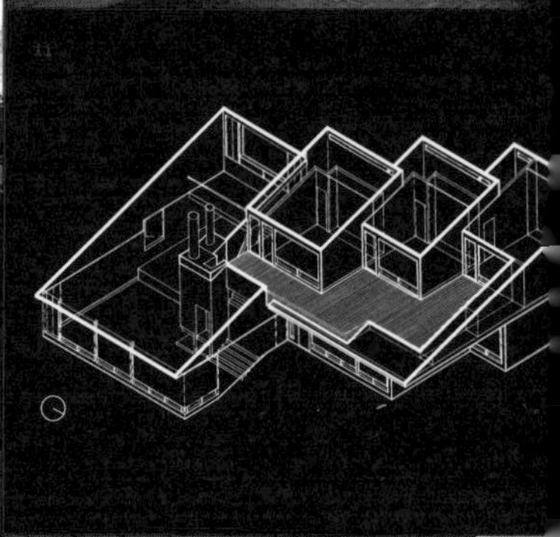

9

12

which rises from the one-story glass elevation on the garden to the rear of the balcony on the second floor. The sweeping wooden ceiling floats above the glass and unifies the dynamic space. Each of the three smaller facets contains a private bedroom suite and its own sheltered deck, so that there are private as well as public exterior spaces.

8 living room looking to garden
9 living room
10 glass corner
11 axonometric
12 second floor balcony
13 ventilation panels
14 kitchen from living room
15 living room looking toward stair
16 second floor balcony

15

14

1967

staggered house

4

Staggered House This country house is set on an extremely steep rocky hill above a small mountain lake. The house begins on the top of a plateau, 50 feet above the water, at the spot where cars must stop. It then cascades down the hill, becoming in effect a stairway to the lake. • The central spine gives access to wings alternating down the hill at half levels to make the stairs gentle, reduce construction blasting, and create a composition of one-story elements that comprise the façade as a whole.

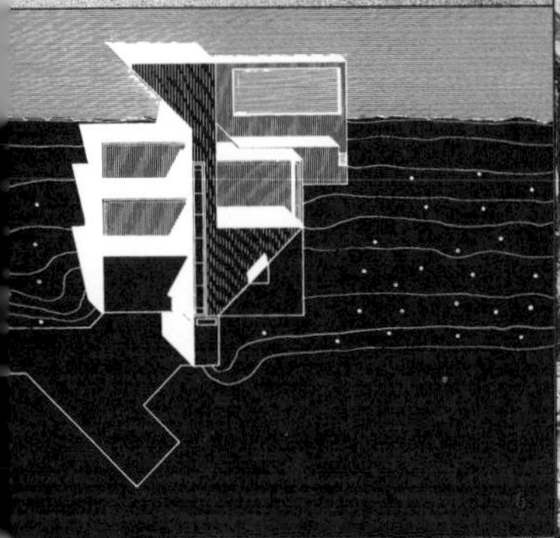

stepping down hill
house from south
lake looking south
pool deck
entrance
roof plan
side elevation
staggered decks
house from north

The large rectangular plan is centrally lit by a continuous skylight above the stair. • Every room in the five alternating wings faces the lake, opening onto a deck that is the roof of the wing below it. The spine continues as an exterior stairway to the edge of the water, where a deck surrounding a pool set in the lake completes the geometry as the platform of a sixth wing.

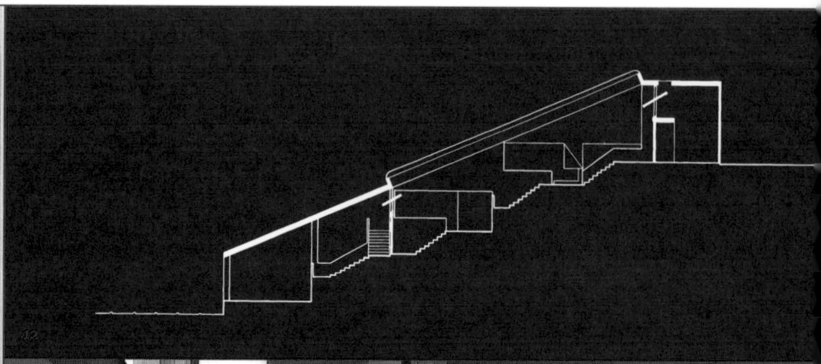

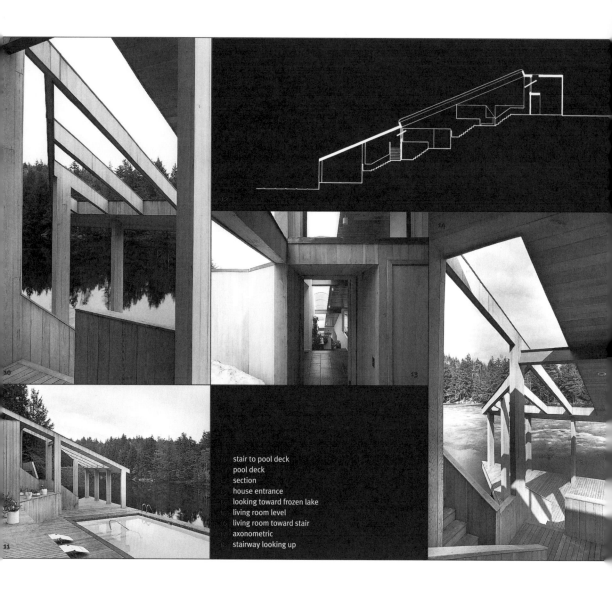

10 stair to pool deck
11 pool deck
12 section
13 house entrance
14 looking toward frozen lake
15 living room level
16 living room toward stair
17 axonometric
18 stairway looking up

15

16

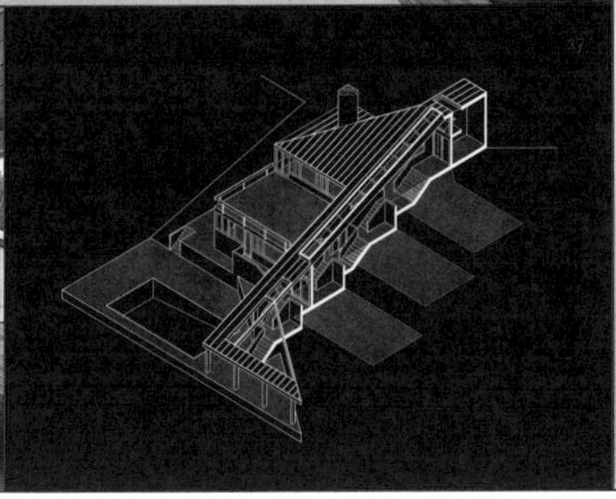
17

18

1969

cluster housing

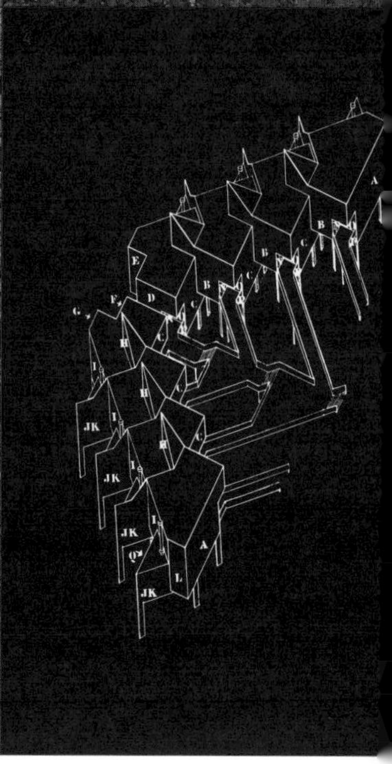

Cluster Housing Looking for a way to develop cost-effective housing to meet social needs, architects in the late 1960s frequently turned to modular and prefabricated construction. It was a time of optimism associated with the government's Great Society programs, several of which attempted to foster social change through low-cost housing. In that spirit I created ARDEC (Architectural Research and Development Corporation) to develop new techniques in a design-build development of attached

3

5

6

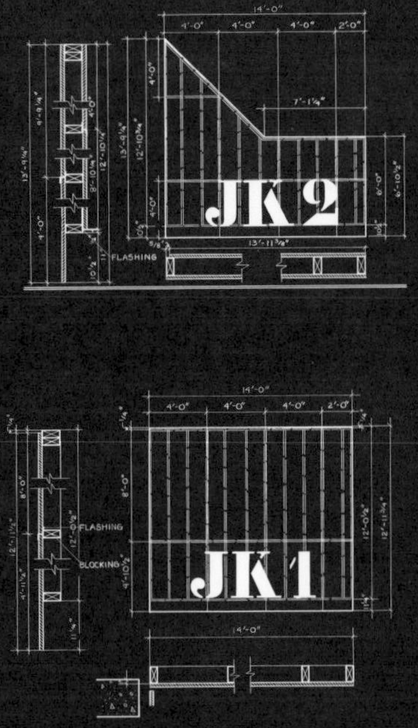

7

8

1 site plan analysis
2 model from above
3 model from north elevation
4 axonometric
5 site installation
6 panel shop drawings
7 site installation
8 panels ready for installation

housing. • Composed of prefabricated panels, the units reduced both maintenance and construction costs by simple assembly and shared utilities and services. Cluster siting also made it possible to avoid sprawl and preserve the natural environment by creating a quasi-urban density in a rural setting and maintaining the common land in perpetuity. • To simplify the fabrication of an architecturally complex geometry, the construction documents consisted of shop drawings describing each wall panel in detail

9

10

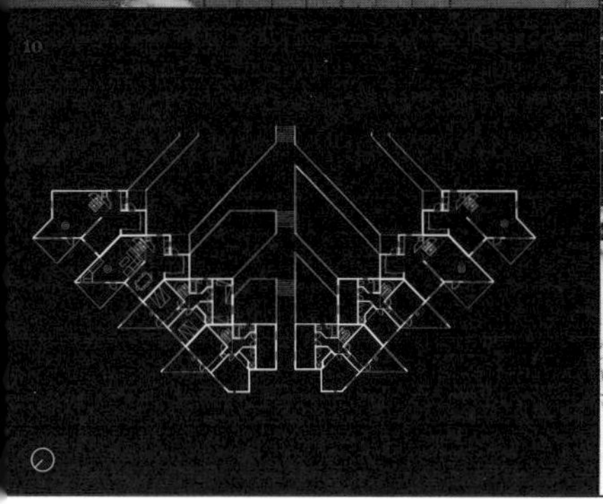

9 entrances to units
10 first floor plan
11 view from ravine
12 view from sky slope
13 living room from balcony
14 assembly key
15 view toward entries
16 section
17 living room

12

11

on a separate sheet of paper. Each one was keyed to the axonometric whole like a puzzle pre-solved for the builders who had only to follow the indicated sequence of installation of each panel. Even on the steep site, the panels were easily lifted into place by a crane, and the building was quickly finished with ready-made windows, dry wall, and cabinetry.

13

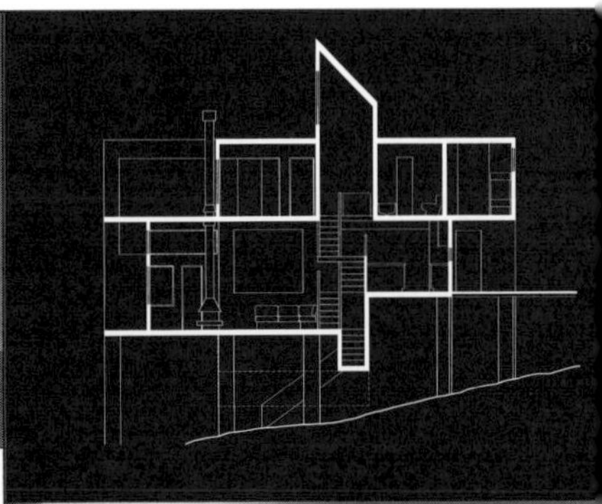

17

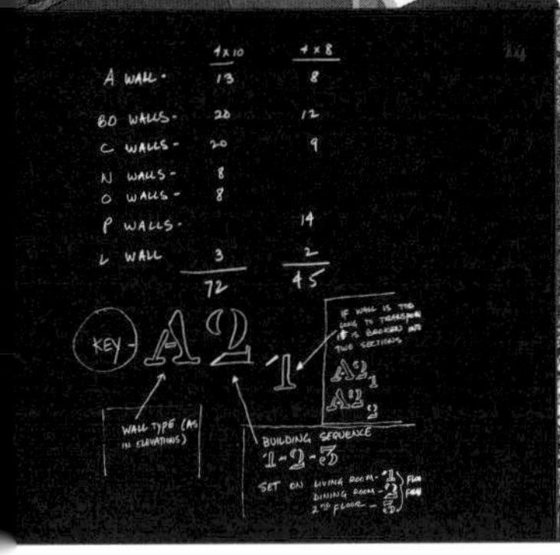
4x10
4x8
A WALL - 13 8
BD WALLS - 20 12
C WALLS - 20 9
N WALLS - 8
O WALLS - 8
P WALLS - 14
L WALL 3 2
72 45
KEY - A2 1
IF WALL IS TOO LONG TO TRANSPORT IT IS BROKEN INTO TWO SECTIONS
A2 1
A2 2
WALL TYPE (AS IN ELEVATIONS)
BUILDING SEQUENCE
1-2-3
SET ON LIVING ROOM - 1
DINING ROOM - 2
2ND FLOOR - 3

15

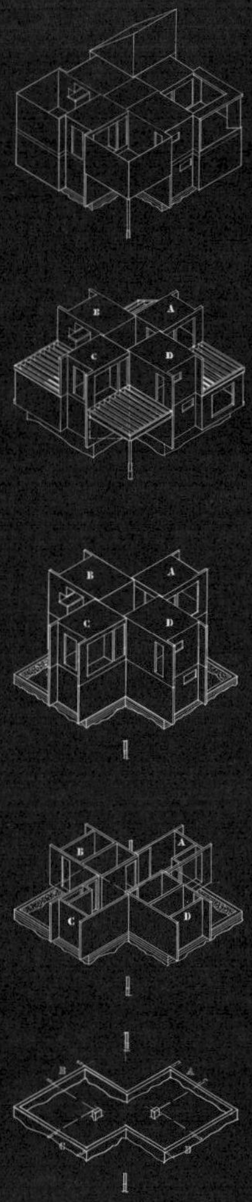

1970

modular housing system

2

Modular Housing System A further step toward complete prefabrication, this modular system combined a series of prefabricated panels and three-dimensional boxes. The factory-built boxes contained all finish carpentry and interior finishes of the stairs, closets, kitchens, and bathrooms, including plumbing and electrical connections. These tightly concentrated modules were assembled with the flat panels on site to form larger spaces like the living rooms and bedrooms, thus reducing ship-

nbly sequence
nbling modules
e family prototype
tory house
tory house
parent overlay

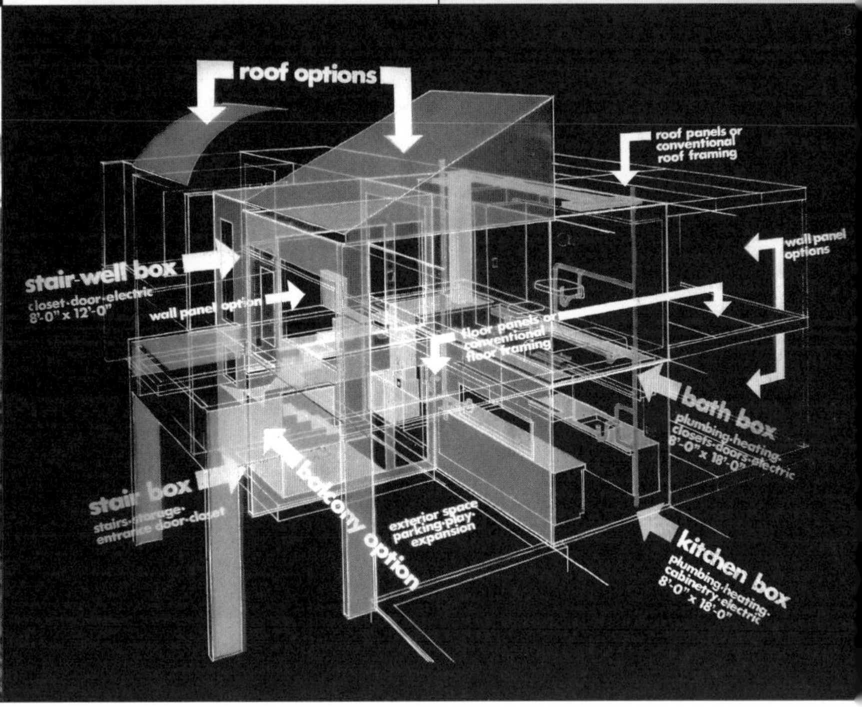

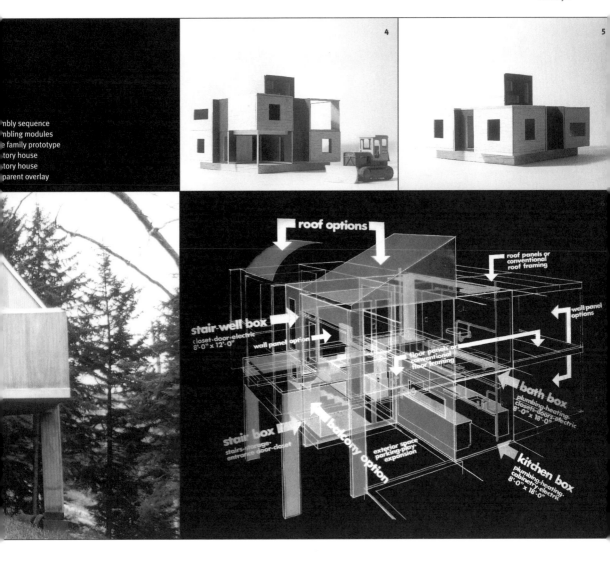

ping volume and costs to a minimum. Simple shop drawings similar to those for the cluster housing made it possible to prefabricate the system in local lumberyards rather than in expensive factories. • Although the prototype unit was built as a single-family house, the system was intended to deliver multi-family buildings for the many low-cost housing programs of the time. • In fact, such low-cost housing seldom moved beyond the experimental stage, in part because economic fluctuations prevented the

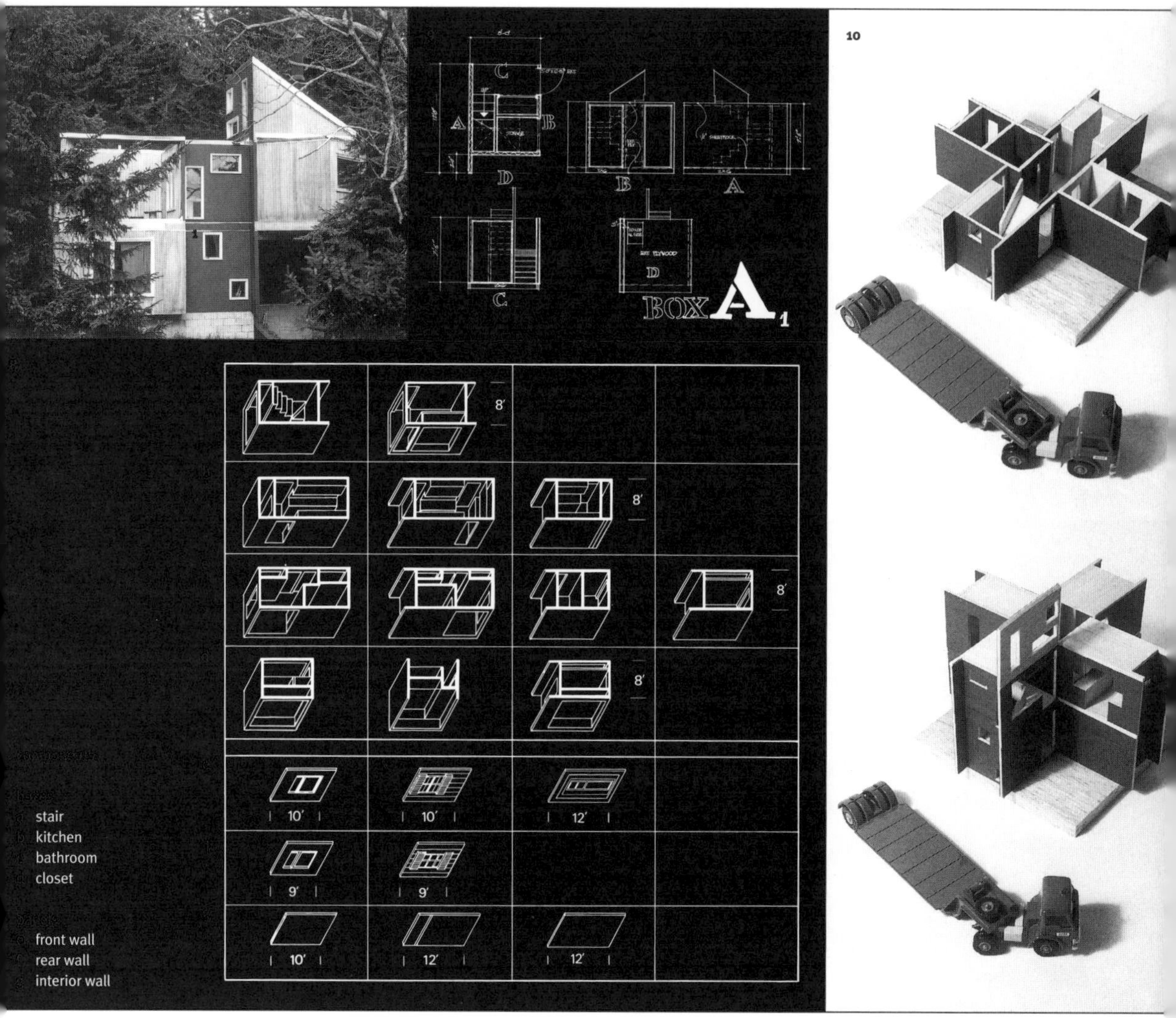

development of a stable market for standardized housing but also because communities, almost without exception, resisted the social implications of low-cost developments in their midst. I see this as a deficit in social policy, planning, and urban texture that has yet to be remedied in the United States. Our recent projects in affordable housing continue our early efforts to overcome these persistent obstacles.

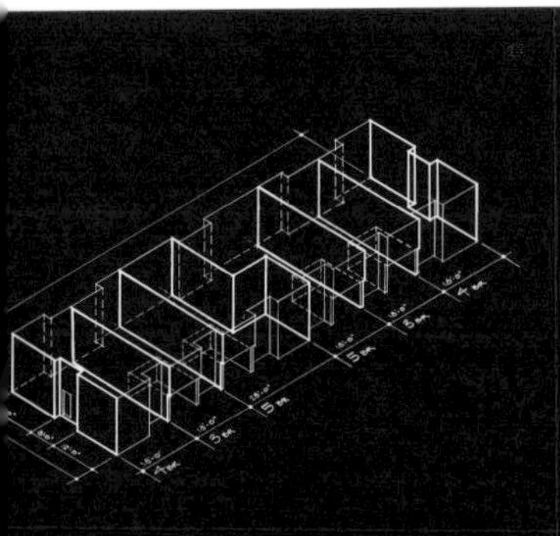

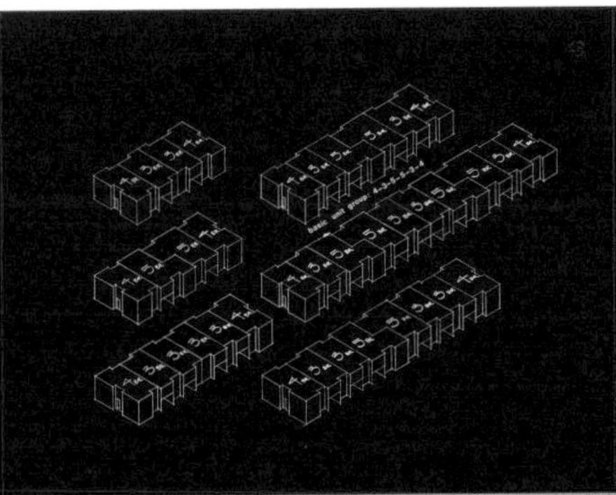

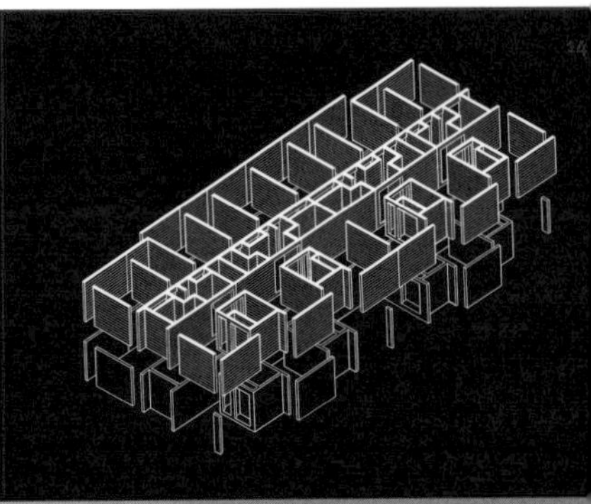

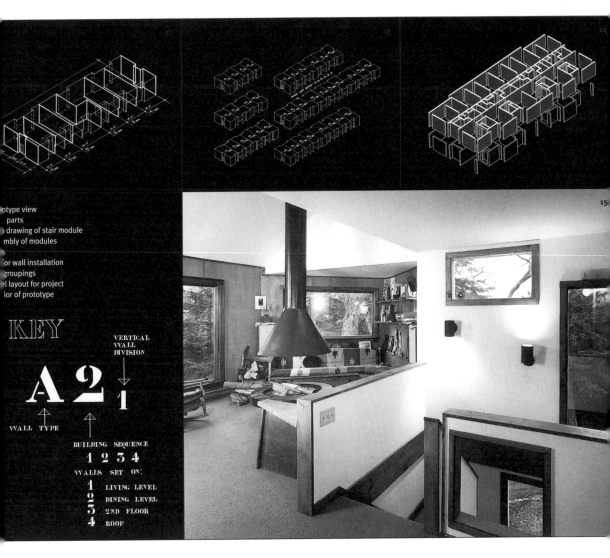

otype view
parts
drawing of stair module
mbly of modules
s
or wall installation
groupings
l layout for project
ior of prototype

KEY

A 2 1

WALL TYPE

BUILDING SEQUENCE

VERTICAL WALL DIVISION

1 2 3 4

WALLS SET ON:

1 LIVING LEVEL
2 DINING LEVEL
3 2ND FLOOR
4 ROOF

15

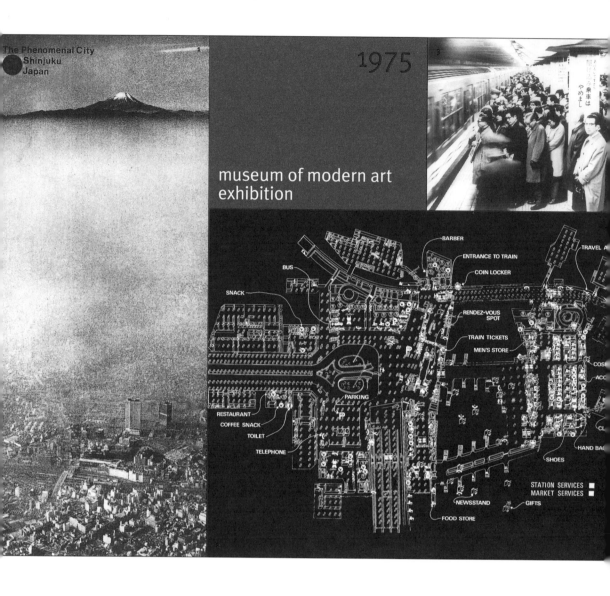

1975

museum of modern art exhibition

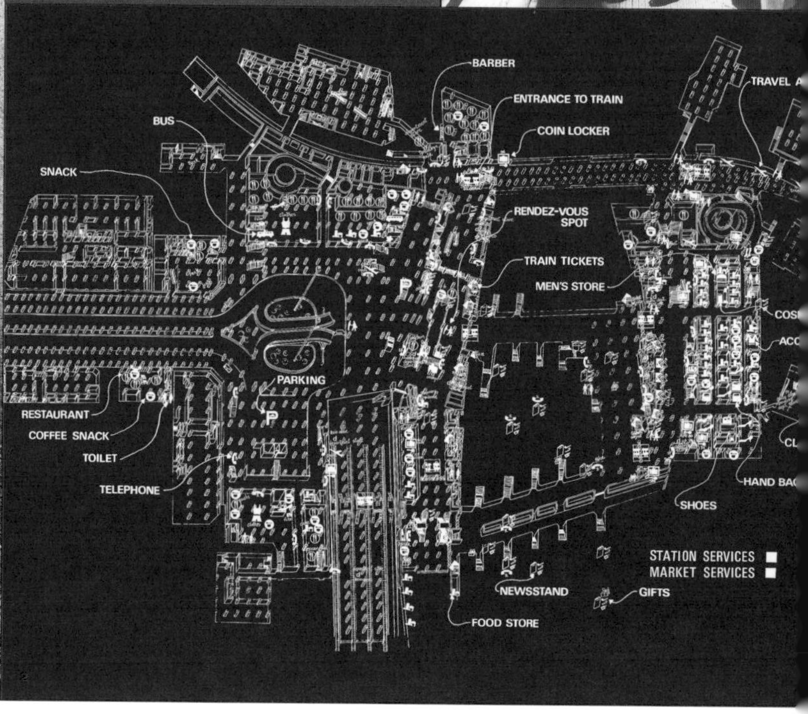

Museum of Modern Art Exhibition Working in Japan from 1972 to 1974 gave me an appreciation of sequential space, asymmetry, and experiential – as opposed to formal – logic that characterized many of my later buildings. I further developed these ideas with Arata Isozaki, Fumihiko Maki, Kisho Kurokawa, and others in seminars I organized at Columbia University in the 1970s. • The city of Tokyo exemplified the diversity of an ad hoc urban planning process that worked from the bottom up

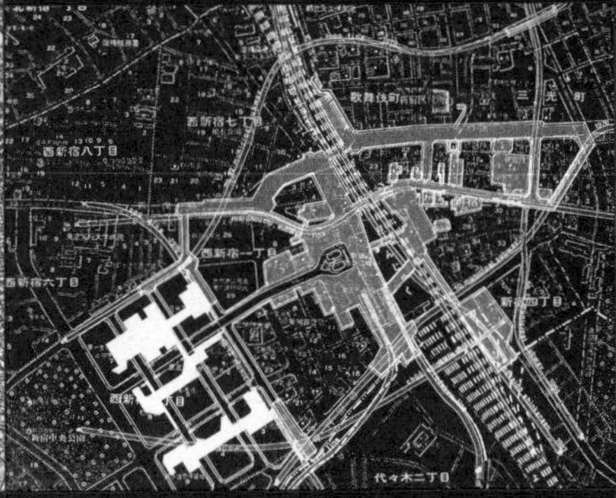

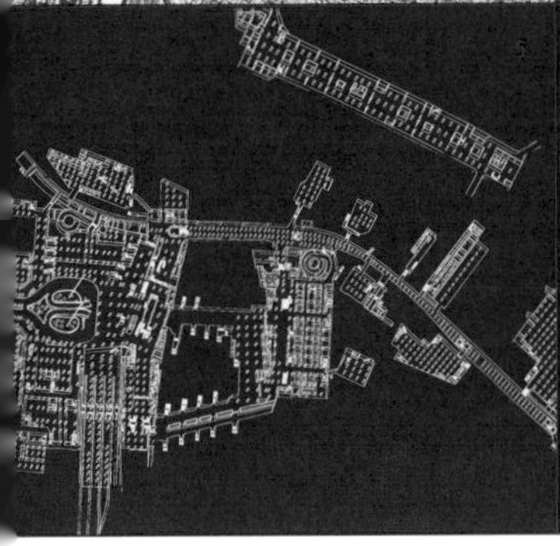

moma exhibition poster
subterranean food shops
commuters at rest and in motion
aerial view of shinjuku
plan of underground area
transportation network
exhibit panels and views

in contrast to the top-down principles associated with European planning. The ordered – though not rational – plan based on the public transportation and pedestrian traffic that underlay the complex, rich, and seemingly chaotic cityscape of Tokyo became the basis for an exhibition on "Shinjuku: the Phenomenal City," which I curated with Henry Smith and Koji Taki at the Museum of Modern Art in New York in 1975.

1978

hillside hotel

3

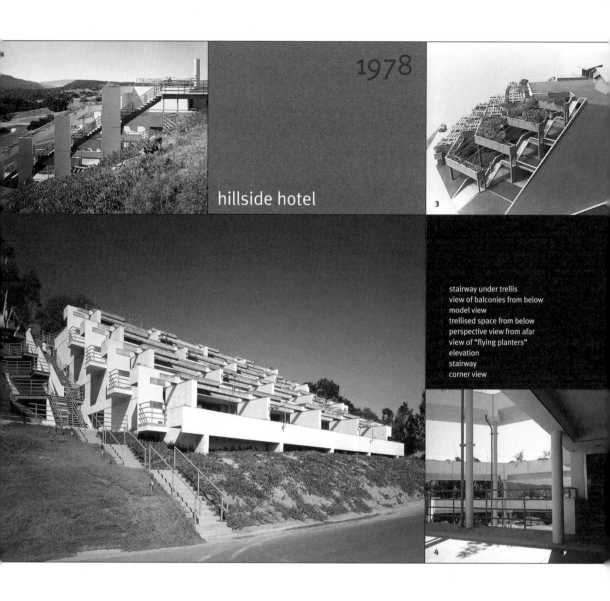

1 stairway under trellis
2 view of balconies from below
3 model view
4 trellised space from below
5 perspective view from afar
6 view of "flying planters"
7 elevation
8 stairway
9 corner view

4

Hillside Hotel Returning to the United States, I received three commissions that posed similar challenges to those I had encountered in Japan in designing a 500-room hotel in Guam for a large Japanese architecture-construction firm. In two hotels and a medical center we were asked to design large buildings with demanding programs and fixed, low-range budgets that would seem to preclude any distinctive architectural expression or innovation. In each instance the typical plan and forms were reinterpreted,

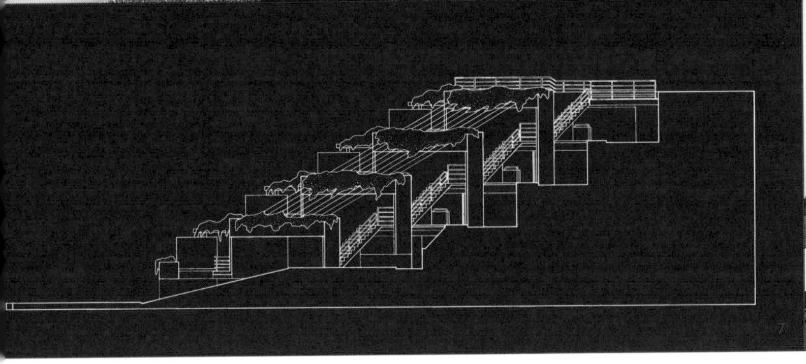

using siting and landscape to unsettle the predictability of the building and subvert the repetitive plan. • For the Hillside Hotel in California we added 175 rooms to the existing resort complex with the objective of minimizing the impact of the new buildings on the sensitive landscape and plantings. Toward this end, the new rooms were embedded in the slopes of the hill, stepping down to provide a terrace for each room with golf-cart access from the rear of the unit. Planters and wood trellises produced a web of natu-

10 stairway down
11 private decks
12 green roof with mountains beyond
13 view from hotel room
14 section

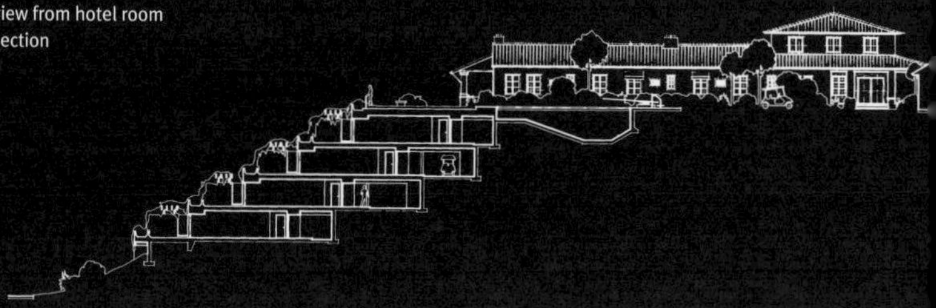

ral vegetation that appeared to cover the side of the hill when viewed from the valley below. This was the first major project that embodied my commitment to the principle that landscape must be integral to the design, an approach that became characteristic of our later work.

1979

waterfront resort

1 axonometric
2 view from ocean
3 entrance to interior court
4 plan of existing hotel and addition

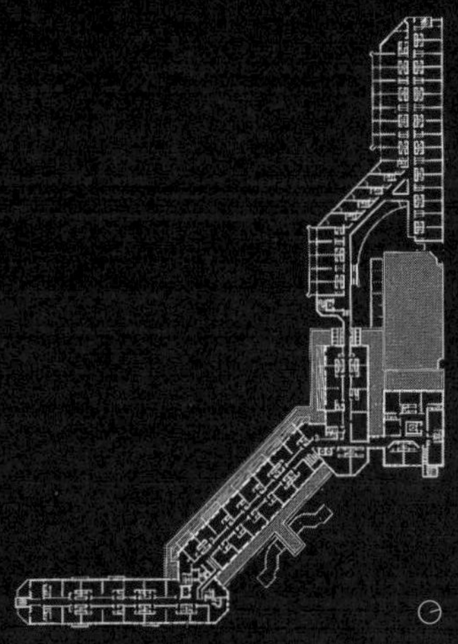

Waterfront Resort For this hotel in southern Florida, the task was to add 139 rooms and a convention center and at the same time restore the original 250-room Spanish-style building built by Henry Flagler in the 1920s. The challenge was to create quality architecture in the ordinary environment of a big hotel chain. The resulting complex combined a painstaking restoration of the gracious mood of the old hotel with an assertively new wing that had all the amenities of a contemporary Caribbean resort.

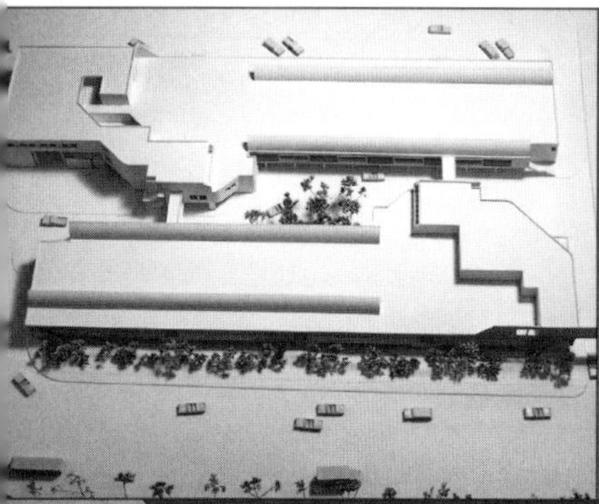

1983

medical center

1. model view
2. view looking east
3. perspective looking east
4. interior drive looking east
5. interior drive looking west
6. view from bridge
7. north & south elevations
8. night view
9. corridor with doctors' suites
10. research labs

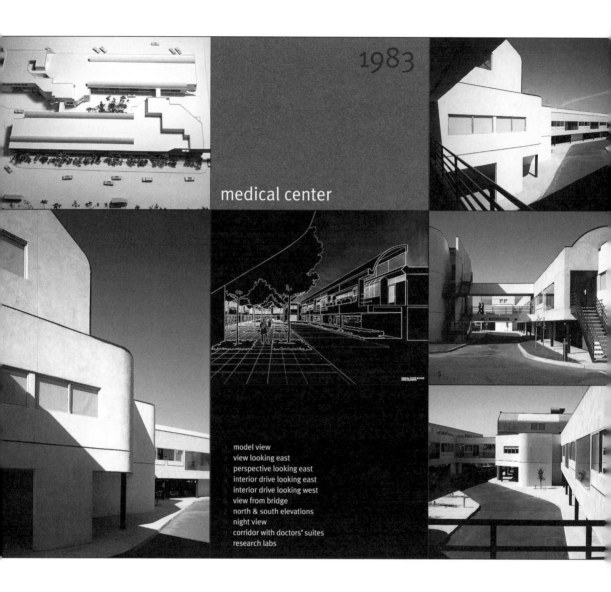

Medical Center In a joint venture with James Stewart Polshek and Partners, we designed a medical center for 65 doctors of different specialties next to the hospital on the main street of a small California city. The 70,000-square-foot building was elevated over its parking lot and conceived as a model for a medical mall, at that time an unfamiliar building type. The program had to accommodate changing specialties, group and individual practices, and the eventual possibility of its transformation into

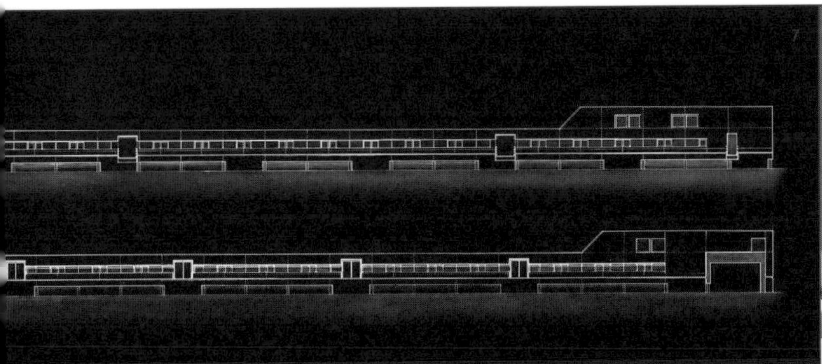

a single unified HMO. To provide this flexibility we developed structural and mechanical systems that could be modified over time without requiring major structural change.

1980

farmhouse renovation

west elevation
view from the street
axonometric from west
axonometric from north
bedroom view
second floor plan/bedroom elevations
view toward mountains

Farmhouse Renovation A crumbling 1820s wood-frame farmhouse with only one room on each floor required complete restoration and an addition almost equal in size to the original to provide a master bedroom, library, kitchen, and bathrooms. To respect the original shape – which was like the iconic house of a child's drawing with its simple single gable, front door, and chimney – the extension echoes the pitched roofs, adding three new gables that integrate the elevation of the old and new parts of the

house. • The corner cut into the master bedroom brings the mountains into view and creates a large glass façade that inverts the shape of the gables in an ironic complication of traditional geometry. The void created by the cut provides a large triangular skylight for the first-floor library. • The result is a tiny house that is traditional in its restored portions, unabashedly modern in the new spaces, and works as a seamless whole.

1980

two-sided house

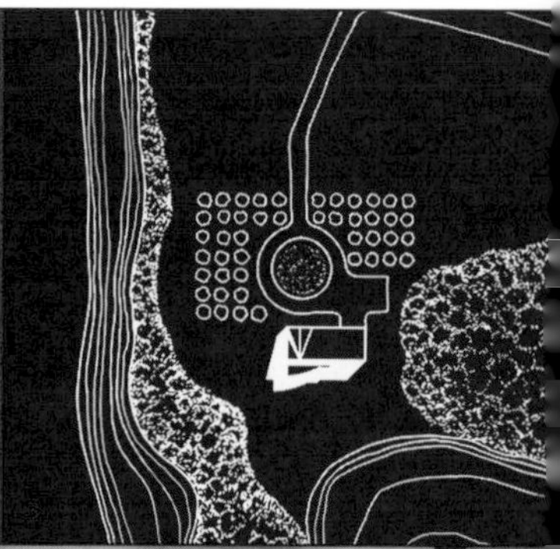

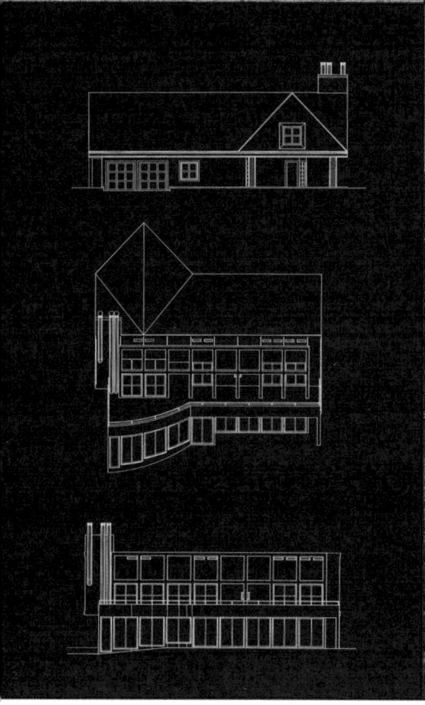

Two-sided House The combination of postmodernism and prescriptive traditionalist zoning in the 1980s made modern design unwelcome in many communities. In response, we designed a series of "pitch-roof houses," which drew on the traditional American notions of "home" but also created a strong sculptural presence and unadorned clarity that reflected the best modernist principles. Thus each of these houses consciously combined the familiar with the bold. • The Two-Sided House is a three-dimensional

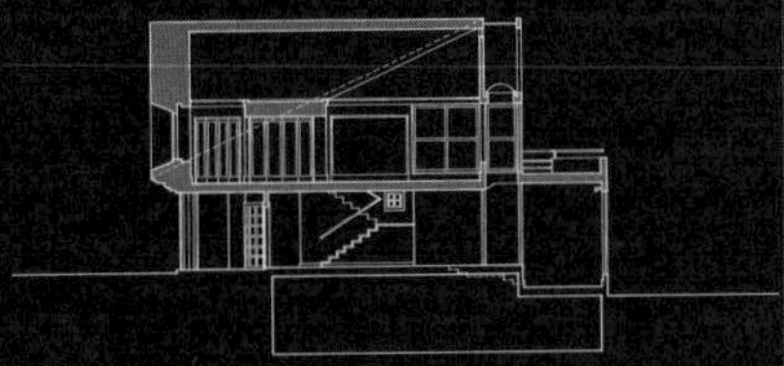

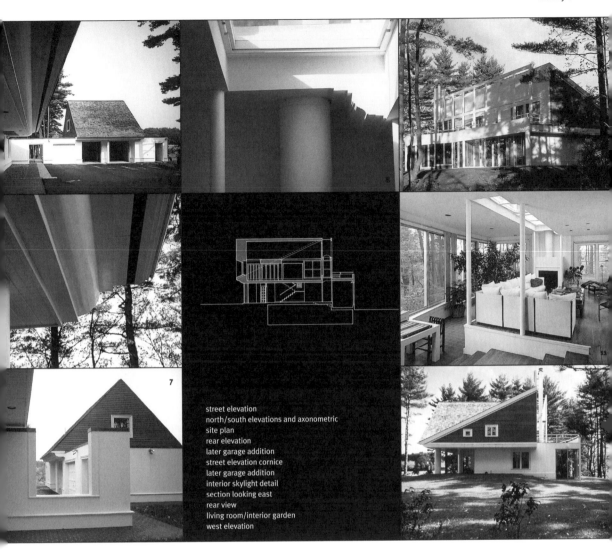

street elevation
north/south elevations and axonometric
site plan
rear elevation
later garage addition
street elevation cornice
later garage addition
interior skylight detail
section looking east
rear view
living room/interior garden
west elevation

polemic that literally expresses the schizophrenic split between the modern impulse on the one hand and the nostalgic need for the appearance of tradition on the other. The house demands a double reading by creating two contradictory façades: a public gabled front, which plays off the design requirements of a conservative suburban town, and a private glassed back that meets the family's wish for modern forms, space, and light.

Three Gable House Here the exaggerated pitched-roofs become tectonic forms in a residence built within the constraints of a typical builder's house, with inexpensive materials, conventional construction, and the largest amount of space in the least costly shape. Like most of these houses, the plan is a simple rectangle; one-third the space, including the garage, is in the basement; and the predictable driveway (and basketball hoop) marks the automobile approach. • The design plays with conventional

1. proverbial driveway with basketball hoop
2. site plan
3. later garage addition
4. south view
5. entrance elevation
6. first, second, and third floor plans
7. house from street
8. interior stair
9. axonometric
10. second floor corridor balcony

forms. Outside, the columns and gables of the façade transform the builder's pattern into an almost monumental form that gives the house a sculptural presence well beyond its economic means. Inside, the traditional room arrangement shifts laterally to accommodate the symmetry of the exterior; the typical double-loaded corridor of the second-floor bedrooms breaks out as a balcony into the two-story living room; and the living room becomes a witty expansion of the conventional formula.

1987

house for music

entry detailing
axonometric
approach
view from entry court
site plan
entry canopy and rain collectors

House for Music This house in a New York City suburb combines two pitched-roof gables with a formal rational window scheme that subverts the picturesqueness of a traditional façade. Again the double reading creates a modern sculptural form in a conventional context. • A flowing interior plan with a courtyard that is rotated off-axis results in a skewed interior corridor that gets wider toward the public spaces and narrower toward the service side of the house, producing a functionally impelled

asymmetry. • The asymmetry reflects the need for an acoustically sophisticated concert space for chamber music with seating for 125 people as well as an intimate house-within-a-house for private family living. Spaces like the library, family sitting room, and upstairs corridor all open onto the two-story living room and provide additional seating for the concerts. These ancillary spaces break the geometry of the living-room walls and provide acoustical complexity to enhance musical color.

• The entrance courtyard is scaled to accommodate a large number of cars and a formal entry to the house for the concert-goers. Its skewed geometry also provides a view and a path to the waterfront side of the house.

12

13

7 grand piano with balcony corridor above
8 second floor sitting room
9 living room toward pool and sea
10 axonometric looking up
11 stairwell from second floor
12 pool trellis
13 central hall
14 stairway to second floor deck
15 trellis view to sea
16 rear view

1981

jewelry boutique

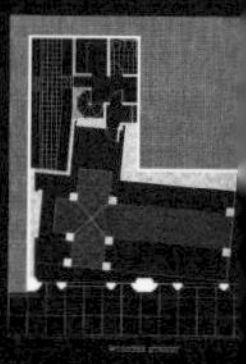

sales desk
main display corridor
jewelry cases
plan

Jewelry Boutique Under the sign of postmodernism in the 1980s, architecture rediscovered its premodernist past. Although we resisted the direct transcription of historical styles, we took advantage of the liberation from the restrictive ideologies of high modernism. • Here a purist environment accommodated postmodern elements in the vaults made of acoustically transparent stretch fabric and implied masonry plaster walls.

1982

vault house

1 front door
2 axial space
3 side room
4 ocean view

Vault House A similar combination of modern and postmodern elements makes the central vault of this seaside house into a sculptural form that organizes the plan and focuses its composition on the ocean view. The vault forms an interior plaza, and the two wings facing it close the house off from the neighboring buildings that crowd it on either side of a particularly cramped site.

1985

corporate headquarters

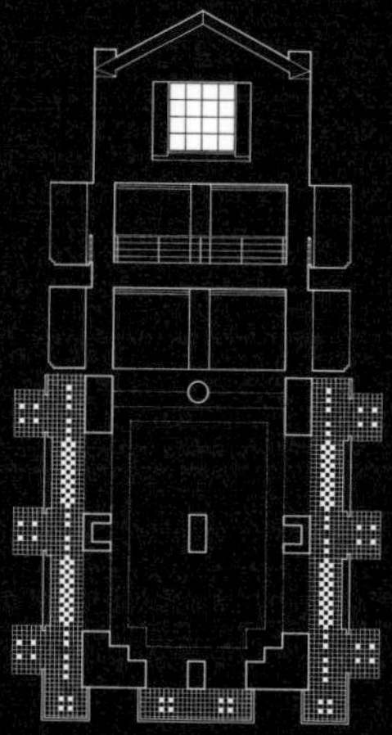

1. street entrance
2. lobby
3. plan/elevation of lower floor
4. art wall
5. stair

Corporate Headquarters This total renovation transformed two adjoining five-story factory buildings in lower Manhattan into corporate offices for a high-tech computer company, which wanted its art collection integrated with efficient work space that fostered a progressive corporate culture and created a distinctive appearance. Central multi-functional spaces showcase the art and encourage free-flowing personal interaction, while the ironic broken pediment in the entryway suggests a counter-cultural identity for the firm.

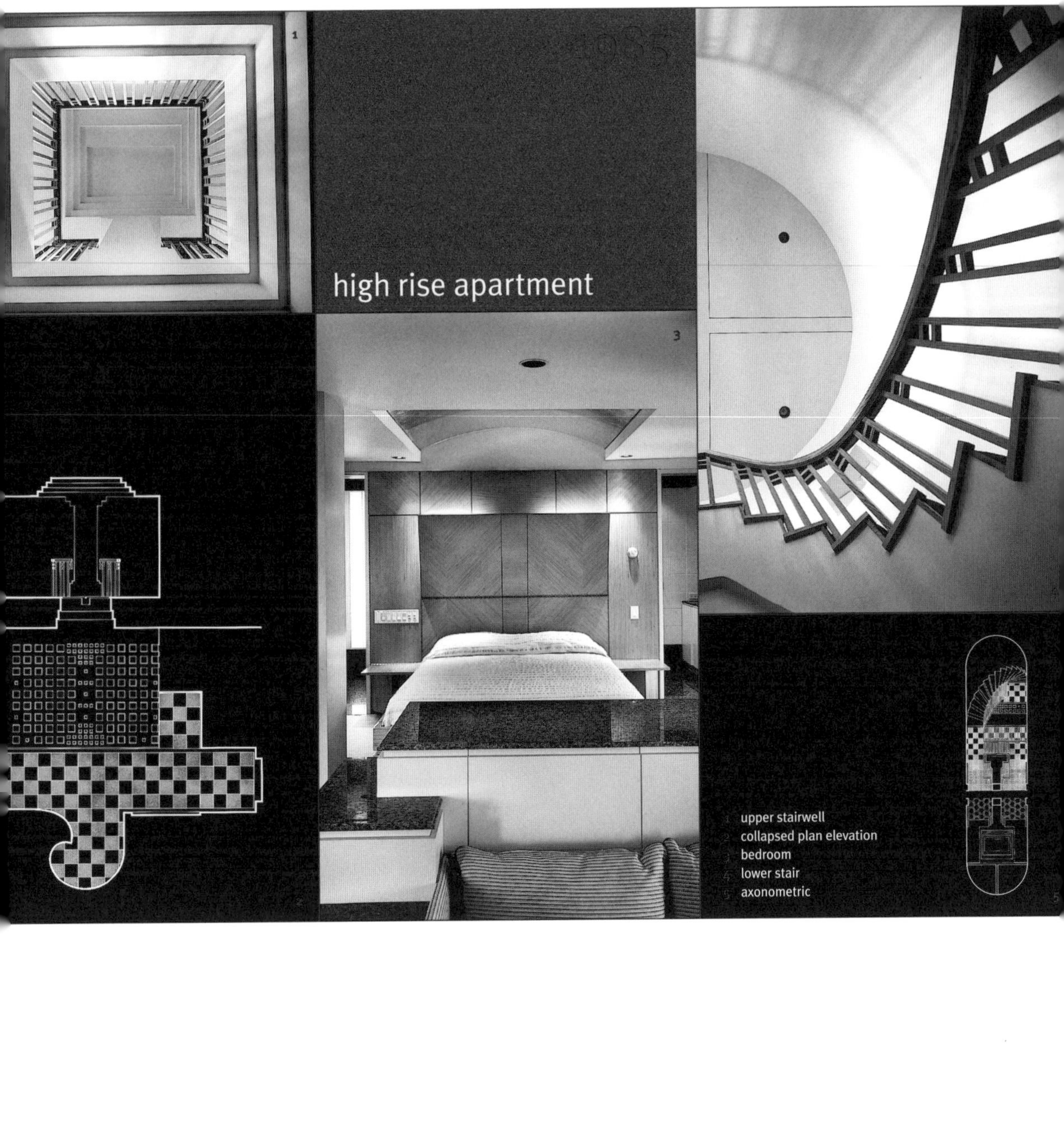

high rise apartment

1 upper stairwell
2 collapsed plan elevation
3 bedroom
4 lower stair
5 axonometric

High Rise Apartment This renovation of a Manhattan penthouse apartment included adding a master bedroom in the rooftop water tank of the building. The main focus is the series of stairways – one circular, one rectangular – which create a three-story sculptural space through a play of geometric forms. The result is a lavish suite high above the city skyline with a distinctive character and spatial presence.

1

1986

university business school

2

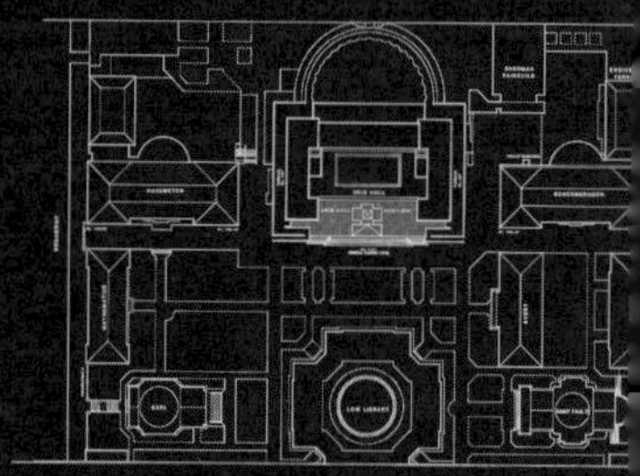

1 existing building and early construction
2 new façade
3 new building from campus walk
4 site plan
5 façade detail
6 perspective
7 new building with pre-existing steps

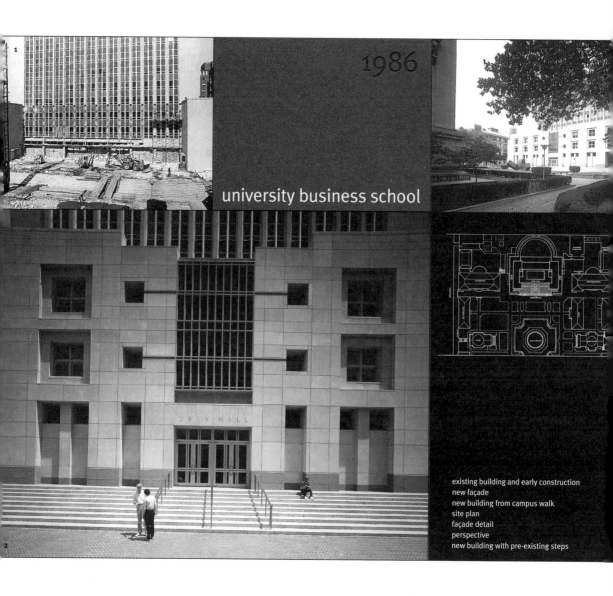

University Business School Confronted with two extreme instances of building in a context of recognized historical significance – one, a famous university campus plan designed by McKim, Mead & White, the other an archetypical suburban neo-Norman church – the goal was to combine a postmodern respect for the original architectural intent with the principles of the modern impulse. • The addition to the Columbia Business School presented a two-fold contextual challenge. The requested addition stood

5

7

opposite the original Palladian rotunda designed by McKim, Mead & White as the centerpiece for the new Columbia campus in 1903, but it was attached to a nine-story aluminum and glass high-rise, a 1964 developer-designed building that violated every aspect of the original campus design and composition. • The university first asked for simple extensions on either side of the existing business school, which in my view would simply have attached "ears" to the ungainly building. Instead we reorganized the interior

8

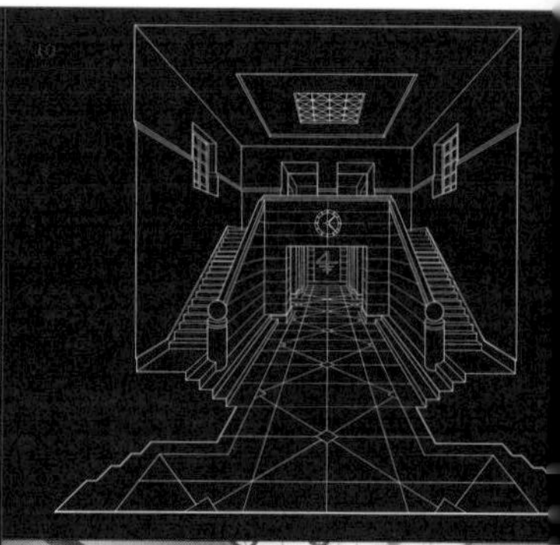
10

11

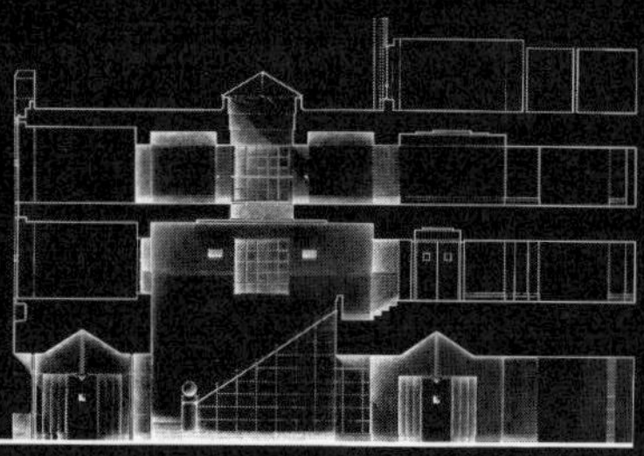
9

plan and circulation and designed a new entrance hall and façade, which in fact created a "mask" that concealed most of the offending building from campus view. • The limestone-clad façade established the appropriate scale and character to engage in the kind of contextual conversation with the Palladian rotunda across the courtyard that McKim, Mead & White had originally envisioned. We set the new windows in groups of two and extended their surrounds beyond their floor levels in order to match the

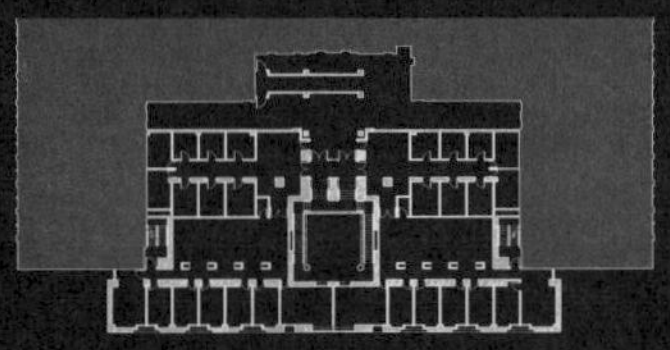

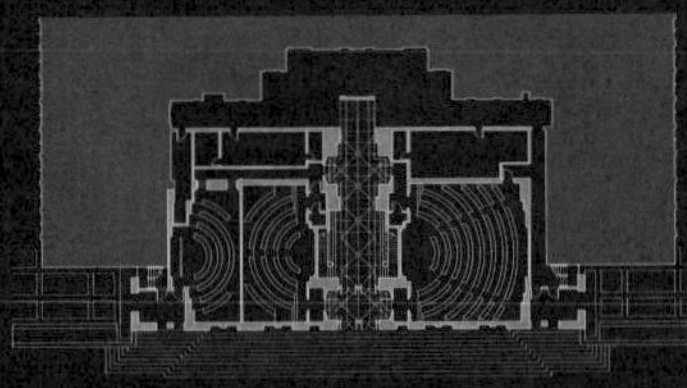

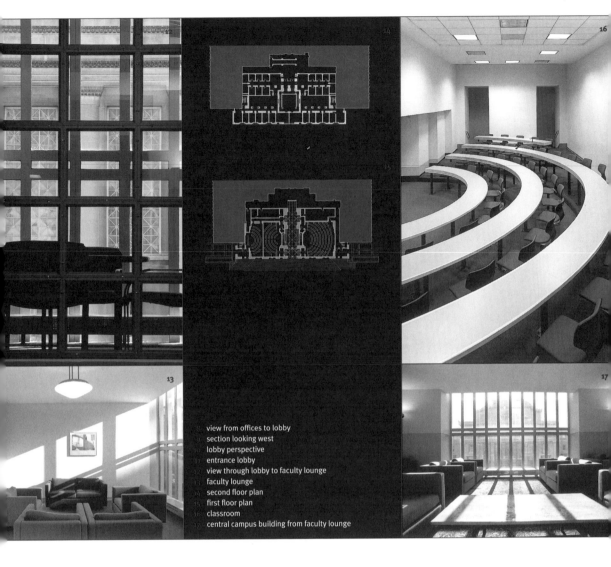

8 view from offices to lobby
9 section looking west
10 lobby perspective
11 entrance lobby
12 view through lobby to faculty lounge
13 faculty lounge
14 second floor plan
15 first floor plan
16 classroom
17 central campus building from faculty lounge

unusually tall windows of the original campus buildings. The central figure, a curtain wall that spans two floors, is meant to read as both opaque, in deference to the neighboring façades , and also transparent, in a gesture to the modern preference for open and continuous space.

1989

suburban church

Suburban Church After a fire destroyed a 1920s neo-Norman church set within a larger complex in a New York suburb, some of the parishioners wanted very much to evoke, or even replicate, the old building. Others sought a new church that was lofty, light, large, and open. Yet another group were most interested in creating the acoustics for professional performances on the new English organ they were planning to purchase. A further demand came from the town requirement to limit the building

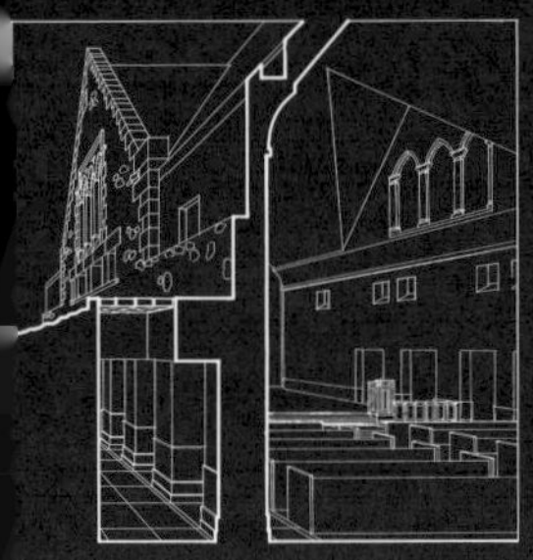

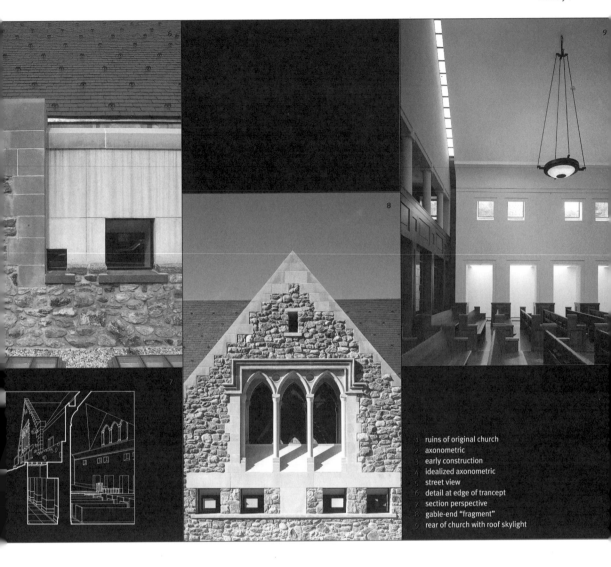

1 ruins of original church
2 axonometric
3 early construction
4 idealized axonometric
5 street view
6 detail at edge of trancept
7 section perspective
8 gable-end "fragment"
9 rear of church with roof skylight

to one story to preserve the "residential scale" of the community. • This was the perfect situation in which to combine modernist principles of light and space with postmodern devices that evoked the semiotics of tradition. To maintain the one-story height, the nave was sunk to create a soaring 45-foot-high space. Lit by clerestory windows at street-level, the interior was light, pure, and unadorned. To link the church with its past, we placed a "literal fragment" at the gable end of the transept facing

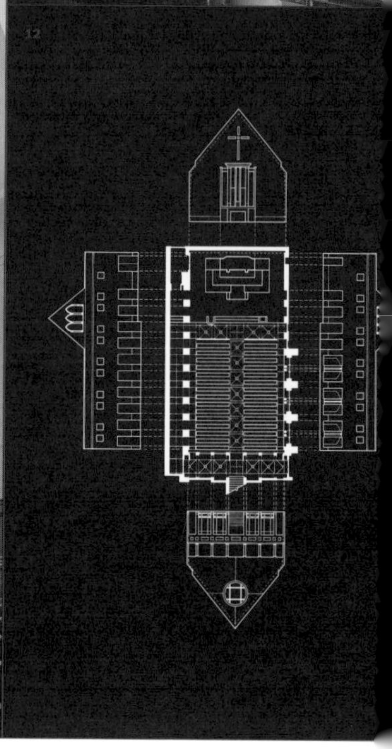

the street. Created from the stone rubble salvaged from the fire, the fragment became a mnemonic device, a distilled image of original Norman architecture of centuries past as well as an evocation of the church so recently destroyed. In this context, the modernist design was masked by the Norman fragment on the street elevation and celebrated in the interior of the church. Since completion, the building has become renowned for its acoustics and is now a sought-after space for organ concerts.

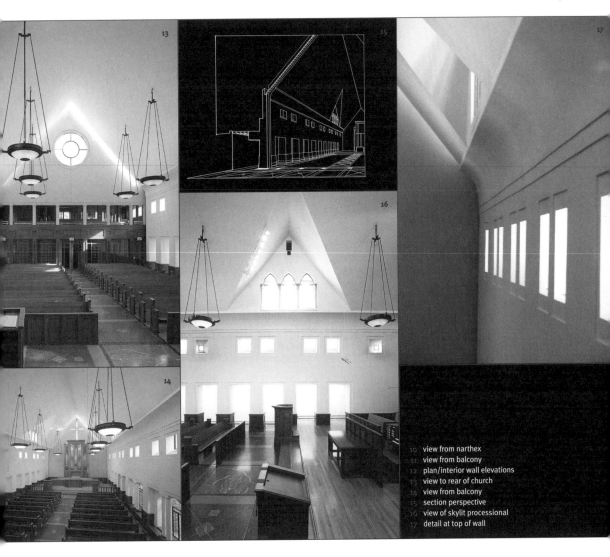

10 view from narthex
11 view from balcony
12 plan/interior wall elevations
13 view to rear of church
14 view from balcony
15 section perspective
16 view of skylit processional
17 detail at top of wall

1 plan of sanctuary
2 sanctuary looking toward ark
3 balconies and skylight

1990

suburban synagogue

3

1

Suburban Synagogue The new sanctuary creates a space that is egalitarian, in that all seats are equally distant from the central lectern, and ascetic, with the only ornament the changing moods created by the movement of sun and clouds visible through the central skylight. The strong geometry of the circular seating enclosure set within the square plan of the building, the perforated screen behind the altar, and the symmetrical balconies all suggest the purity of spiritual observance.

1993

first composite house

1

5

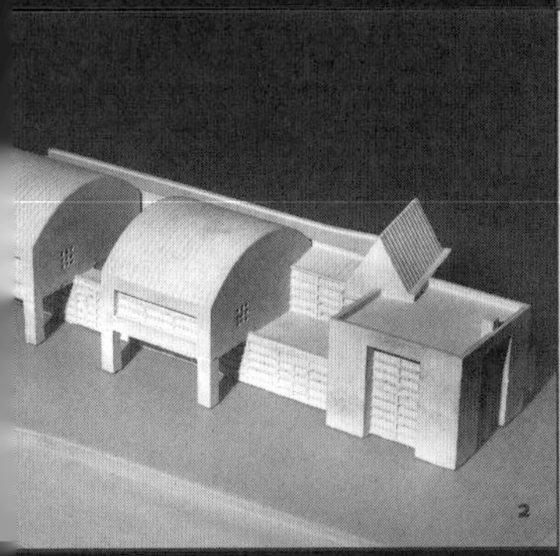

2

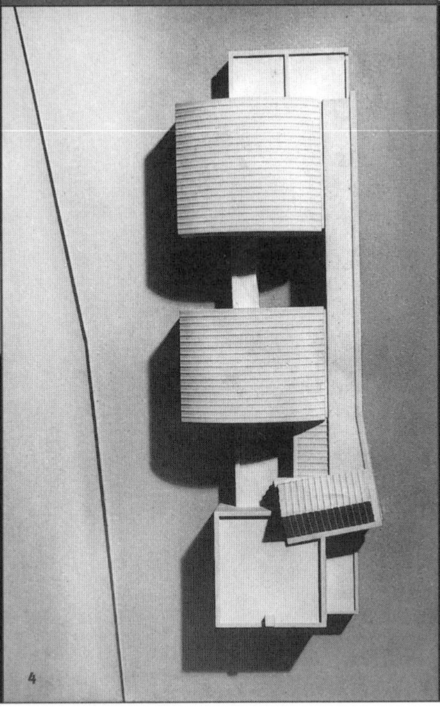

4

3

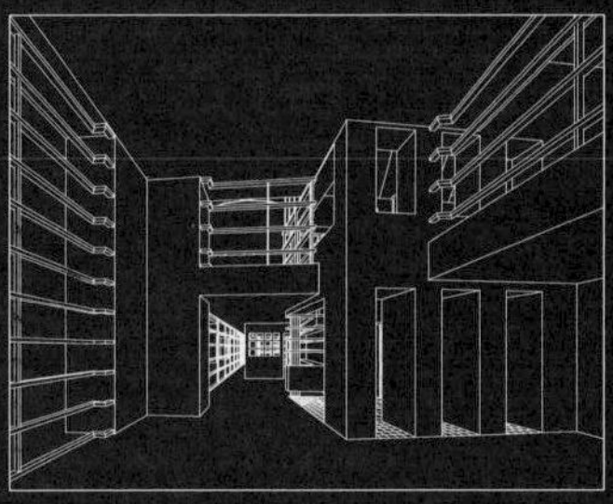

6

1 perspective from deck
2 view of model
3 perspective of living room with deck above
4 roof view
5 model from street side
6 interior perspective

First Composite House This suburban waterfront house is the first in a series of large houses whose form was divided into smaller components to reduce the scale of the building and express the function of its parts. Circulation patterns, groups of related rooms, and courtyard spaces were juxtaposed to create a sculptural composition that humanizes what would otherwise be a very large house.

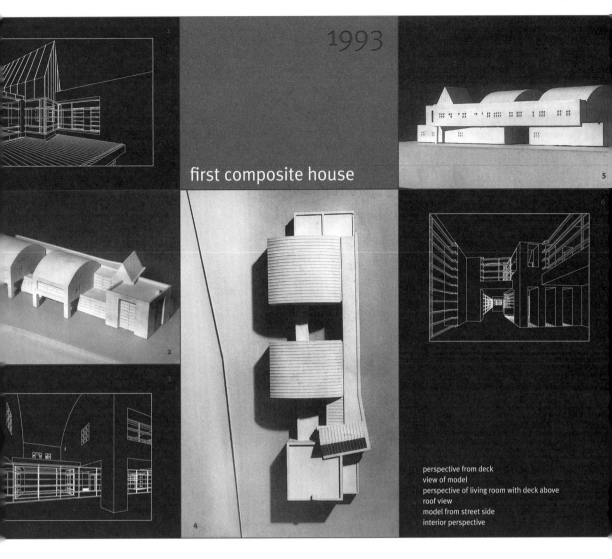

1998

early learning center

1 rain collector detail
2 classroom
3 playground elevation
4 framing with glue-lam beams

Early Learning Center This preschool building is divided into three bays to create a scale and rhythm congenial to small children. Each classroom is easily identified, but the overall form is eccentric enough to avoid an institutional feeling. Vaulted ceilings are lit from below with soft reflected light, and the bright-yellow façade is inviting and playful.

featured works

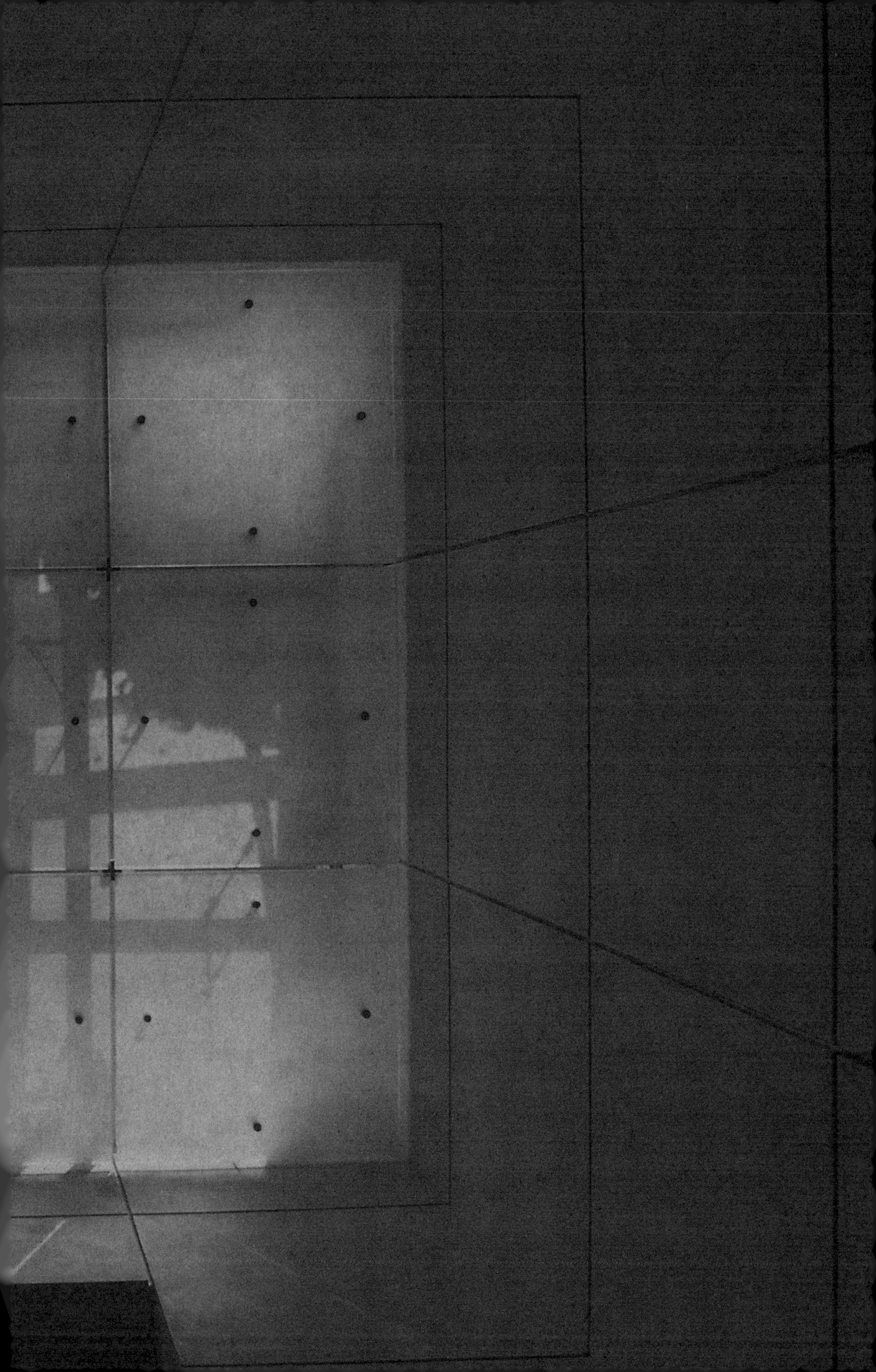

featured works The 1990s brought new opportunities for architecture, ushering in a period of dynamism and diversity of design in many countries. Several factors combined to create this moment, including economic trends, environmental sensitivities, new construction techniques, and a noticeable broadening of public interest in architecture. A wealth of engaging projects and engaged clients also happened to coincide with the end of postmodernism, as architects sought once again to redefine their art in new and creative ways.

For me this provided more occasion to pursue the principles of the modern impulse in a series of designs that are different one to the other but nonetheless constitute a linked exploration of the formal and poetic possibilities of an evolving modernism suited to millennial times.

Adding to the Masters Always an important factor in the architectural equation, context becomes the first determinant of design when the task is adding directly to an existing building – especially when that building is historically significant. A dialogue must be developed based on sympathy for the old and recognition for the new in order to produce a

whole with an integrity of its own. The addition should not demean or confuse the original by imitating it, but rather enhance it through appropriate use of materials, structure, and scale. If successful, the new and the old both retain the authenticity of their respective times while the whole becomes greater than the sum of its parts.

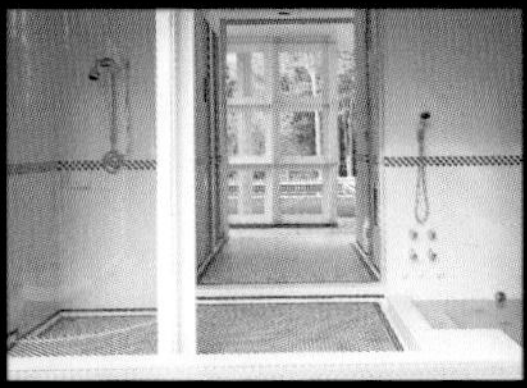

mies

house

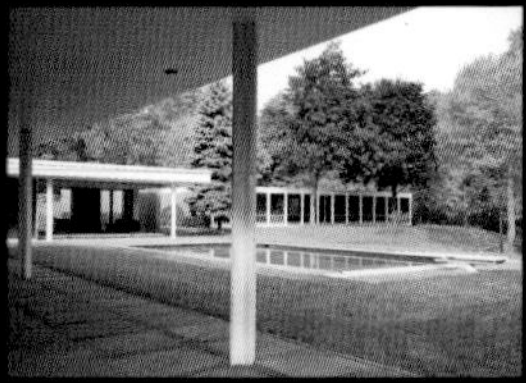

additions

Mies House Addition **1984, 1989**
Weston, Connecticut

01

The idea of "adding to" an iconic building by Mies van der Rohe was daunting. With respect to this example of high modernism – by then a historical object – the design had to be contextual. With respect to the new owners, it had to meet their present-day needs better than the original Mies house could. The task was to engage modernism as tradition and treat the International Style in a historicist mode. To do this, we turned the same materials Mies used to similar architectural ends, preserving the modernist spaces and open plan but using contemporary construction techniques to meet the new programmatic demands. The goal was for the complex to read as an integrated whole that respected the original even as it expanded it.

Mies designed this private residence in 1955, based on his earlier model for workers' housing and using window-wall units left over from the construction of his famous Lake Shore Drive Apartments in Chicago. One of only three existing Mies houses in the United States, it was bought in 1981 by an owner who wanted to expand it for use as a weekend retreat. Five years later, a new owner came back to us, requesting a permanent family residence. In the first phase, we built two linked pavilions, and in the second, we restored and enlarged the original Mies house.

By leaving the original house intact, it became part of a composition of buildings that included two separate but linked pavilions inspired by the plan of Mies's Barcelona Pavilion of 1929. One pavilion contains two guest rooms, a sauna, and a Japanese bath; the other, a large common room, with a kitchen, for meetings and entertaining. The two are linked by a perforated steel screen which also marks the precinct of the outdoor pool.

The early modernist fascination with Japanese architecture provided another point of reference. Japanese elements appear in the raised platform floors and exterior walls that slide into glass pockets, leaving the rooms completely open to the outdoors. While the Japanese allusions are literal, the materials are high-modern glass, steel, and aluminum. Mies, who used glass as a surrogate for walls, might have approved of their elimination altogether, a feat not yet technically available to him.

The contractors required constant supervision to achieve the small tolerances necessary to create the minimalism that gave the famous impression of "less is more." Our role in the construction process marked the beginning of what later became AR/CS, the construction side of our practice which enables us to realize our designs at lower cost and less aggravation for the clients.

FUJI RDPIII
FUJI RDPIII
RDPIII ⇨ 2
RDPIII ⇨ 3

DPIII 003
FUJI RDPIII
RDPIII ⇨ 4
RDPIII ⇨ 5

AF DEFI (10.2X12.7)
11943
FUJI

FUJI
11943
AF DED

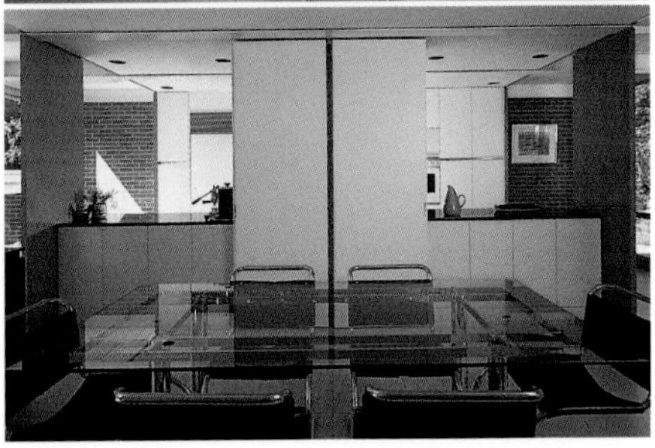

FUJI
11943
AF DFAA (10.2X12.7)
3

usonian

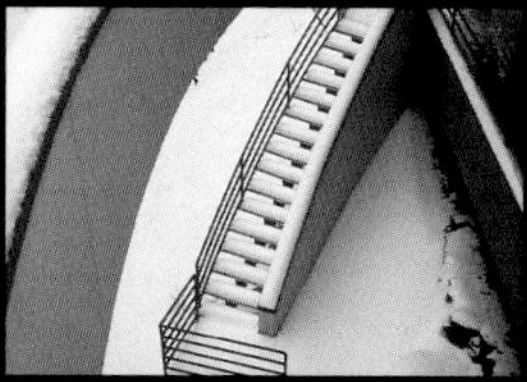

house

addition

Usonian House Addition **1994**
Pleasantville, New York

02 Here the task was to enhance the Wrightian elements of an imperfectly conceived Usonian house while correcting its deficiencies and expanding its program. Unlike the Mies house, this was no icon, but the rather poorly built 1954 work of a Wright disciple. The contextual challenge was not so much to preserve the original design as it was to improve it, to make the Wrightian elements stronger and the connection to the surrounding woodland more direct. Set on a steep, forested site, the top floor - with its carport, open plan, slanted roof, and views of the woods - possessed the best features of Wright's Usonian ideal. But the rest of the original three-story structure was awkward in appearance and provided no access to the outdoors.

The new barrel-shaped addition wraps around the lower two floors, forming a plinth for the top floor which retains the one-story reading, whose horizontality highlights the authentic Wrightian idea. Partitions were removed and glass added to the top floor to enhance this purity of expression. Most of the program was relocated in the addition, its stucco façade distinguishing it from the Wrightian wood and glass above. The roof of the addition becomes a terrace under the canopy of forest, providing usable outdoor space where there was none before. The house has an elegant and practical living and dining floor; the four bedrooms are on the lower level, with the children's room and playroom separated from the master suite, all with views of the encircling woods.

FUJI
15743
AD GCBF (10.2×12.7)

Country Houses These residential projects represent a transition between the peaked-roof houses of the postmodern eighties and the modernist boldness of our houses of the late nineties. Here the combination of modern

forms with the farmhouse shapes evokes earlier additions to the backs and sides of rural dwellings, but there is little pretense of any conversational blending between the two.

farmhouse

with

lap pool

Farmhouse with Lap Pool **1995**
Worcester, New York

03

This 18th-century white frame farmhouse, situated in an open field with a view of two silos and a hillside beyond, presented a picture-perfect image of American rural vernacular architecture. The owners asked for an addition that would be twice as large as the original, and would include an art gallery and lap pool.

The context demanded a design that would sustain multiple readings, allowing the original farmhouse to remain prominent in the composition without limiting the sculptural possibilities of the new structures. The new forms evoked the outbuildings traditionally added to the rear of farmhouses, and their shapes and materials linked them to the barns and silos on the site. As a whole the house remains abstract while responding to the context. The same design principles developed earlier for the Mies and Wright projects operate here with an anonymous vernacular building, enhancing the original both by respect and contrast.

Four separate forms contain the new living room, master-bedroom suite, gallery, and pool, their separateness reducing what might otherwise be the overwhelming size of the new structure. To maintain an appropriate scale between the old and the new, the 15-foot-high, 90-foot-long lap pool building is suppressed one level, so that the pool opens onto a sunken garden and terrace, creating a sense of privacy without obstructing the landscape with fences or walls. The buildings each respond to larger landscapes of their own, extending the house into exterior spaces that are defined by a combination of built and landscape form. Architecture does not stop at the outer wall of the building but integrally includes the spaces created by reshaped earth and the surfaces composed of plantings.

The resulting composition now functions as a family homestead and retirement retreat, as well as a center for the display of local artists' work. The two functions are spatially and symbolically separated but not remote from one another.

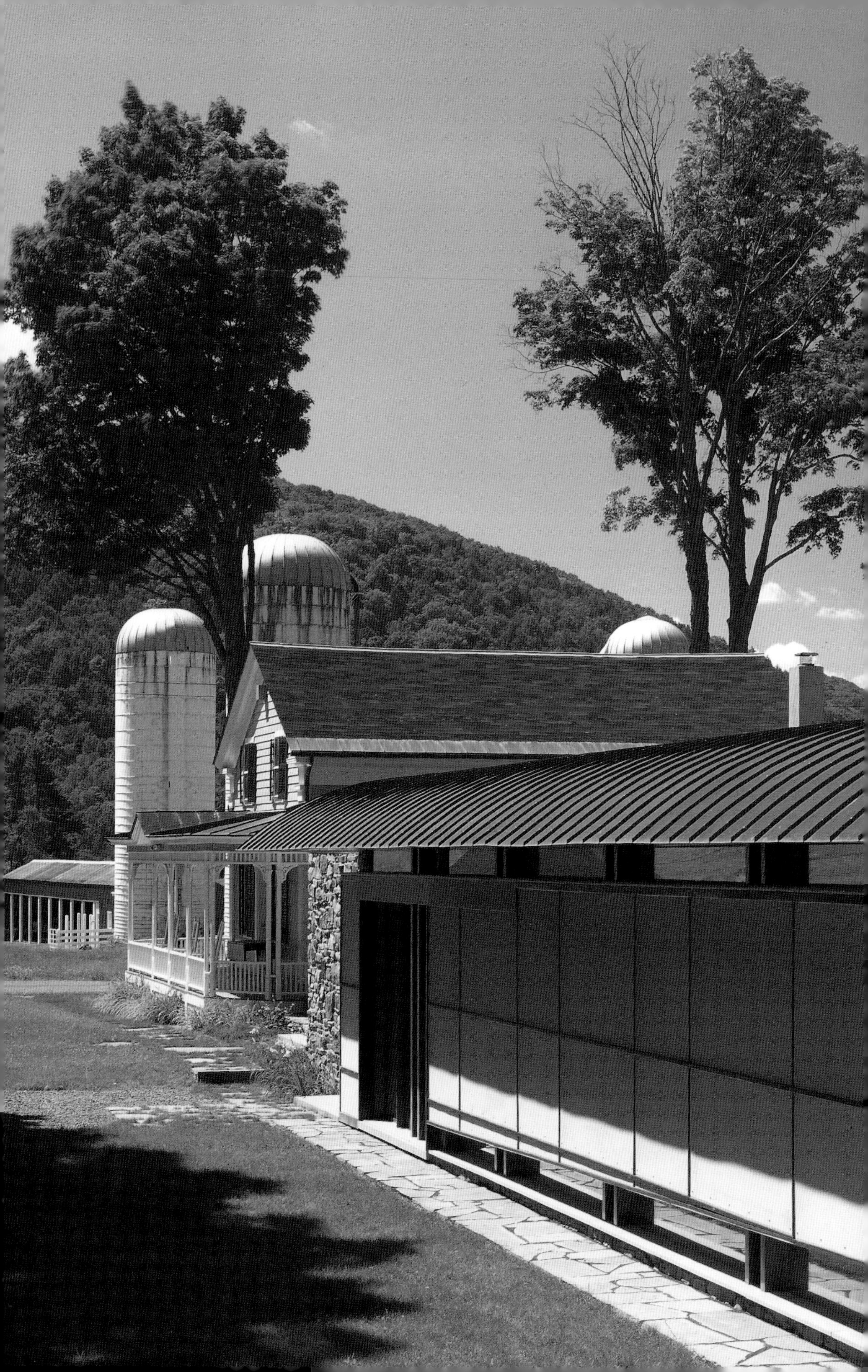

FUJIFILM RDPII
11552

FUJIFILM RDPII
11552

FUJIFILM RDPII

KODAK EPP 6005
47
6

KODAK EPP 6005
52
10
PP 6005

FUJIFILM RDPII
11552

linear

house

Linear House **1996**
Millerton, New York

04

New England farmers built their houses directly on the road that was their link to markets and to town. They kept domestic activity as close as possible, planting vegetable gardens and raising chickens nearby, so that the household became a small precinct of order isolated from the spaces of the surrounding countryside. Today, when proximity to the highway holds little appeal, the most desirable rural landscape offers privacy, views, and the invitation to wander.

To enlarge this early 19th century farmhouse for a family of four with growing children, the relation of house to site was inverted to suit a late 20th century idea of nature. The new addition is an 80-foot extension that stretches back from the original house on the road and makes the transition in plan and section to the natural landscape which had before been invisible and inaccessible.

The two contexts – one of landscape, the other of vernacular style – were related in the simple, metal shed-roof of the addition, which echoes the utilitarian aspect of the rural idiom. And the new exterior walkway from the second floor of the old house to the pond and orchard level uses the topography in the same way that local barns once gave easy access to the hayloft.

The addition is a pure linear shape, with two glass façades hung on a rationalist post-and-beam structure. Only one room deep, its formal scheme allows each room to view the waterfall on one side and a new rock garden on the other, while the cross-ventilation makes air conditioning unnecessary. The linear plan also maximizes privacy; the new rooms are not contiguous, and the new wing, with two bedrooms, study, and family room, provides separate space for children and guests. A new kitchen connects the common living functions of the old house and the new, both of which are designed to accommodate an informal family lifestyle filled with activity both indoors and out.

FUJIFILM RVP
54856

bridge

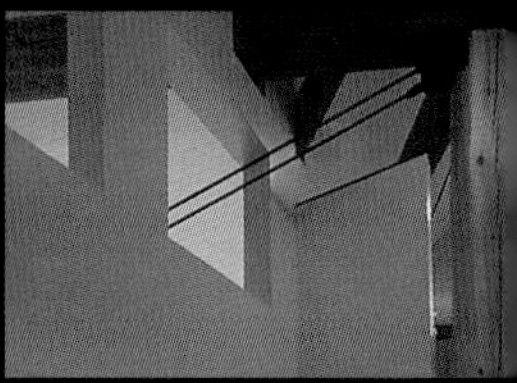

house

Bridge House **1996**
Olive Bridge, New York

05

This country retreat for an urban family sought to reconfigure the shape and function of the typical vacation house, which is often just a regular house built somewhere else. Here the design expresses, boldly and forthrightly in space and form, the uses and structure of what is in effect a guest-and-gathering house. The site and program demanded bridges both conceptual and physical: bridges between historical forms, styles, and materials; as well as between topographies, uses, and generations.

The house consists of three identifiable forms, each with its own stylistic expression and distinctive use of materials. The main façade is a large, three-story cube, faced in thin concrete panels akin to cut stone, suggesting the Palladian formality of colonial American architecture. A clapboard-sided, steeply pitched roof-form intersects the cube at an oblique angle, its shape a gesture to 19th-century regional farmhouses. This form is penetrated by a long, narrow, elevated wing clad in corrugated metal typical of a low-cost rural building in the 20th century. The whole is a composition that evokes three centuries of American country architecture.

From the roof terrace on top of the cube, a long bridge leads to the bluestone cliffs and connects the groomed lawns and rose garden below with the natural rocks, waterfalls, and forests beyond. The interior of the house concentrates the common areas in the large living room in the cube, places intermediate spaces like the library, billiard room, and study in the pitched-roof form, and segregates the five bedrooms in the linear wing for privacy. Each bedroom faces the corridor, has windows overlooking the woods, and is separated acoustically by an intervening bath. The plan accommodates several generations of family by providing different kinds of common space for different ages and family units, and sleeping spaces for 24 people.

Both interior and exterior spaces are characterized by elements of whimsy and surprise, so that the spatial experience is variable and playful – not so much a house as a place for fun and camaraderie in the woods.

FUJIFILM RDPII 11854

Composite Houses The 1990s saw another resurgence of the modern impulse, freed of the postmodern constraints of representation and also of the ossified modernism that had impelled postmodernism in the first place.

This series of “houses in parts” reflects this liberation in their plastic forms, innovative plans, and reinterpretations of domestic living. In addition, the trend toward larger family houses demanded an architectural solution that would “domesticate” their size and scale. This provided an opportunity for tectonic invention and sculptural play in the parts that comprised the whole.

lake
house

with

court

Lake House with Court **1997**
Highland Park, Illinois

06

Situated on a bluff overlooking Lake Michigan, this design responds to the beauty and bluster of the lake by creating two worlds. One is oriented to the sunrise, water, and changing views of the lake, while the other is turned inward toward a courtyard that captures the warmth of the sun and provides a contrast to the severe lakefront weather. The strong forms of the house express the two worlds: its curved courtyard façade tears away from the glassed, three-story rectangle facing the lake. The important rooms - living room, dining room, family room, master bedroom, office, and hallways - have exposure to both the courtyard and the lake. A three-foot-thick brick wall curves through the house, a modernist metaphor for the separation of the man-made from the natural.

The house subverts the traditional suburban pattern, which presents the front yard, front façade, and garage to the street. Here, very little of the large house is visible to the community. The circular courtyard, separated from the street by a garden wall, replaces the customary open and unused front yard with a private exterior landscape. Cars enter from the side behind the curved brick wall that contains the garage, directly accessible to the house but out of sight.

The house is designed as a sequence of layers, in which the seasons and weather are as much a part of the experience as the normal activities of daily life. The plan lends itself to large-scale entertaining and family reunions, and also creates comfortable quarters for a couple living by themselves.

AR/CS built the house, proving the effectiveness and efficiency of combining design and construction in one continuous, controlled process.

FUJI
RDPII 6
FUJI RDPII
5

Kodak EPR 3171

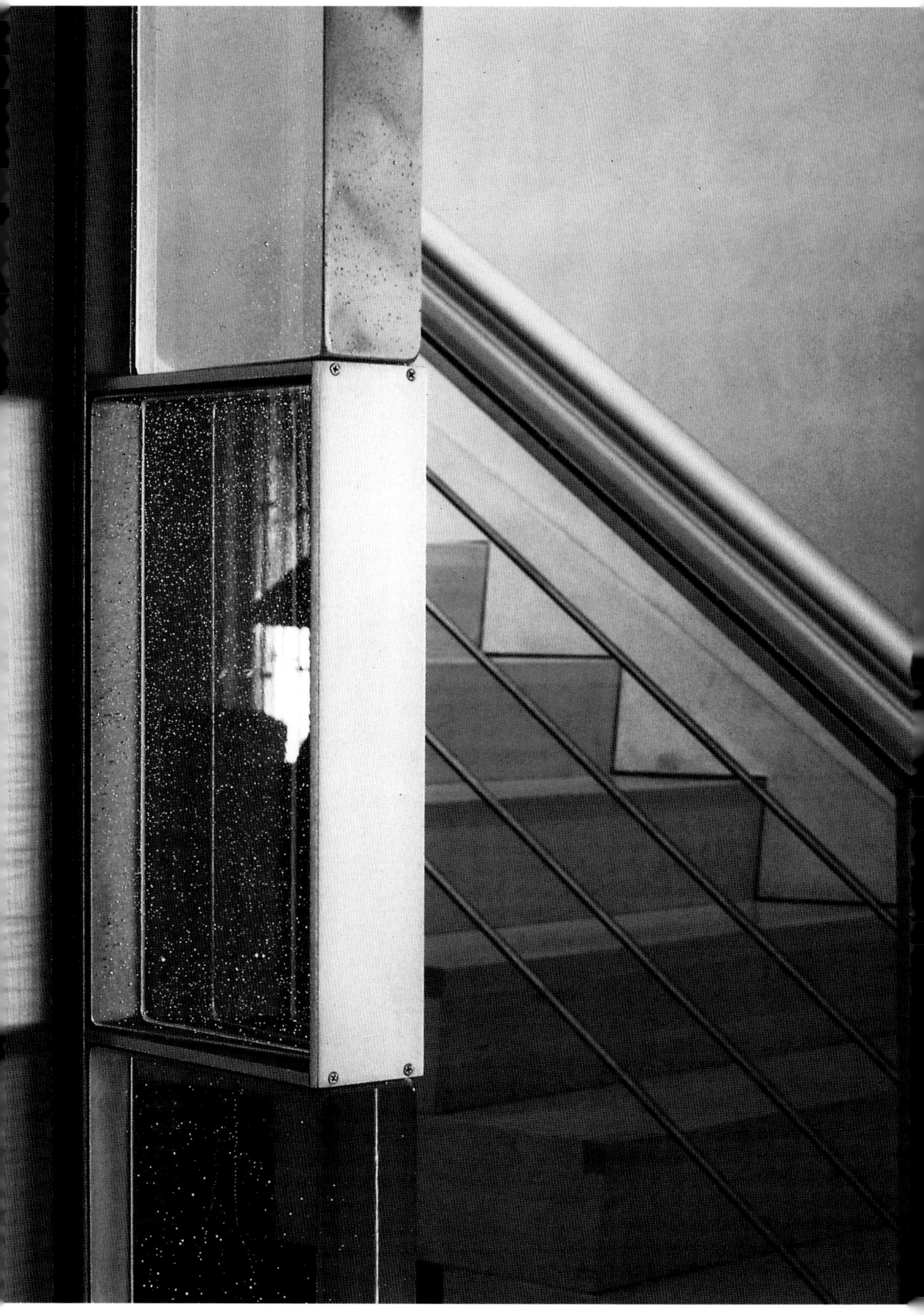

Kodak EPY 6271

Kodak E100G 0171

Kodak E100G 0171

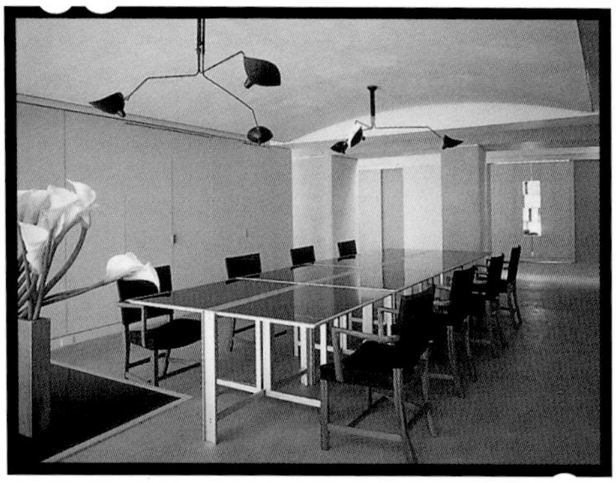

double

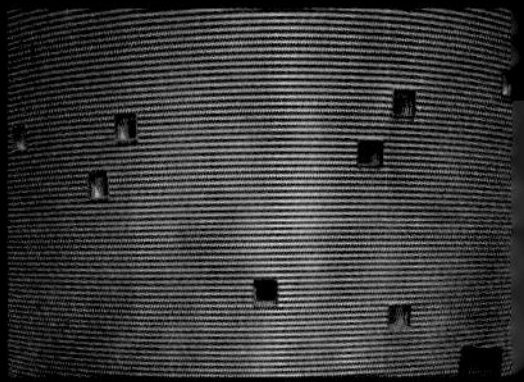

house

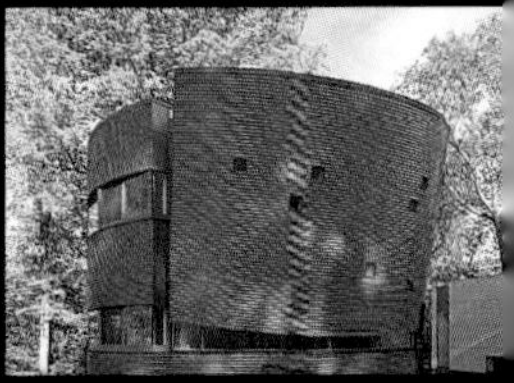

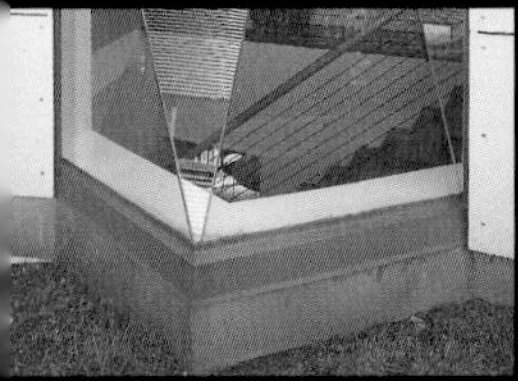

Double House **2002**
New Canaan, Connecticut

07

This house is a dialogue between two shapes: the cylinder containing the children's bedrooms with whimsical spaces and 180-degree views; and a rectangular form for the more formal public spaces and the master bedroom suite. Both geometries are manipulated so that an inflection of the rectangle and a peeling away of the cylinder mark the vertical circulation within and provide views of the other building across the lawn.

By dividing the 7,200-square-foot structure into two volumes – nicknamed the crate and barrel – and submerging the service spaces, the composition minimizes the bulk of the house and produces varied views and experiences of the landscape. It also encourages parental privacy on the one hand and a sense of independence for the children on the other. Over time, the cylinder can accommodate other uses, such as studio and office space and visits of adult children and their families.

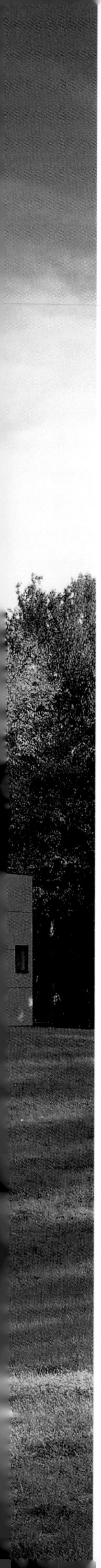

FUJIFILM RDPIII 02452

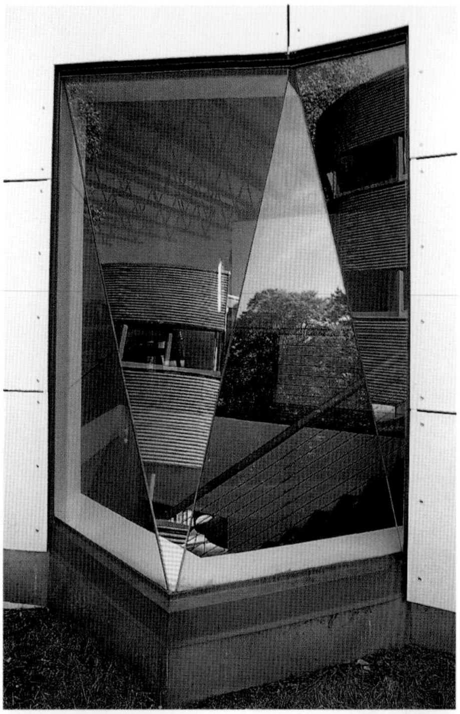

bar

house

08

The simple and strong geometric shape of this house – which is a bar set boldly across, rather than nestling along, the valley floor – stands up to the rugged and majestic mountains that surround it. Despite its strength, the house is partly submerged in the ground, as if to lock it into the landscape. The views up and down the valley dominate the interior spaces, but they are tempered in different ways by the varied size and placement of the windows and the shape of the rooms.

The winter weather is severe, and the sun reaches the bottom of the narrow valley only from the south. The bedrooms and the family room are located in a single-loaded corridor on the south side of the second floor. The linear program gives each room southern exposure and provides spectacular views of the valley. An exterior stair is elongated on the northern side, leading to an open-air roof deck, allowing light into the second floor and providing the bedrooms with cross-ventilation. The living room on the ground floor has scenic views on three sides. A garage and guest apartment are located on the other side of the driveway, and an overhang of the house provides protection in inclement weather.

floating

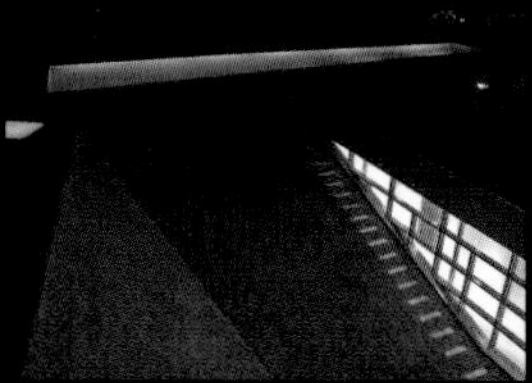
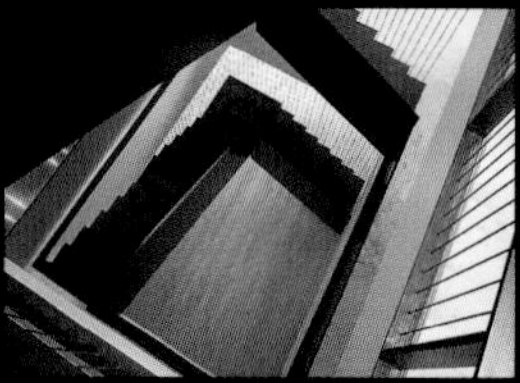

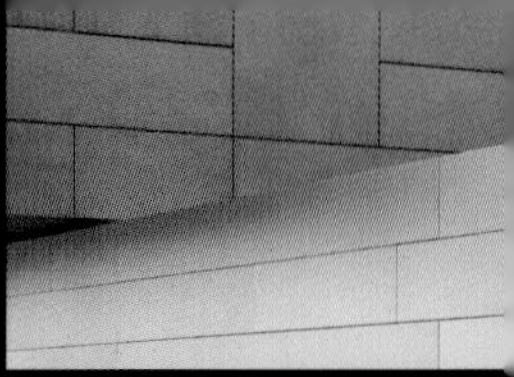

box

house

Floating Box House **2005**
Austin, Texas

09

This house stands on a stunning native landscape of landmarked live oaks and frames the modern urban skyline of Austin in the distance.

The forms of the house consist of a floating box, the stainless steel structure on which it sits, and the partly buried base. The guest bedrooms, media room, and service areas are located in the buried section. An underground garage assures that the landscape remains free of automobiles and driveways. The floating box, which is the top floor, contains the family bedrooms.

Between the ground plane and the floating box is an entirely transparent glassed enclosure that gives the living room, dining room, and kitchen unobstructed views of the natural surroundings on one side and the Austin skyline on the other. The stainless-steel structure holds the mechanicals for the house and produces the illusion of a wall-less space with a floating form above.

Moving through the building, the sectional complexities add to the spatial experiences inside and outside the house. The sunken courtyard, formed by a sharp cut in the earth, connects the ground floor to the transparent living room by an upward-sloping grass ramp. This ramp becomes the roof of the buried sections, with skylights cutting through the grass to provide natural light for the spaces below.

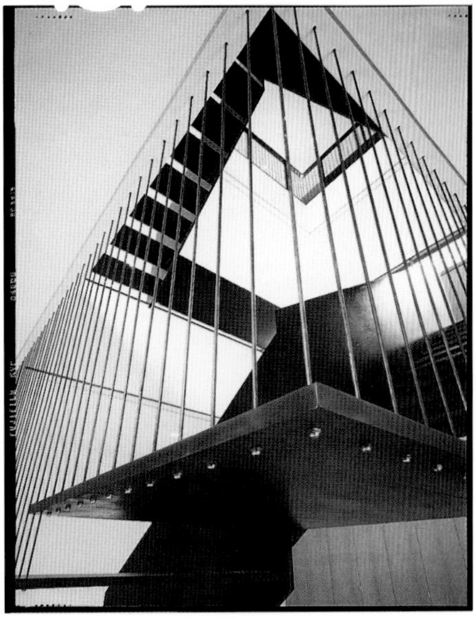

Spec Houses Following the premise that the process of design and construction benefits from the engagement of the architect, we wanted to take it one step further into the world of speculative building. In these projects we acted as developer, architect, and builder, all focused on a commitment to good design. Our experience in designing, building, and

selling emphatically modernist projects suggests that the common wisdom of the market's resistance to innovative design is only partially true. The town of Aspen has since selected us to design, build, and deliver an affordable housing project of 41 bedrooms based on a similar approach.

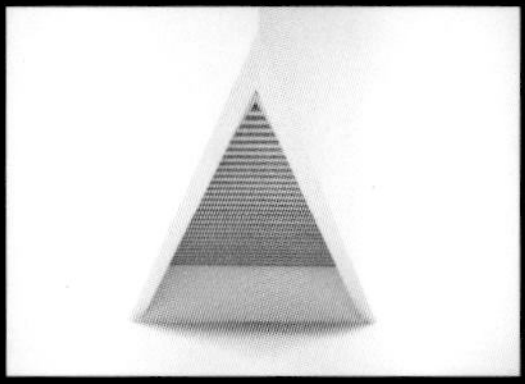

cube

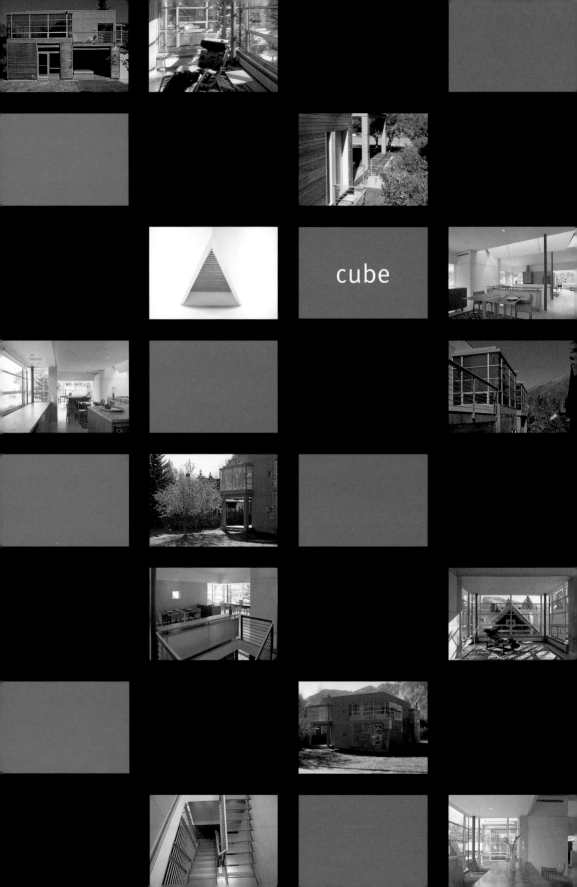

house

10 We chose Aspen as a venue for development for several reasons. It has a remarkable architectural heritage, from the early mining town and Victorian buildings of the late 19th century through the mid-20th-century Bauhaus structures of the Aspen Institute. Despite the recent boom in themed architecture of "mountain design homes," some of rustic logs and stone, others of adobe and Swiss Chalet imitations, it seemed possible in an active real estate market to prove that good modernist design makes economic sense. In addition, the town's residential district presented a small-scale urban context with many of the conditions that exist in larger scale in cities around the country.

The first speculative house was built on a 1/8-acre site, a spatial cube filling its lot on the town grid the way urban residences typically do. The conventional residential plan was inverted, with the living, dining, and kitchen areas located on the second floor of the house, providing spectacular views of the mountains from every corner and lifting the living areas above street level for privacy. Because the corners of the cube are glass, the diagonal views cut across the town grid so that the mountain views are not blocked by the houses across the street.

The cube accommodates a large program, with five bedrooms, a separate caretaker's apartment, and a considerable amount of public space. One-third of the area is below grade to reduce the impact of the house on the street; a central skylight provides light through a glass stairway.

AR/CS built the house, which was sold before it was completed.

zinc

house

Zinc House **2002**
Aspen, Colorado

11 Similarly situated in the historic downtown residential grid, a few blocks from the first project, this house is a series of indoor and outdoor rooms organized around two axes, horizontal and vertical. The horizontal axis is an inside thoroughfare, which runs from the front to the rear entrance, with interior bedrooms and the exterior courtyard opening onto it from either side. Because zoning required a separate structure for the garage, this thoroughfare had to traverse a diagonal from the front entrance to the garage at the rear, producing a tension with the geometry of the street, which we used to create an unexpected spatial experience on the first floor that is echoed in the living spaces above.

The vertical axis is a stairway and ventilating skylight that opens the house, from bottom to top, to light and the circulation of air. Sliding mahogany panels on the outside walls of the living spaces open to make the room seem like a balcony with views of the mountains beyond the gardens below. A horizontal wood beam breaks up the floor-to-ceiling expanse of glass to give warmth and human scale to the high-ceilinged, loft-like spaces. The house was built by AR/CS, making it possible to include features such as the mahogany panel-and-window system.

Kodak E100VS 0461

Kodak E100VS 0461

affordable

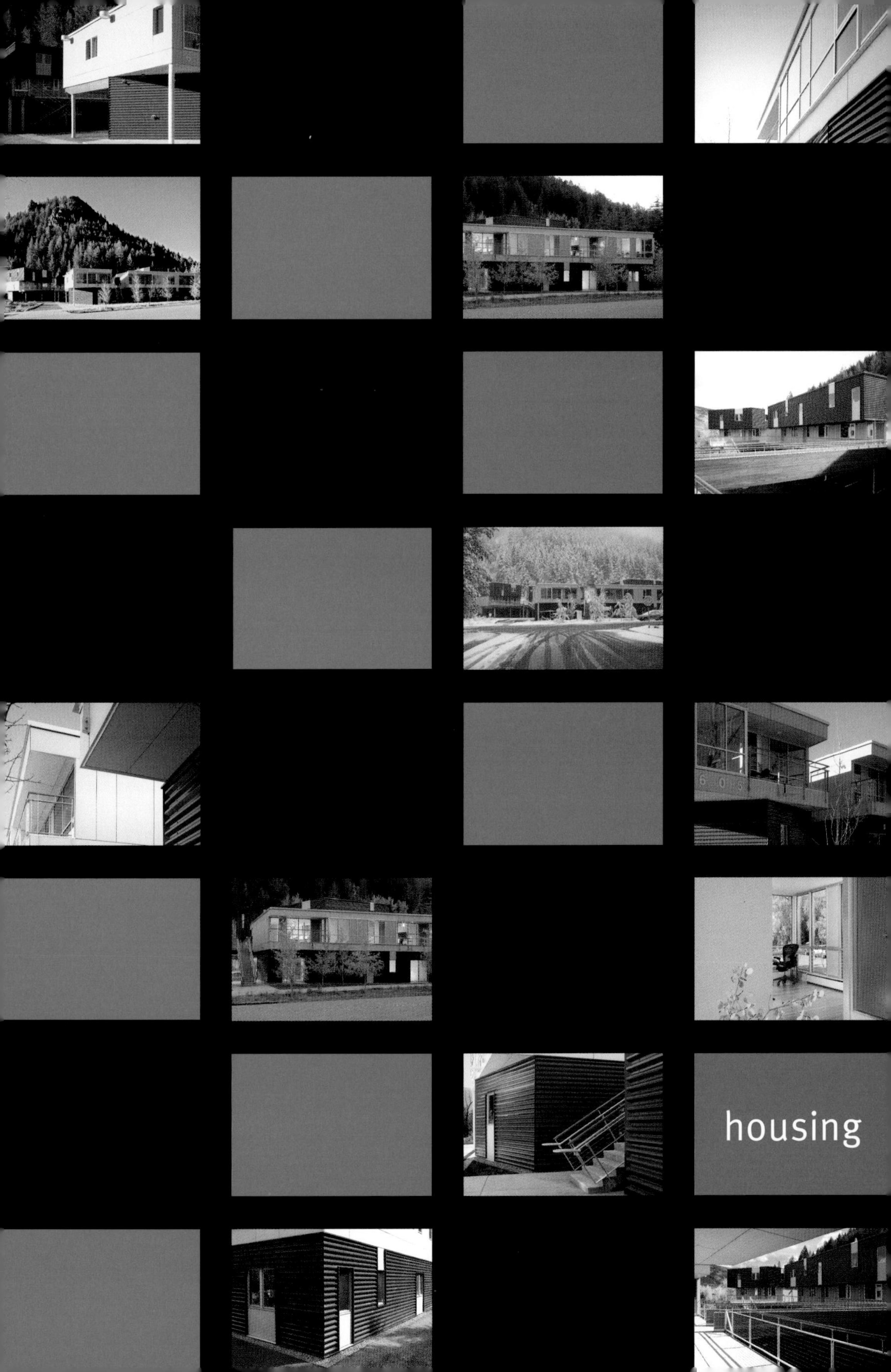
housing

12

In response to the overwhelming need for affordable housing in Aspen, we partnered with the City of Aspen to build a complex of 14 units for working families who previously could not afford to live close to their workplace. Subsidized by the City, we acted as developer, architect and construction manager and delivered it "turn key" to the municipality. As part of the planning process, an open space parcel was created linking together the many public trails surrounding the site.

We were able to convert a brown-field site, previously seen as unusable because of its steep elevation and presence of mine waste rock, into a multifaceted solution to the City of Aspen's need for affordable housing.

A unique housing solution, this complex is a riff on the traditional courtyard scheme. It redefines and expands what is typically a formulaic architectural typology. A skewed geometry allows the building to conform to the streetscape in front and the natural contours and vegetation of the slope above. The project steps up the hill, providing covered parking that is only partially visible from the street. Three angled 'slots' slice through the courtyard block breaking it into an interconnected series of volumes. The 'slots' provide internal circulation and a physical and visual connection to the mountains.

A series of 2nd floor walkways and playful bridges provide multiple connections to the units, public trails and city sidewalks. Multiple circulation routes enhance fire safety and provide privacy by insuring that most units are accessed without passing neighboring apartments. A special wall system combines high performance glass with colorful insulated panels.

An efficient centralized mechanical system, low VOC paints, recycled content carpets, and laminates that did not require finishing resulted in a building that far exceeded the strict sustainability code of the City of Aspen which is based on LEED formulas.

605

6 0 5

605

STOP

Yoshio Taniguchi

EXIT

EXIT

Special Uses Buildings with an unusual program sometimes offer the purest opportunity to pursue the principles of the modern impulse and design "from zero," since no preconceived building type or preimagined image of "house," "school," or "church" inter-

venes in the design process. For this reason, too, these special-use buildings sometimes more clearly reveal the balancing of the attributes of use, structure, context, and social effect with poetic expression than conventional buildings do, providing yet another perspective on the work of architecture.

scholar's

library

Scholar's Library **2004**
Olive Bridge, New York

13 A pure and elegant Platonic cube matches the unity of the building's purpose and form, in both programmatic and metaphorical terms. The first floor is completely closed and contains stacks for a library of books. The second floor, which is entirely open, is a scholar's working study. The study sits on the books below much like scholarship rests on the body of work that precedes it.

The structure expresses this dual character, with the floating roof cantilevered off the second floor to highlight the distinction between the solid and the void. The windows (standard-issue sliding doors) open on all four sides, stacking in opposite corners, to create the feeling of an aerie in the woods. The changing seasons provide the context, with the study "walls" green in the summer, orange in the fall, and white in the winter. An economy of means in cost, materials, and structure result in simplicity and directness with no elaboration. The study is a serene and solitary haven for quiet work that is at the same time immersed in the natural world around it.

In its alignment of use, structure, context, and social effect, this library probably comes close to the ever-elusive perfect diagram that we are always seeking.

広辞苑

横浜市史
神奈川県教育史
NIPPON
PACIFIC RIFT
TEXTUAL STRATEGIES

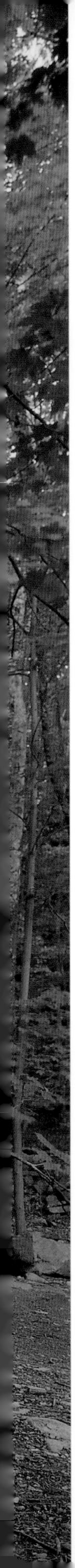

inverted

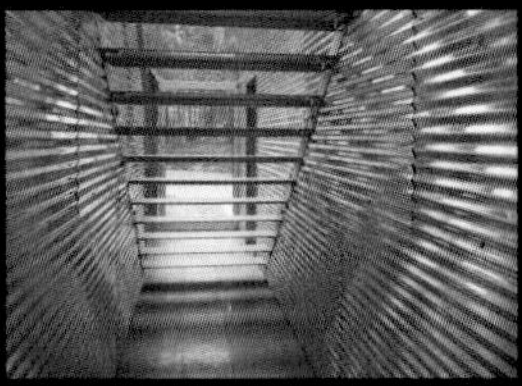

outbuilding

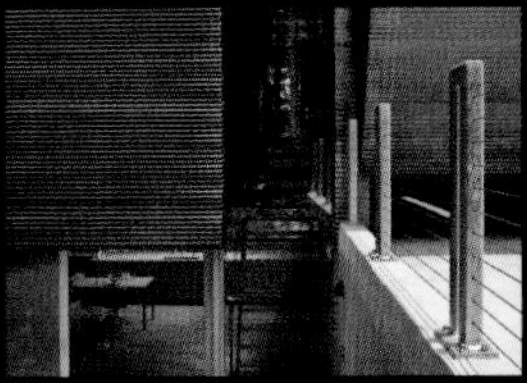

Inverted Outbuilding **2005**
Lake George, New York

14

This unusual program led to a play of strong form and assertive materials in order to unify a massive storage building and two intimate guest studios within a single structure. A long, solid rectangular bar contains the storage and garage space and anchors two cube-shaped guest suites at either end – one living room raised above the bar, the other dropped below it on the slope of the hill, each an inversion of the other. Corrugated copper cladding unites the bar and its mirror-image inversions in a utilitarian material of corrugated metal that is softened by the warmth of copper.

The simplicity of the section, the solidity of the bar, and the transparency of the two inverted glassed living rooms give the building an elegance of proportion and presence. The large airplane-hangar doors of the garage open to become awnings for an outdoor entertainment space, and the upper apartment also acts as a gatehouse overlooking the entrance to the site.

Kodak E100G 0171

SISTERS

Urban Works Having designed houses and apartments in urban settings, we had the opportunity in the 1990s to return to the social mission of modern architecture, which sought to bring good design to all parts of society beyond the monuments of high culture and the grounds of elite institutions. The end of the century brought a renewed focus on the inner city, with non-profit, state, and private groups cooperating to rethink the educational and social services available to urban families and their children. Because of our experience in combining architecture and construction we are committed and able to produce good design at low cost for the underserved of the inner city.

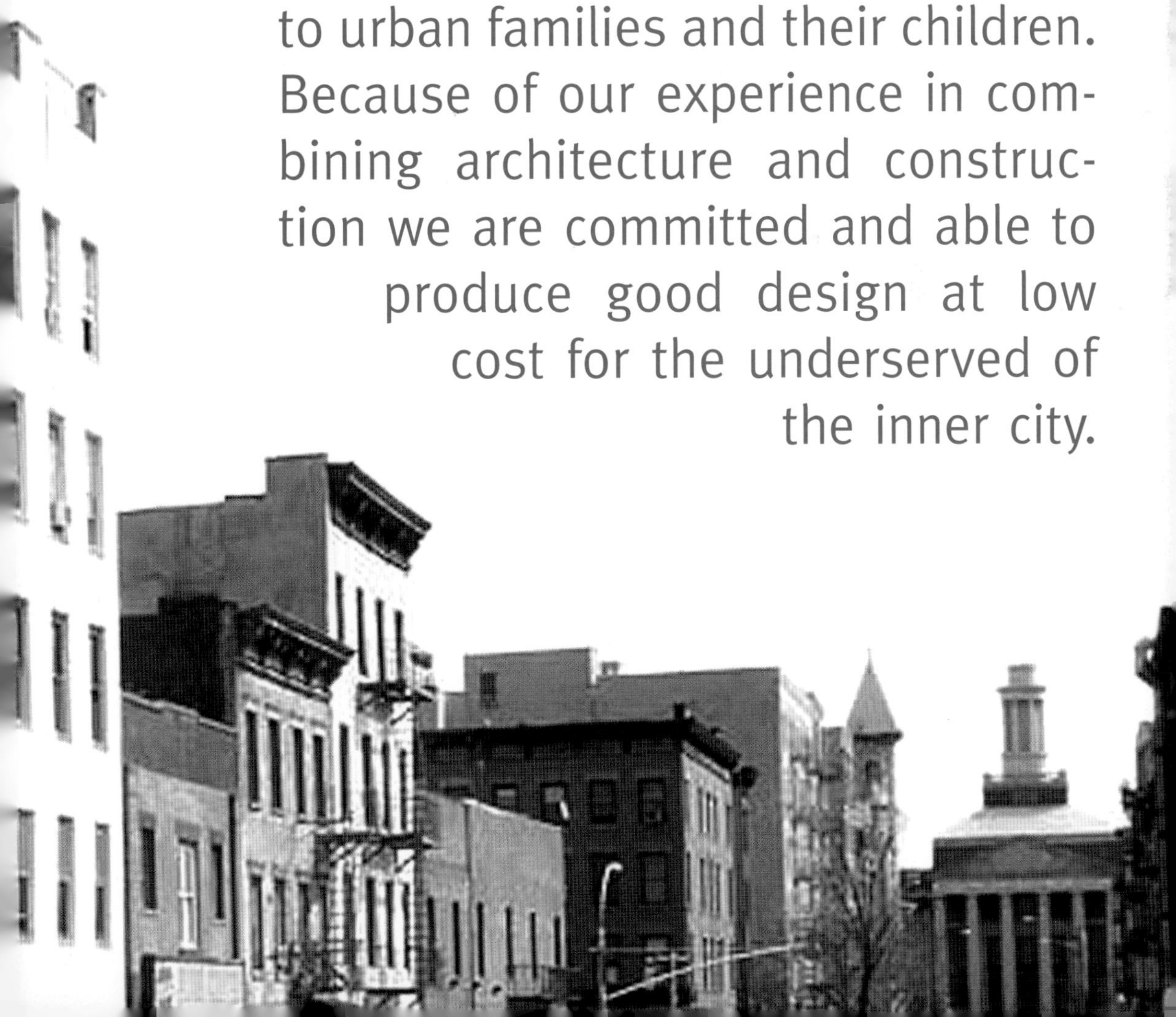

corner

house

Corner House 1998
Brooklyn, New York

15

Building a large new house in an established urban block led to contrasting approaches to the interior and exterior. Facing the street, the house is formal and closed, both for privacy and decorum and to respect the fabric of the neighborhood. Inside, the spaces are dynamic and open, dissolving into a light-filled central atrium that rises the entire height of the building and is animated by the constant activity of a large family moving through and around it.

The exterior alludes to the European family's personal connection to early Viennese modernism, with its stress on simplicity and strength of form. The three-and-a-half story cube is broken into three small compositions, almost mini-houses in themselves, which bring the scale of the façade into proportion with the surrounding buildings. Unlike most corner residences, which treat one street façade as the front and the other as the side, here a coherent sculptural shape turns the corner, terminating each block with equal decisiveness. The third floor at the same corner is cut out to form a terrace enclosed by a trellis and roof garden, with the existing trees along the public sidewalk forming a private sycamore canopy above.

The rooms, including 11 bedrooms for a large extended family, are organized around the central stairway and skylight, which pours light into the middle of the house. To emphasize the separation of public from private space, the main staircase is set off from the entrance hallways by a two-story open wall of wood and operable glass screens. Clean modernist detailing complements a richness of materials, which include mahogany, integrally colored plasters, and stone. The third-floor sunroom, enclosed by steel and glass walls, opens to the terrace, which provides outdoor space – unusual in the city – for children, gardening, and entertaining.

KODAK E100VS
48

KODAK E100VS
54

KODAK E100VS
49

KODAK
53
KODAK E100VS

charter

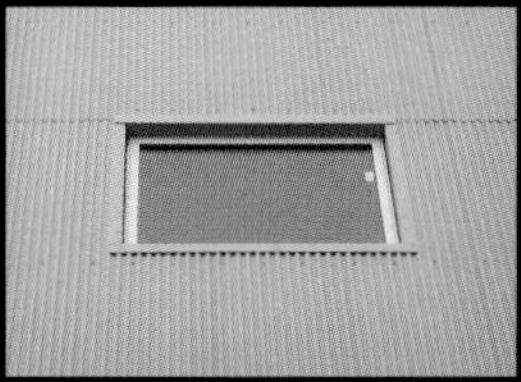

school

Charter School **2004, 2006**
Bronx, New York

16

The challenge was to create a low-cost but college-like campus within a single block in the South Bronx, which would foster the educational ideals of the school for 800 students, their parents, and teachers.

We turned the steep site, which at first seemed almost unbuildable, into an asset by creating a series of linear forms that step up the slope, each one identified as a separate "academy." This avoided the box-like institutional cavern of most school buildings and made the scale student-friendly. The two middle schools, upper school, and a multi-use "gymnatorium" for both school and community activities have their own distinctive architectural form. Like the mission of the school, the self-contained and serious but welcoming spaces represent a retreat from the problems of the inner city as well as the hopes and opportunities that education brings.

Jettisoning the conventions of New York City school construction, we used precast concrete plank and steel for the structural system because it was less expensive, faster to build, and, in conjunction with exposed mechanical systems, allowed for higher ceilings and more spacious classrooms. Instead of the usual costly masonry exterior, we chose light-weight industrial colored metal claddings to mark the different academies. A small expanse of blue polished tile and glass highlights the special shared rooms for music and science, appearing like a beacon for the ambitions of the school.

Kodak E100G 0171

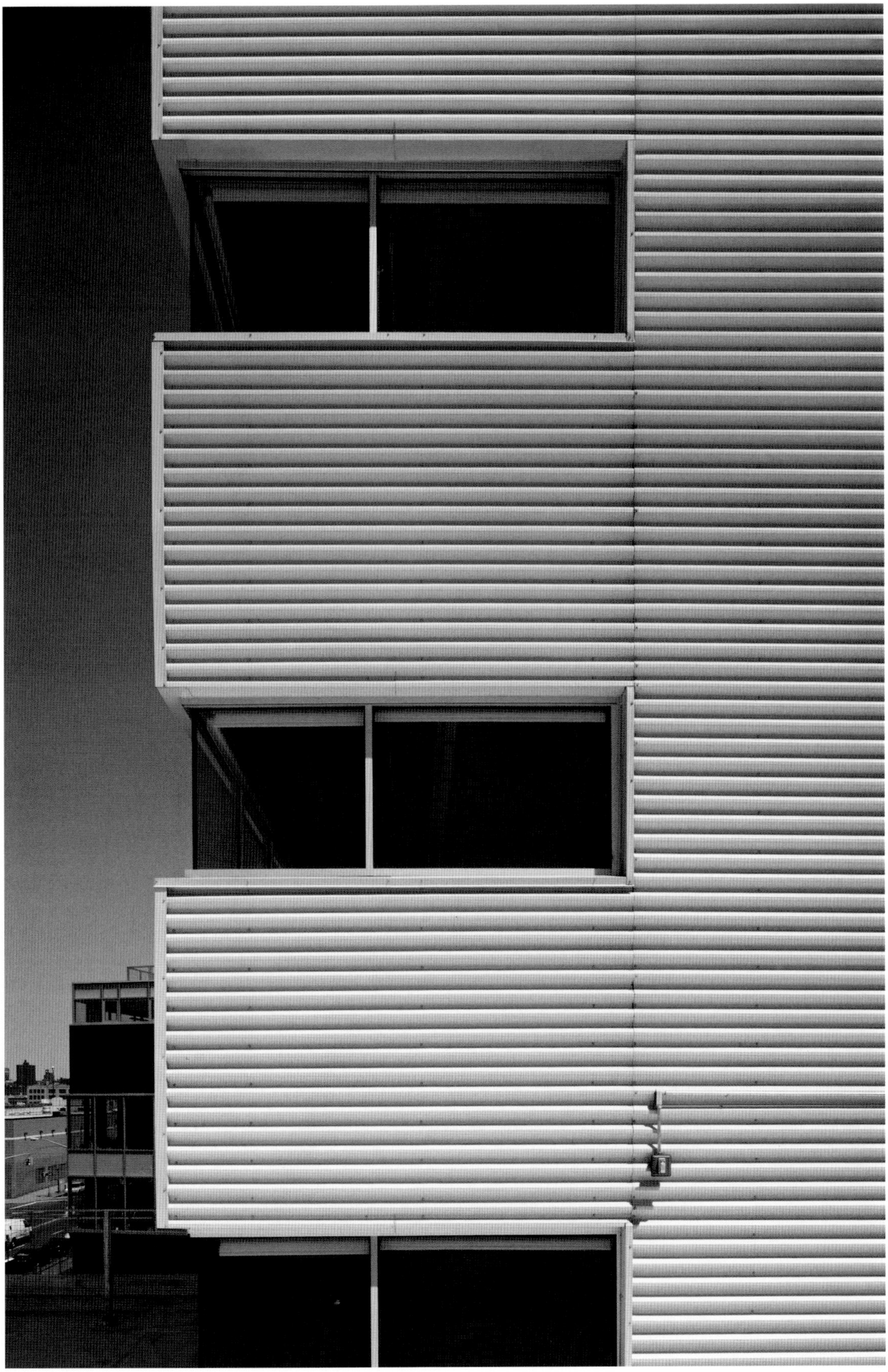

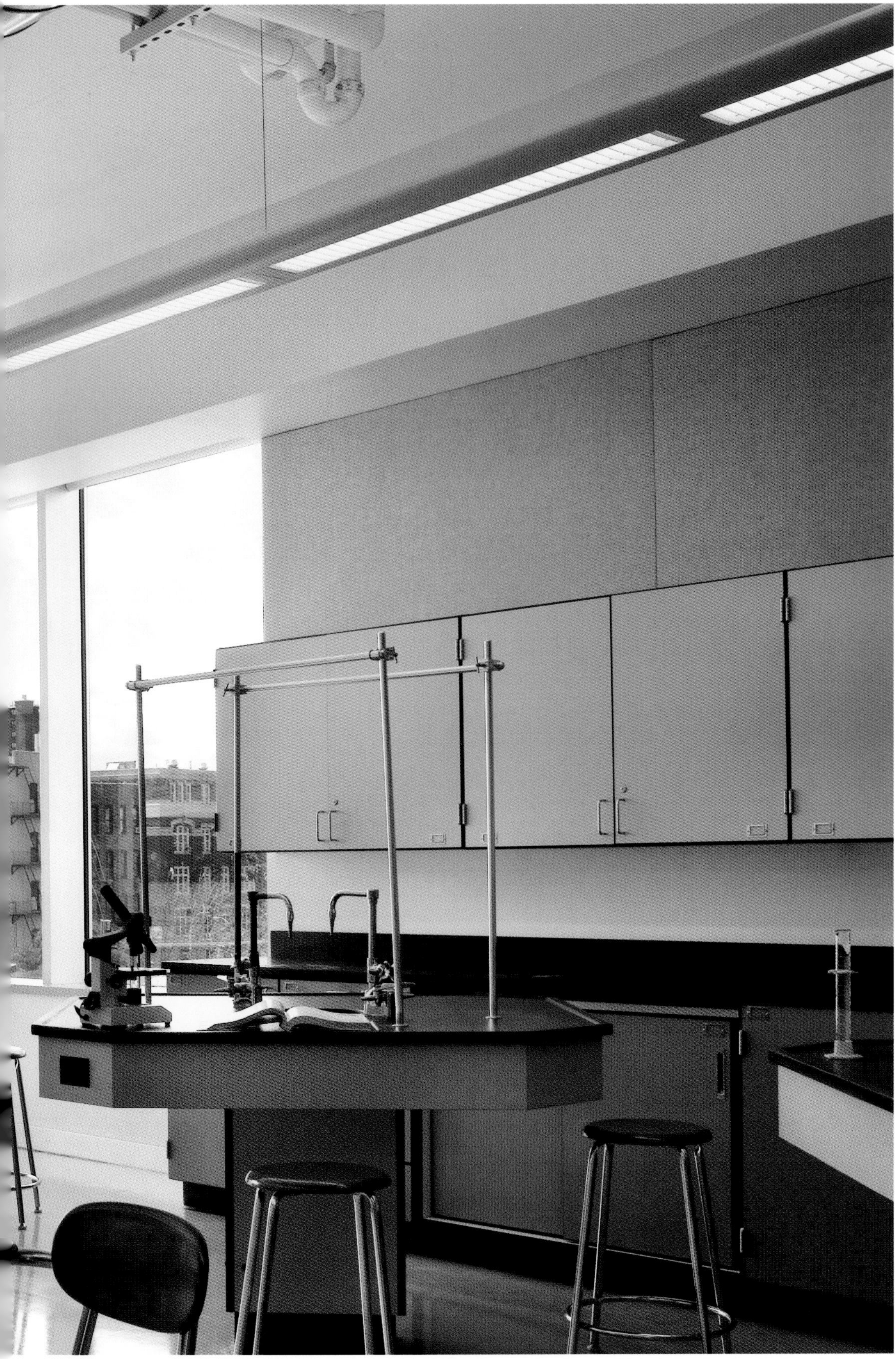

AMIGOS GROCERY

social

services

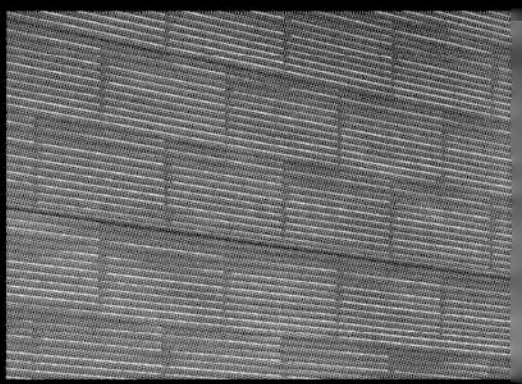

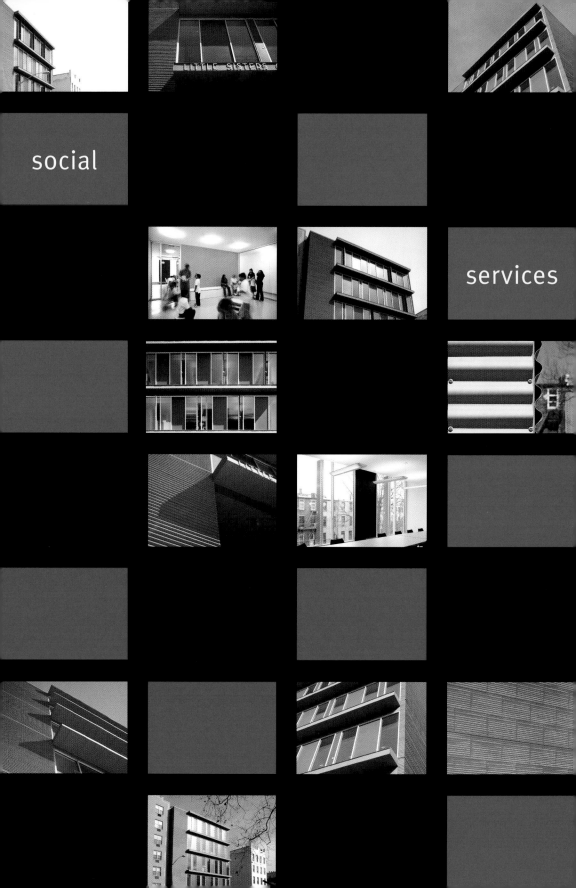

center
HEALTH SERVICE

Social Services Center **2003**
East Harlem, New York

17 This building for a family services center dedicated to community outreach has a welcoming, colorful, and transparent façade that literally reaches out to the community to express the openness of the organization within. The façade is made up of an ordinary exterior door system, large pieces of fixed glass, and insulated brightly colored panels. As the colors brighten and dim with the sunlight and the operable panels open and close with use, the façade constantly changes character, making it an instant neighborhood attraction and conveying the mission of the organization.

A steel structural frame allows for clear, column-free spans to provide unobstructed views and flexibility to reconfigure the interior space to suit any change in the programs. The structural frame and foundations are sized for two additional floors should the organization wish to expand the building in the future.

Despite the extremely limited budget, low-cost materials and attention to construction techniques enabled us to create a visible and welcoming refuge for the low-income families who depend on the center for its services, which include home nursing care, a food pantry, family advocacy, day care, and a thrift store.

LITTLE SISTERS OF THE ASSUMPTION FAMILY HEALTH SERVICE
333

LY HEALTH SERVICE

LITTLE SISTERS

LITTLE SISTERS OF THE ASS

TION FAMILY HEALTH SERVICE
333

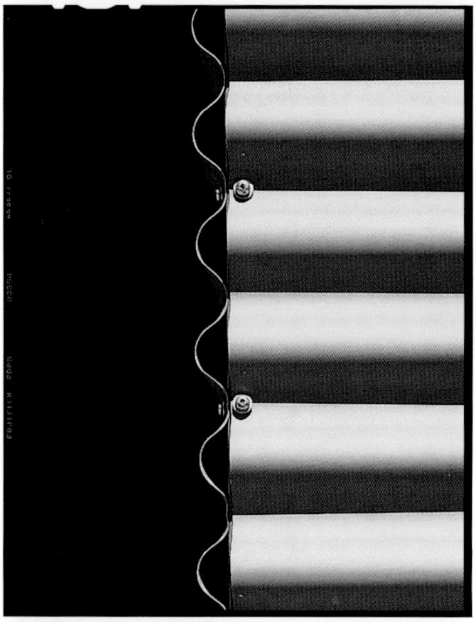

documentation

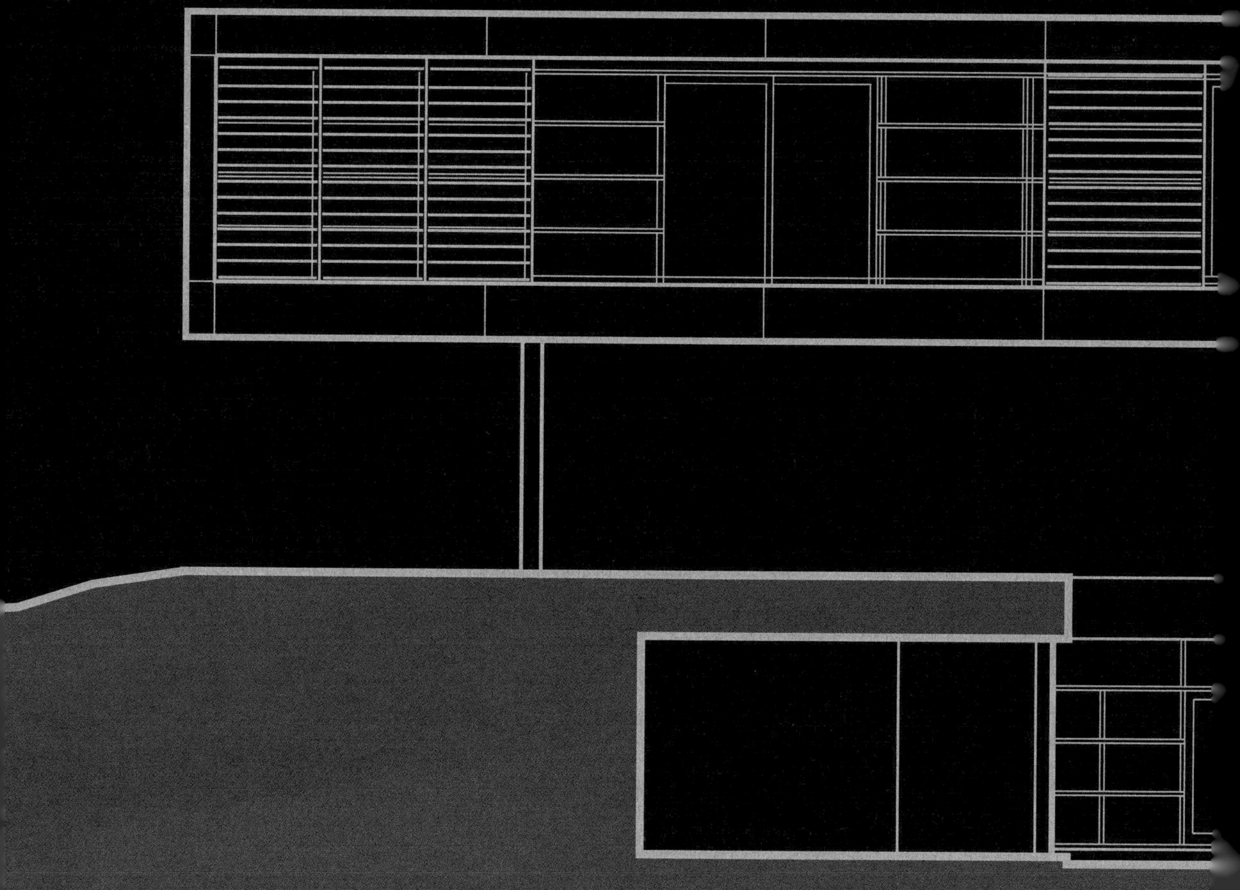

documentation Drawings, models, and renderings are the language of architectural imagination. In my case, I begin with small sketches – ideograms – that often number in the hundreds and then move immediately to scaled models which are worked and reworked – literally, smashed and remade – in three dimensions. Unlike most architects in our firm, I do not use the computer.

The drawings and models developed at different stages of the design process record the evolution of architectural thought for any given project. When numbers of these representations are juxtaposed to one another, they constitute a discourse that, despite the different design resolutions of the individual buildings, reveal a set of underlying principles, a consistency of intent that characterizes an architect's work. To facilitate such a reading, the documents for the "Featured Works" in this book are gathered together in the following section.

mies house pavilion and addition

Weston, Connecticut

Pavilion
Project Team: Cary Davis, Kent Larson, Louis Turpin
Lot Size: 5.5 acres (2.2 hectares)
Building Size: 2,050 sf (190 m^2)
Date of Design: 1981
Construction Completed: 1986

Addition
Project Team: Cary Davis, Kent Larson, Louis Turpin
Building Size: 1,500 sf (139 m^2)
Date of Design: 1986
Construction Completed: 1989

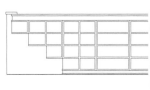

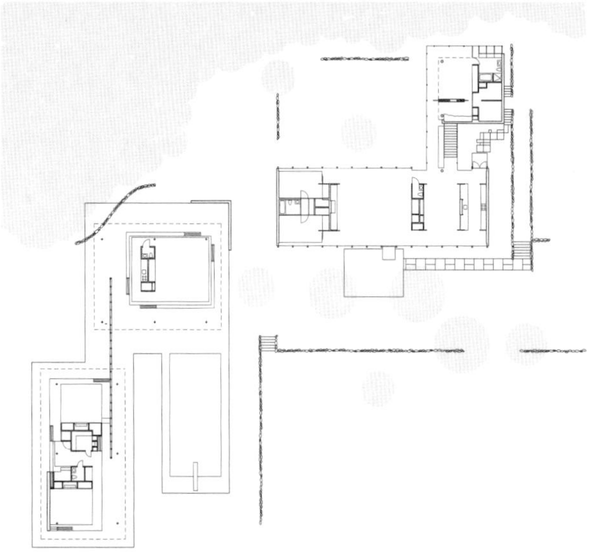

site plan

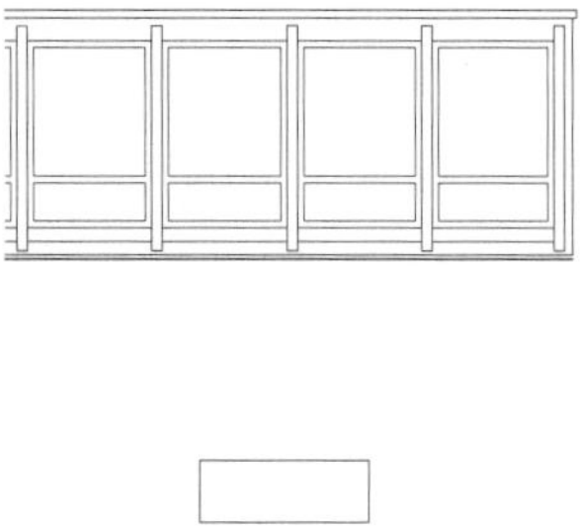

1955

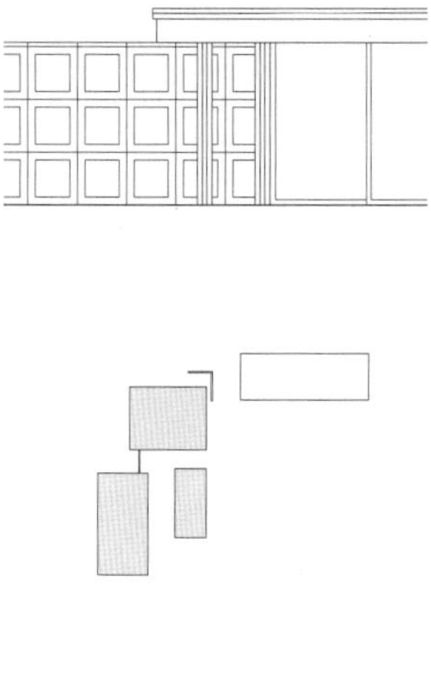

1986

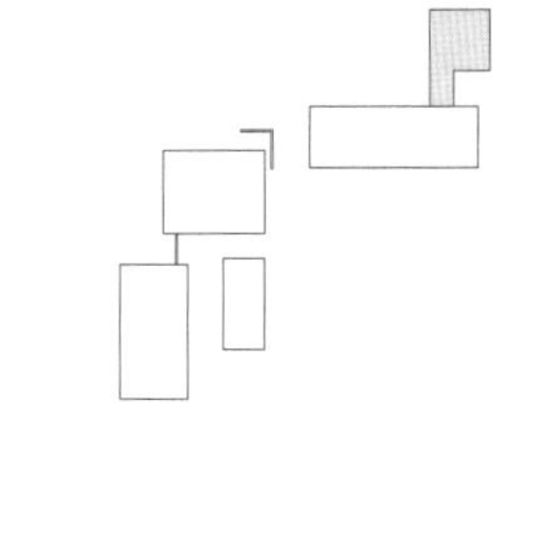

1989

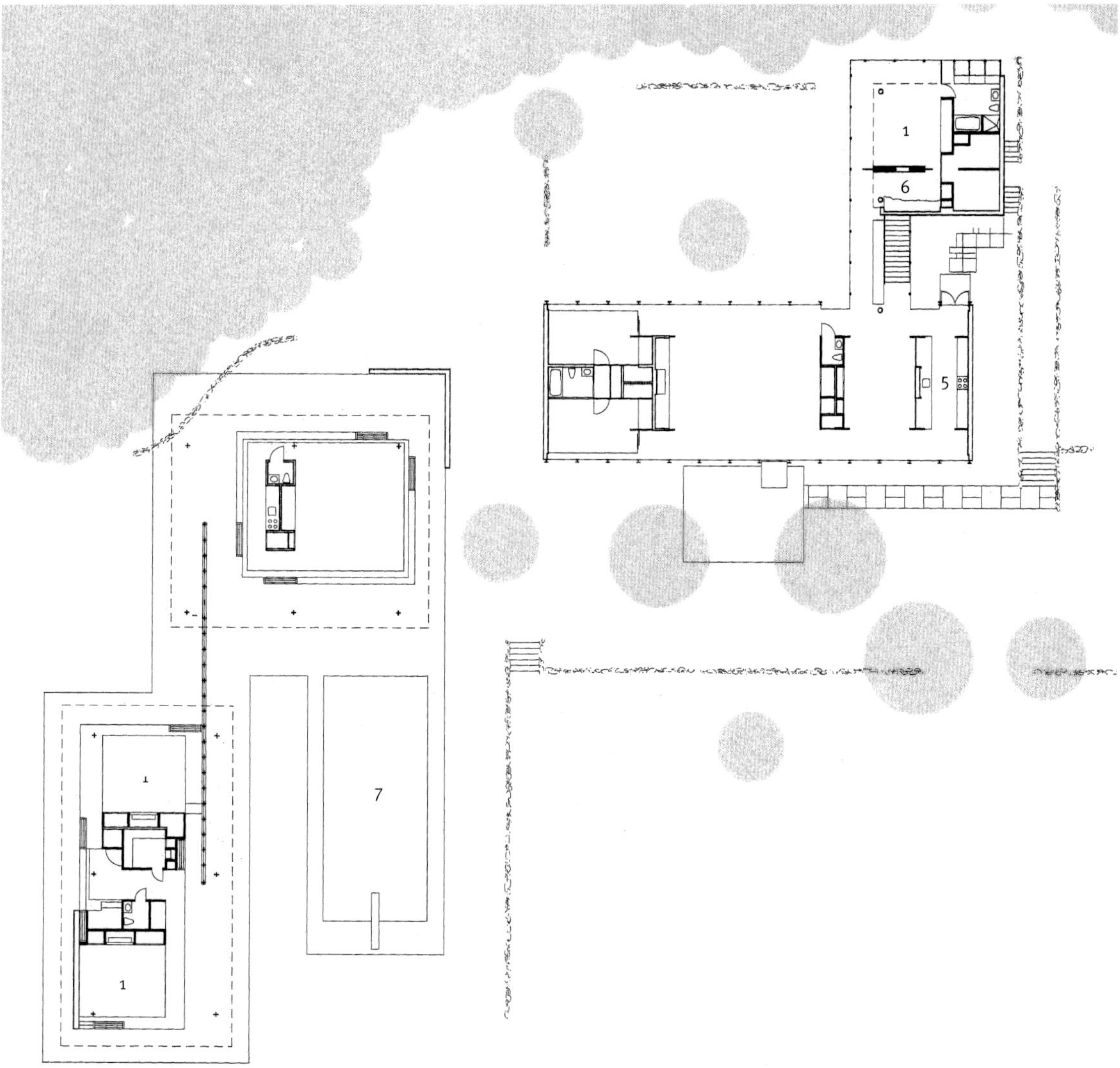

plan

1 bedroom
2 guest pavilion
3 living
4 dining
5 kitchen
6 study
7 swimming pool

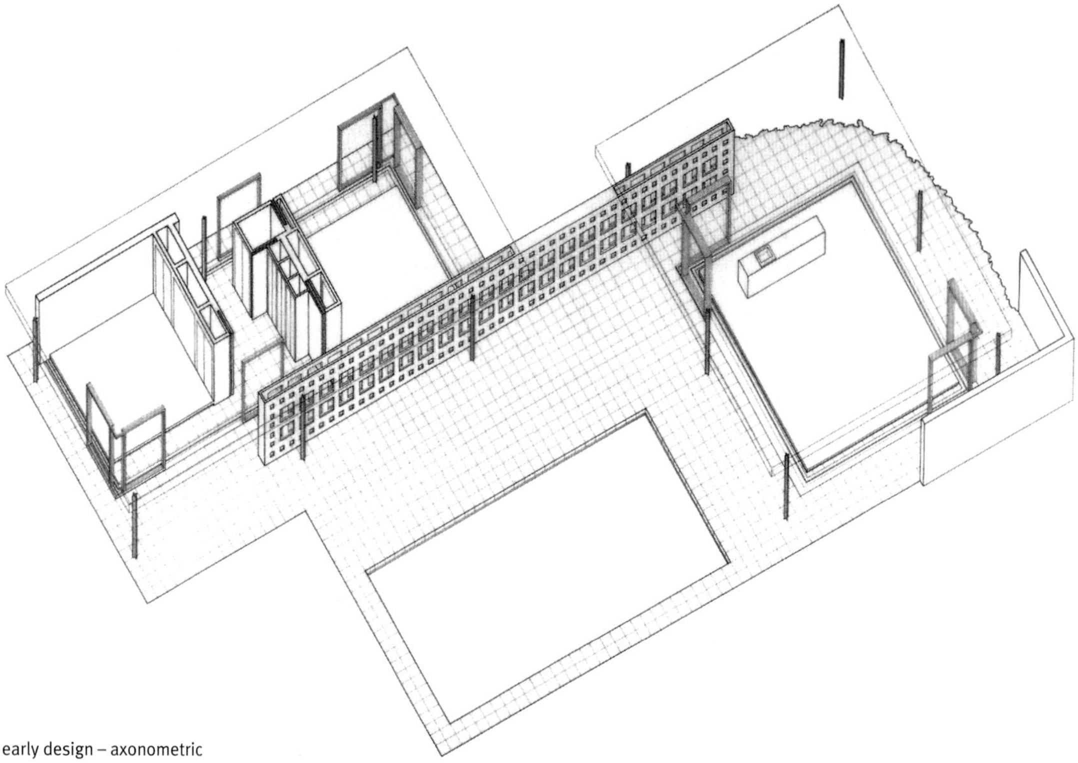

early design – axonometric

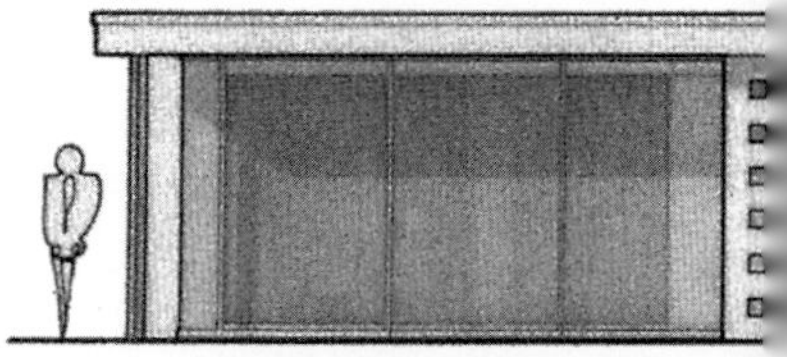

early design – northeast elevation

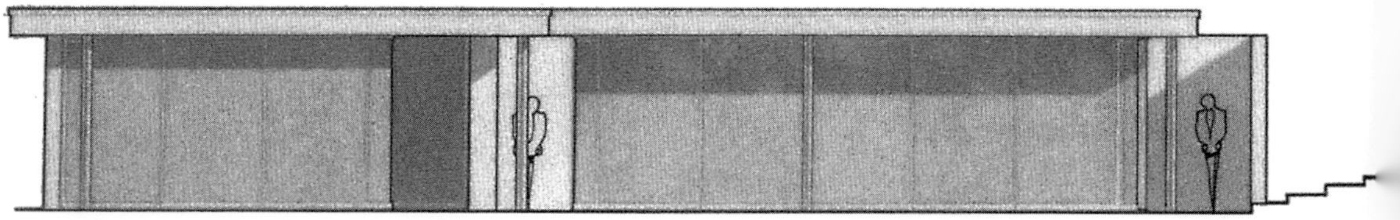

early design – southeast elevation

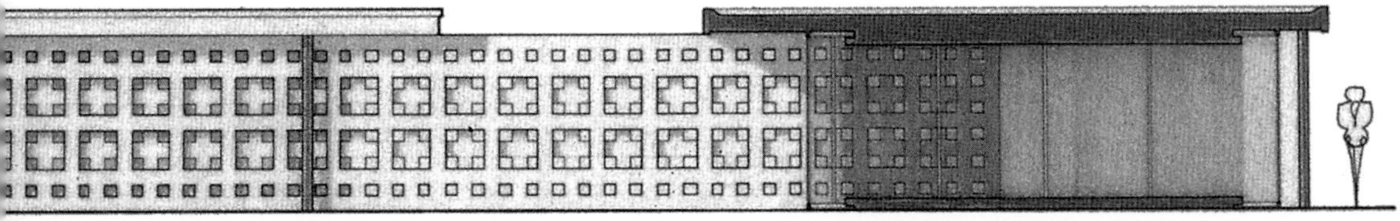

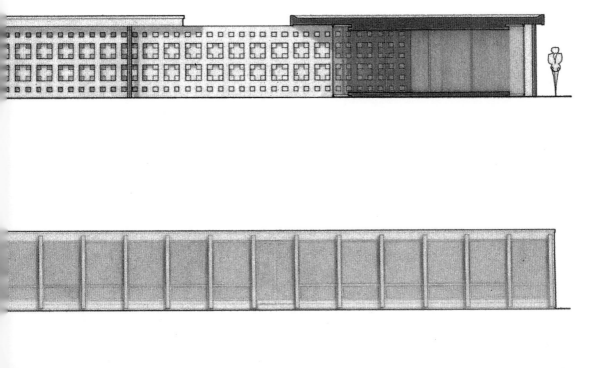

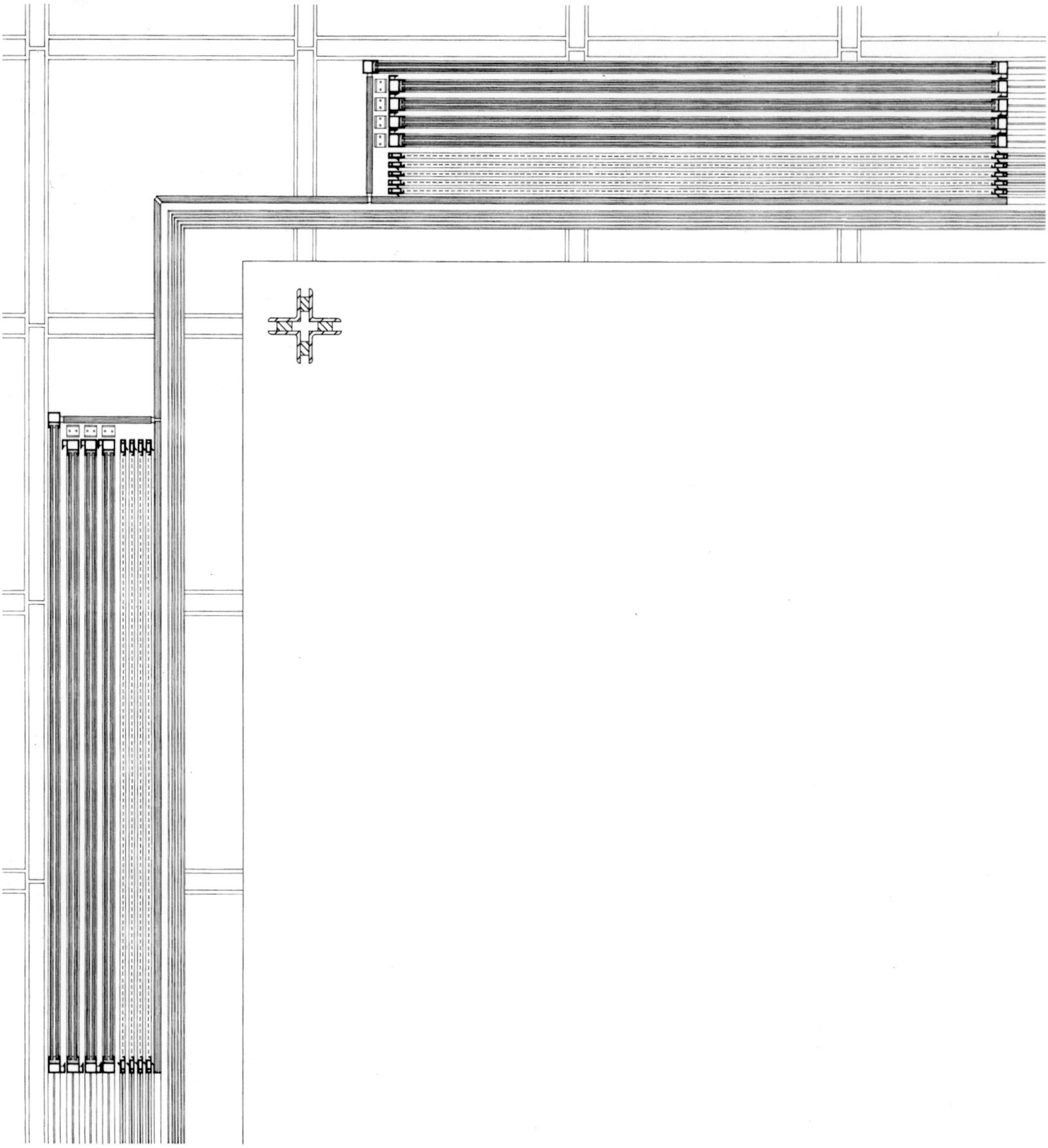

plan and section of glass pockets at pavilion

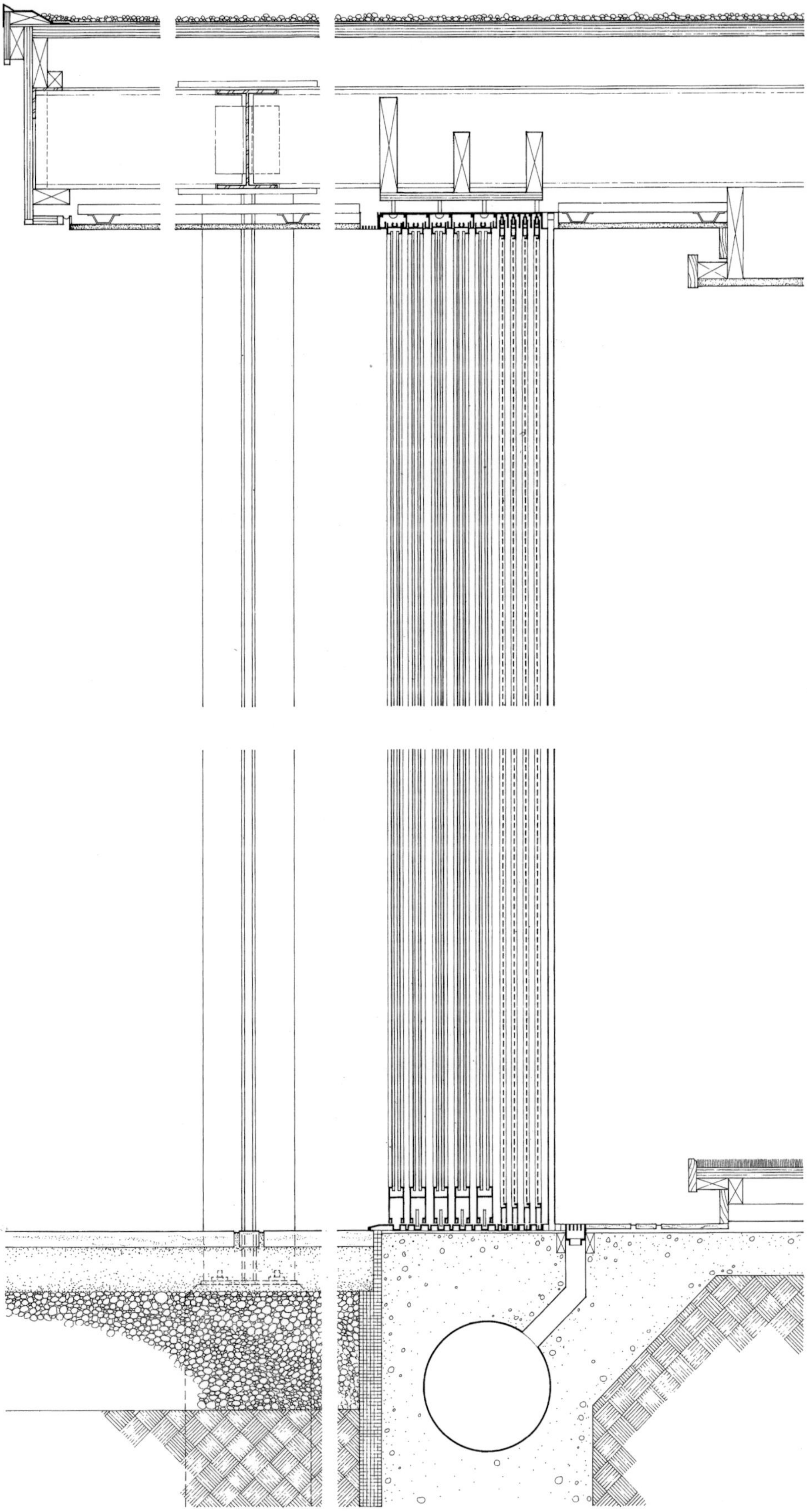

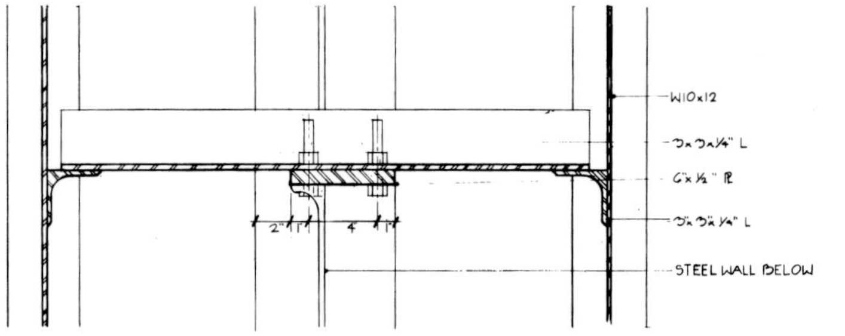

(1) PLAN SECTION

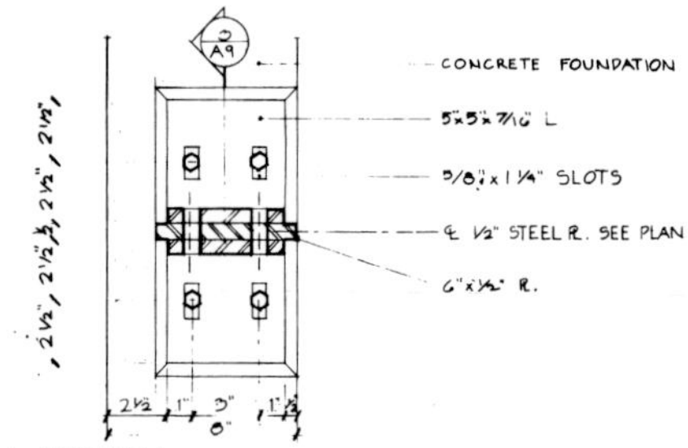

(2) PLAN SECTION

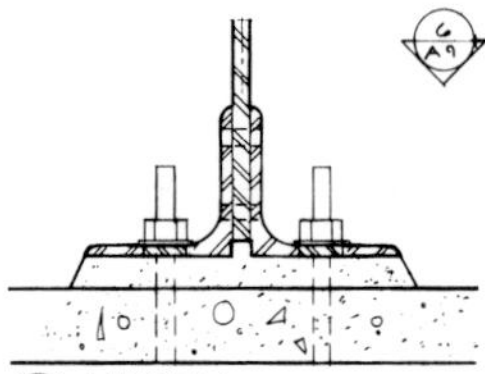

(3) SECTION

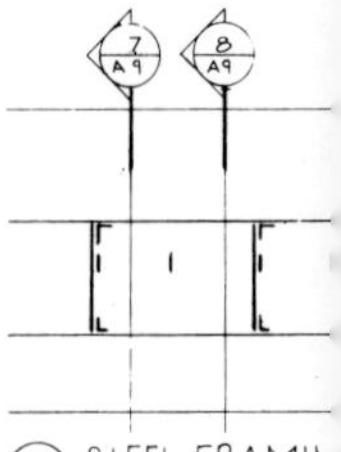

(4) STEEL FRAMIN

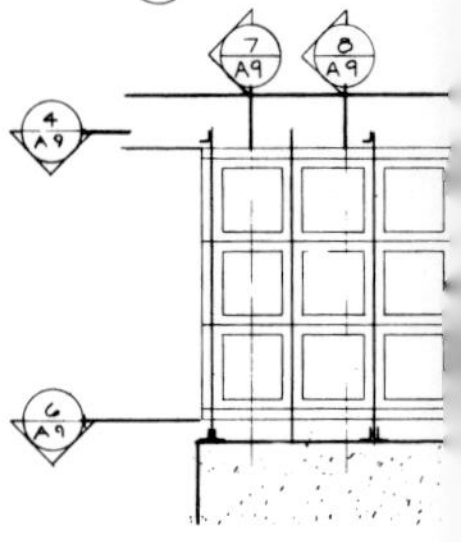

(5) ELEVATION

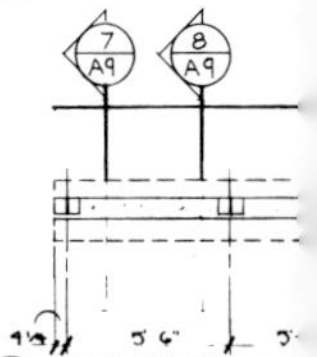

(6) FOUNDATION

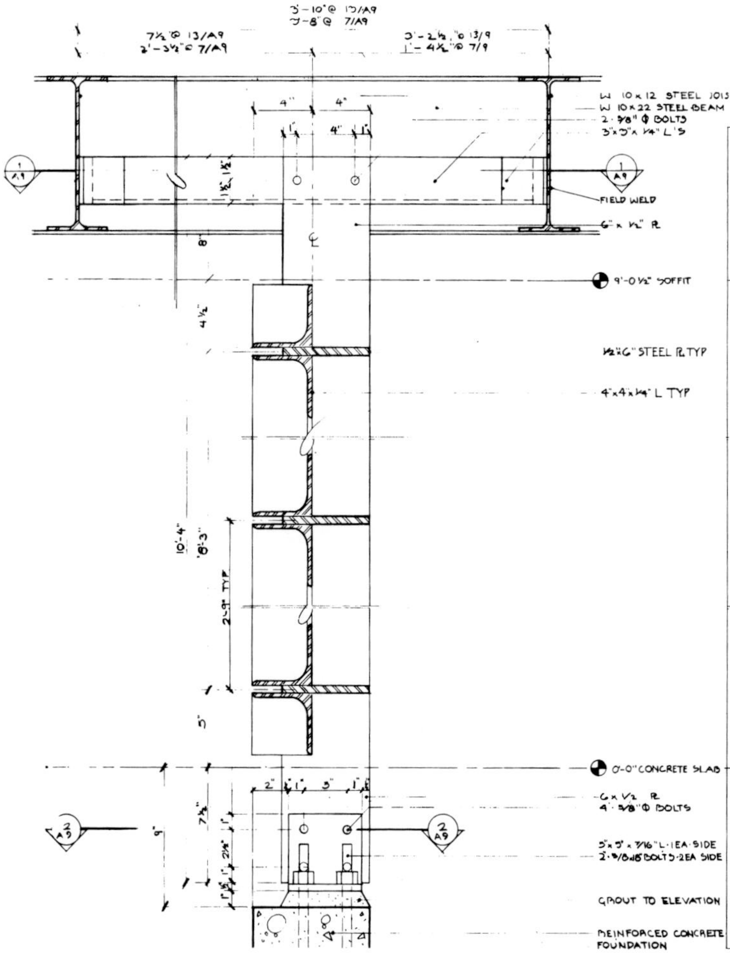

(7)(13) SECTION

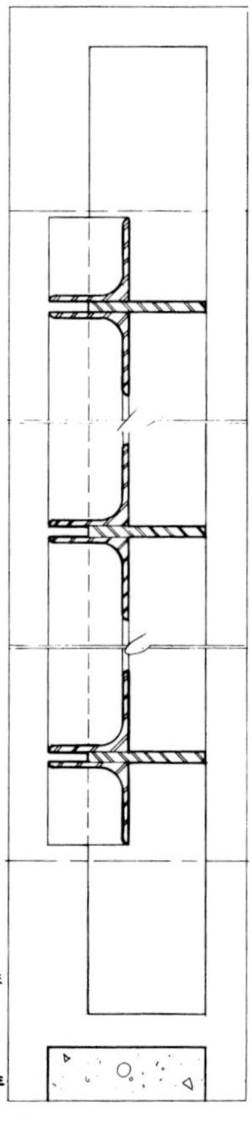

(8)(14) SECTION

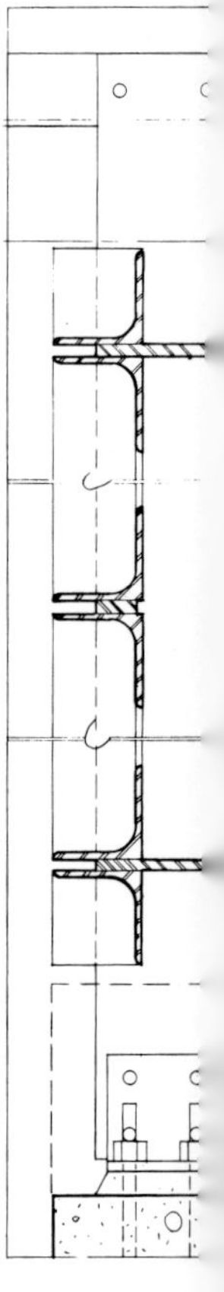

(9) SECTION

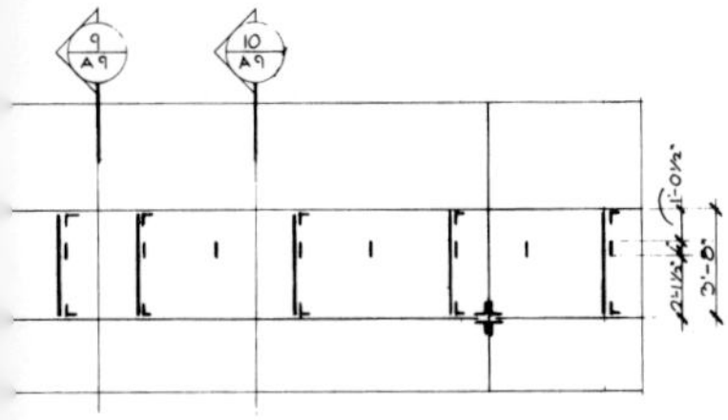

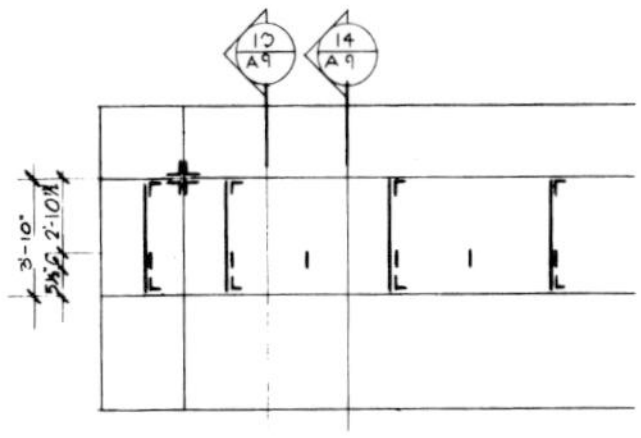

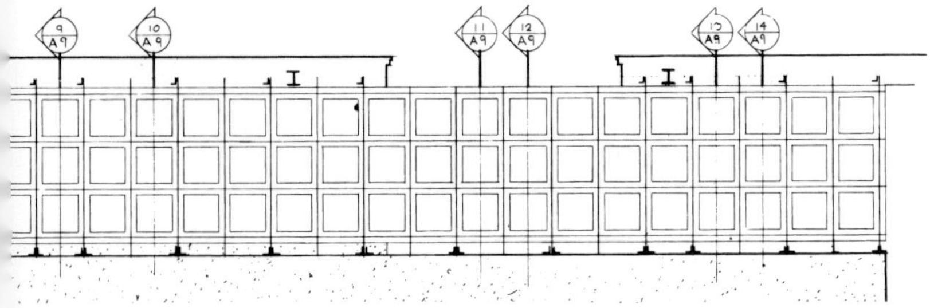

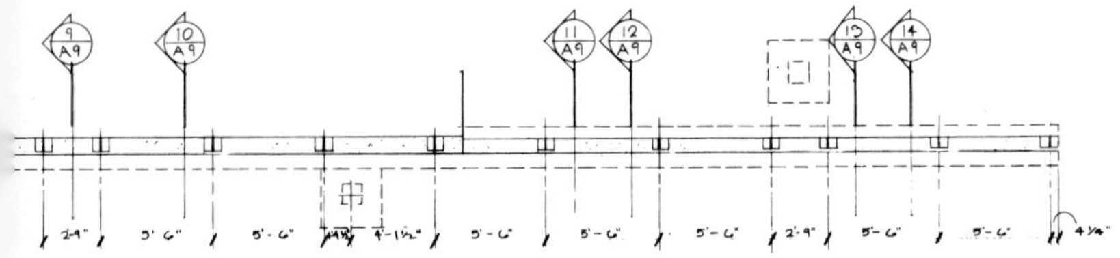

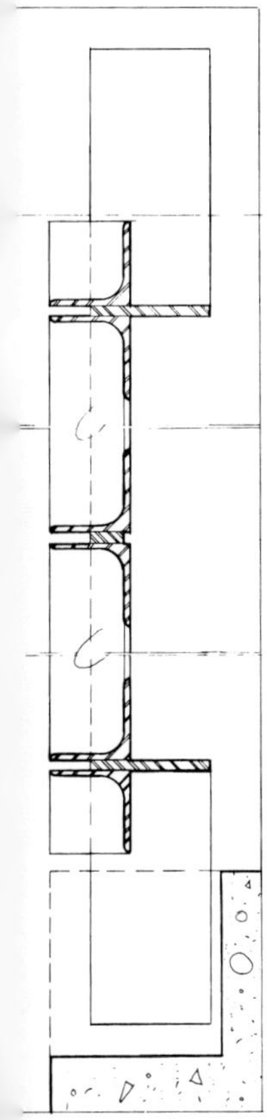

10 SECTION

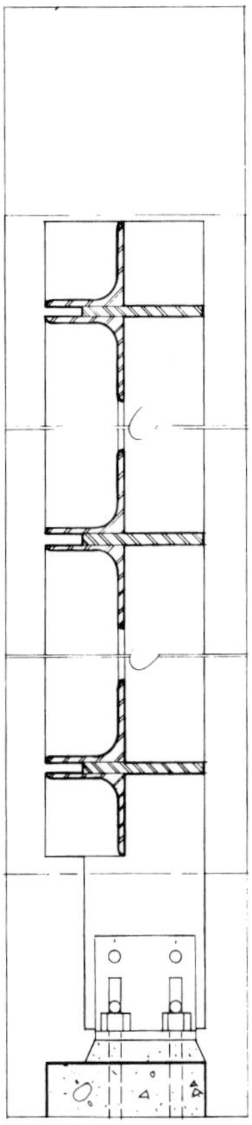

11 SECTION

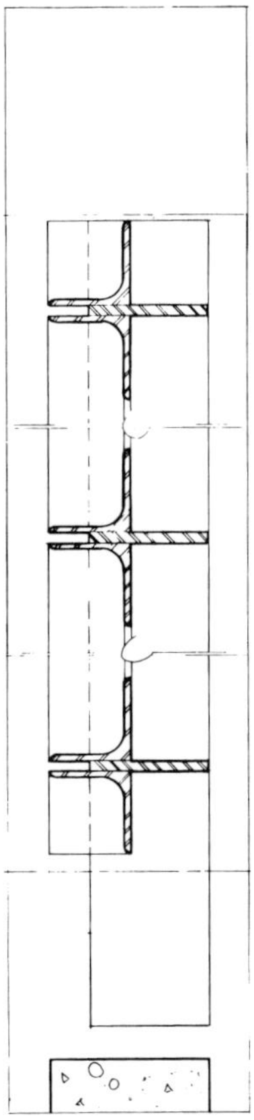

12 SECTION

early design model

digital rendering of pool area

digital rendering of pool pavilion

digital rendering of screen

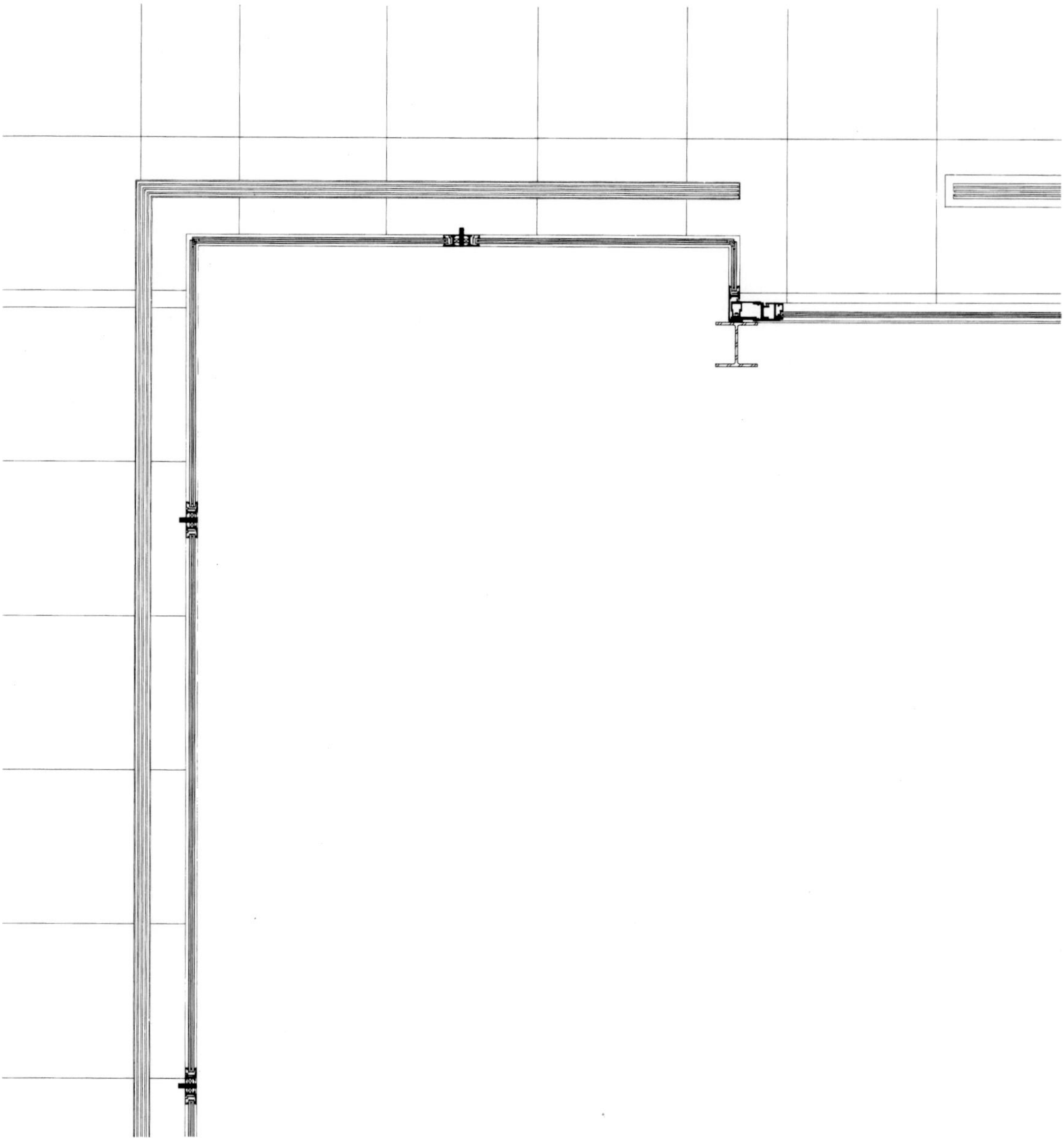

plan and section of second addition glass wall

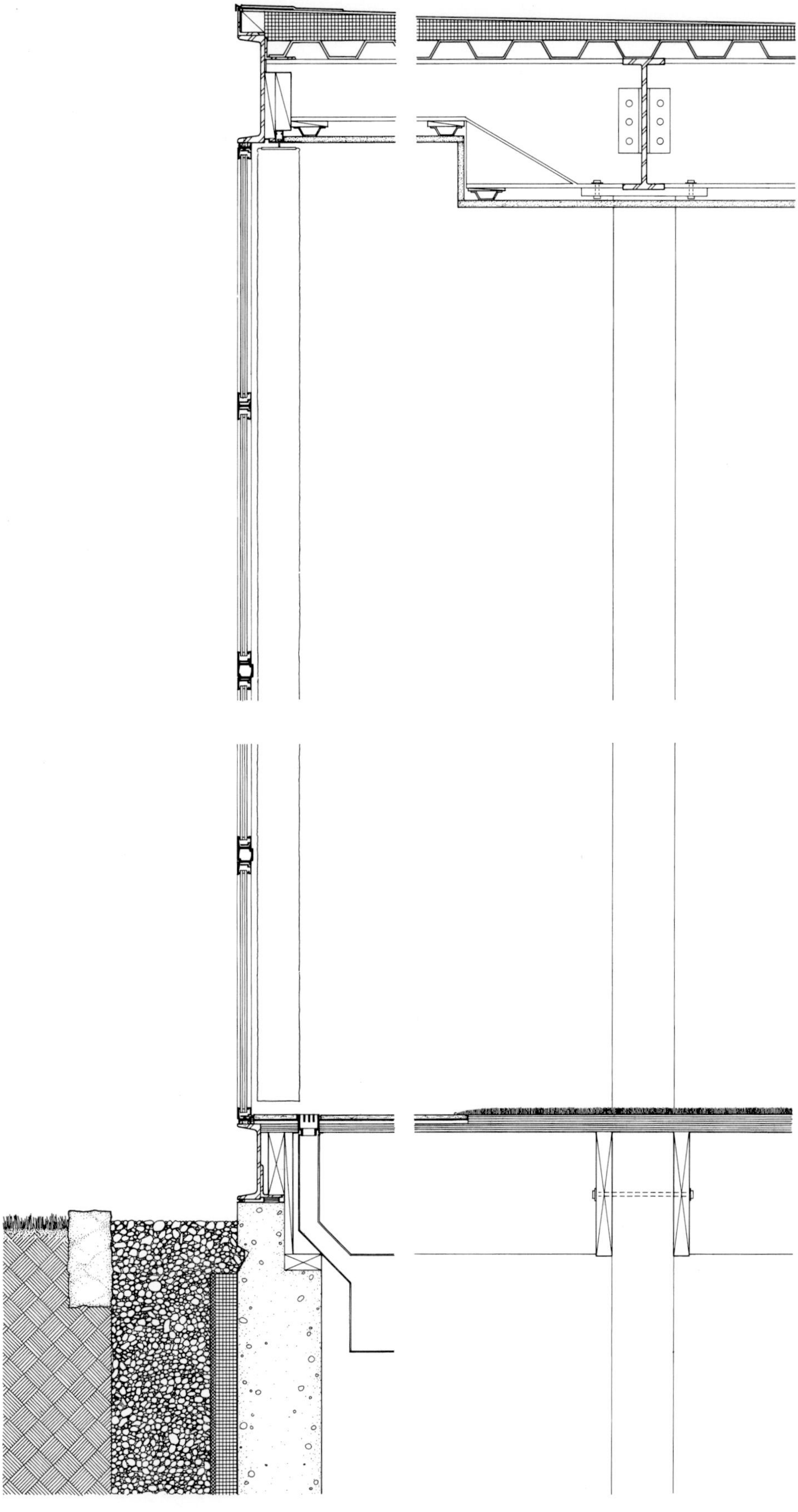

usonian house addition

Pleasantville, New York

Project Team: Wendy Pautz
Lot Size: 1.25 acres (5,059 m^2)
Building Size: 3,500 sf (325 m^2)
Date of Design: 1992
Construction Completed: 1994

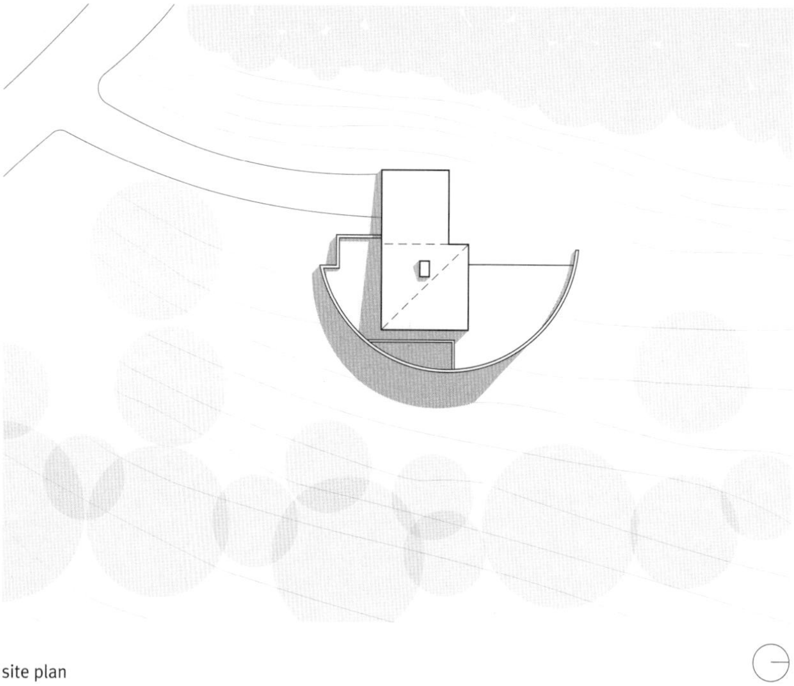

site plan

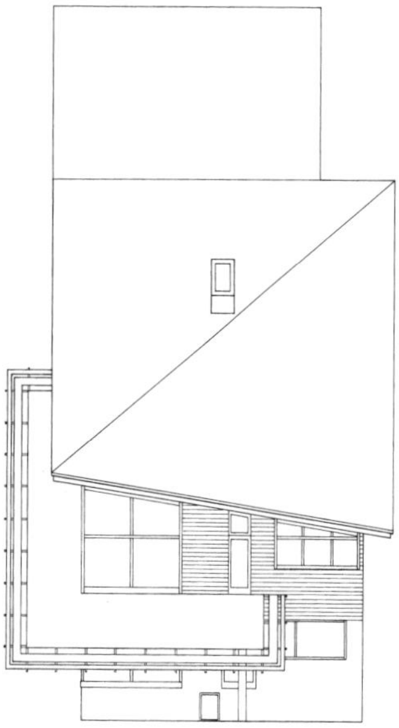

axonometric of existing house

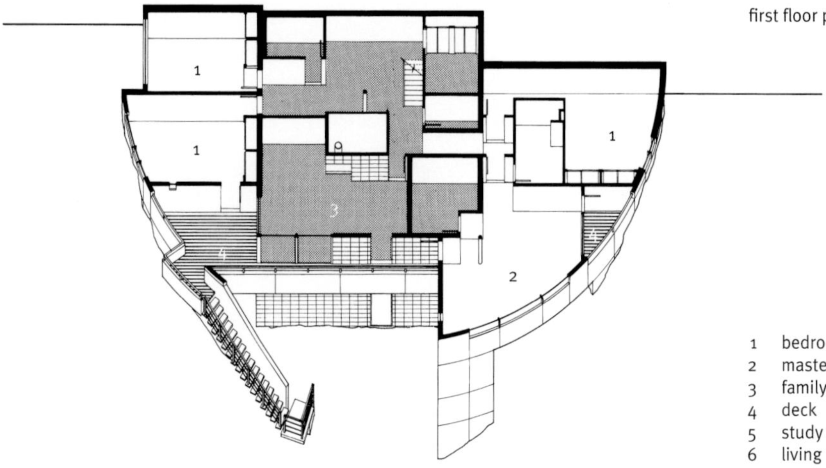

first floor plan axonometric

1 bedroom
2 master bedroom
3 family room
4 deck
5 study
6 living - dining - kitchen

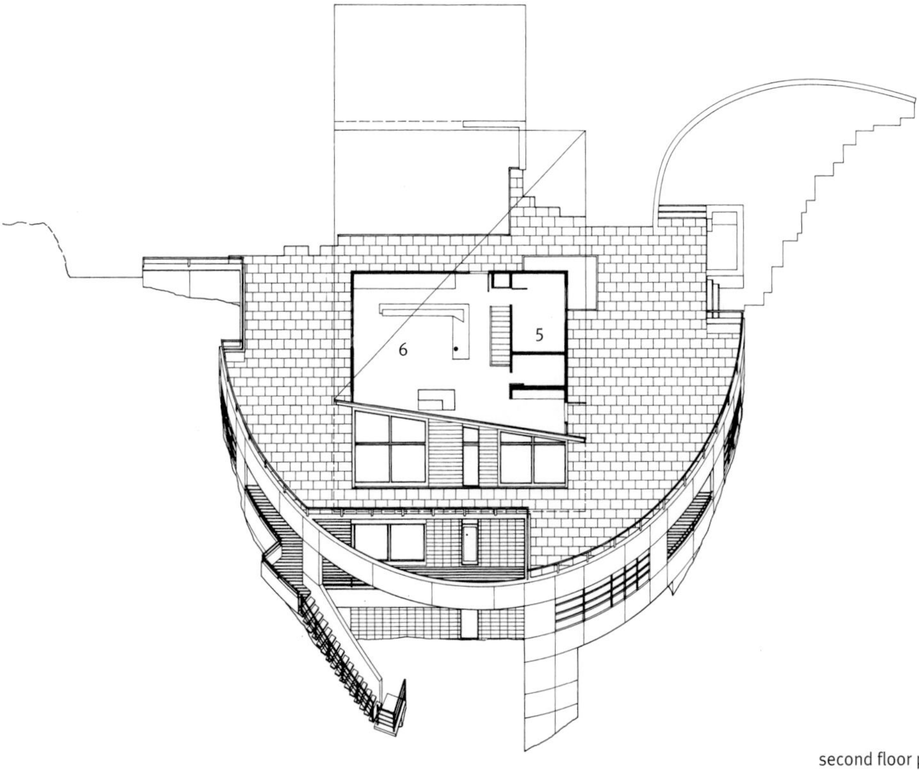

second floor plan axonometric

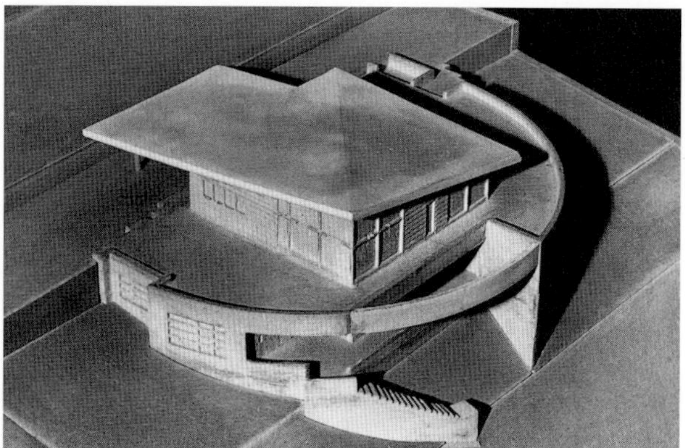

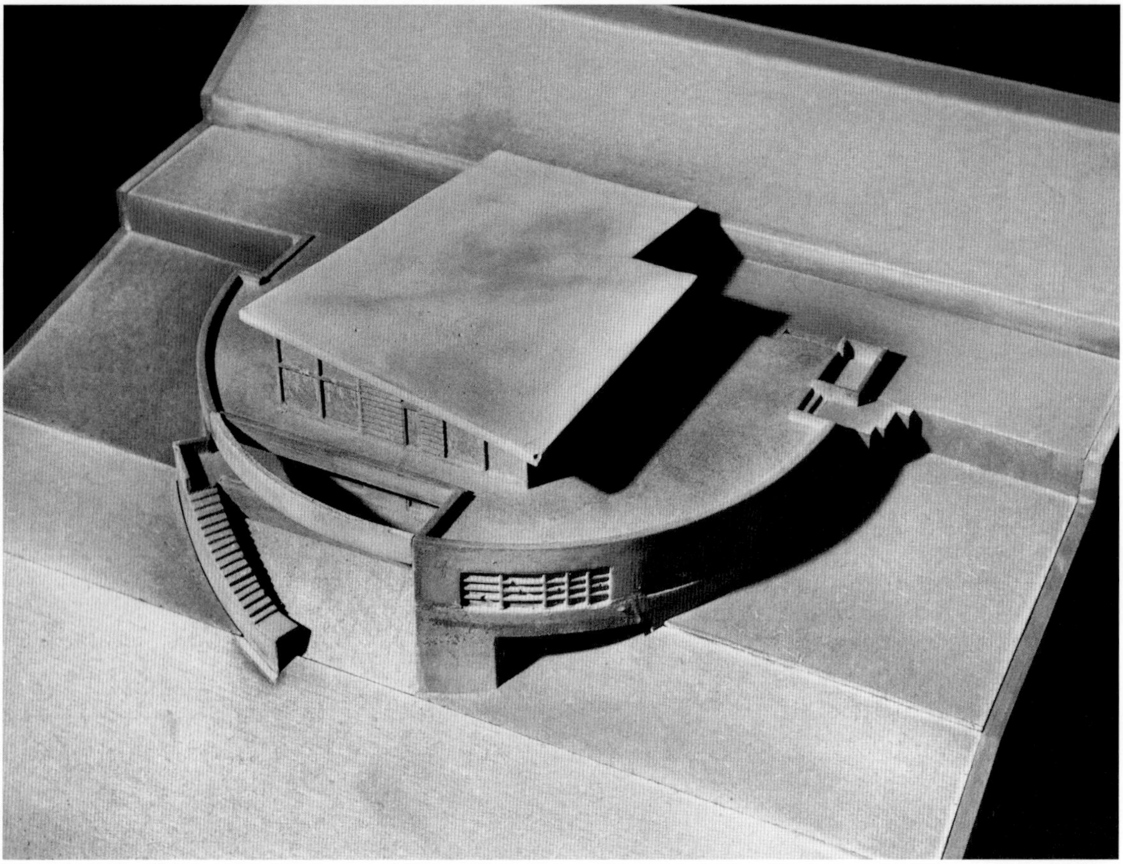

plaster model views

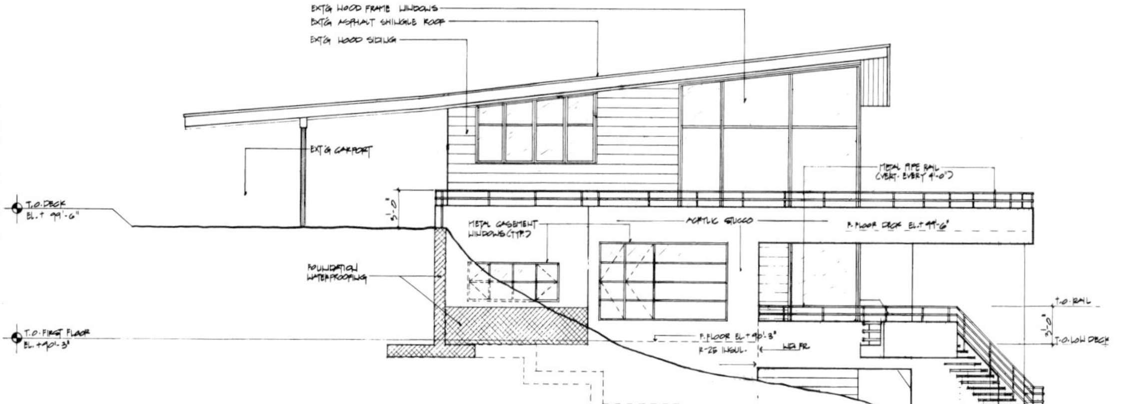

south elevation

farmhouse with lap pool

Worcester, New York

Project Team: Fritz Read, Jim Walker
Lot Size: 500 acres (202 hectares)
Building Size: 5,000 sf (465 m^2)
Date of Design: 1992
Construction Completed: 1995

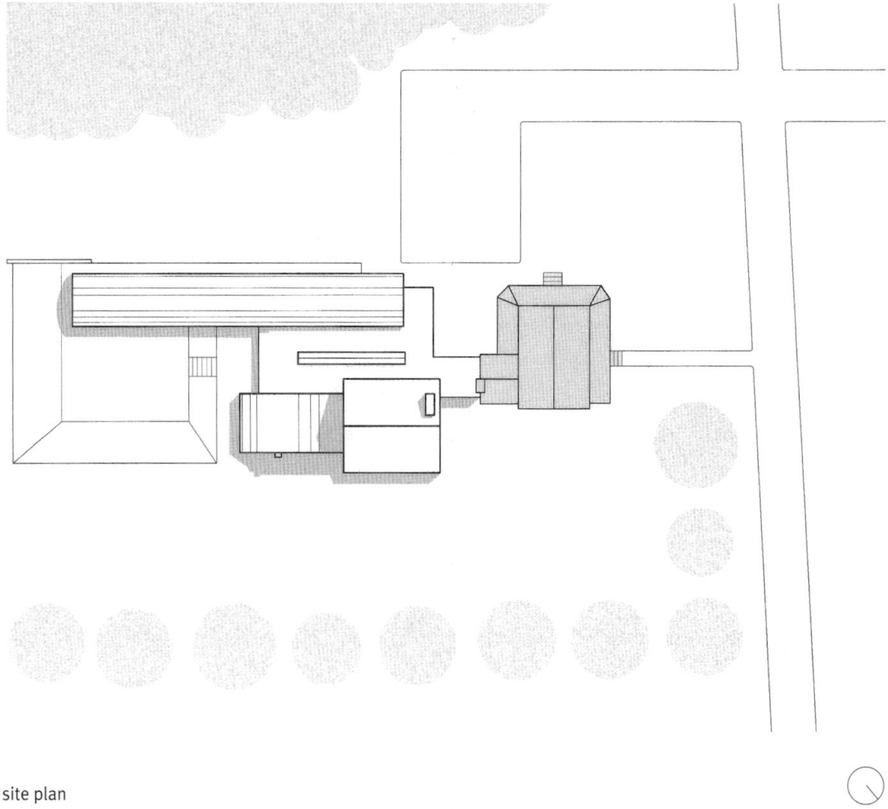

site plan

03

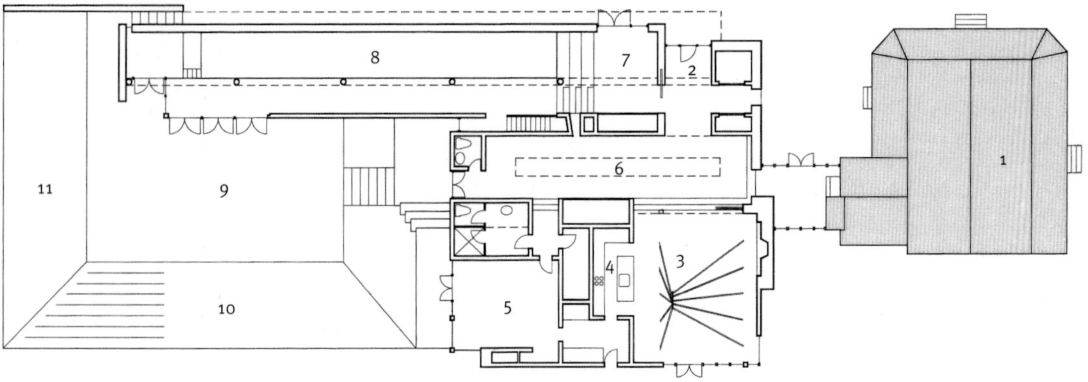

floor plan

1 existing farmhouse
2 entry
3 living
4 kitchen
5 bedroom
6 gallery
7 pool sitting area
8 lap pool
9 sunken terrace
10 slope
11 rose garden

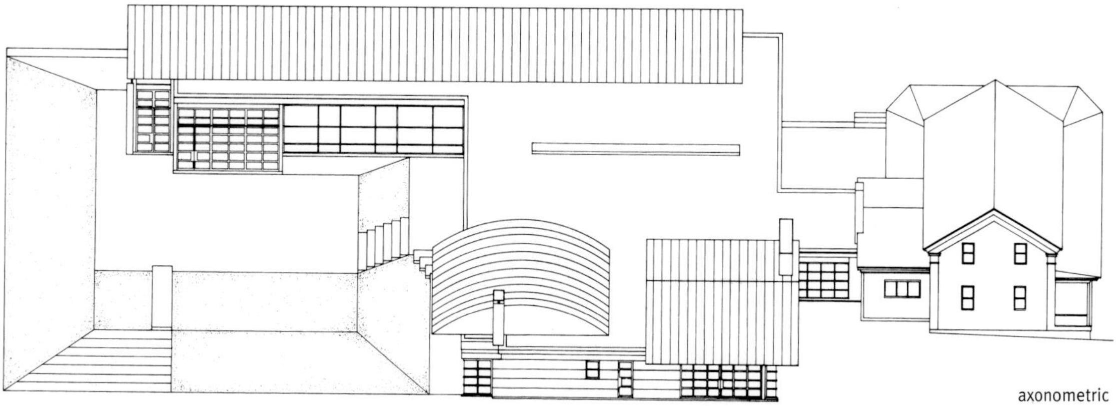

axonometric

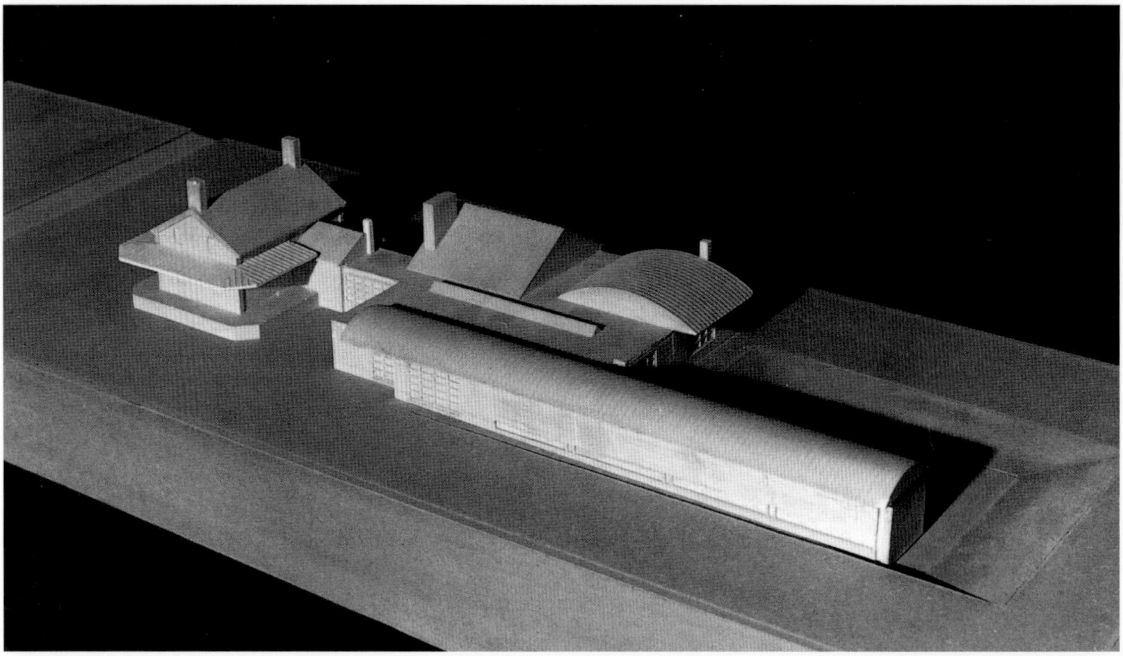

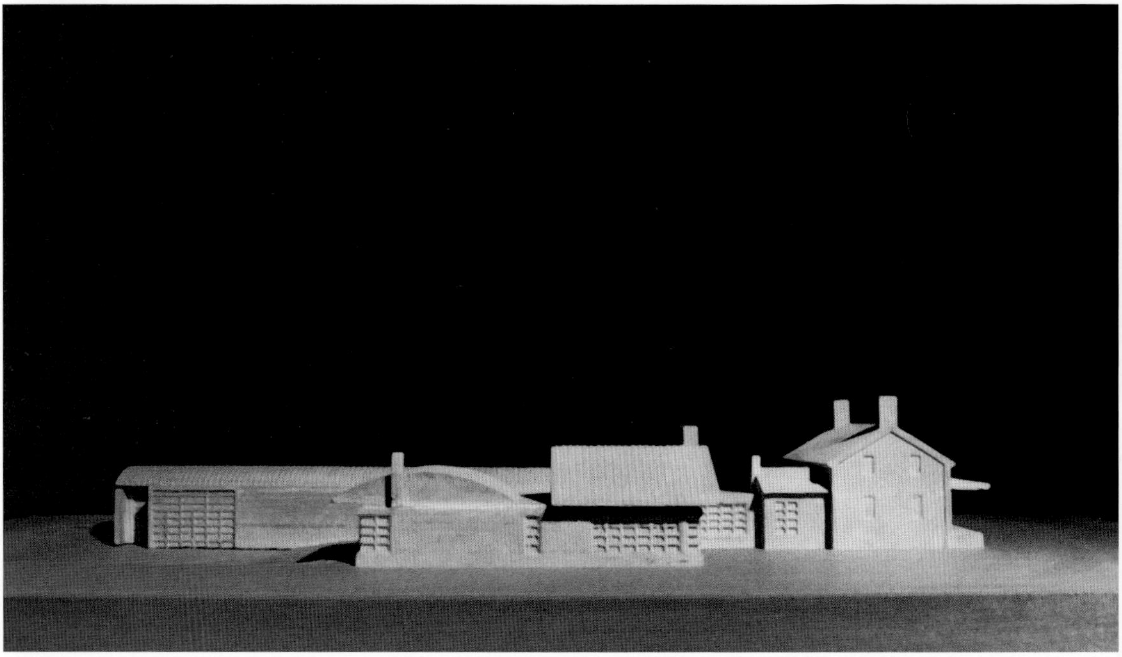

plaster model views

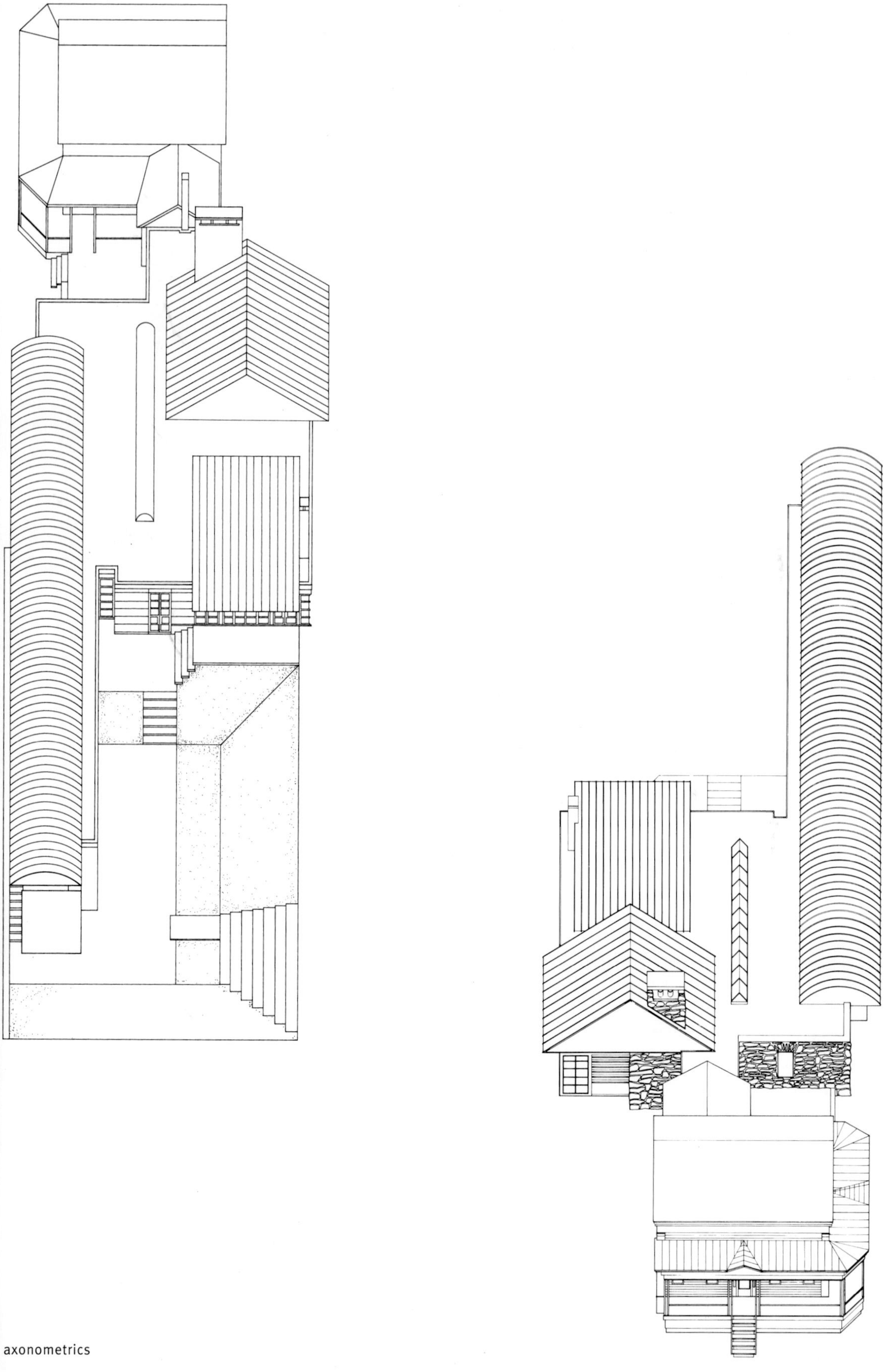

axonometrics

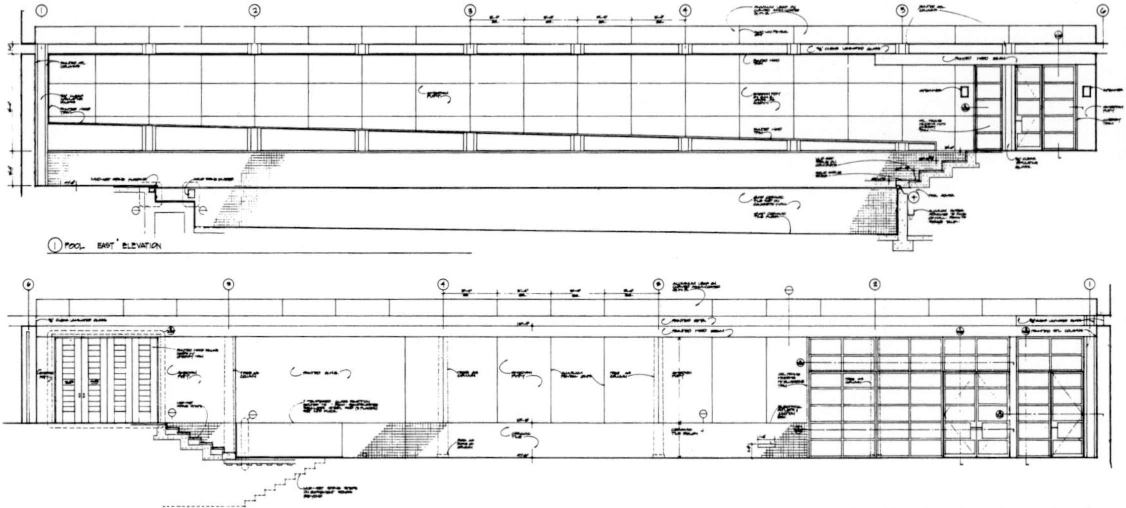

pool west and east section – elevations

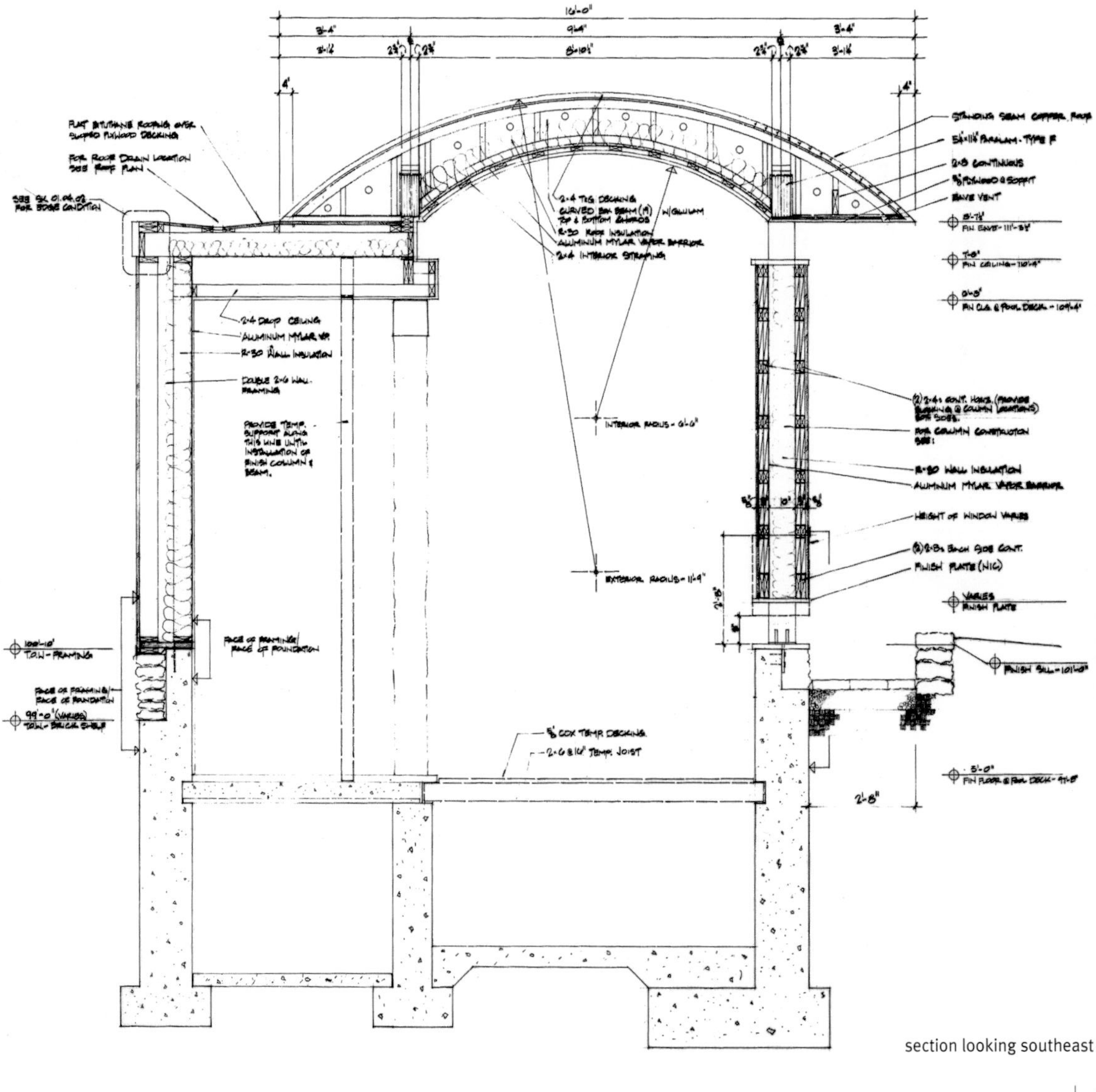

section looking southeast

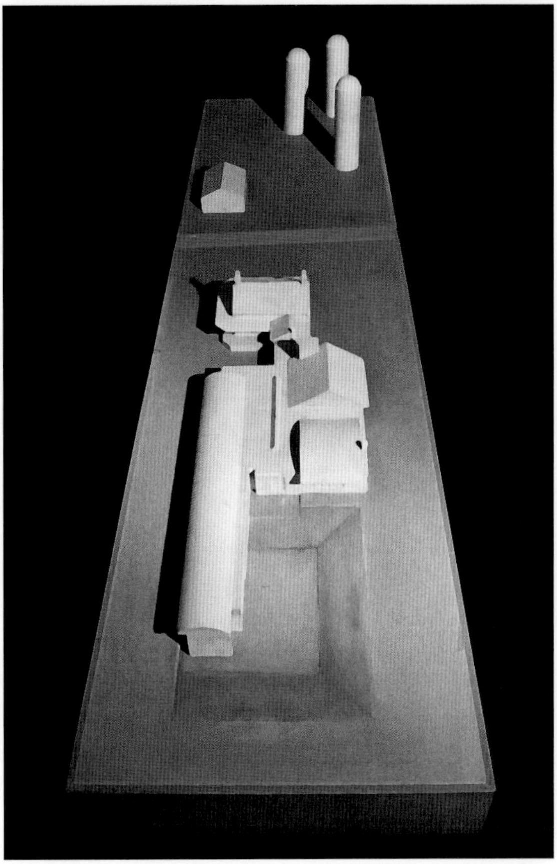

aerial view of model

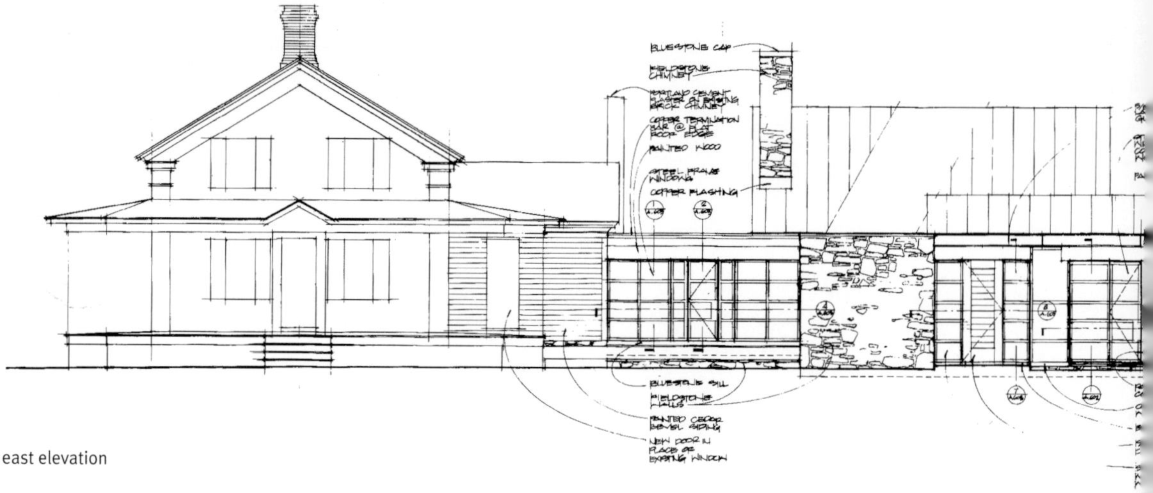

east elevation

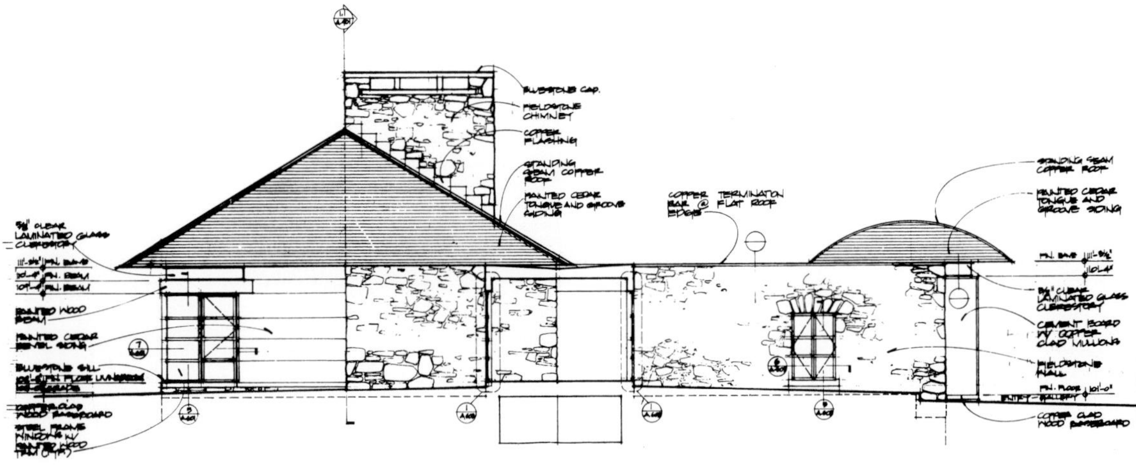

north section – elevation

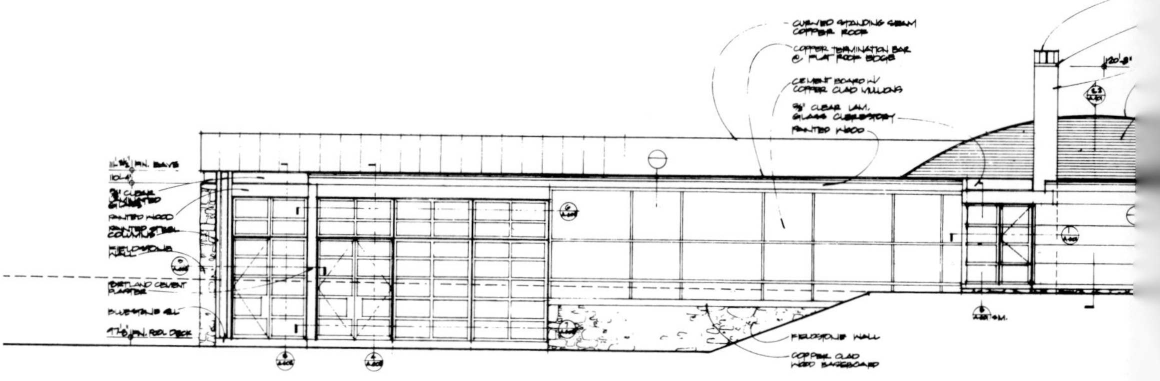

west elevation

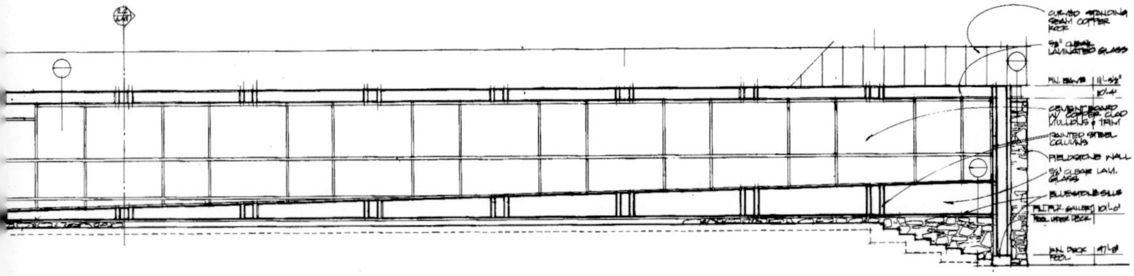

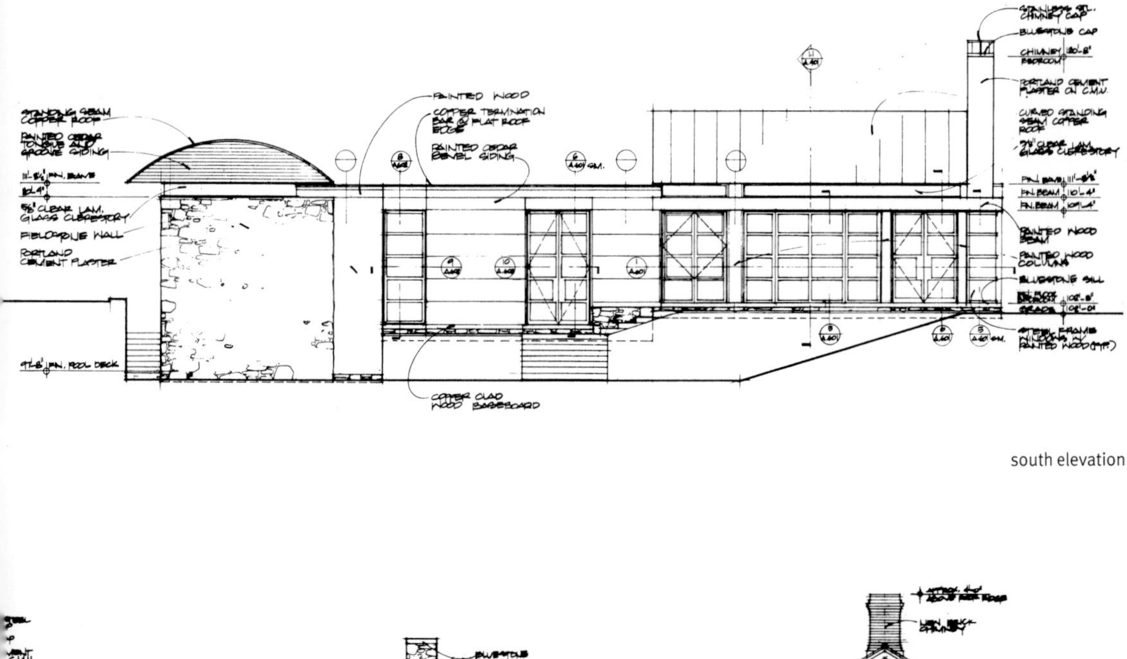

south elevation

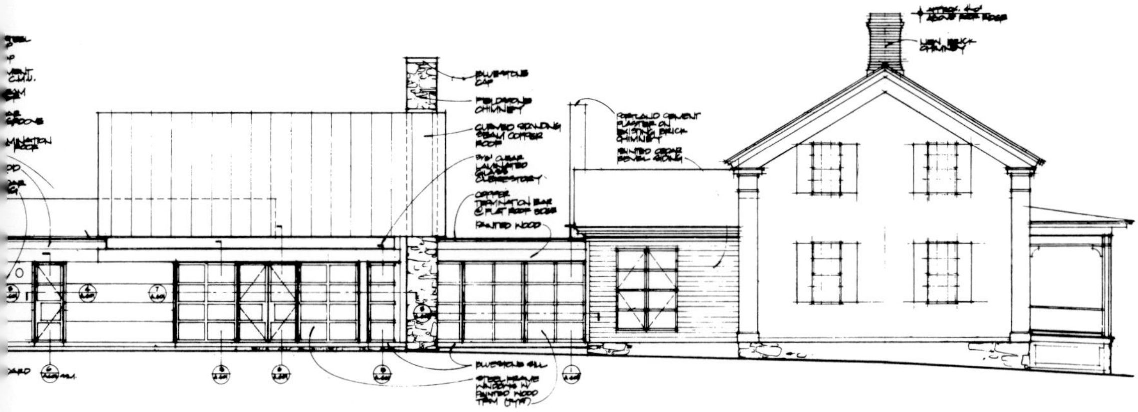

linear house
Millerton, New York

Project Team: Suki Dixon
Lot Size: 50 acres (20 hectares)
Building Size: 2,500 sf (232 m^2)
Date of Design: 1993
Construction Completed: 1996

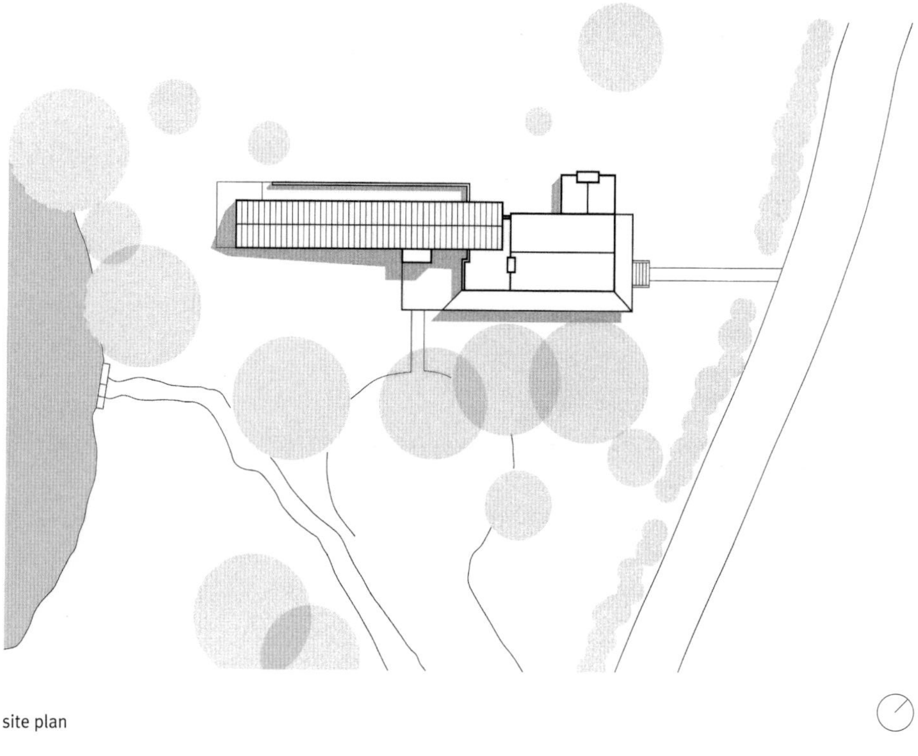

site plan

04

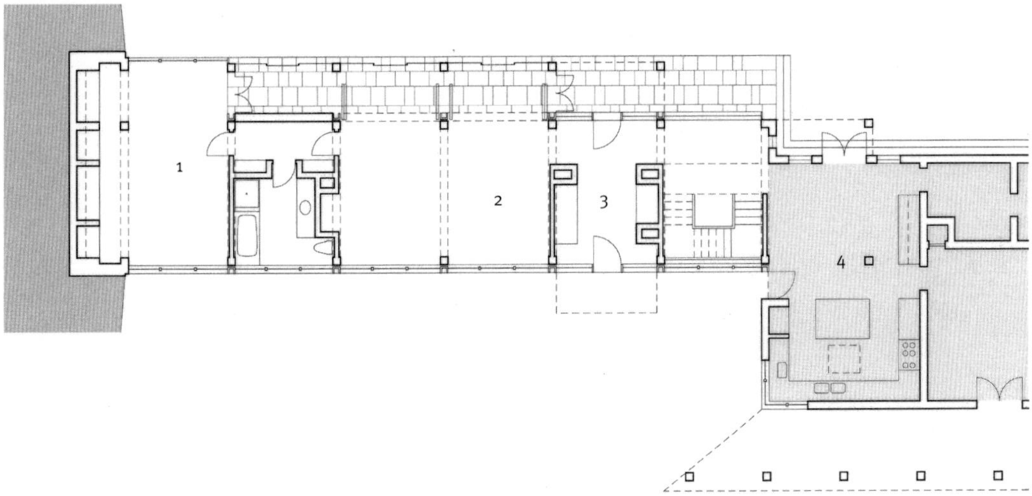

first floor plan

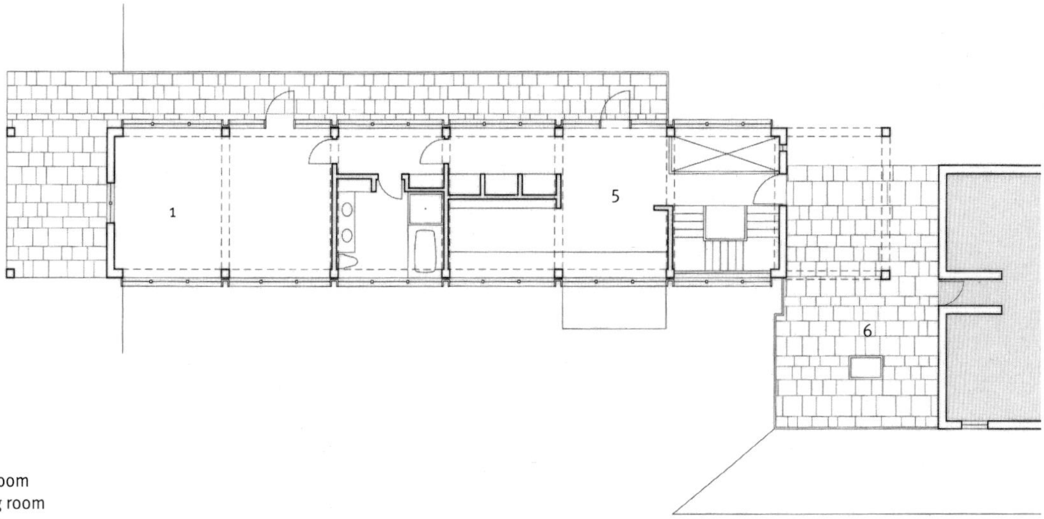

1 bedroom
2 living room
3 entry
4 existing house
5 study
6 terrace

second floor plan

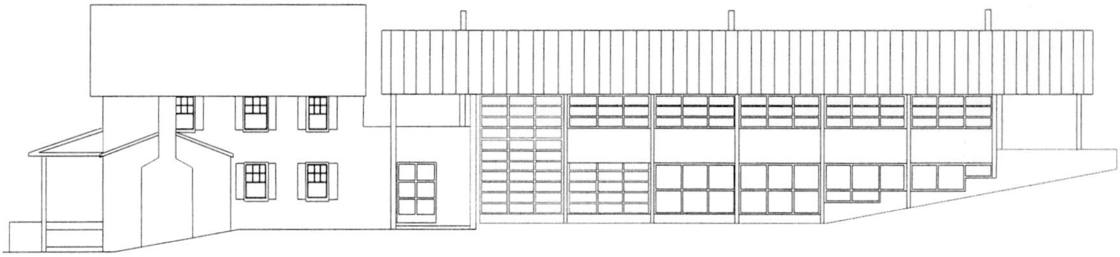

north elevation

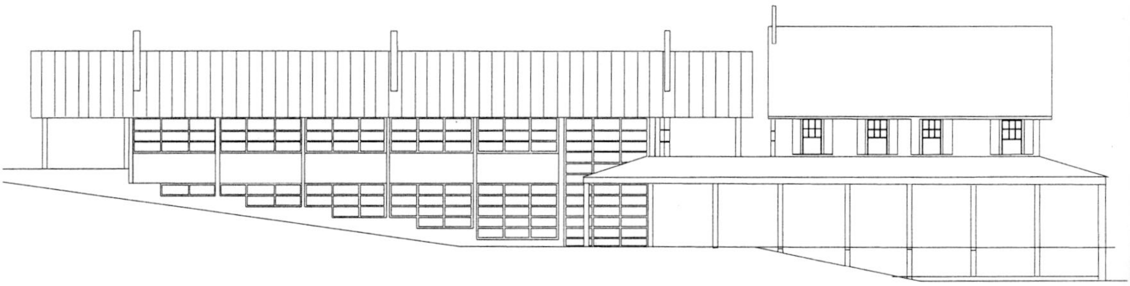

south elevation

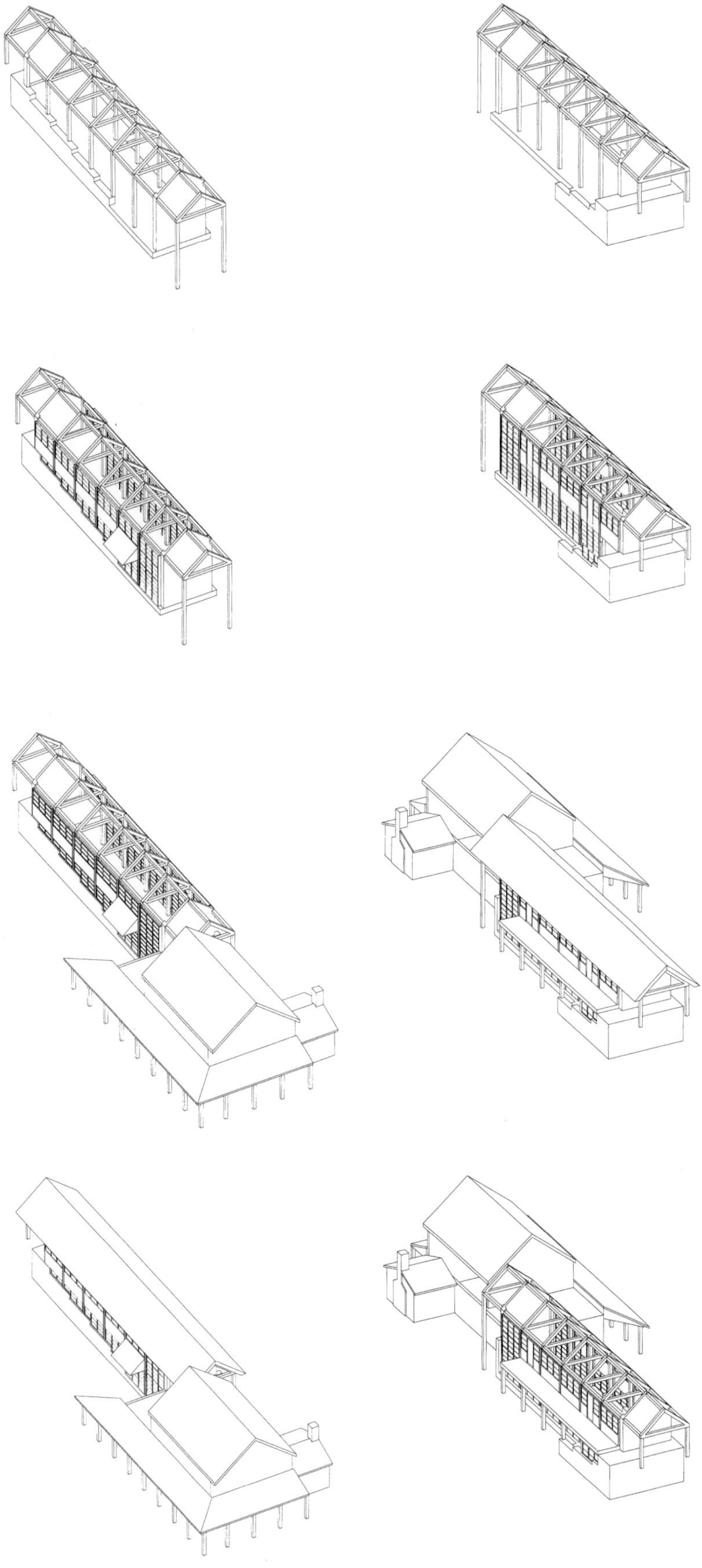

axonometrics showing structure

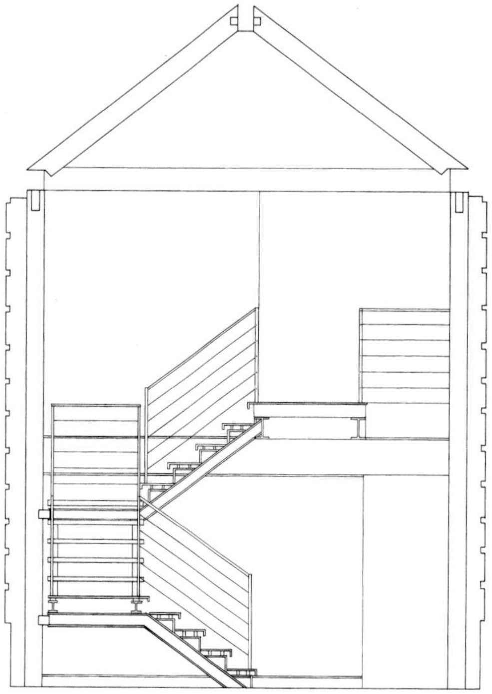

section looking southwest

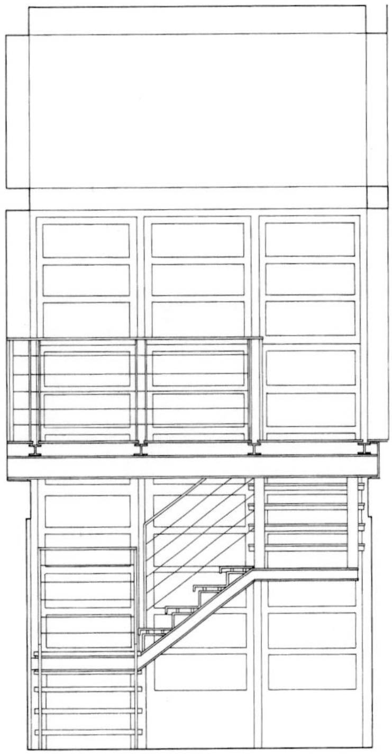

section looking southeast

plan section of curtain wall at columns

1 5/8" plywood
2 5/8" gypsum board
3 8 x 8 wood column
4 3" x 3" x 8" angles
5 2 x 6 stud wall 16" o.c.
6 5 1/2" batt insulation
7 3/4" rigid insulation
8 exterior siding

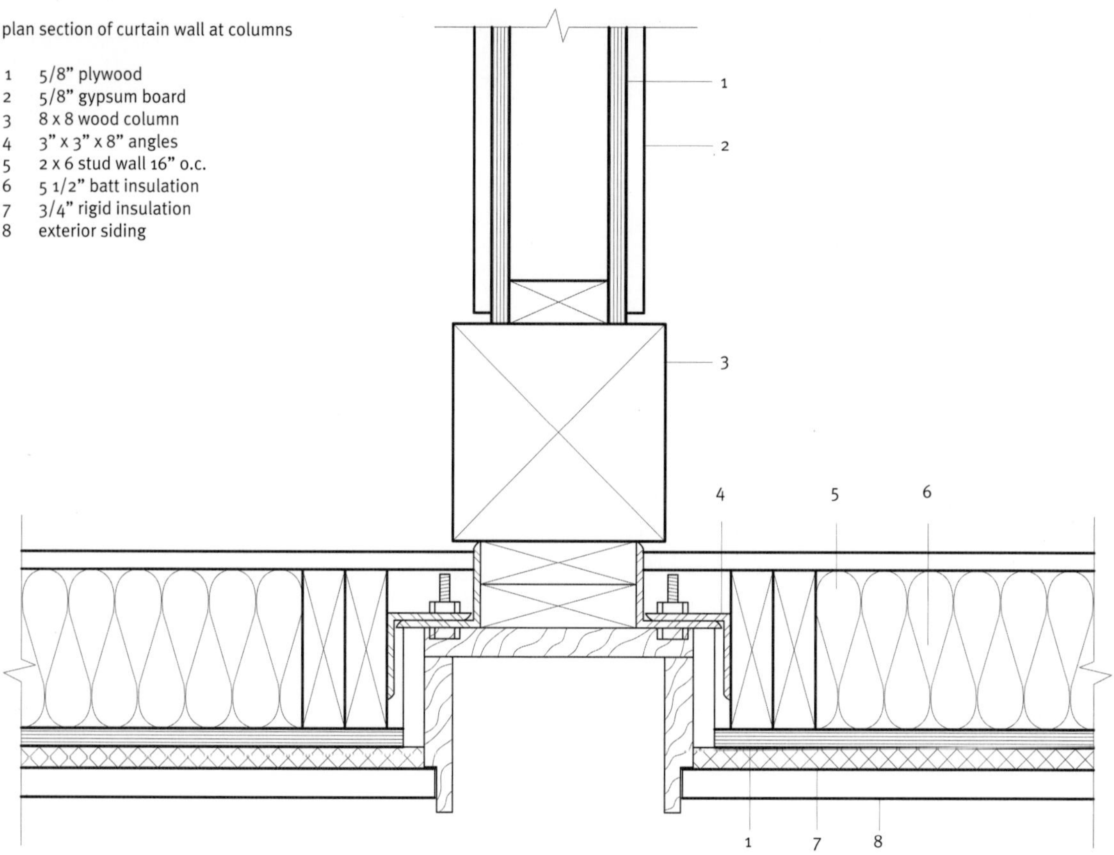

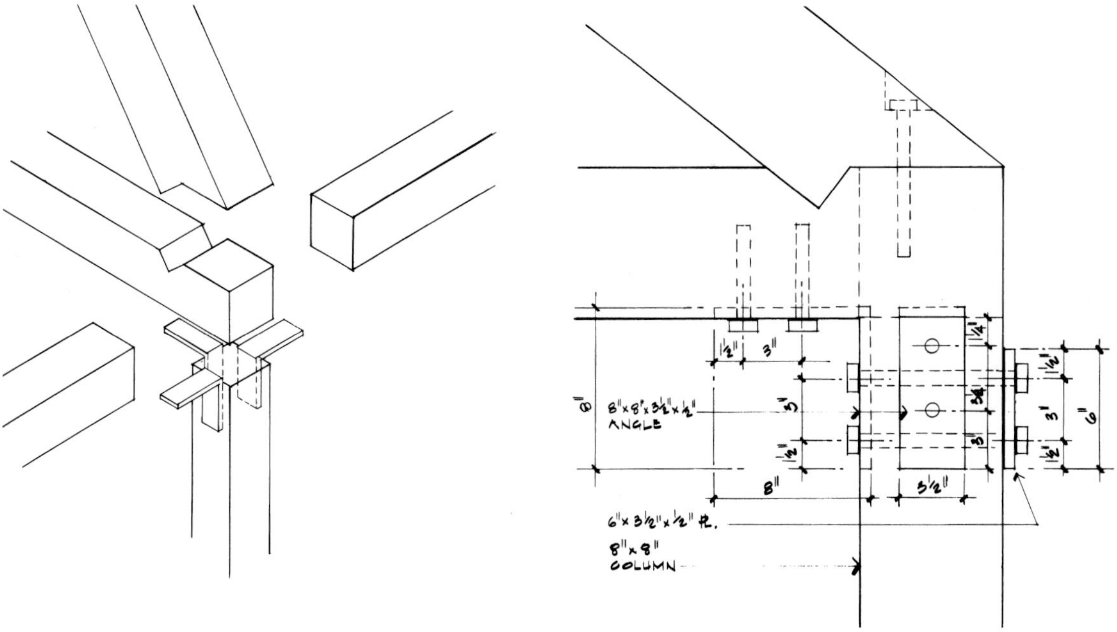

heavy timber connection detail

bridge house

Olive Bridge, New York

Project Team: Thomas Gluck
Lot Size: 18 acres (7.3 hectares)
Building Size: 5,800 sf (539 m2)
Date of Design: 1992
Construction Completed: 1996

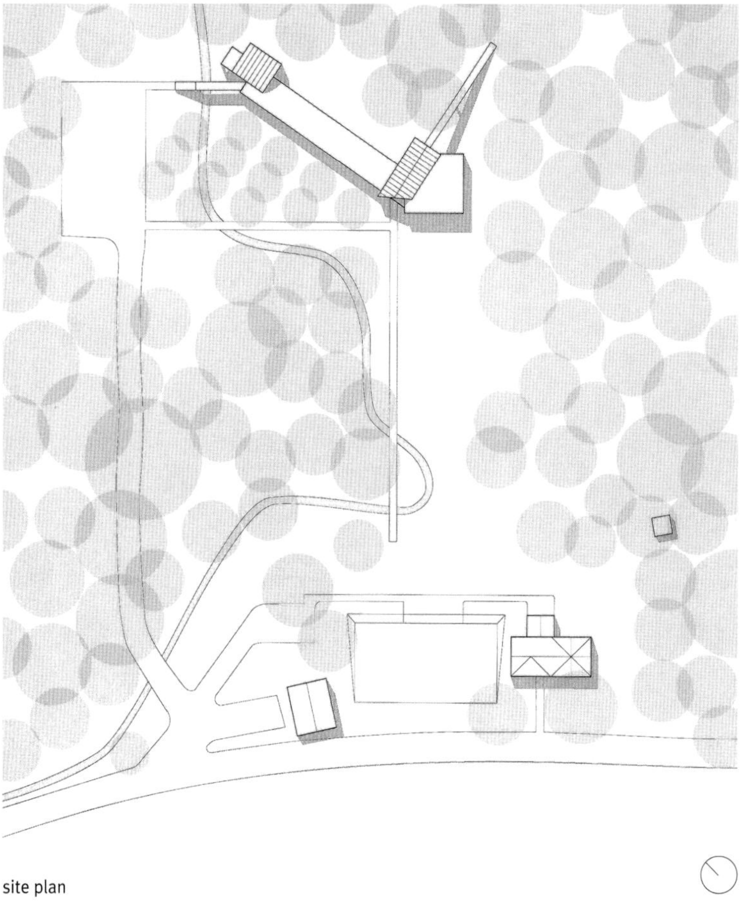

site plan

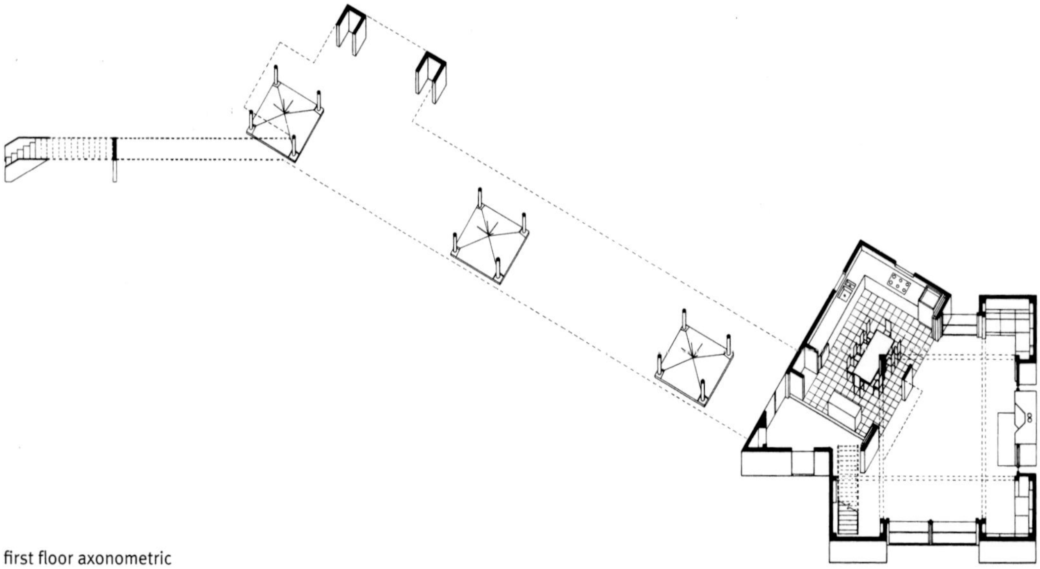

first floor axonometric

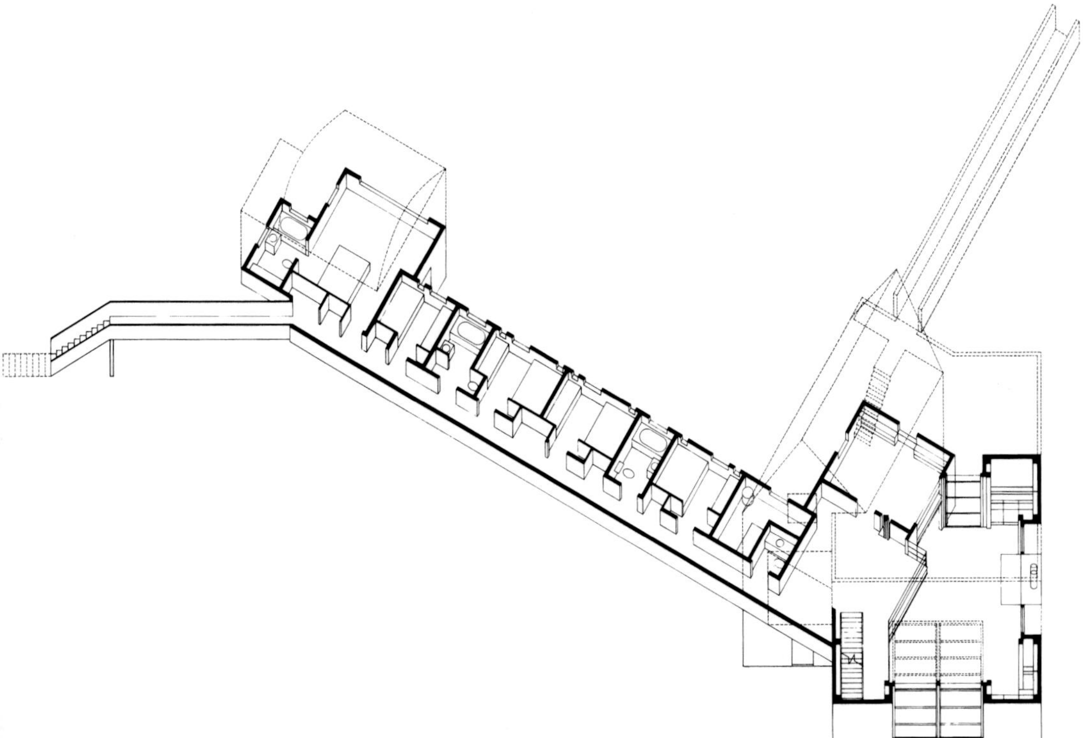

second floor axonometric

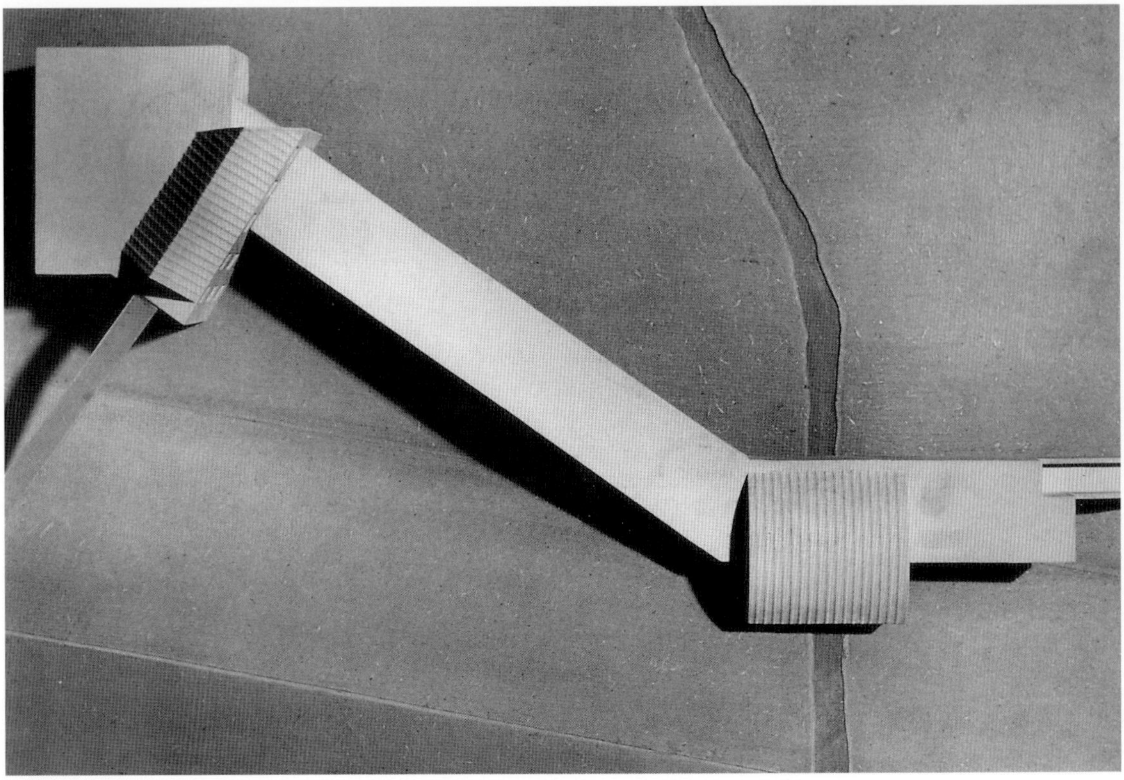

plaster model view from above

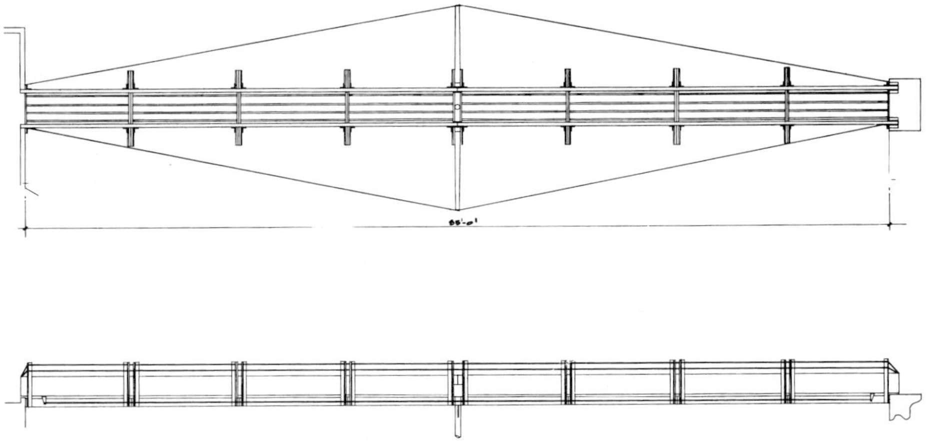

bridge plan and elevation

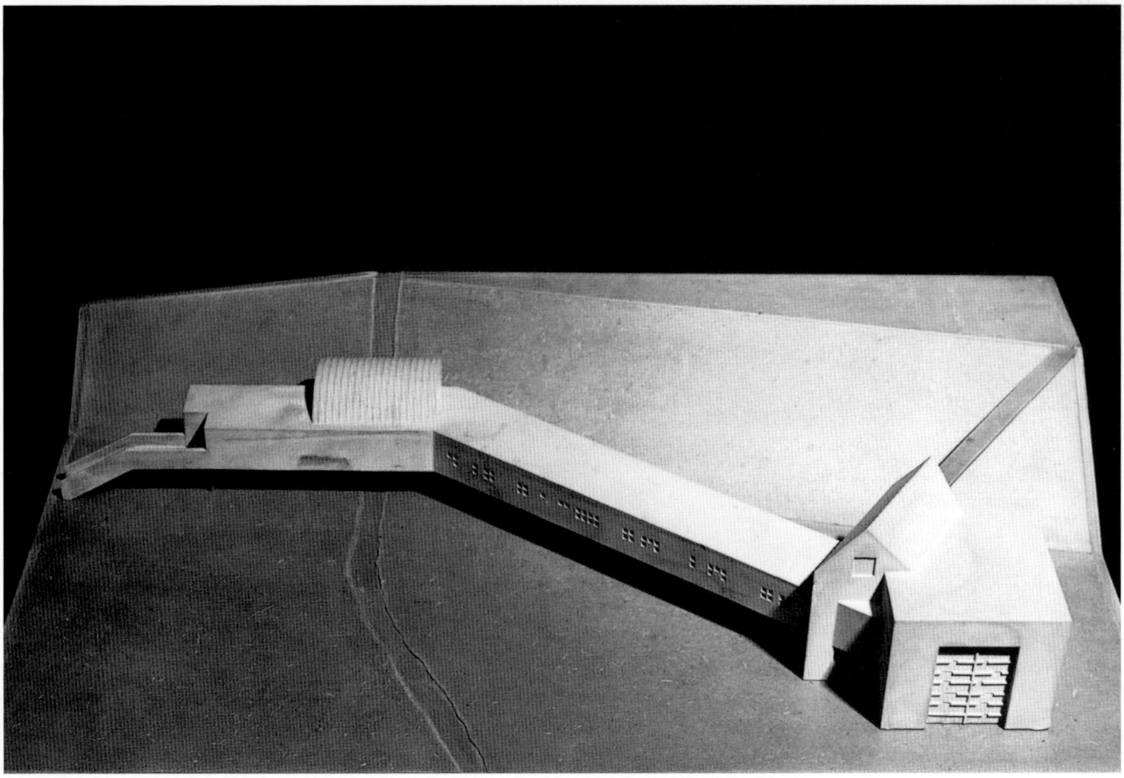

model view from west

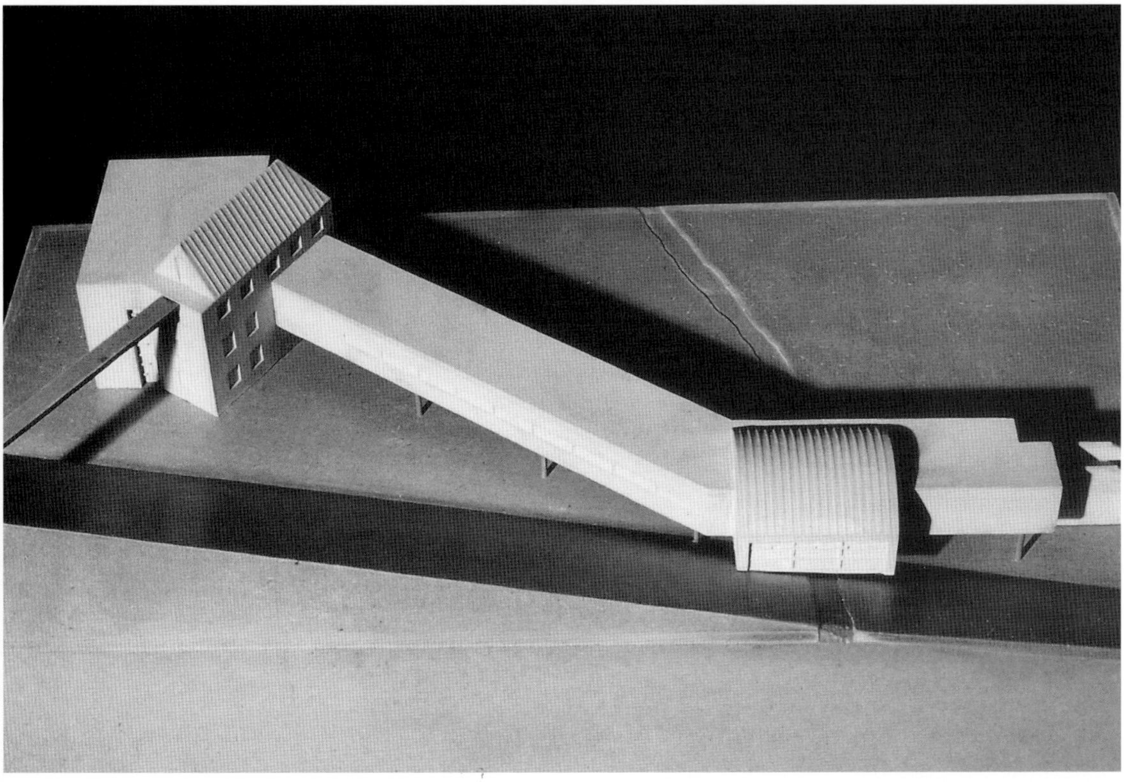

model view from east

lake house with court

Highland Park, Illinois

Project Team: Miranda Burton, Craig Graber, Wendy Pautz, Jim Walker, Fred Wolf
Lot Size: 1.3 acres (5,260 m²)
Building Size: 12,800 sf (1,189 m²)
Date of Design: 1993
Construction Completed: 1997

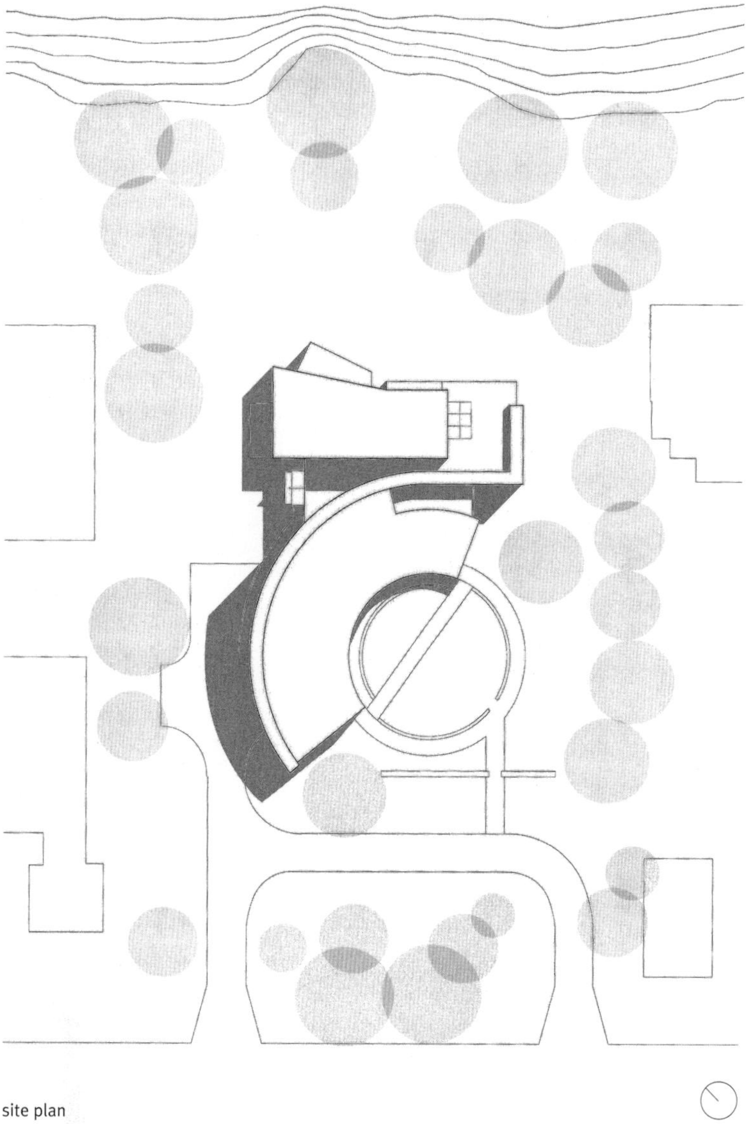

site plan

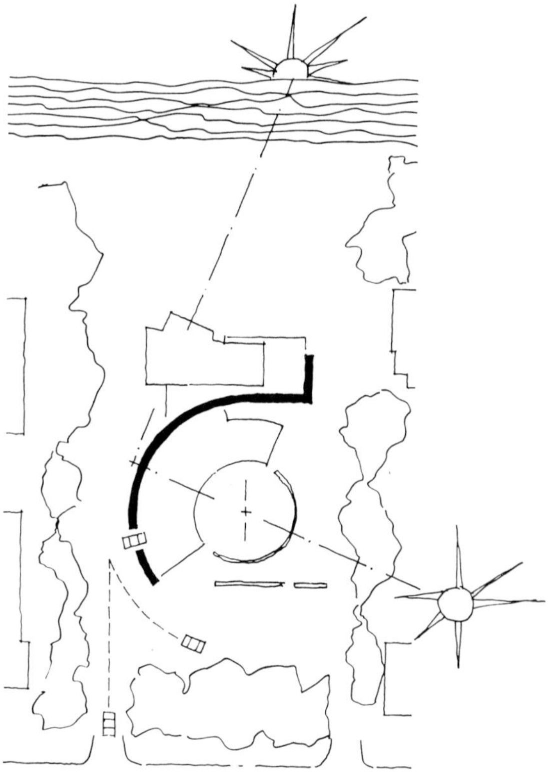

sun movement sketch

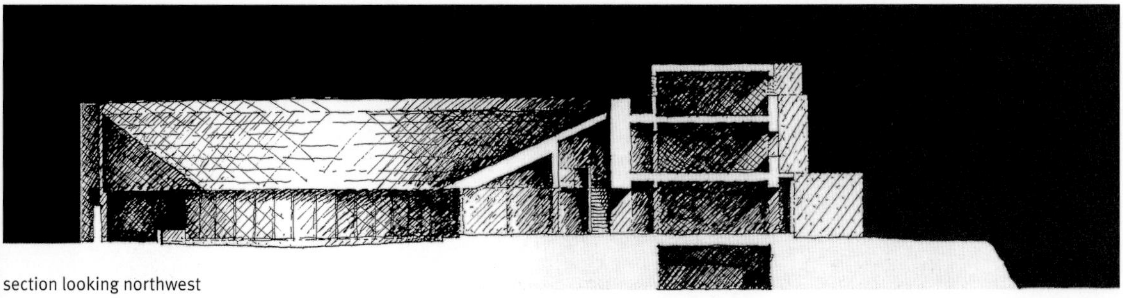

section looking northwest

early model views

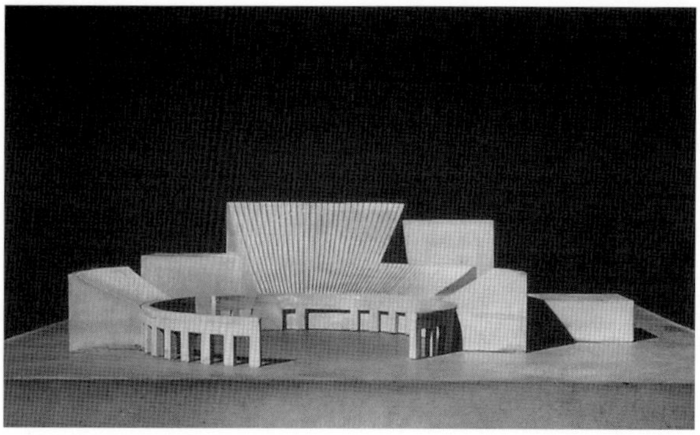

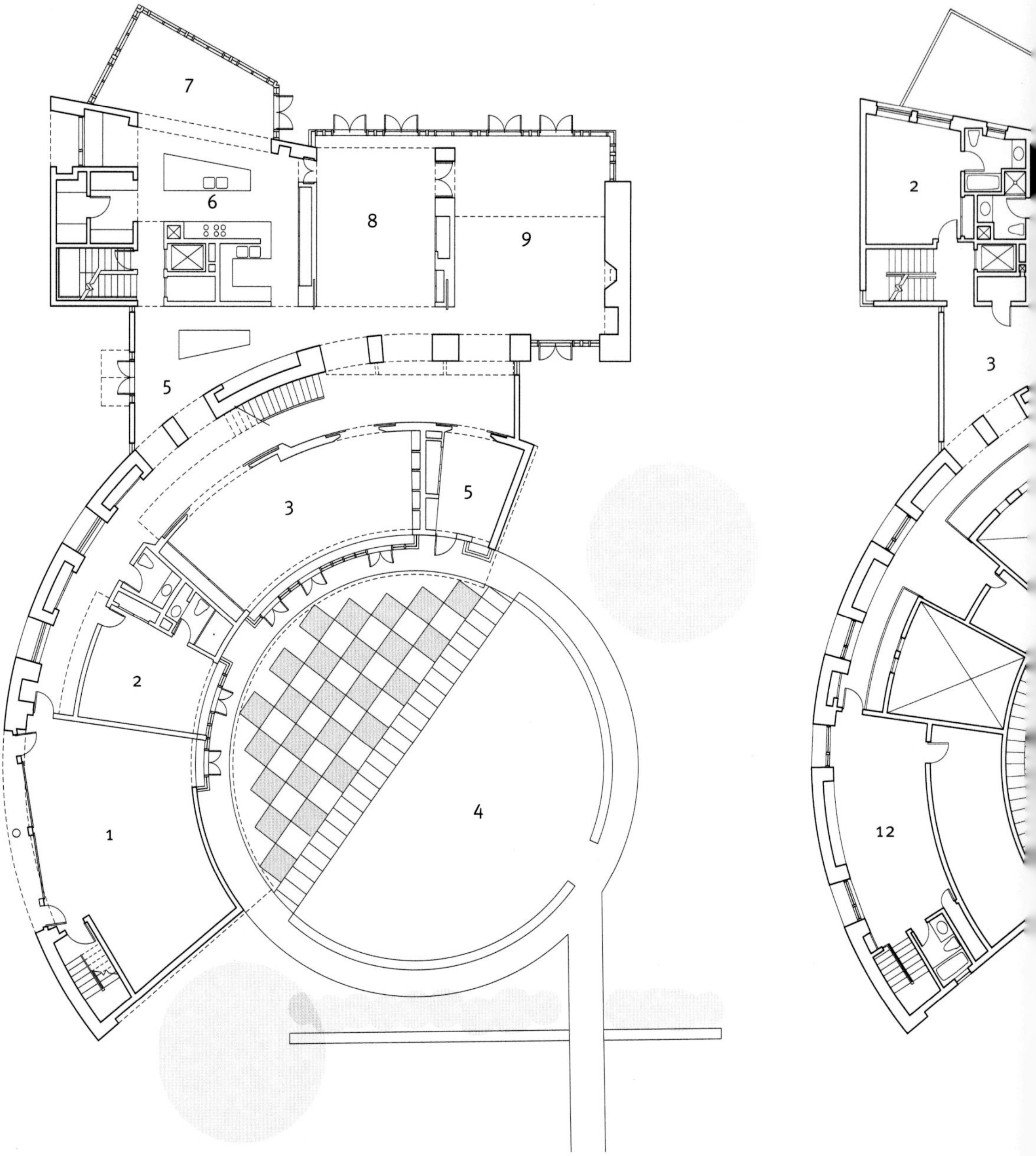

first, second, and third floor plans

1 garage
2 bedroom
3 sitting
4 courtyard
5 entry
6 kitchen
7 breakfast area
8 dining
9 living
10 master bedroom
11 office
12 apartment

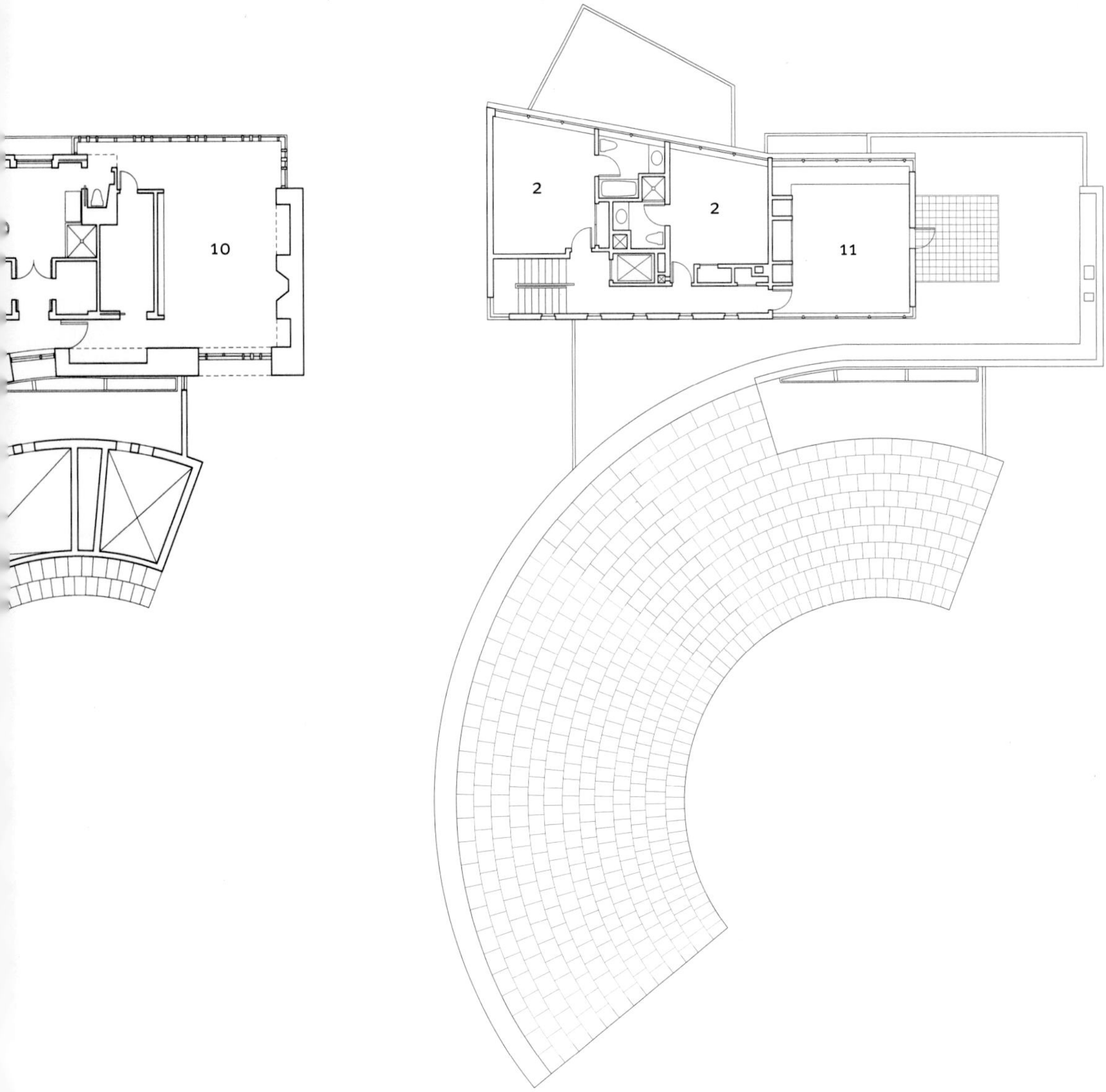
10
2
2
11

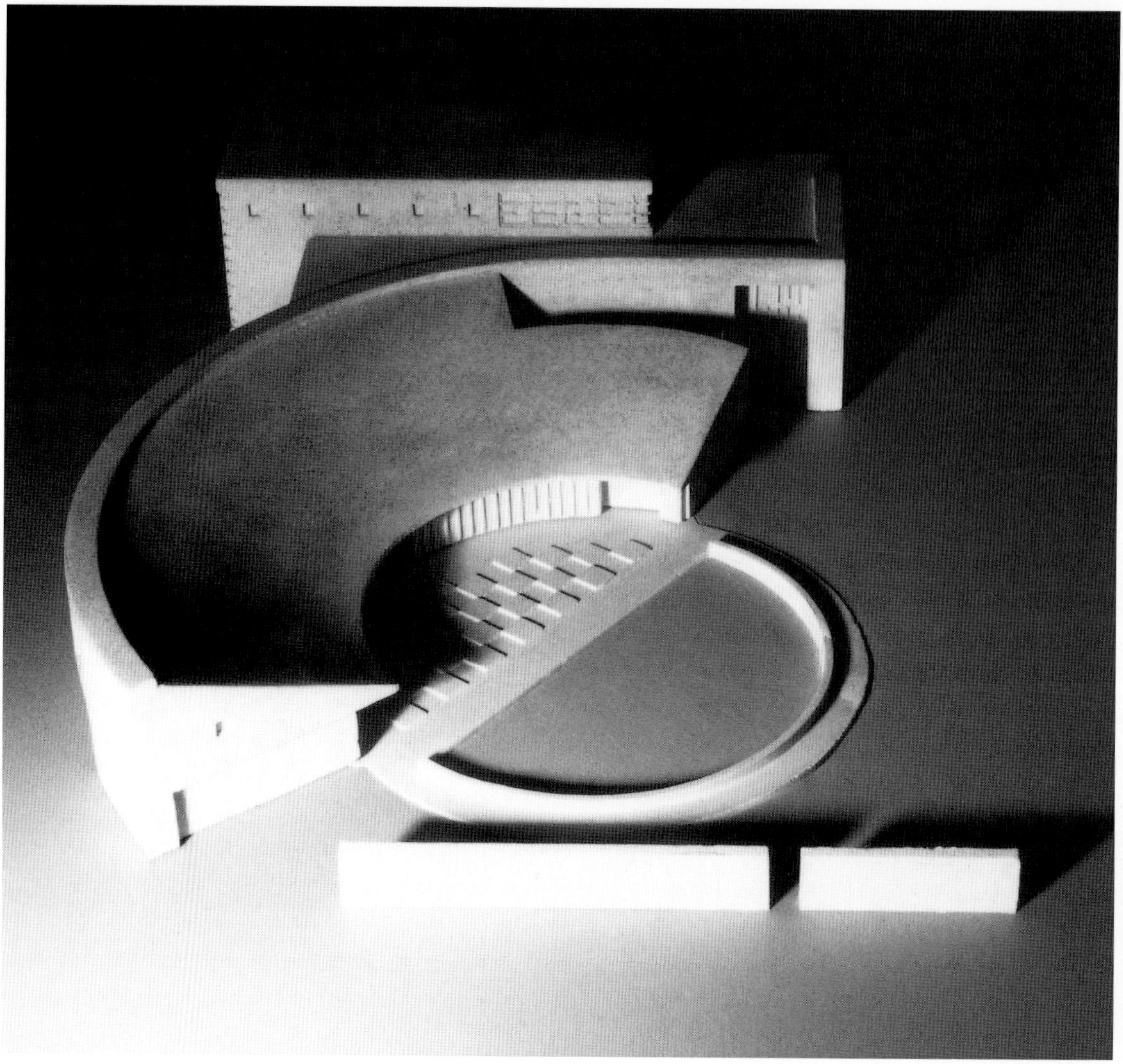

final design models

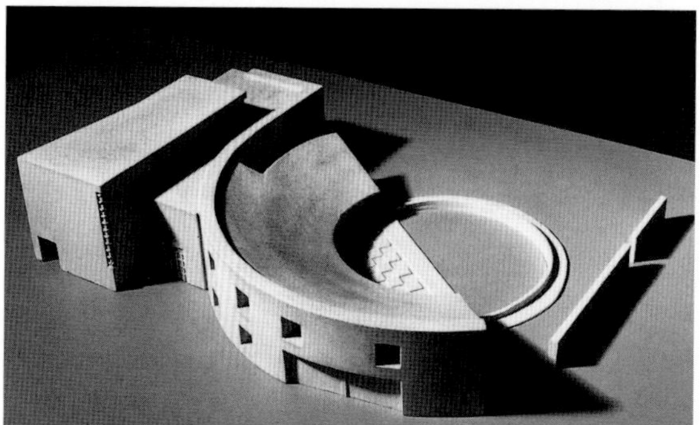

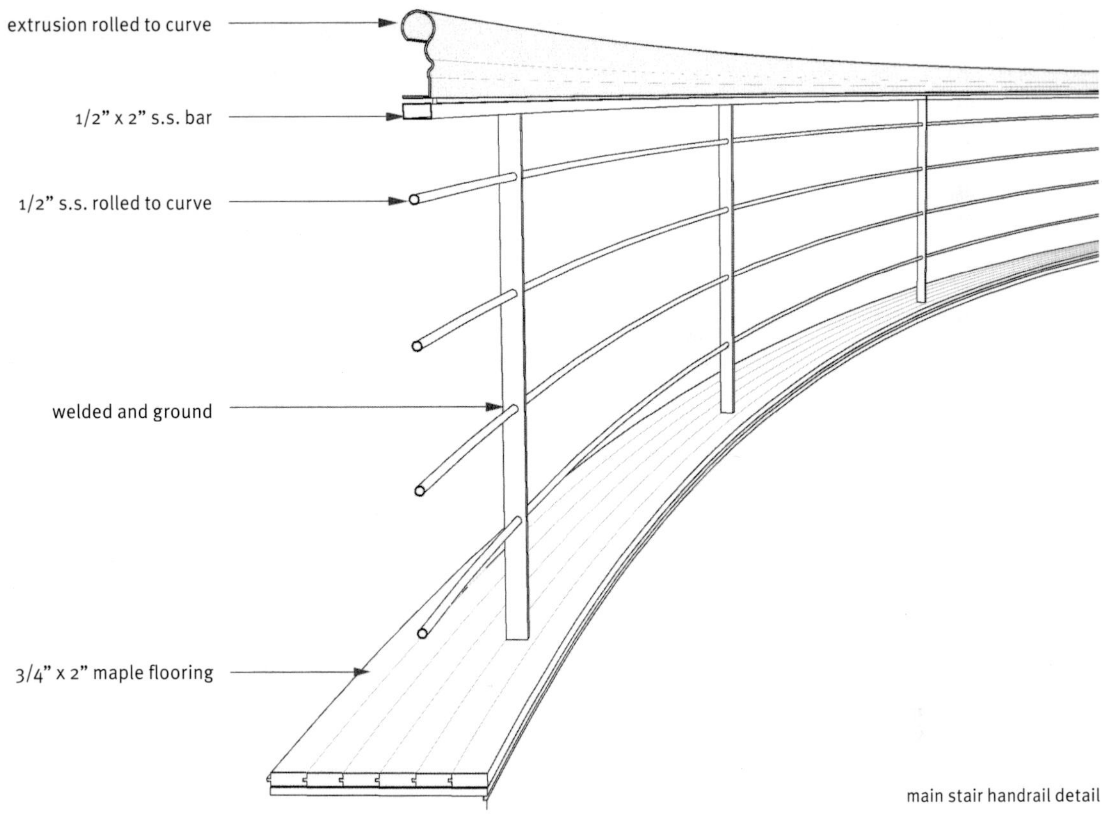

main stair handrail detail

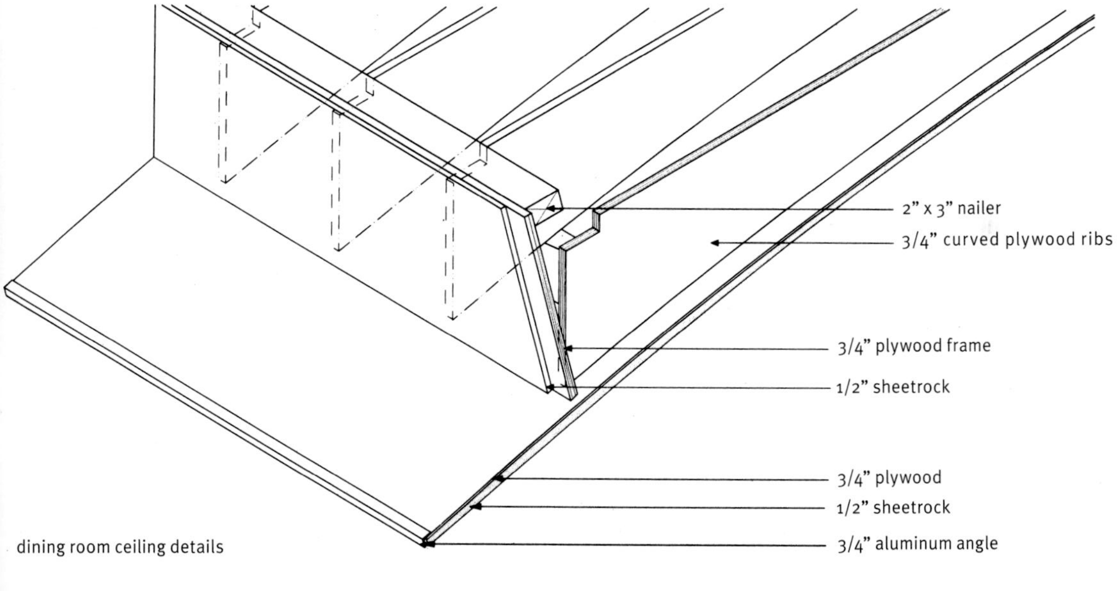

dining room ceiling details

double house

New Canaan, Connecticut

Project Team: Delphine Aboulker, Mark Dixon,
Maria Elena Fanna, Marc Gee, Peter Guthrie, Richard Lucas
Lot Size: 5 acres (2 hectares)
Building Size: 7,200 sf (669 m²)
Date of Design: 1999
Construction Completed: 2002

site plan

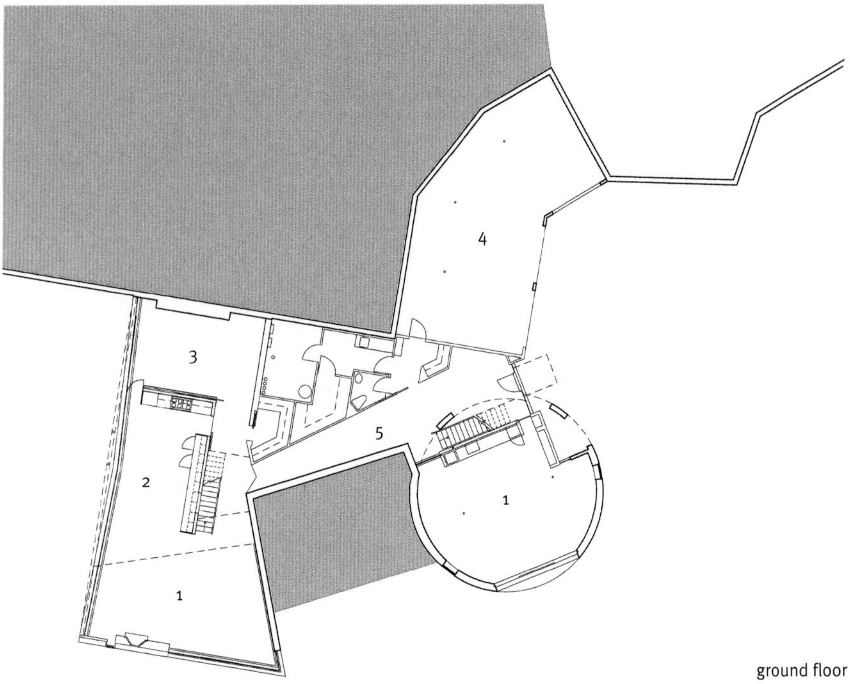

ground floor

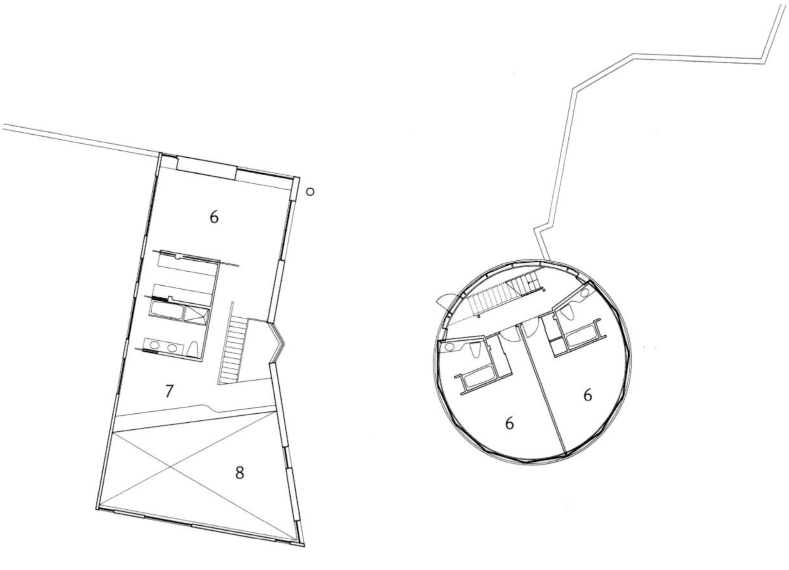

1 living
2 kitchen
3 dining
4 garage
5 gallery
6 bedroom
7 study
8 living room below

second floor

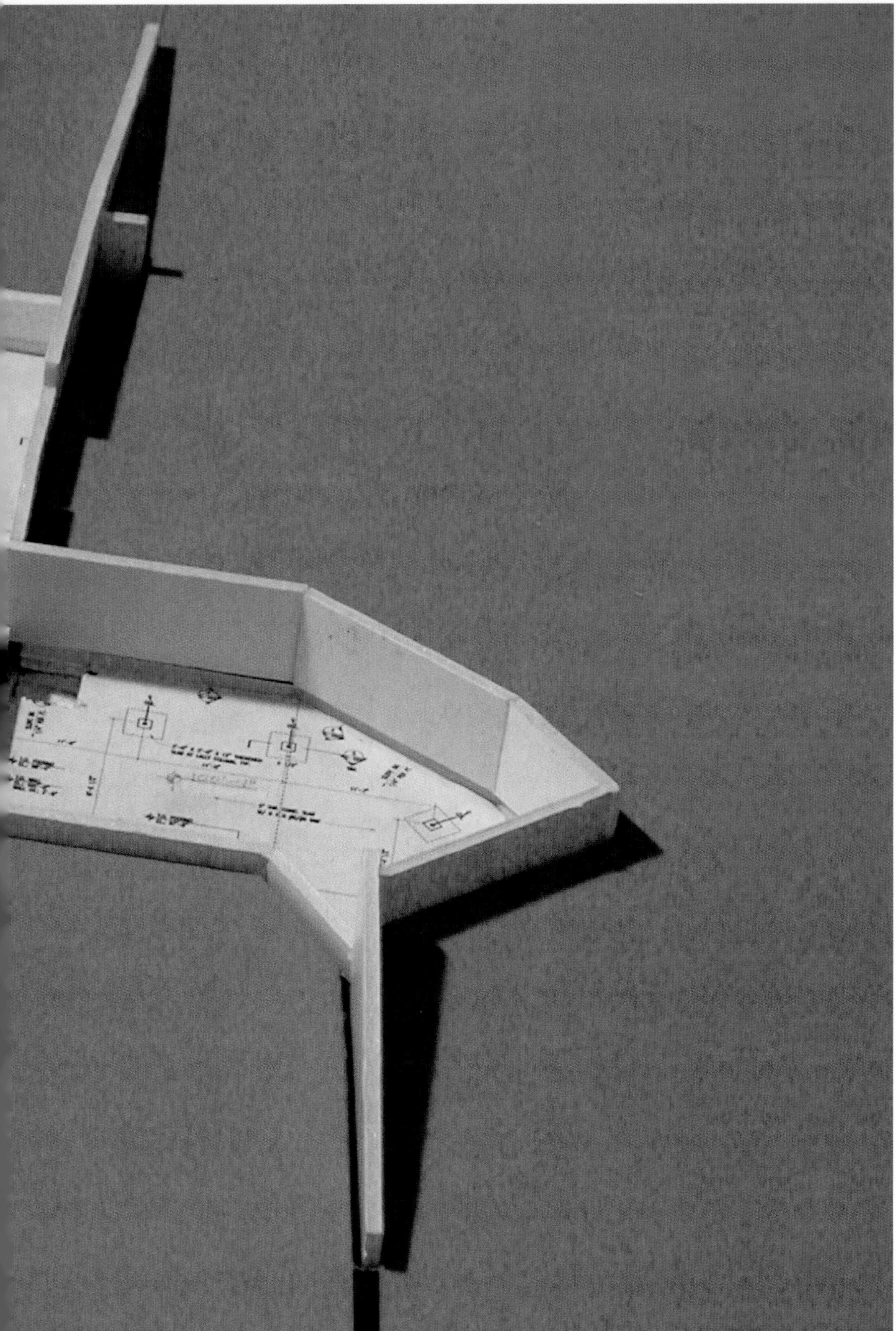

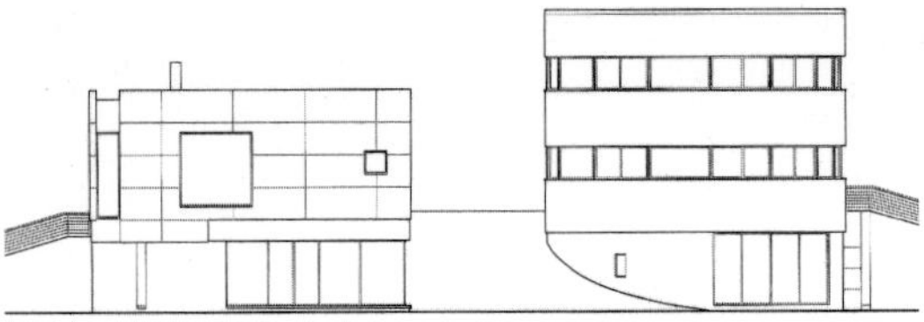

east elevation

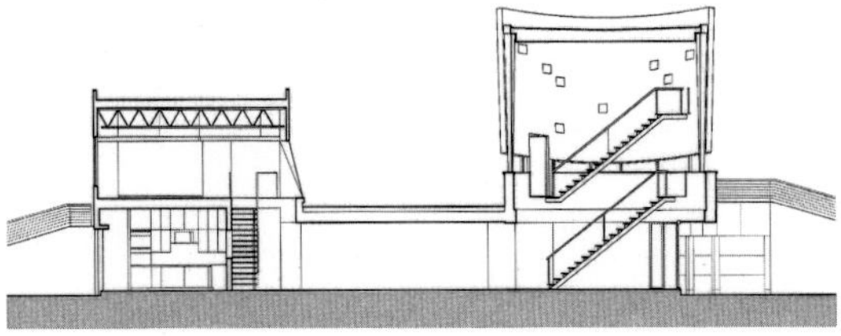

section looking west

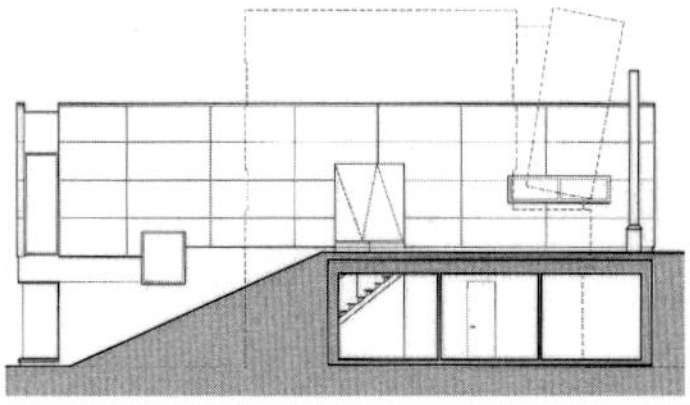

section – elevation looking south

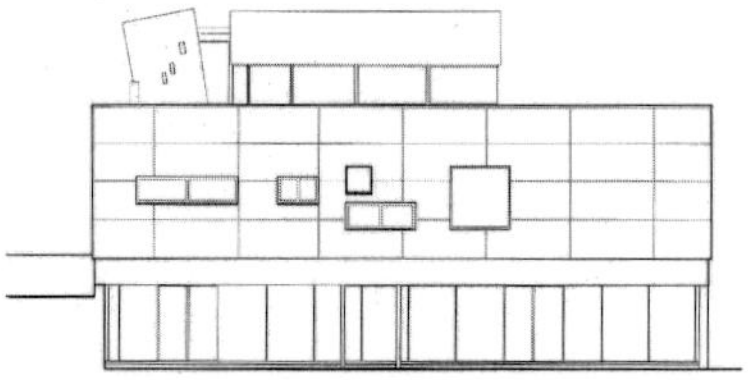

north elevation

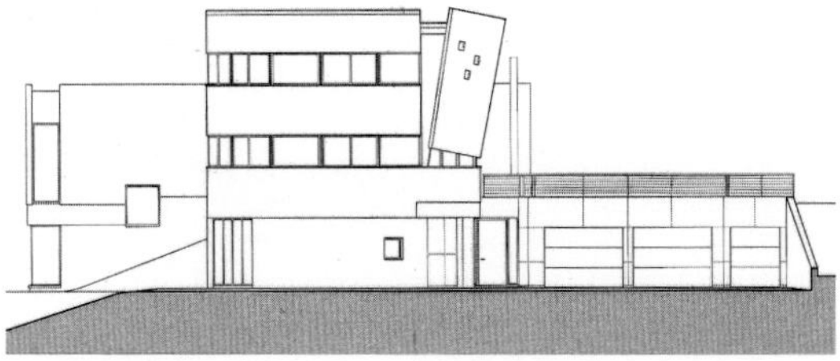

south elevation

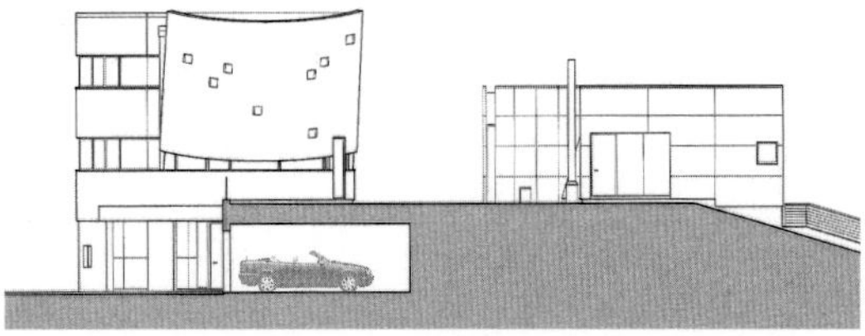

section – elevation looking west

model views

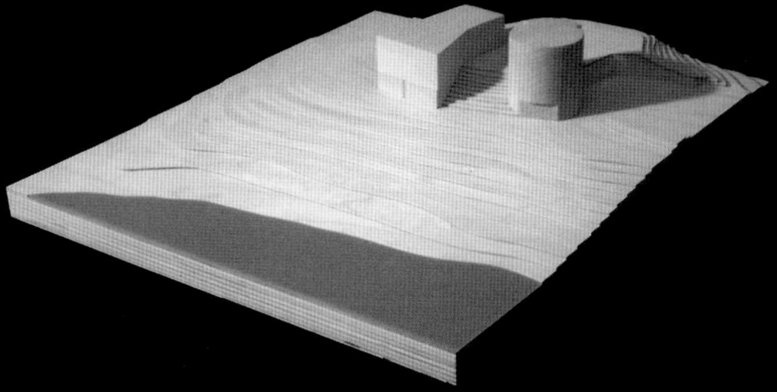

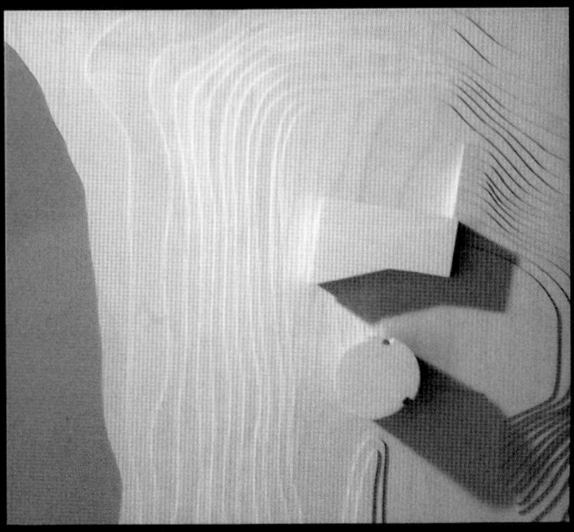

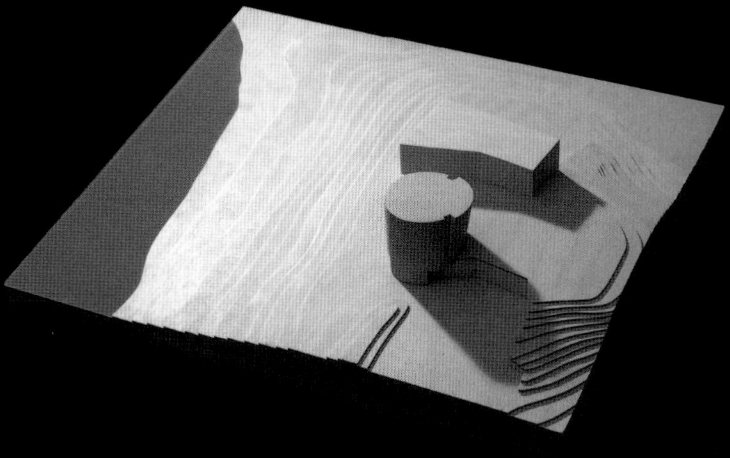

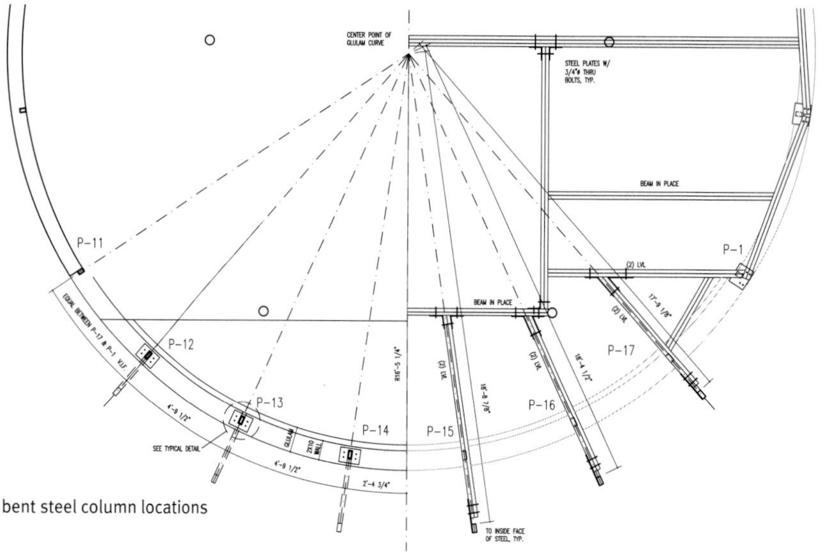

bent steel column locations

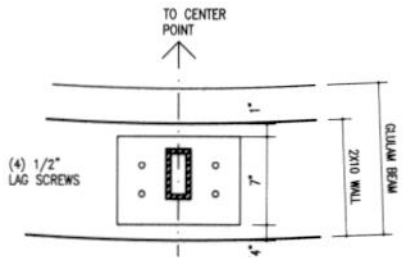

typical base plate detail

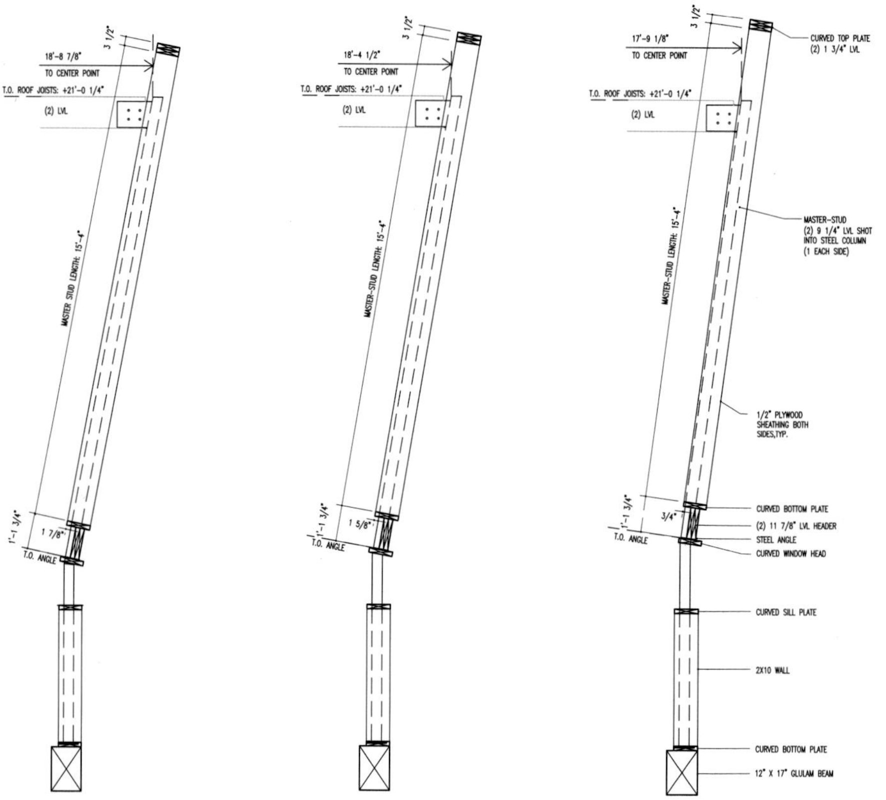

column side elevations

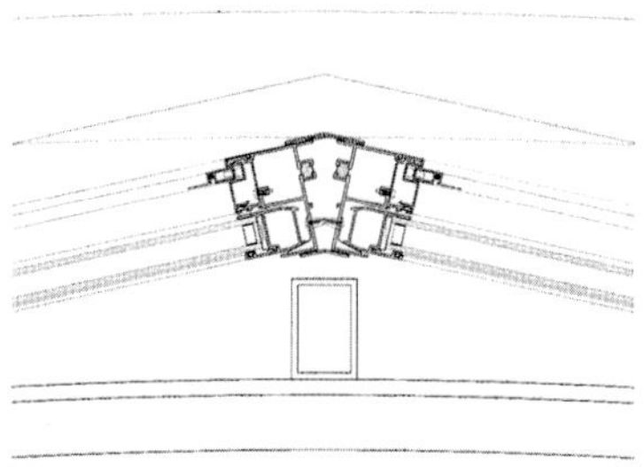

detail at steel supports

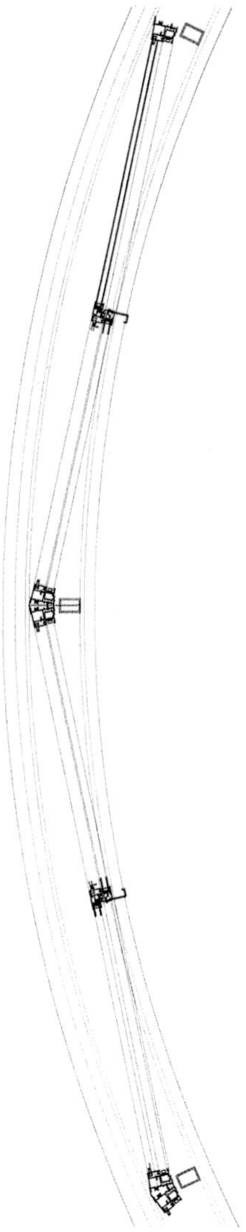

plan of strip windows

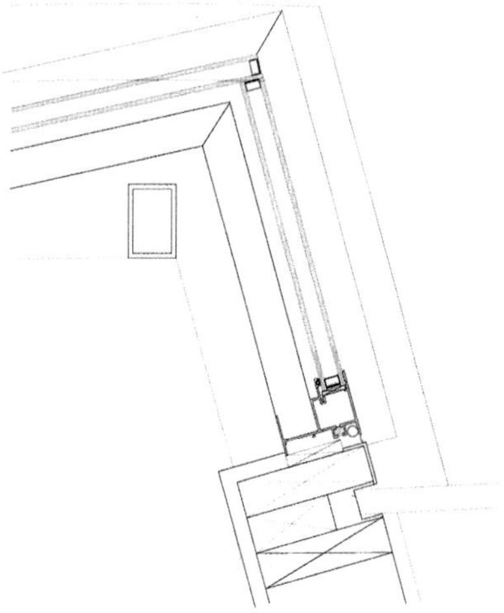

detail at corner vertical fixed glass

glass details at barrel building

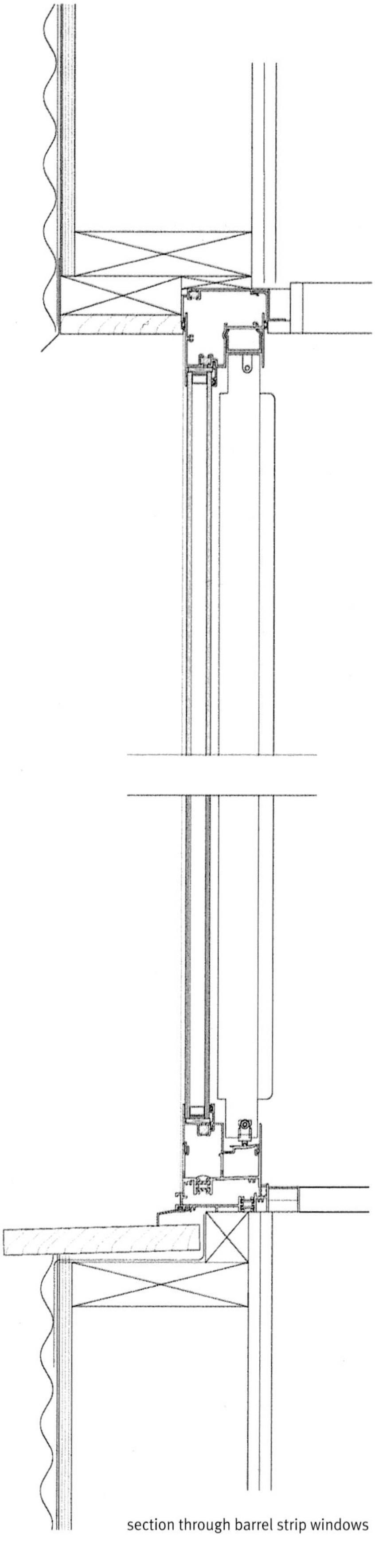

section through barrel strip windows

bar house

Western United States

Project Team: Marc Dixon, Charlie Kaplan,
Jason LaPointe, David Mabbot, Margit Routt, Elaine Sun
Lot Size: 2 acres (8,094 m^2)
Building Size: 5,750 sf (534 m^2)
Date of Design: 2001
Construction Completed: 2004

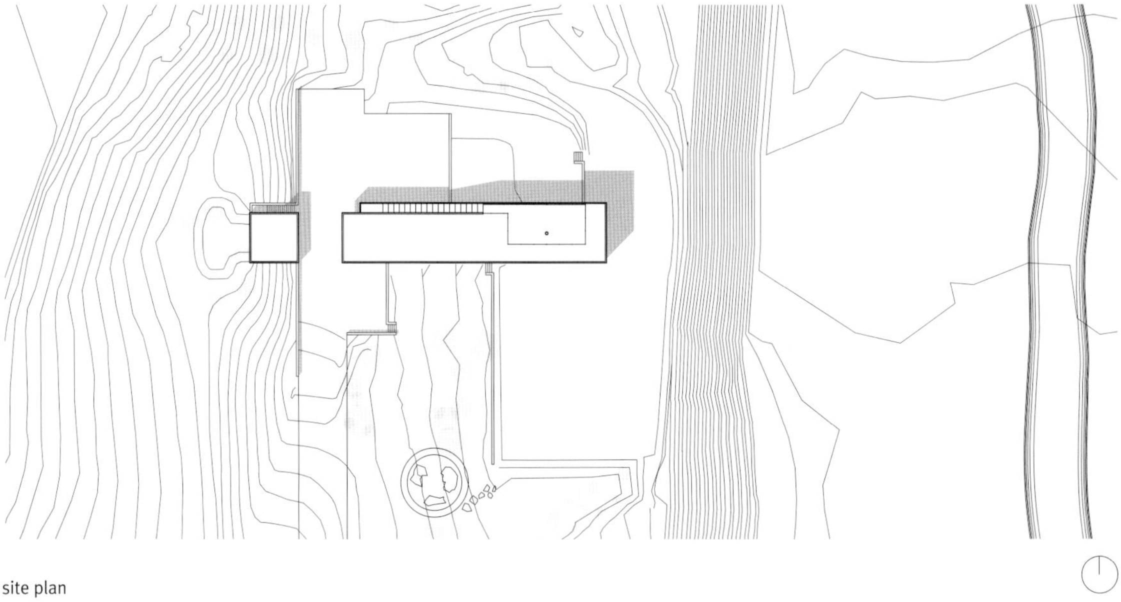

site plan

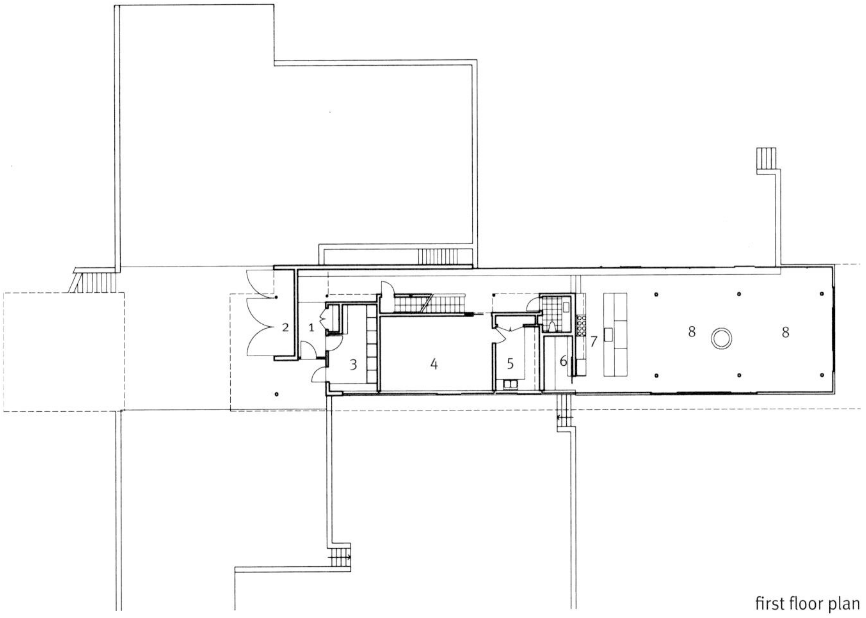

first floor plan

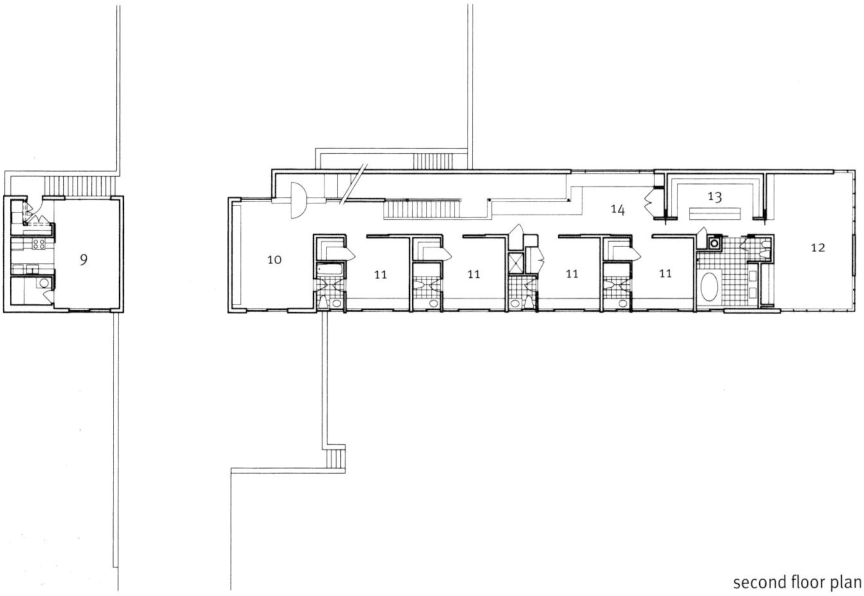

1 entrance
2 storage
3 mudroom
4 gym
5 laundry room
6 pantry
7 kitchen
8 dining / living room
9 guest apartment
10 family room
11 bedroom
12 master bedroom
13 dressing room
14 office / playroom

second floor plan

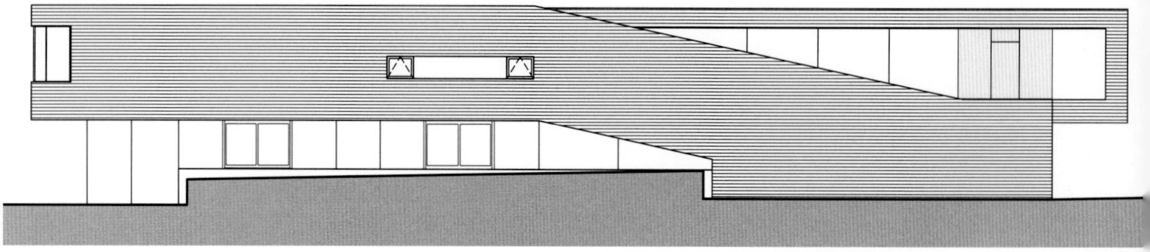

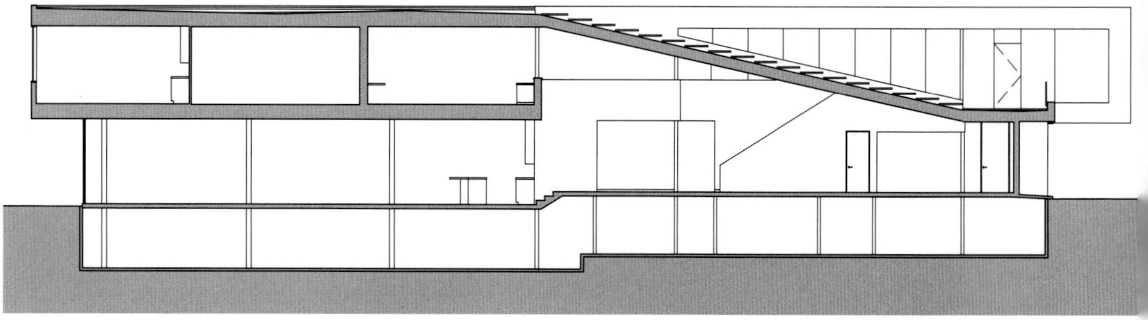

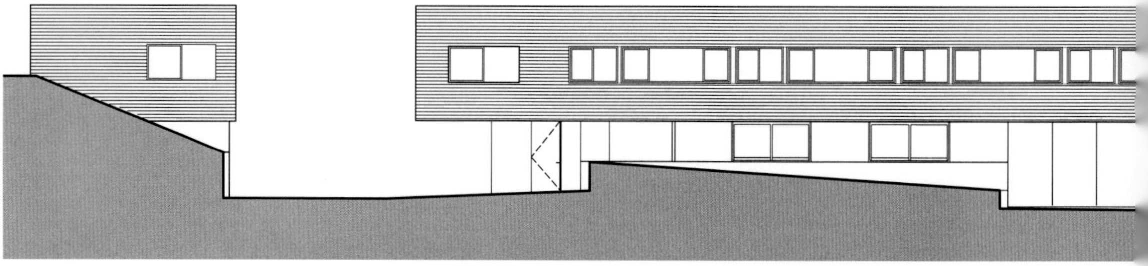

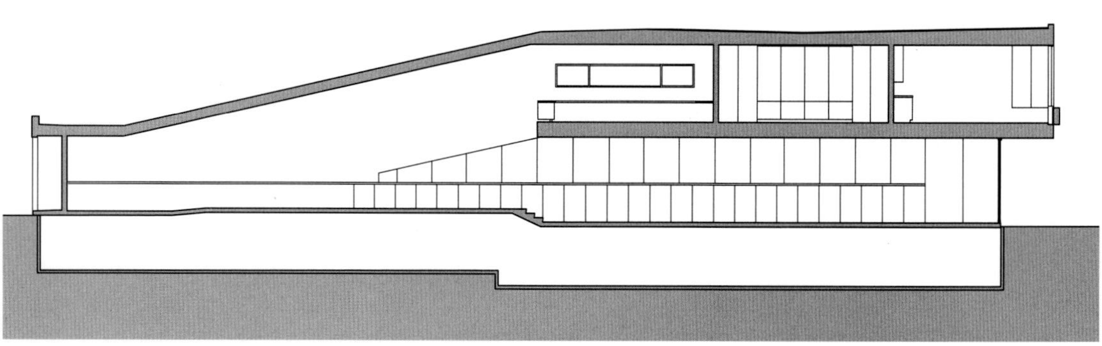

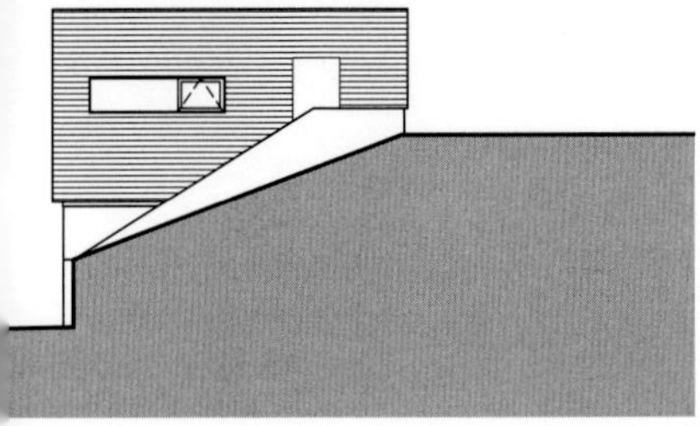

northeast elevation

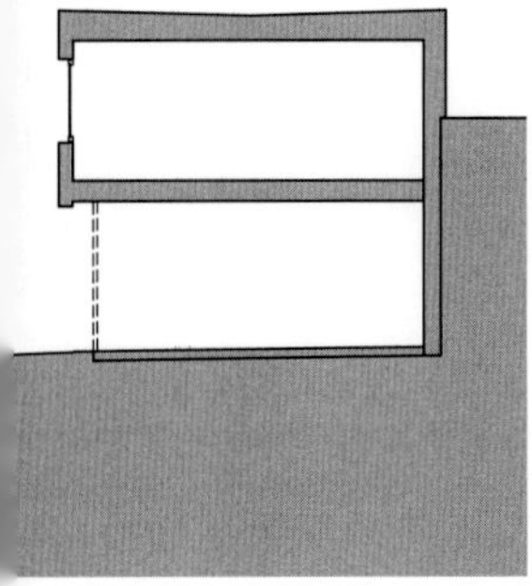

section looking southwest

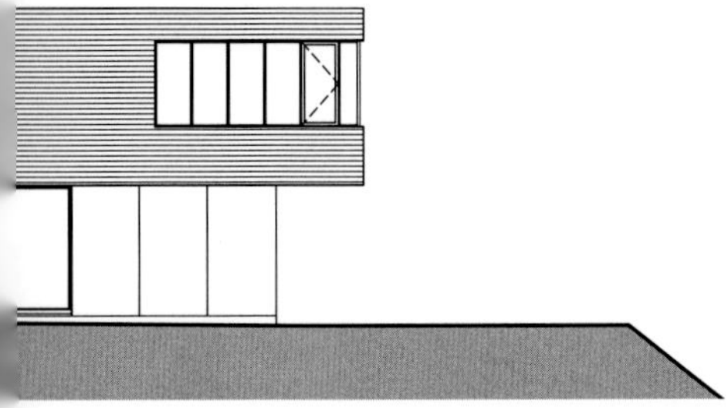

southwest elevation

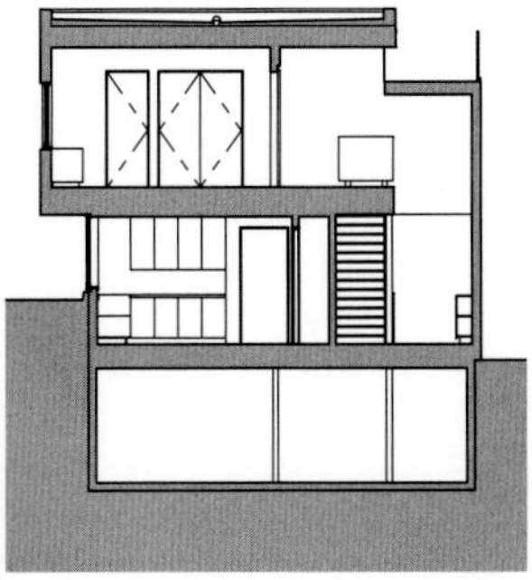

section looking northeast and northwest

floating box house

Austin, Texas

Project Team: Delphine Aboulker, Burton Baldridge, Matt Burgermaster, Maria Elena Fanna, Marc Gee, Richard Lucas, Lj Porter, Stephanie Ragle, Frederik Rissom, Hiroaki Takimoto, Stefanie Werner

Lot Size: 4 acres (1.6 hectares)
Building Size: 12,000 sf (1,115 m²)
Date of Design: 2002
Construction Completed 2005

site plan

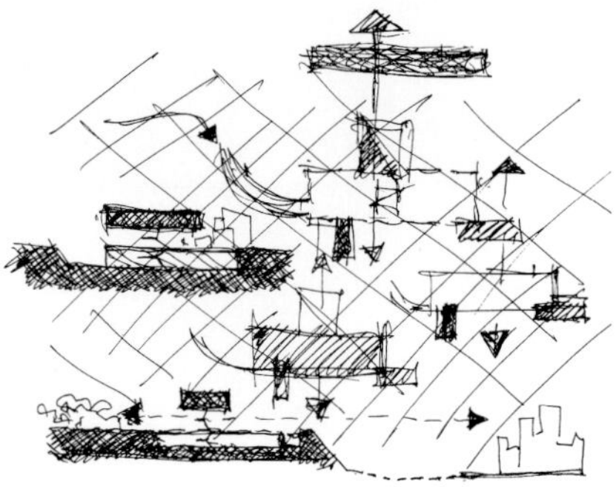

early design sketches

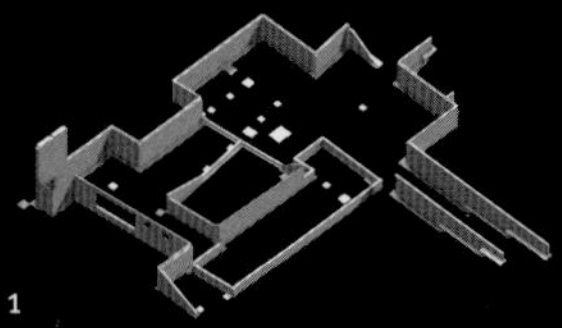

1

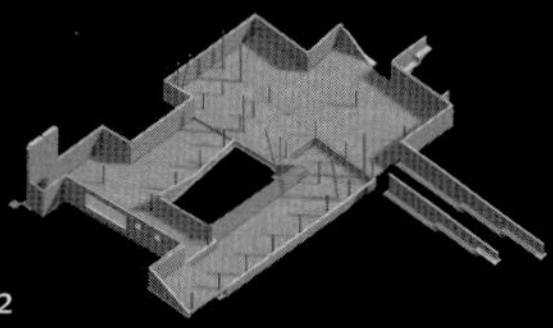

2

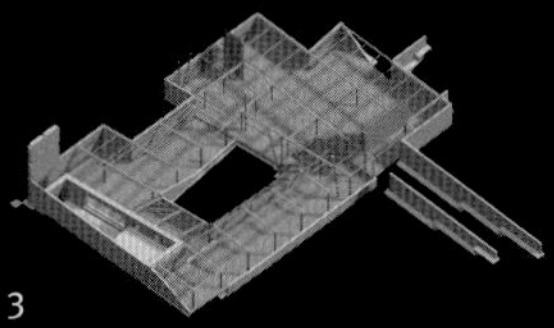

3

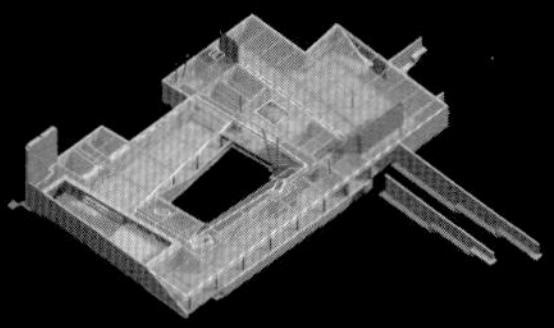

4

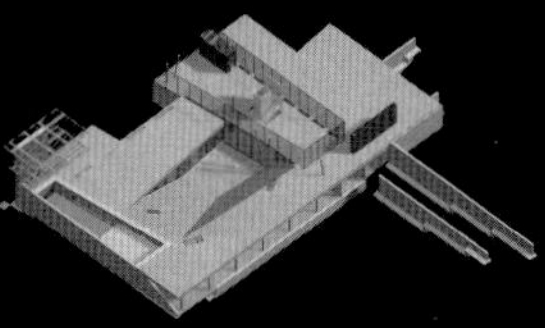

5

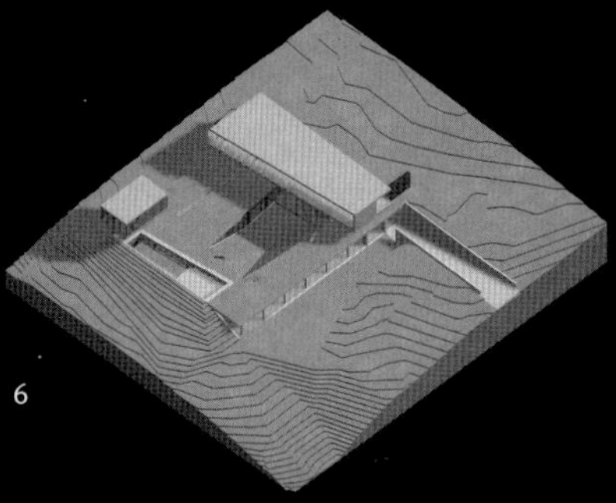

6

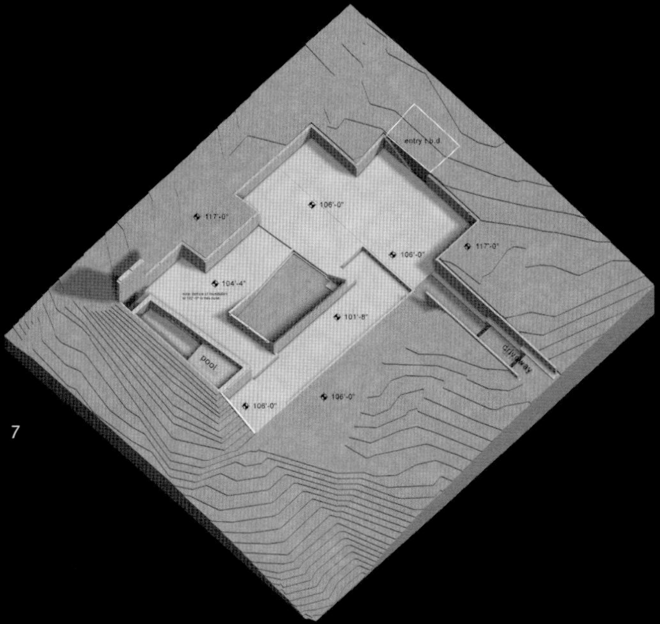

7

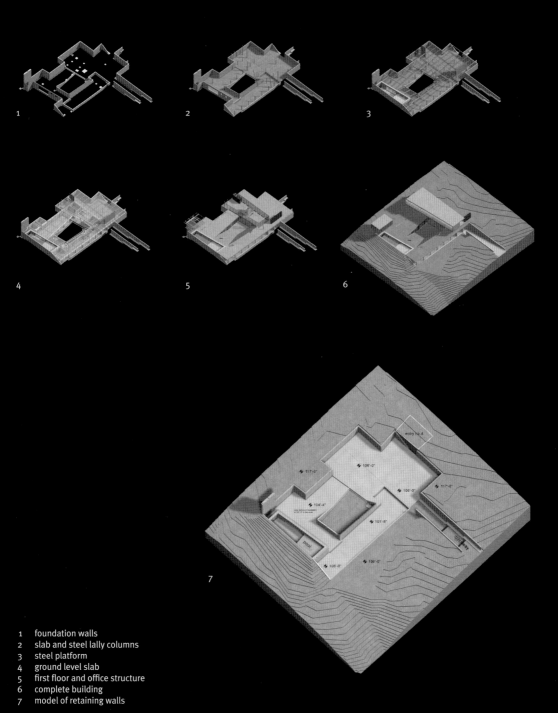

1 foundation walls
2 slab and steel lally columns
3 steel platform
4 ground level slab
5 first floor and office structure
6 complete building
7 model of retaining walls

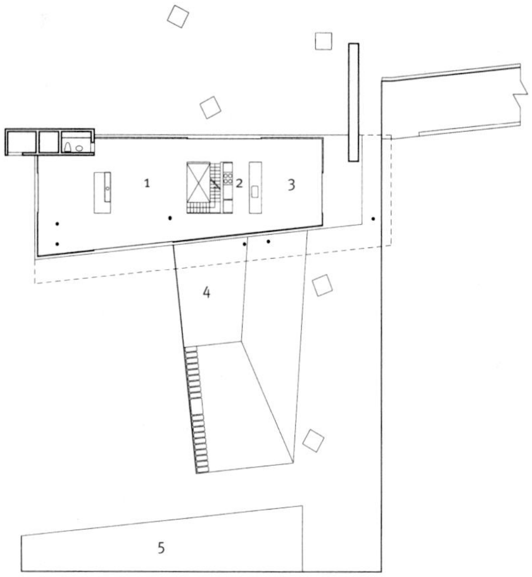

first floor plan

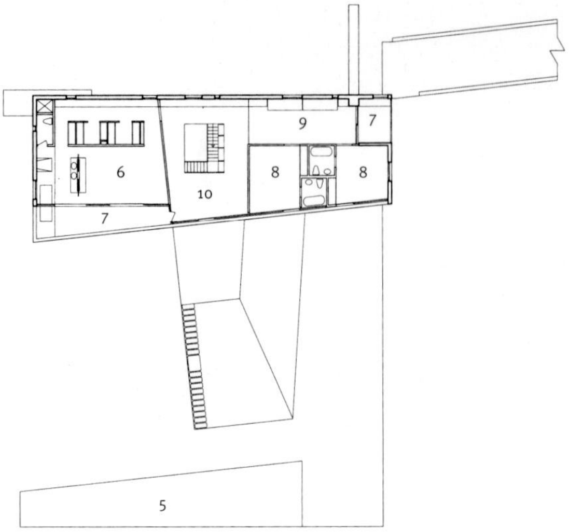

second floor plan

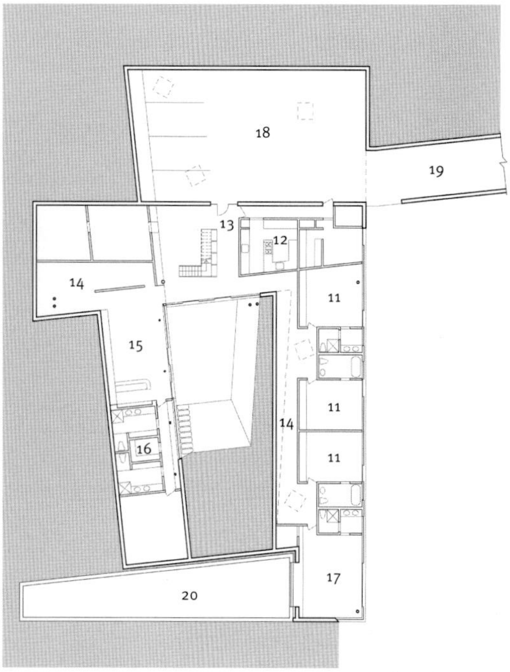

lower floor plan

1 living
2 kitchen
3 dining
4 sunken courtyard
5 pool
6 master bedroom
7 terrace
8 children's bedroom
9 play area
10 sitting area
11 guest bedroom
12 prep kitchen
13 entry
14 gallery
15 media
16 sauna
17 office
18 garage
19 driveway
20 pool above

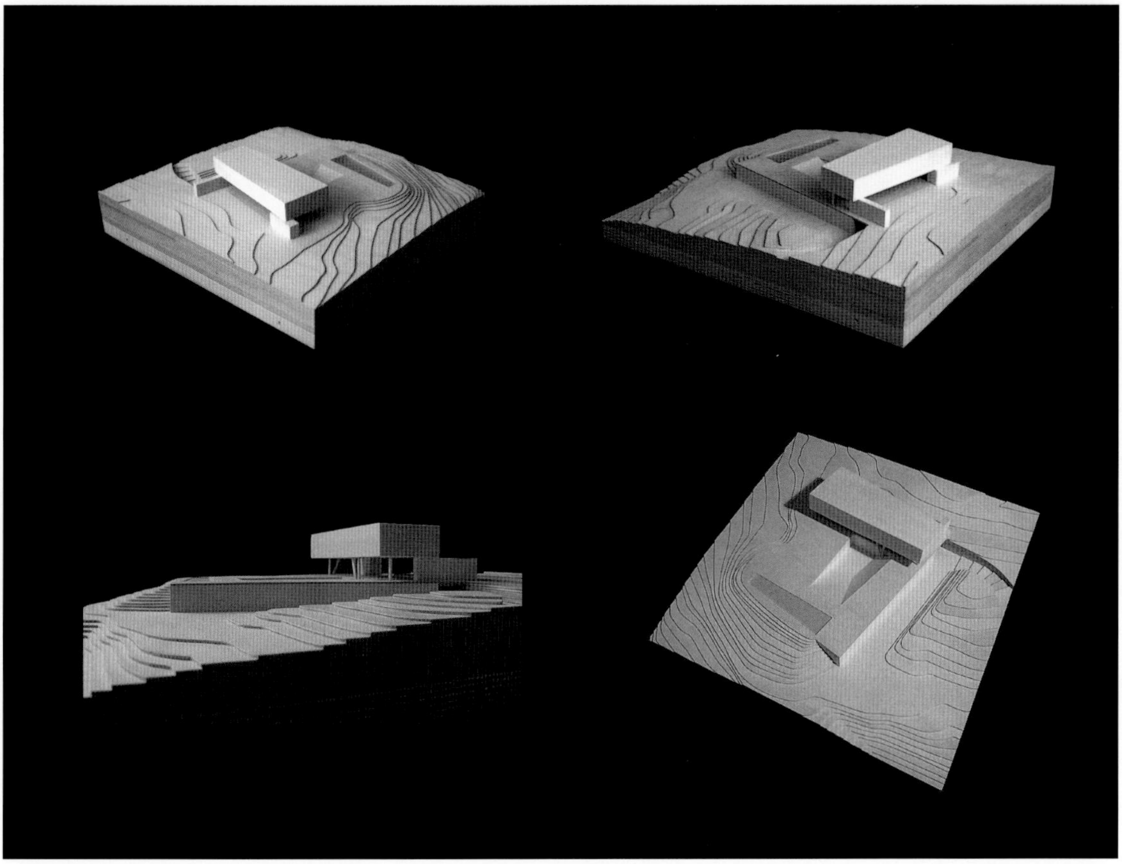

model views

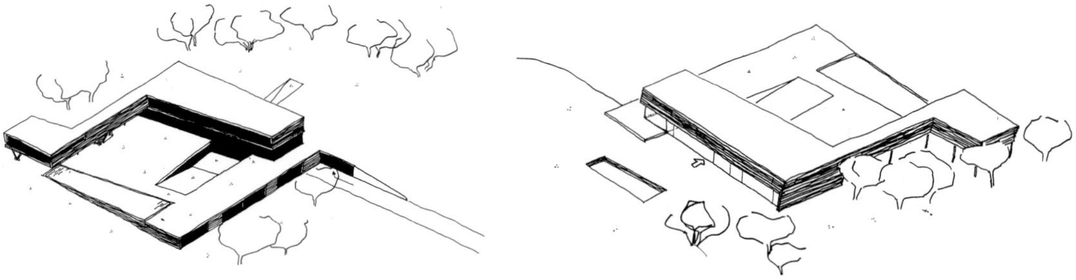

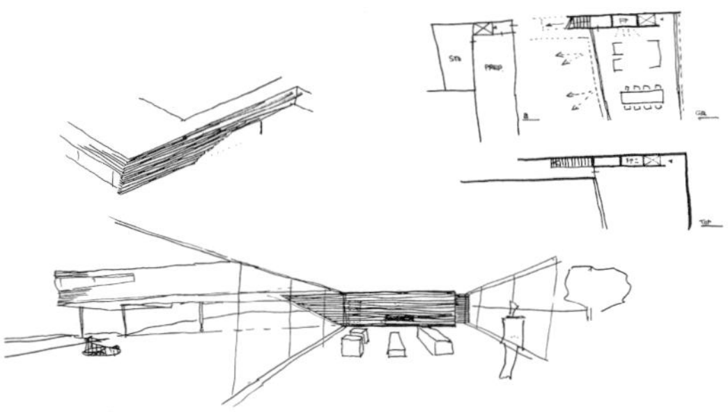

early design sketches

exterior and interior computer design perspectives

section looking south

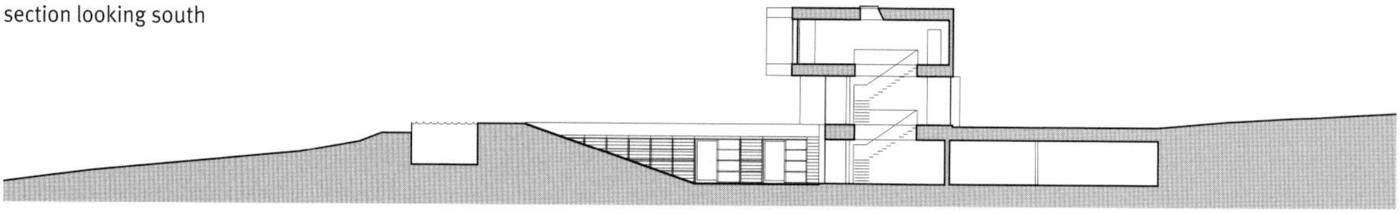

north elevation

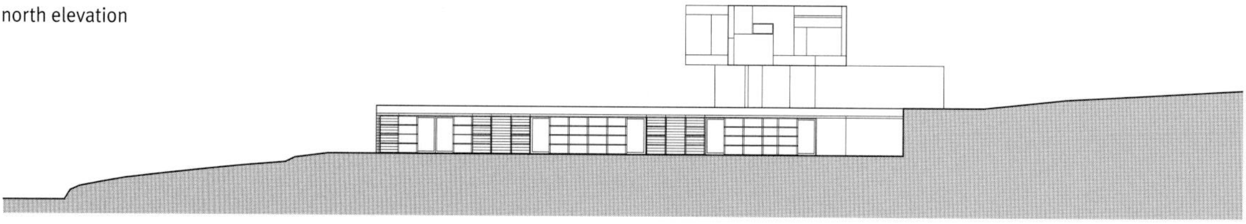

section looking west

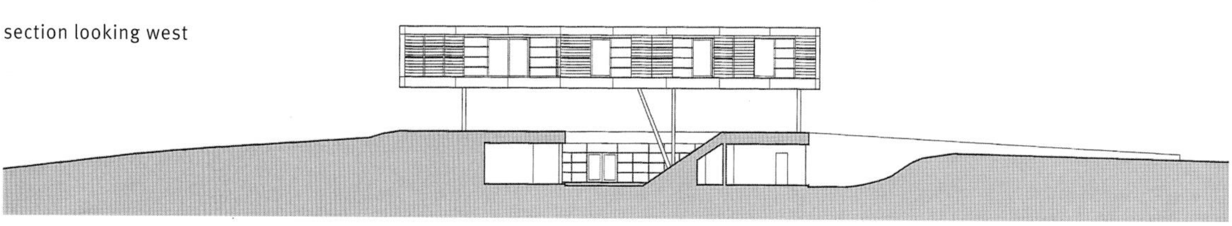

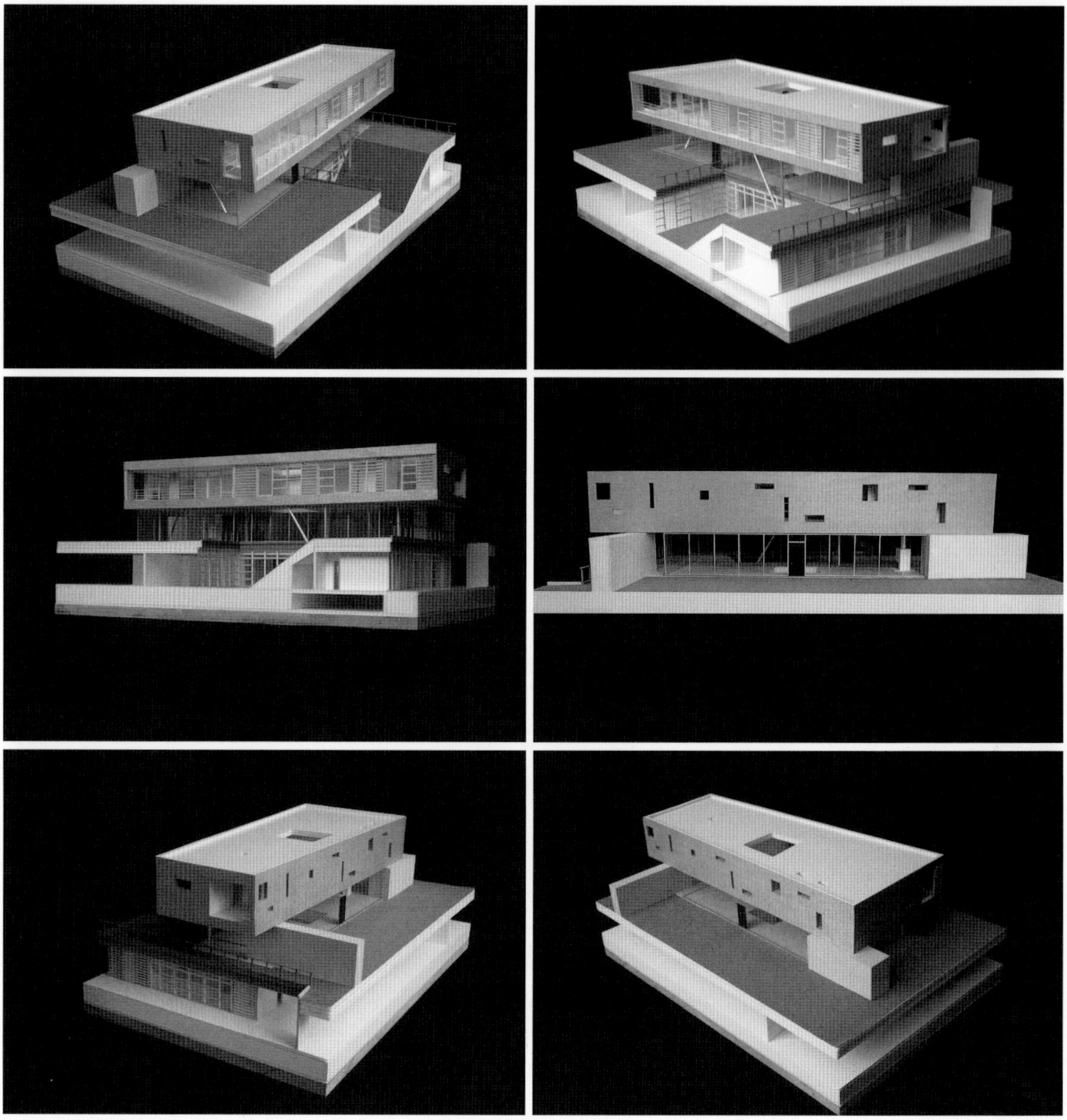

model views

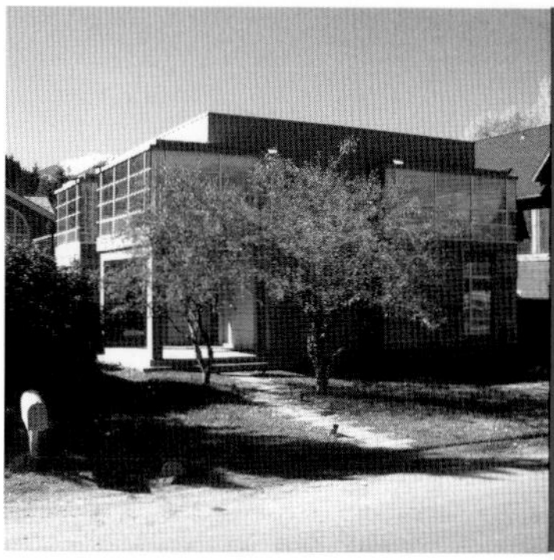

cube house

Aspen, Colorado

Project Team: Suki Dixon, Richard Lucas, Katie Winter, Fred Wolf
Lot Size: 6,000 sf (557 m²)
Building Size: 5,000 sf (465 m²)
Date of Design: 1997
Construction Completed: 1998

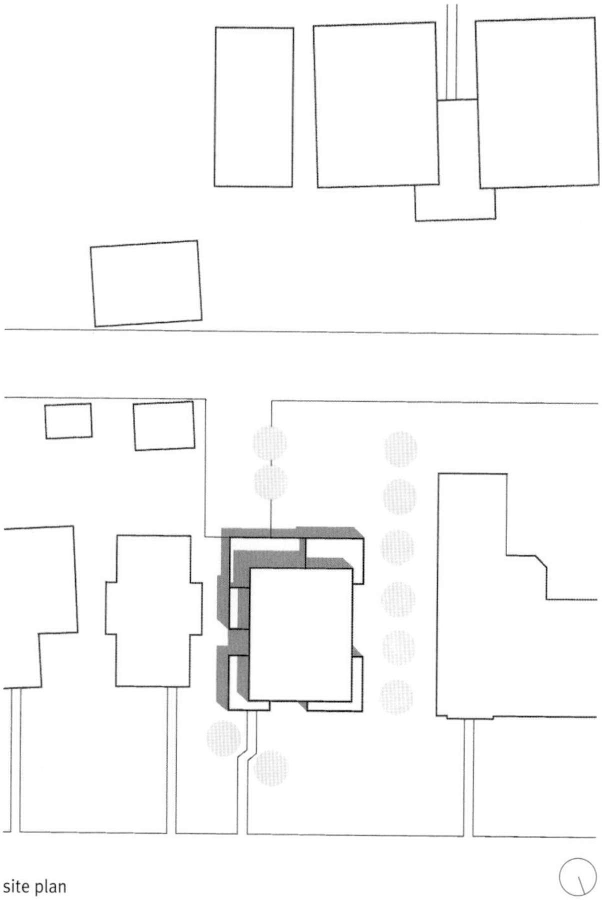

site plan

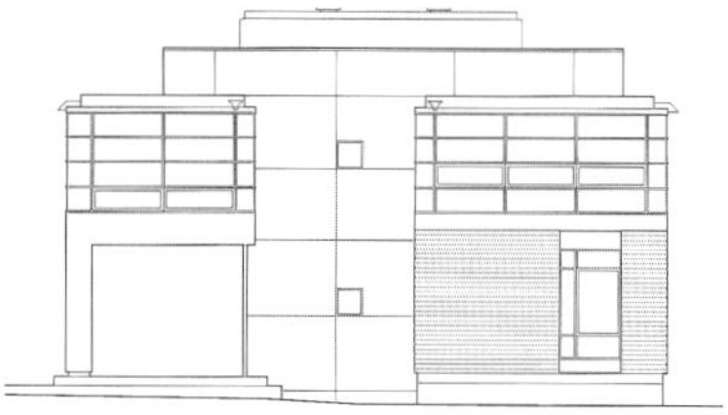

north elevation

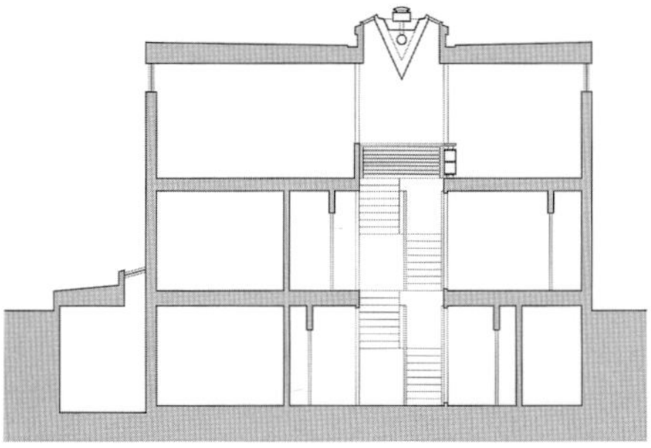

section looking east

10

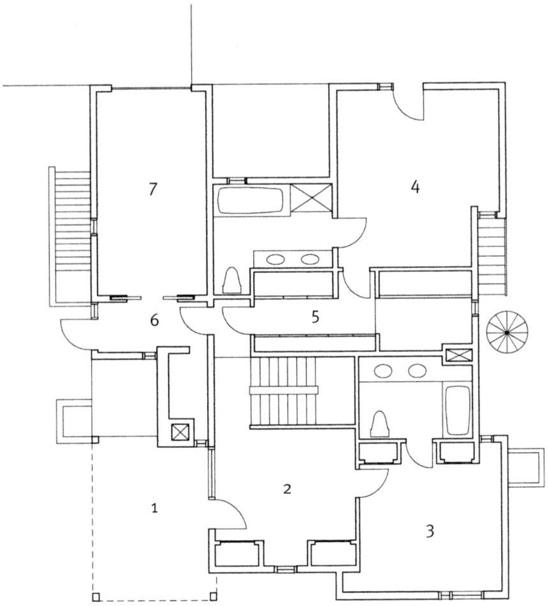

first floor plan

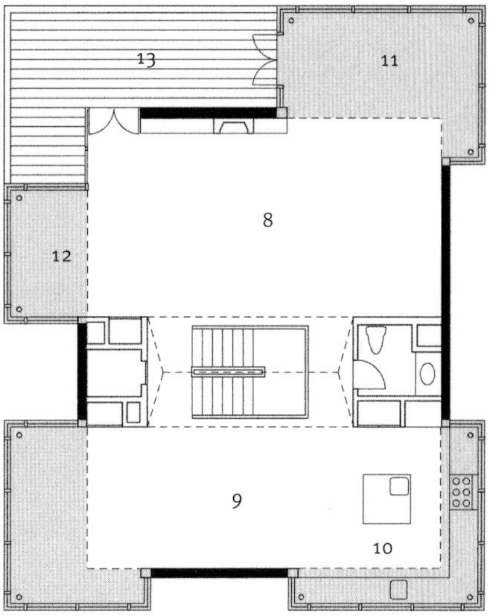

second floor plan

1 entry porch
2 entry hall
3 guest bedroom
4 master bedroom
5 dressing
6 mudroom
7 garage
8 living
9 dining
10 kitchen
11 sitting area
12 study
13 terrace

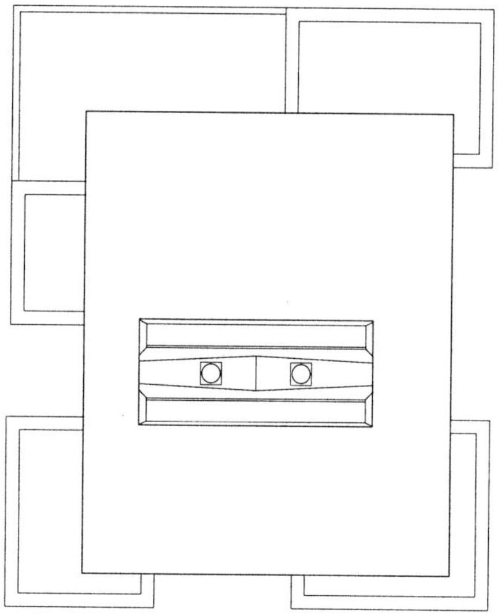

roof plan

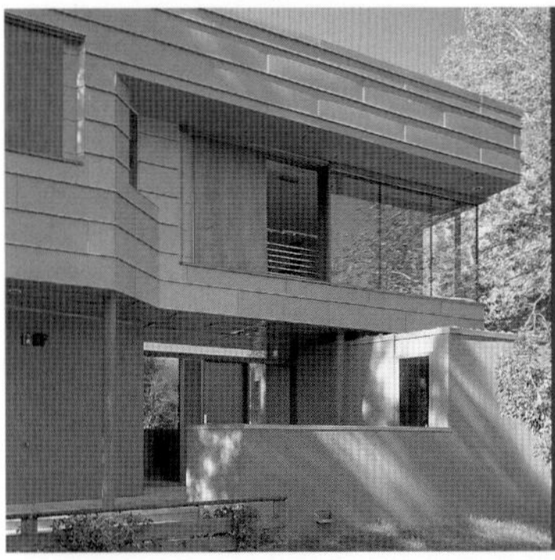

zinc house

Aspen, Colorado

Project Team: Jennifer Bloom, Marc Gee, Charlie Kaplan, Matt Maze, Katie Winter
Lot Size: 6,000 sf (557 m^2)
Building Size: 5,400 sf (502 m^2)
Date of Design: 1999
Construction Completed: 2002

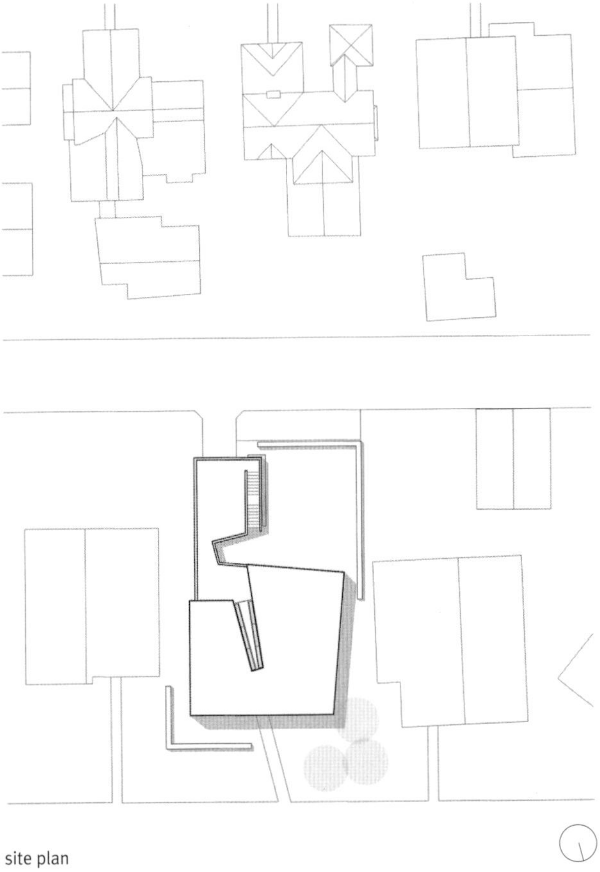

site plan

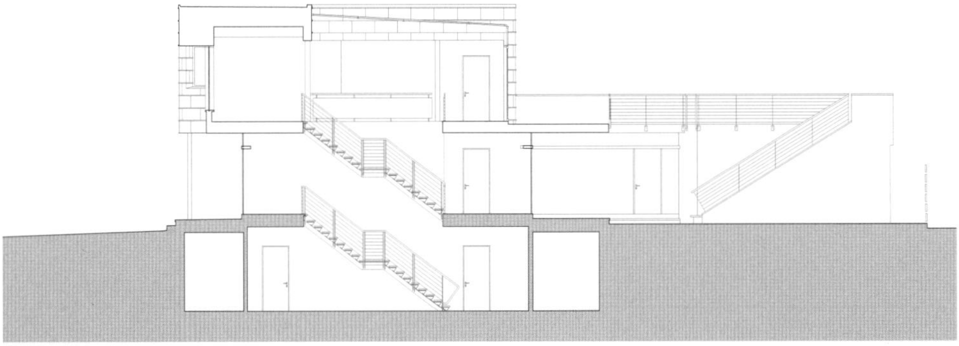

section looking east

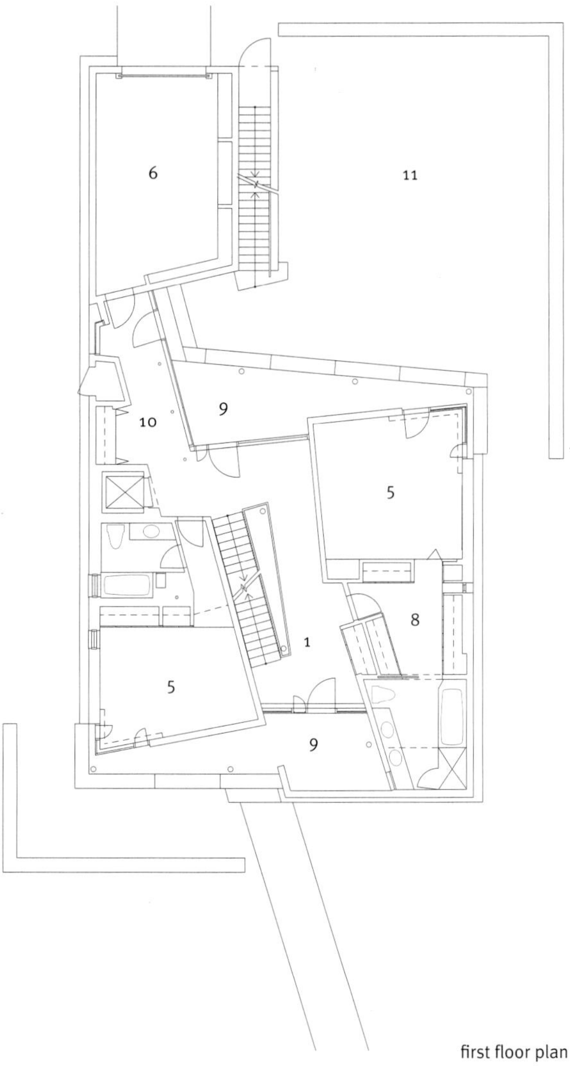

first floor plan

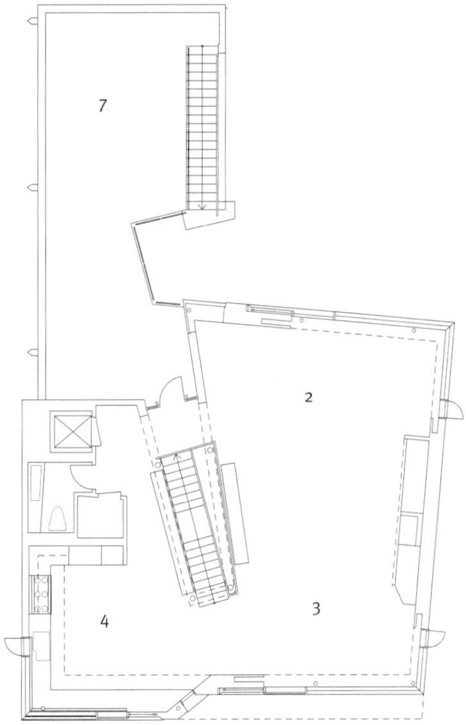

second floor plan

1 entrance
2 living
3 dining
4 kitchen
5 bedroom
6 garage
7 deck
8 dressing
9 porch
10 mudroom
11 garden

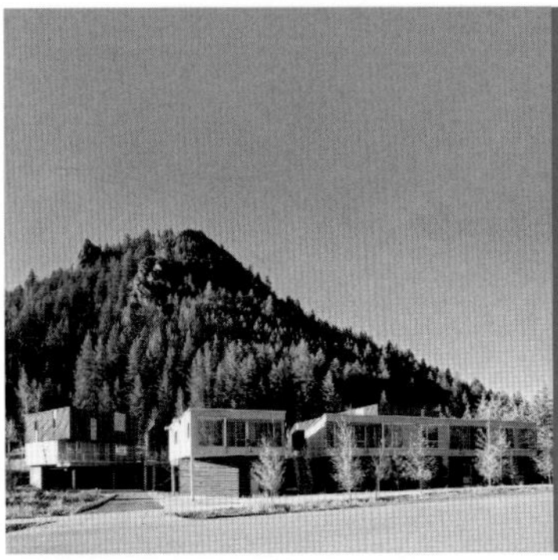

affordable housing

Aspen, Colorado

Project Team: Jennifer Bloom, Charlie Kaplan, Jason Kreuzer, Jason LaPointe, Bethia Liu, Cindy Lordan, Adam Manrique, Hiroaki Takimoto, Stephanie Werner, Katie Winter

Lot Size: 1 acre (4,047 m2)
Building Size: 25,000 sf (2,323 m2)
Date of Design: 2005
Construction Completed: 2006

site plan

12

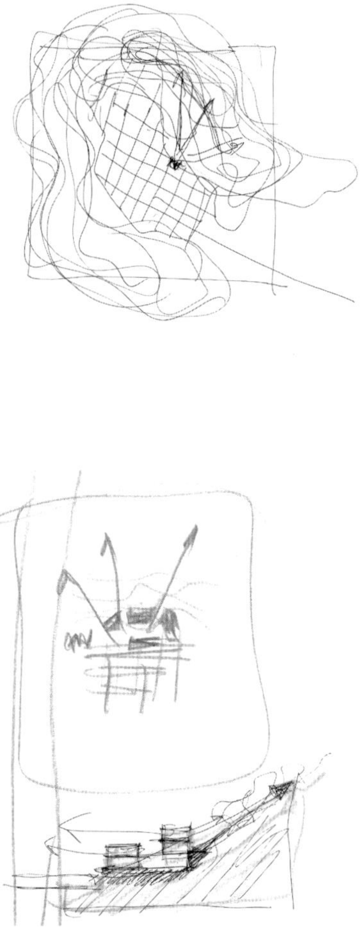

concept sketches

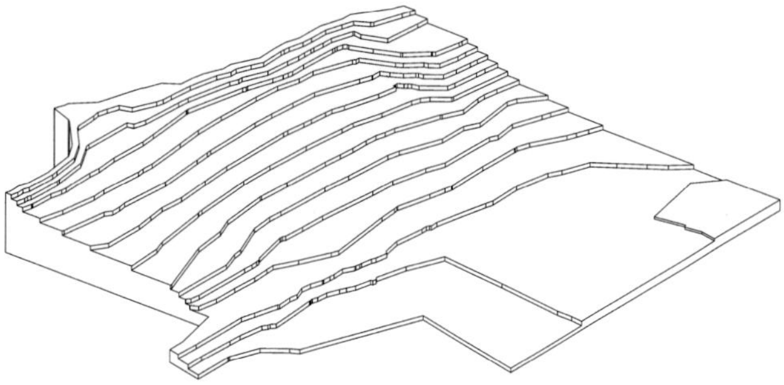

existing topography study

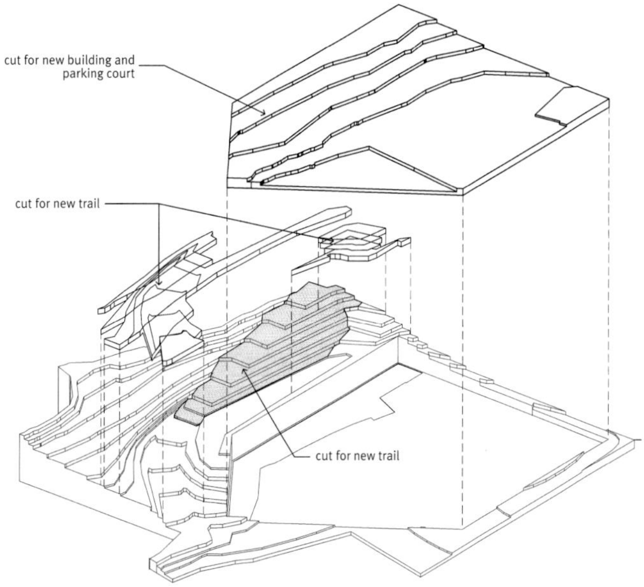

excavation study

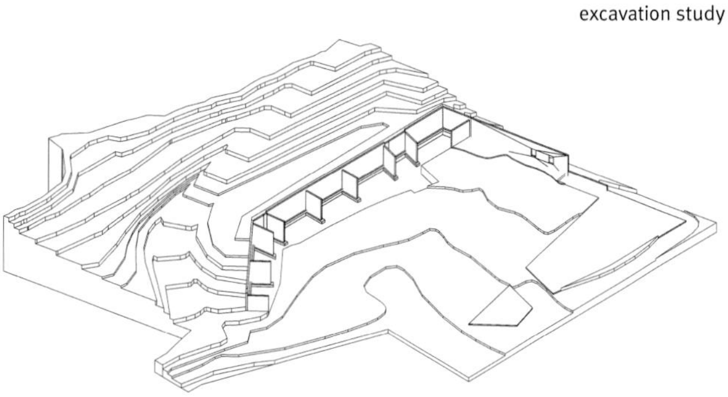

grading/concrete study

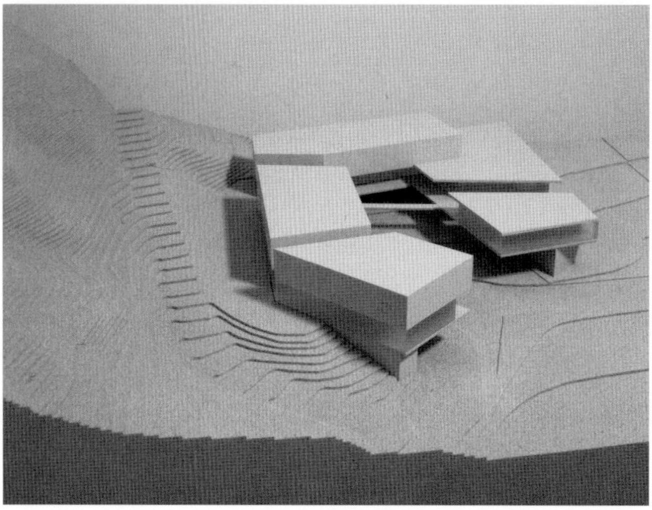

massing model study

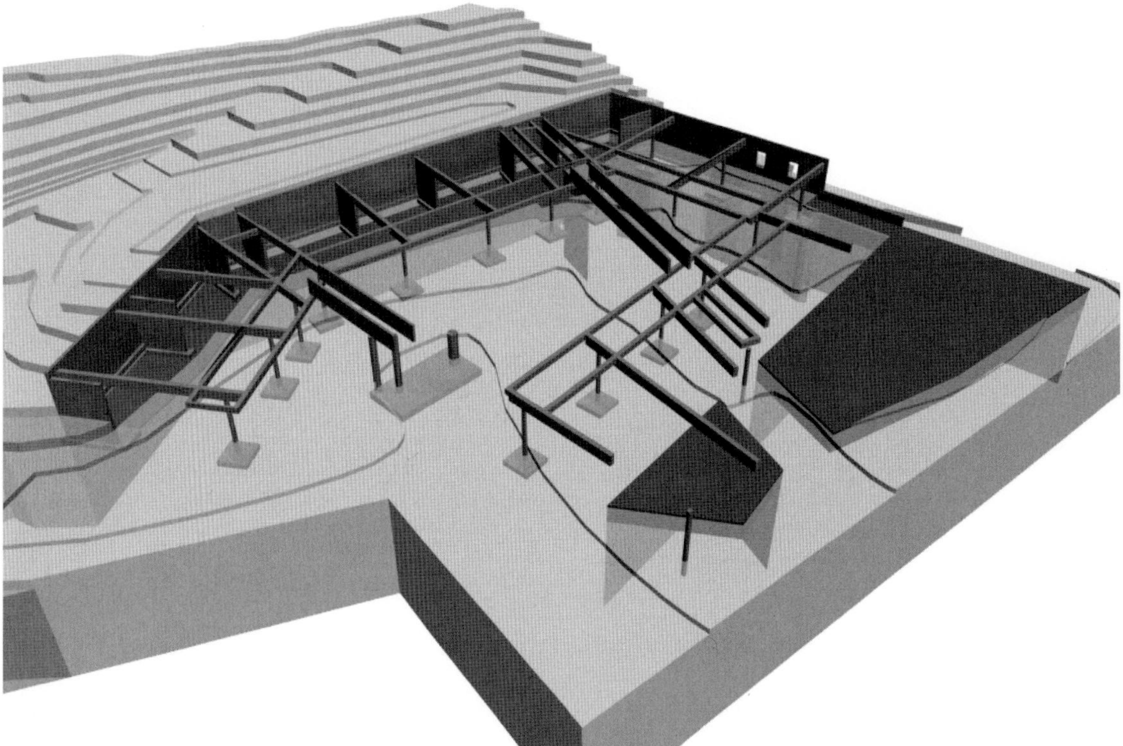

structural study rendering

massing model top view

master rendering

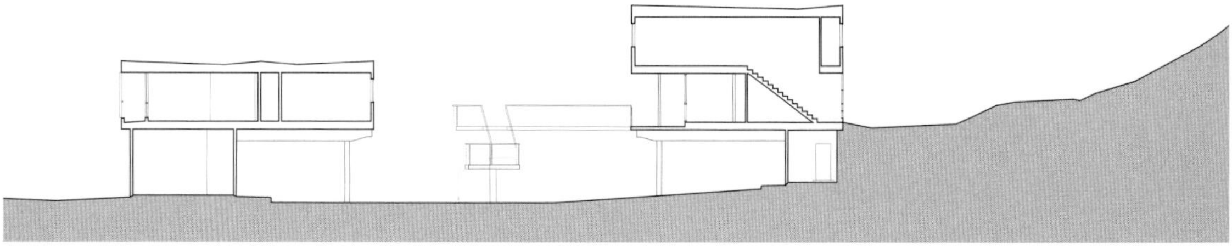

longitudinal section

cladding studies

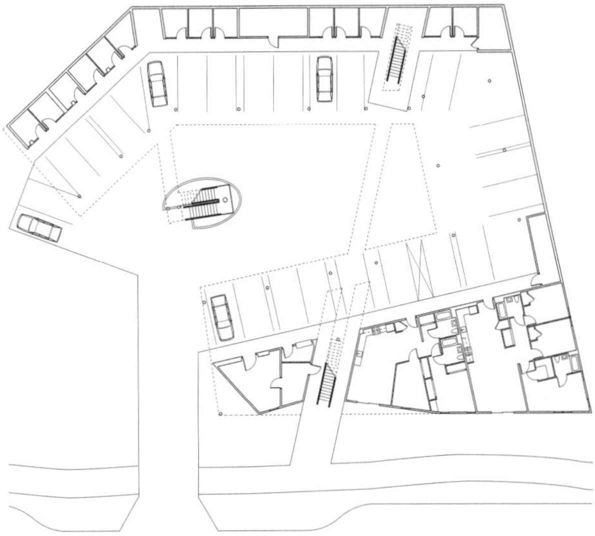

first floor plan

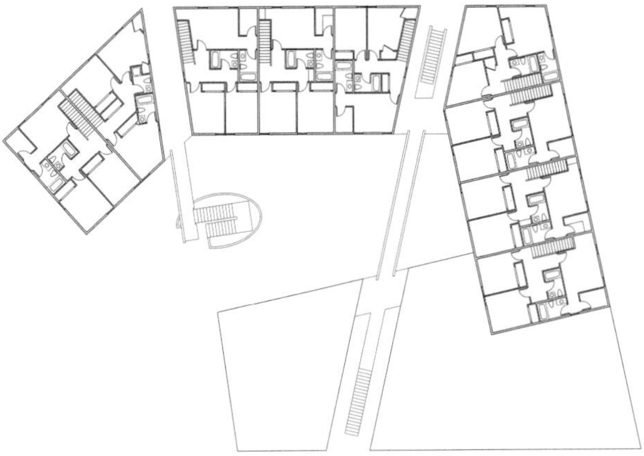

second floor plan

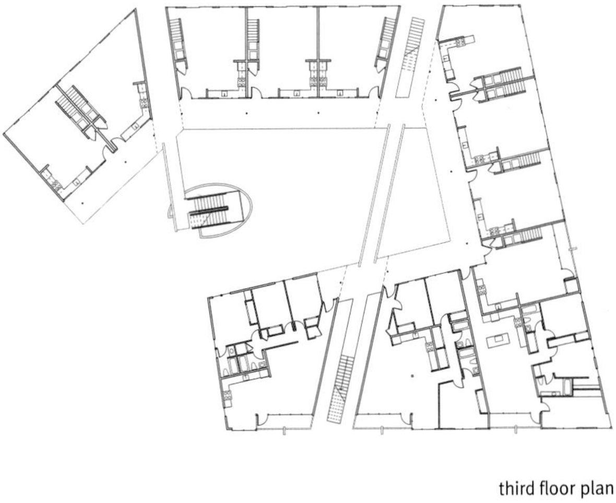

third floor plan

scholar's library

Olive Bridge, New York

Project Team: David Mabbott, Frederick Rissom
Lot Size: 18 acres (7.3 hectares)
Building Size: 800 sf (243 m²)
Date of Design: 2002
Construction Completed: 2003

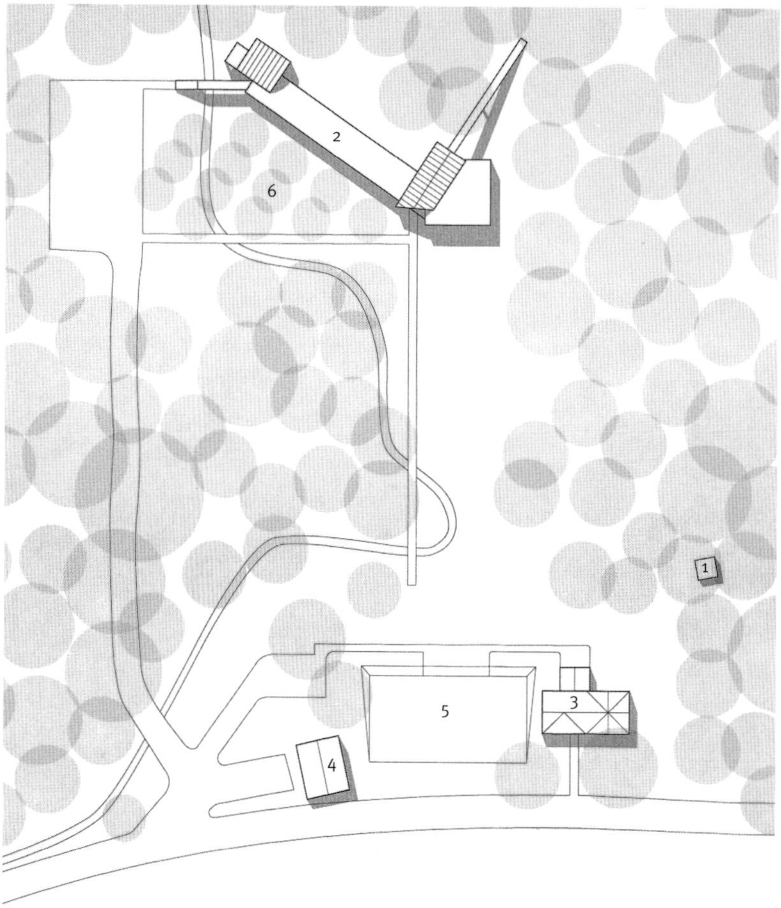

site plan

1 library
2 guest dormitory
3 farmhouse
4 barn
5 badminton court
6 orchard

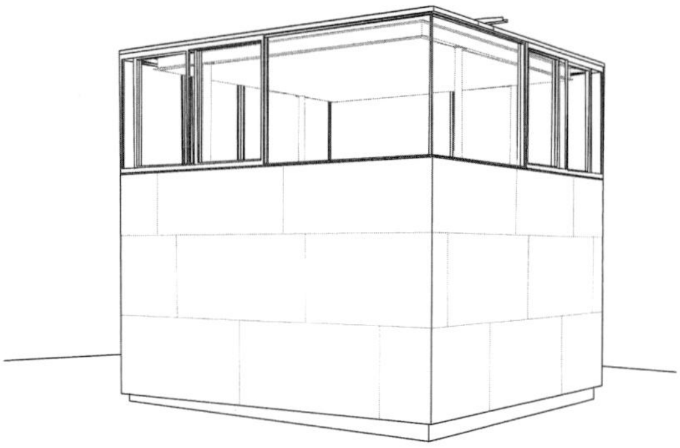

axonometric

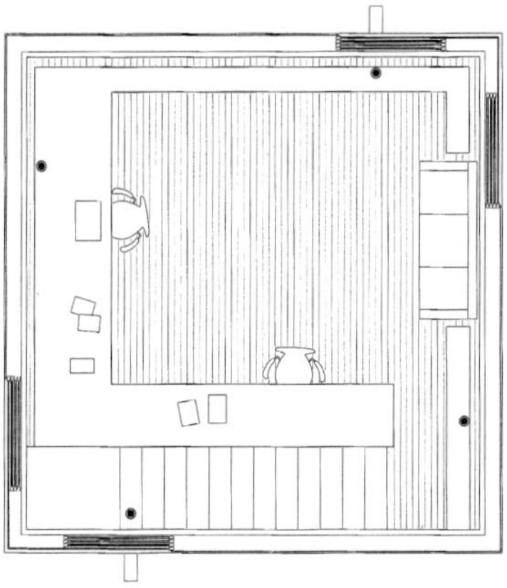

upper floor plan

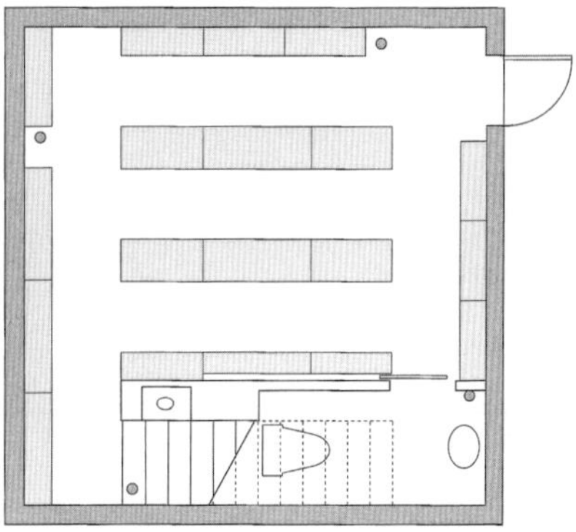

lower floor plan with stacks

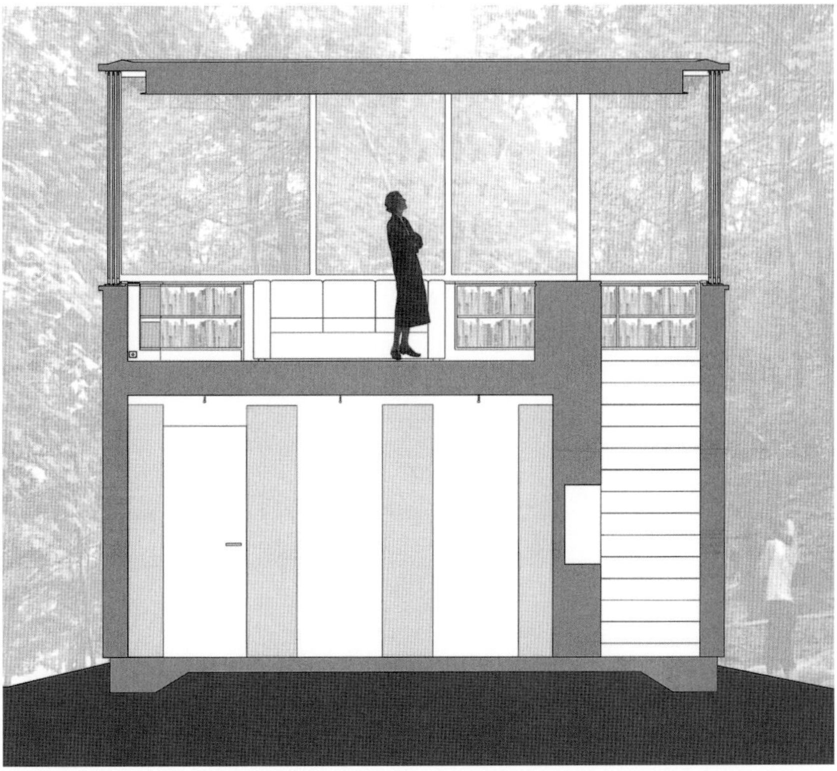

section looking east

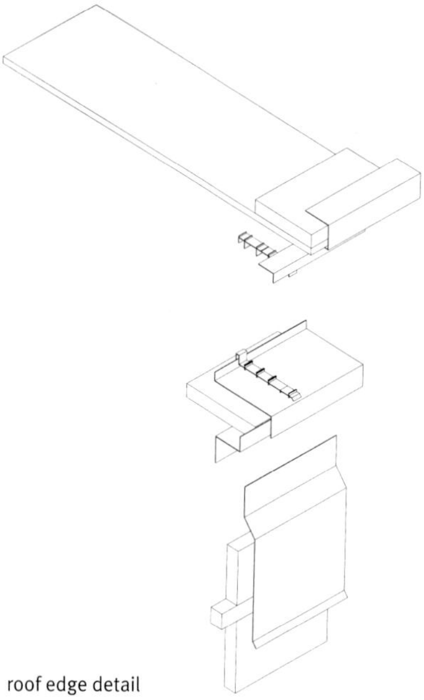
roof edge detail

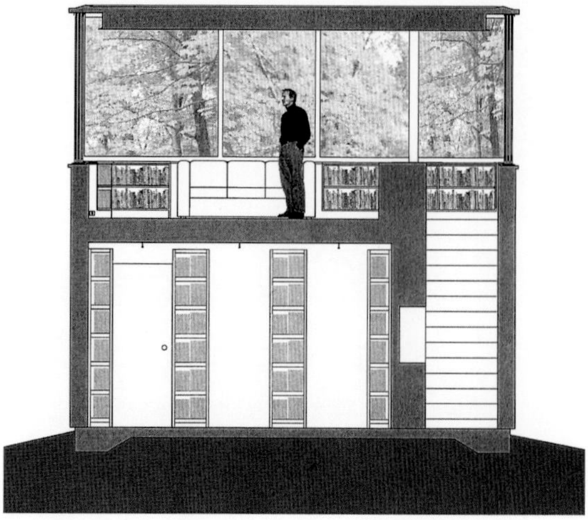
section looking east

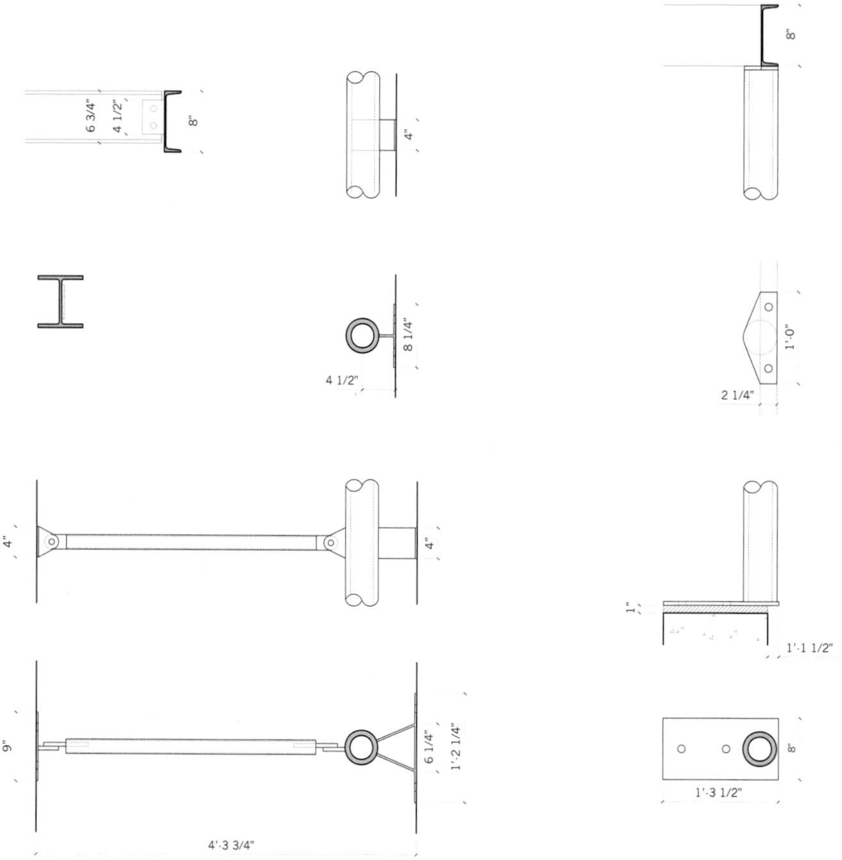

steel details

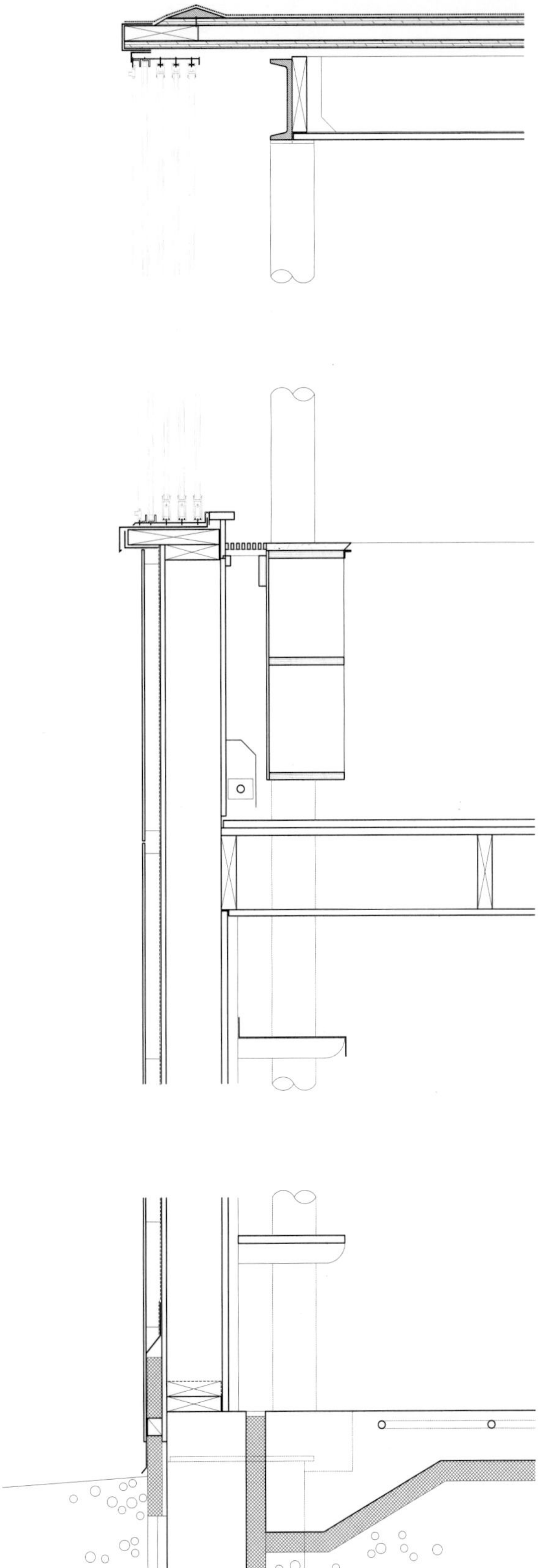

typical section

inverted outbuilding

Lake George, New York

Project Team: Jennifer Bloom, Natalie Wigginton, Thomas Zoli
Lot Size: 1.5 acres (6,070 m^2)
Building Size: 5,600 sf (520 m^2)
Date of Design: 2003
Construction Completed: 2005

site plan

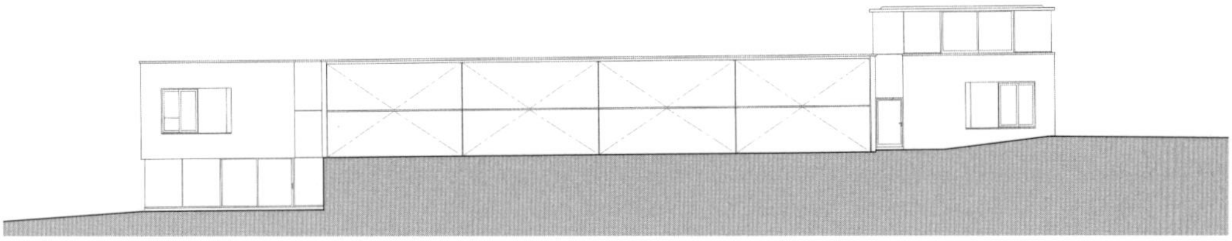

west elevation

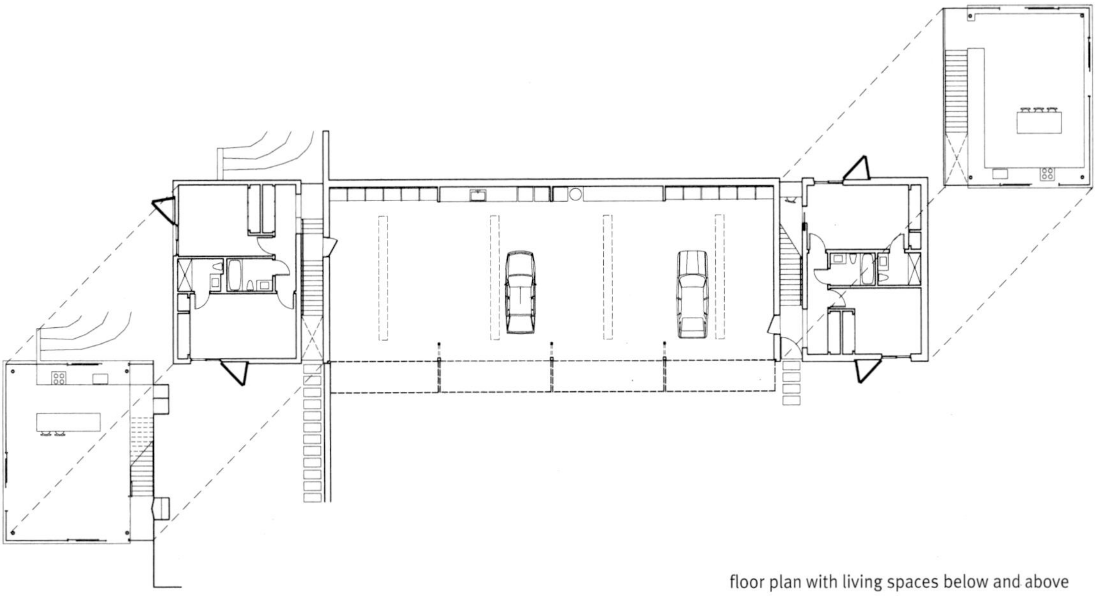

floor plan with living spaces below and above

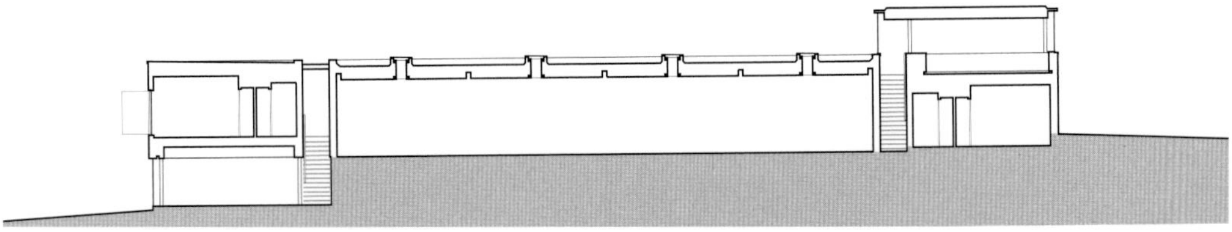

longitudinal section

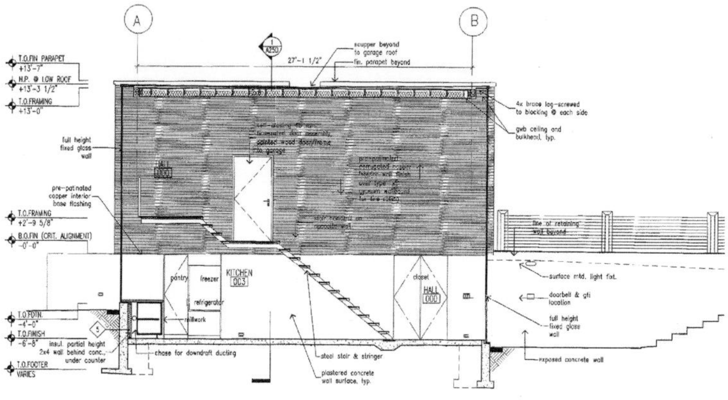

east-west building section north unit

1/4" = 1'-0"

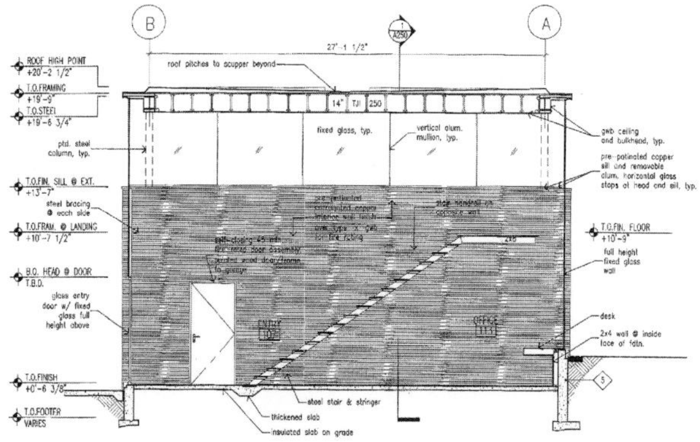

east-west building section south unit

1/4" = 1'-0"

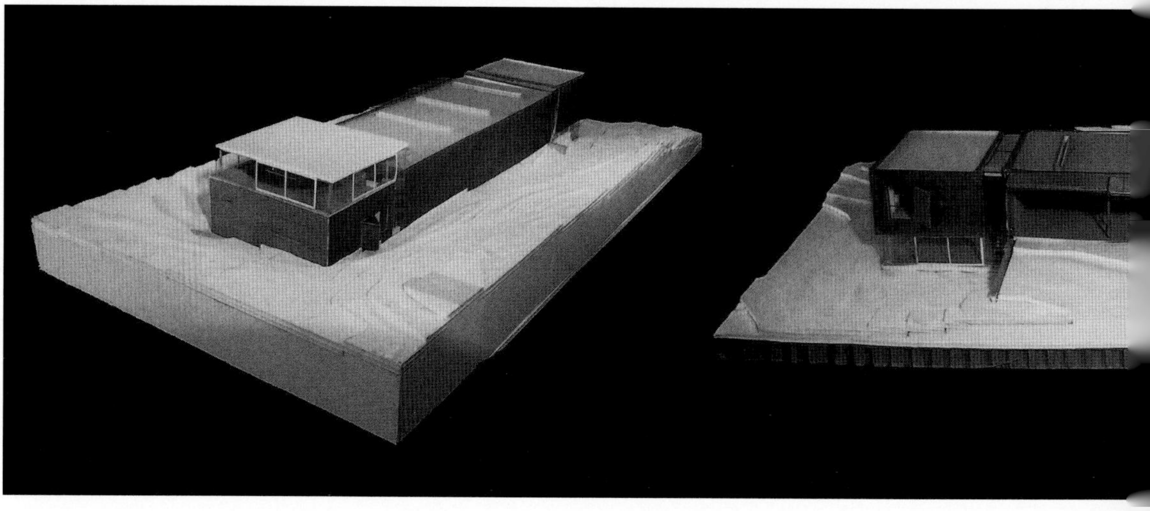

model views

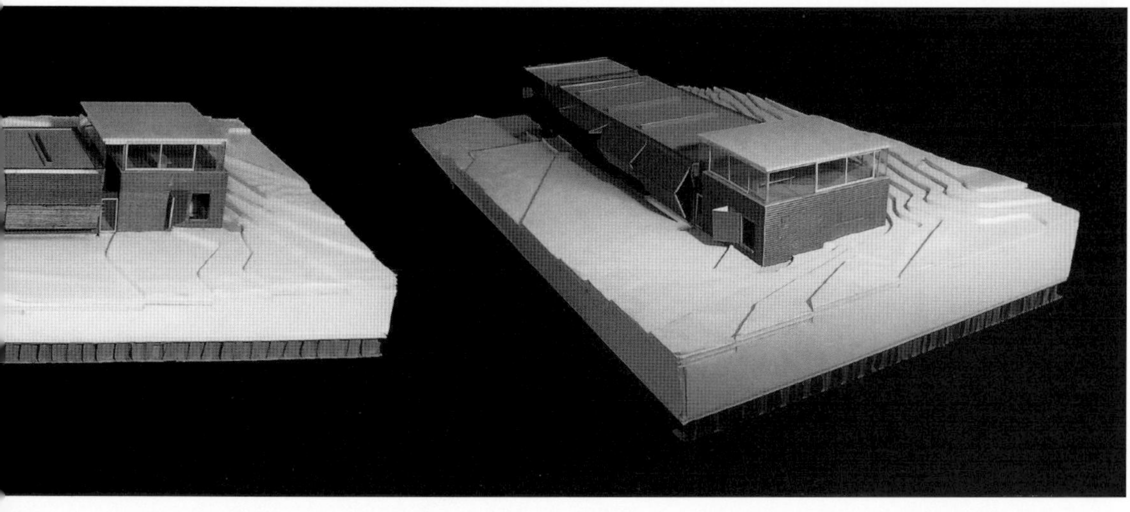

corner house

Brooklyn, New York

Project Team: Suki Dixon, Craig Graber, Katie Winter, Fred Wolf
Lot Size: 5,853 sf (544 m^2)
Building Size: 12,000 sf (1,115 m^2)
Date of Design: 1993
Construction Completed: 1998

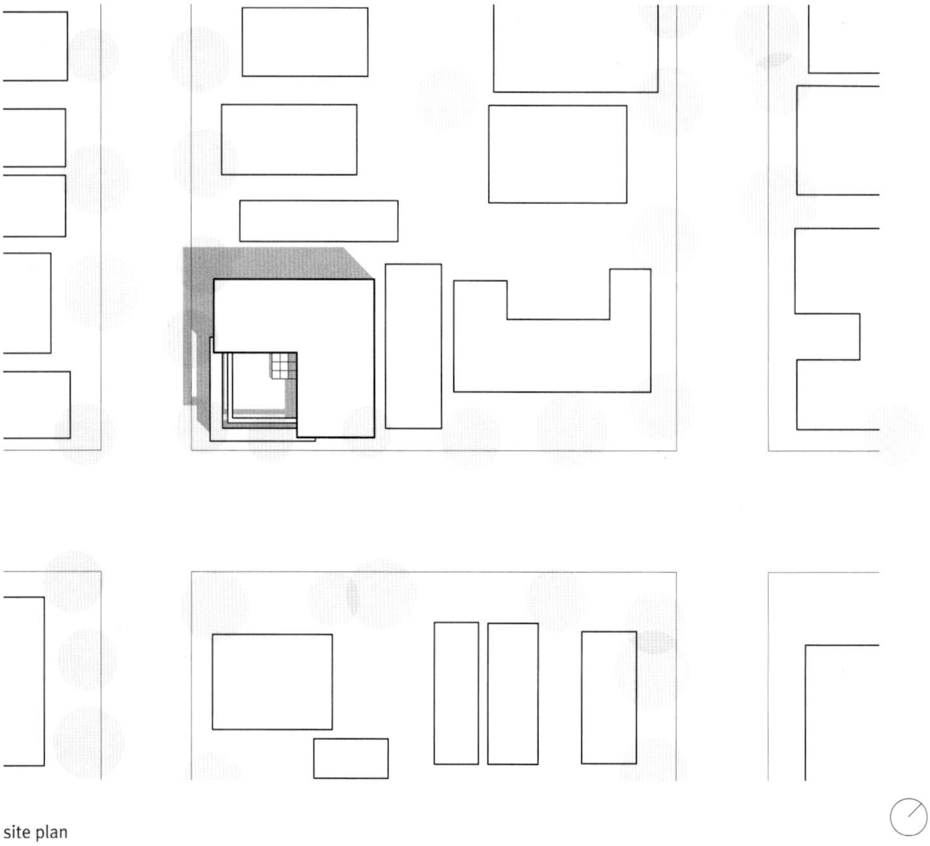

site plan

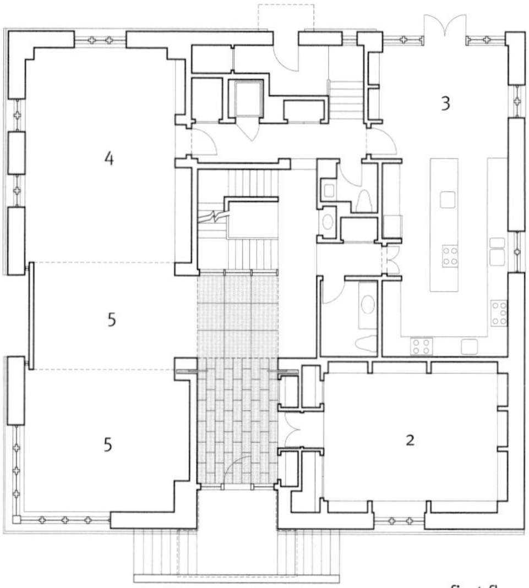

first floor

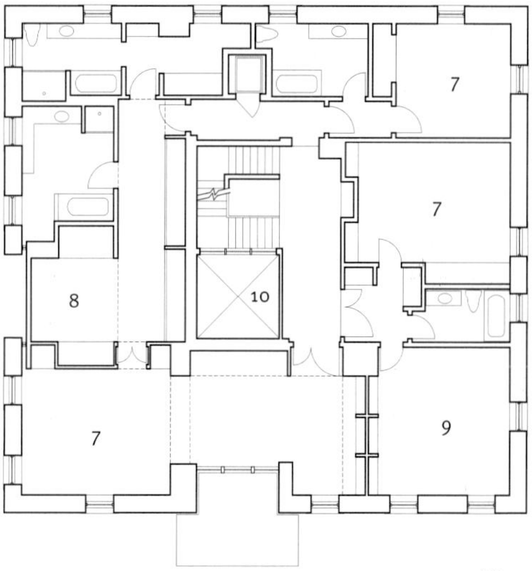

second floor

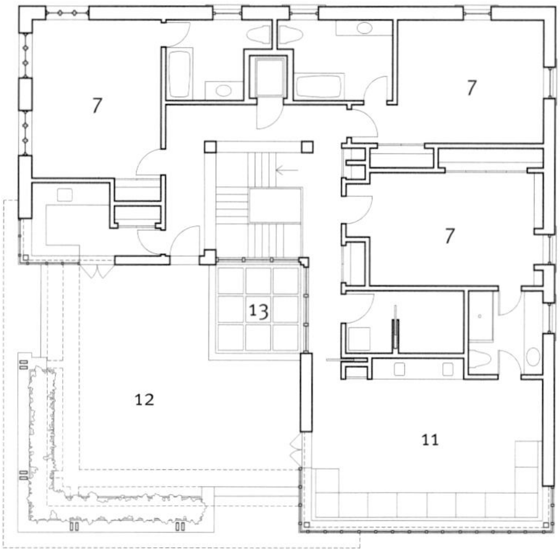

third floor

1 entry
2 library
3 kitchen
4 dining
5 sitting area / living room
6 light well
7 bedroom
8 dressing
9 sitting area
10 light well
11 sunroom
12 outdoor terrace
13 skylight

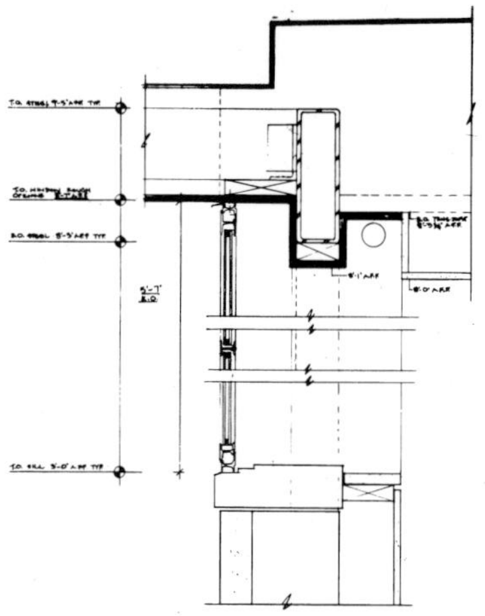

head condition 3 - medium height window

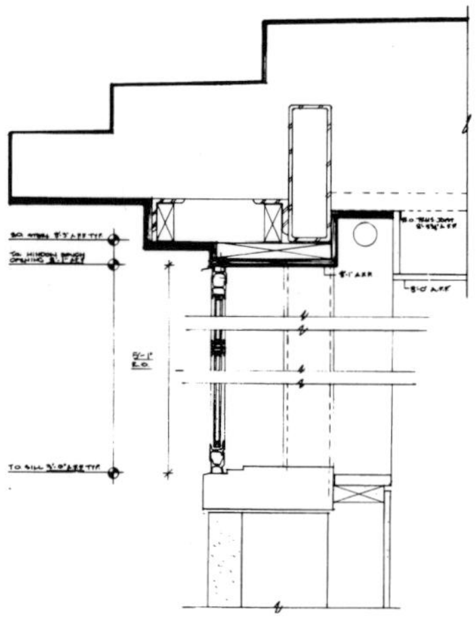

head condition 2 - low windows

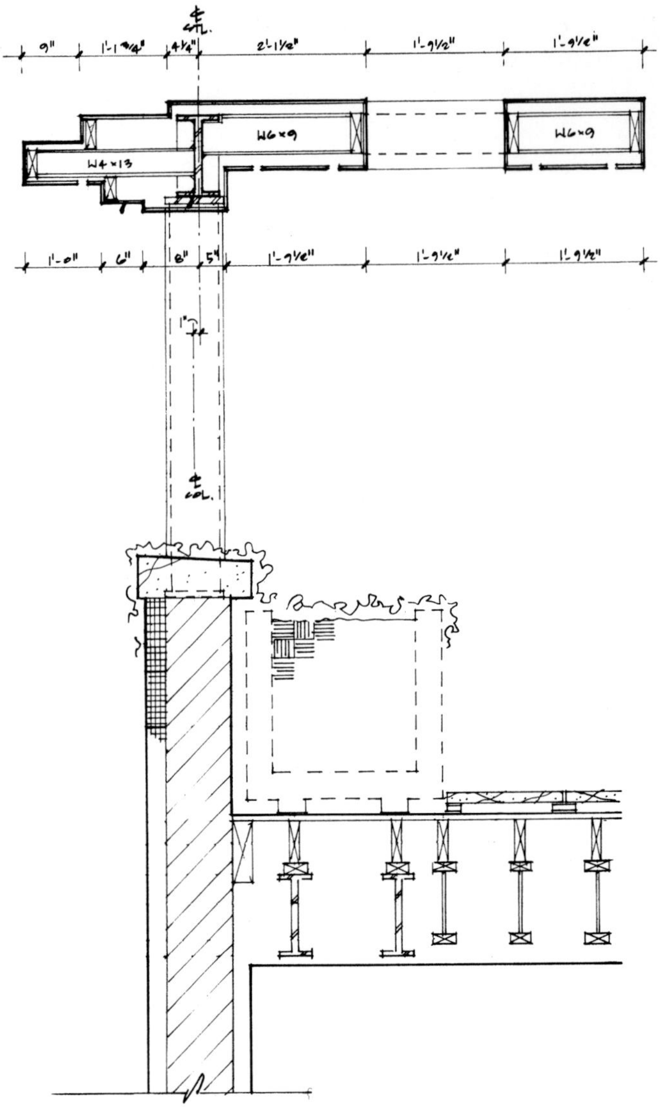

roof terrace section at parapet and trellis

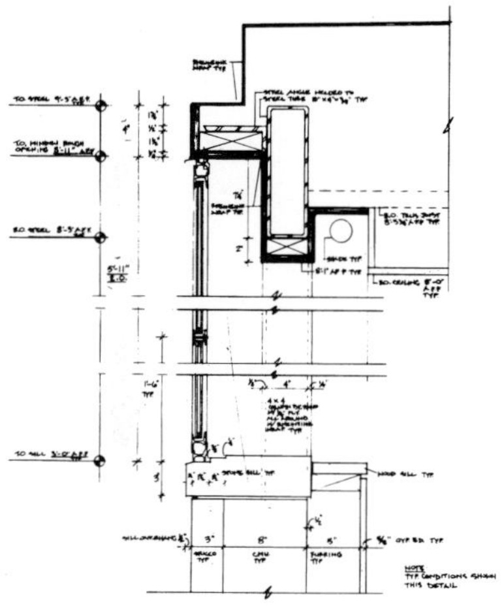

head condition 1 - tall windows

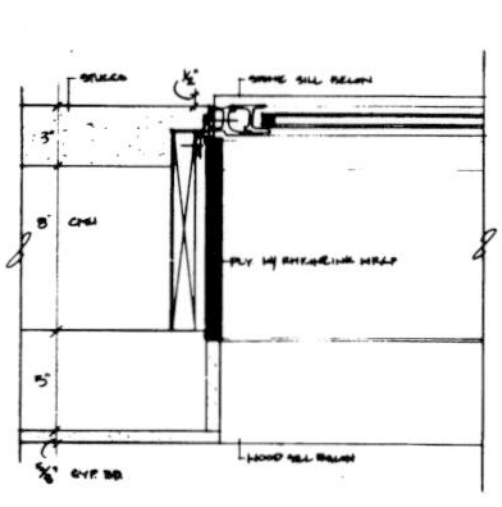

window typical jamb

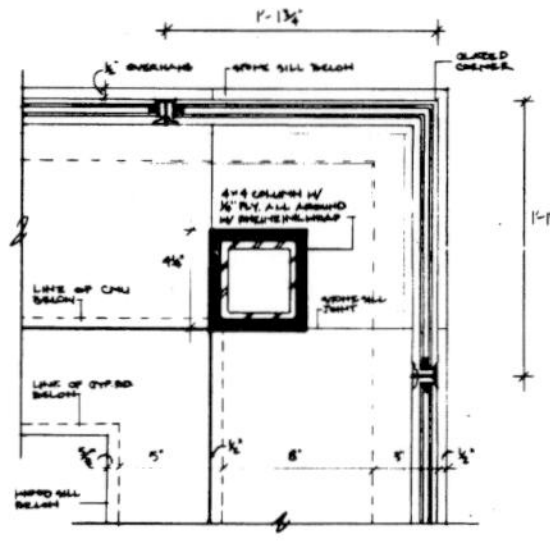

corner condition

street level perspective

model: southeast corner

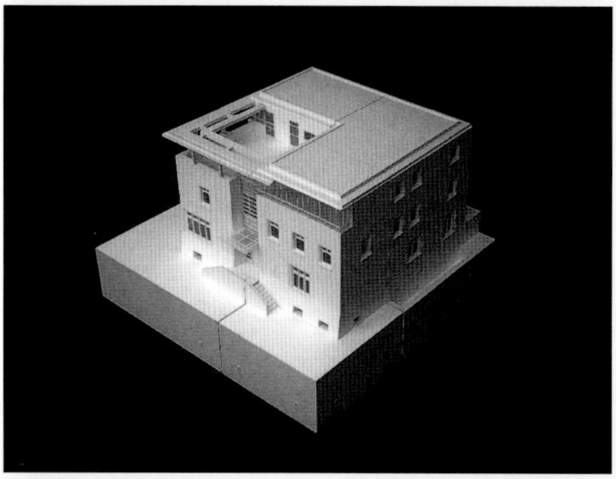

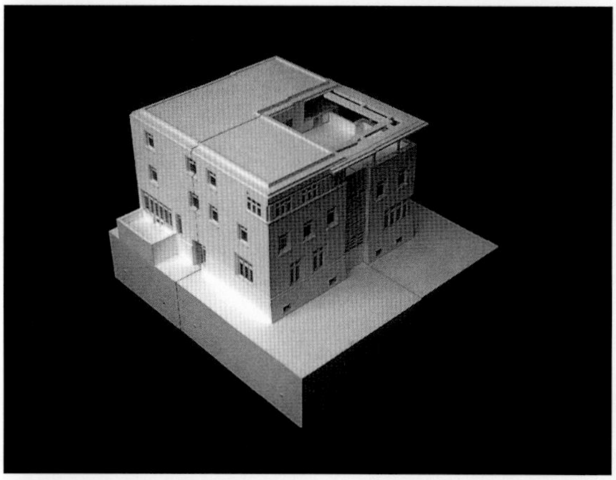

models

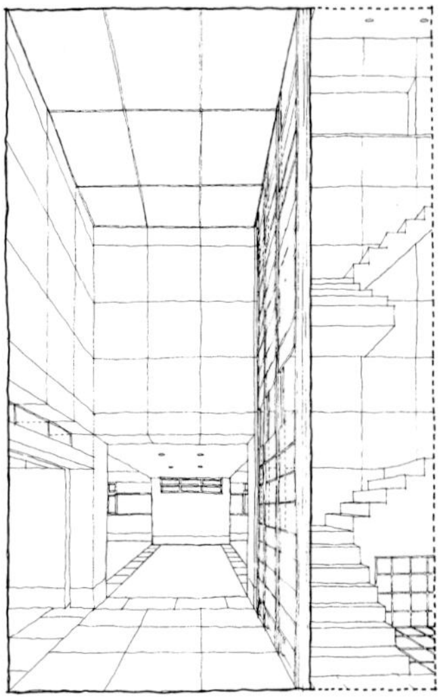

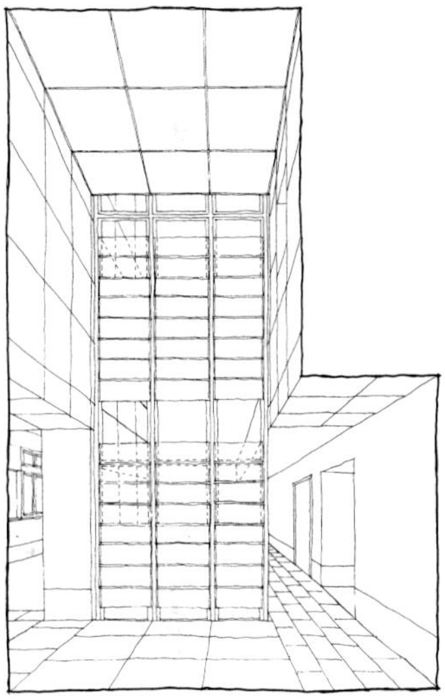

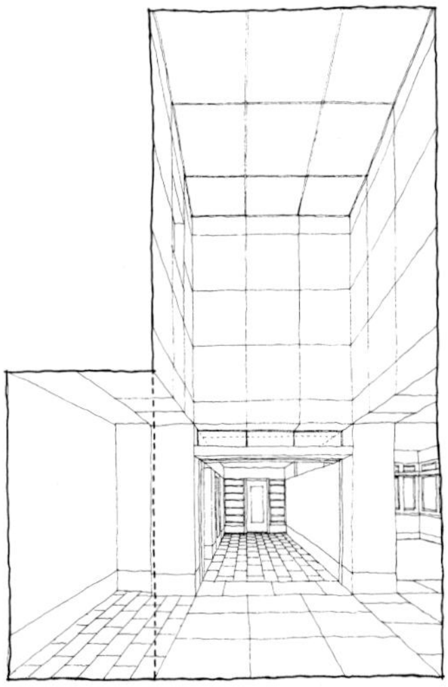

entry hall studies

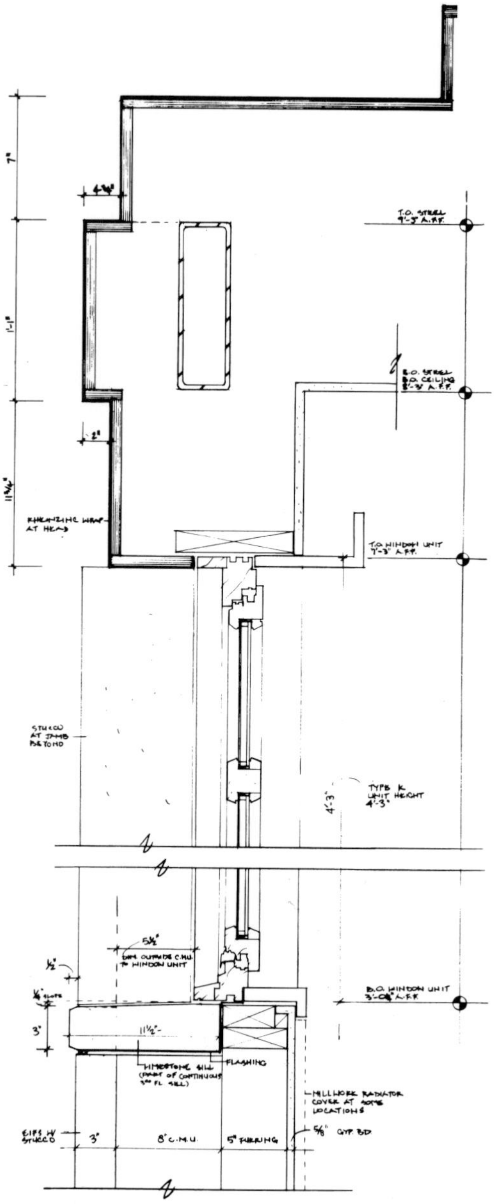

section - type k window - 3rd floor

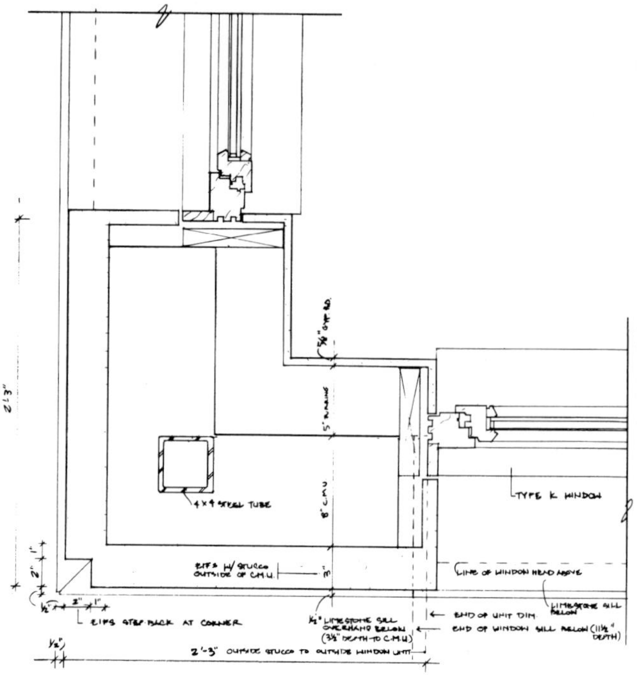

plan section at south corner

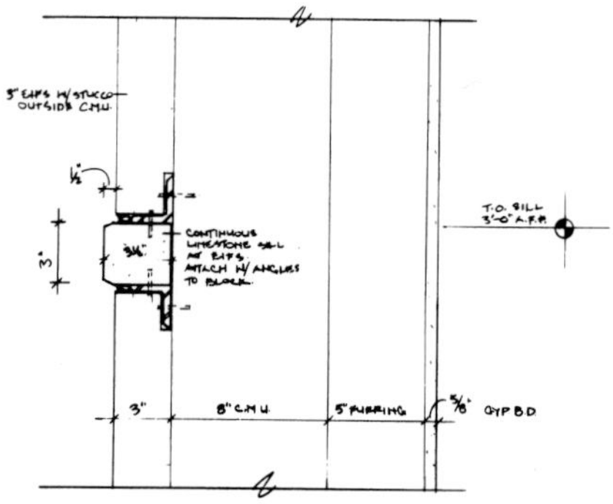

section continuous limestone sill at stucco

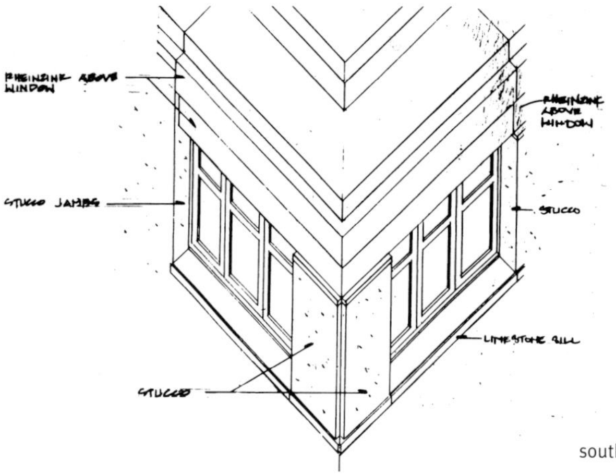

southwest corner axonometric

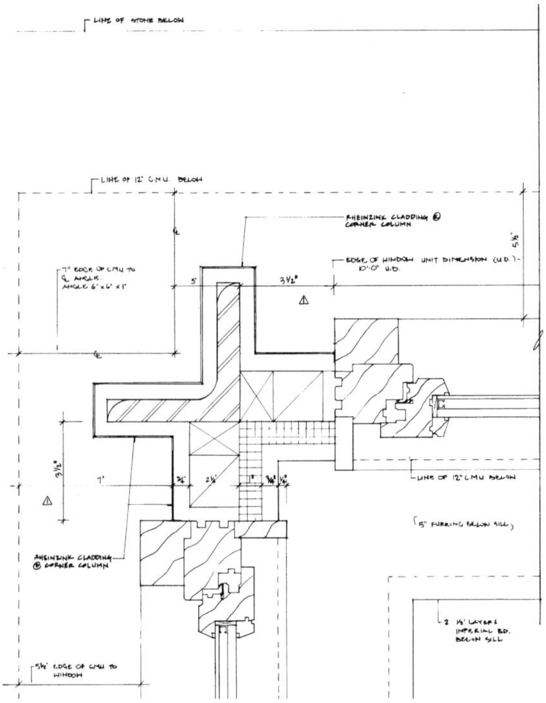

window installation detail at livingroom corner

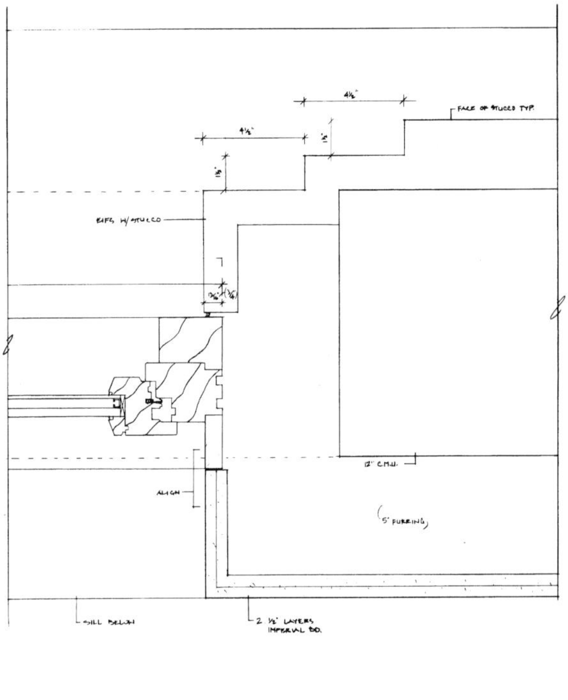

installation detail at first floor jamb

model of window

charter school

Bronx, New York

Project Team: Jennifer Bloom, Kathy Chang, Stephanie Ericson, Charlie Kaplan, Lia Mak, Christoph Plattner, Hiroaki Takimoto, Stacie Wong
Lot Size: 1 acre (4,047 m^2)

Building Size:
phase 1 – 40,000 sf (3,716 m^2)
phase 2 – 30,000 sf (2,787 m^2)
Date of Design: 2002
Construction Completed:
phase 1, 2004 – phase 2, 2006

site plan

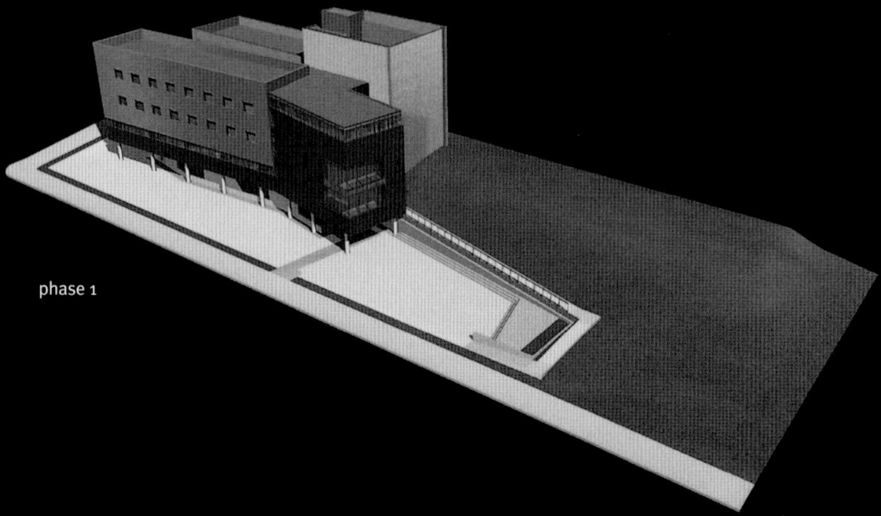

phase 1

phase 2

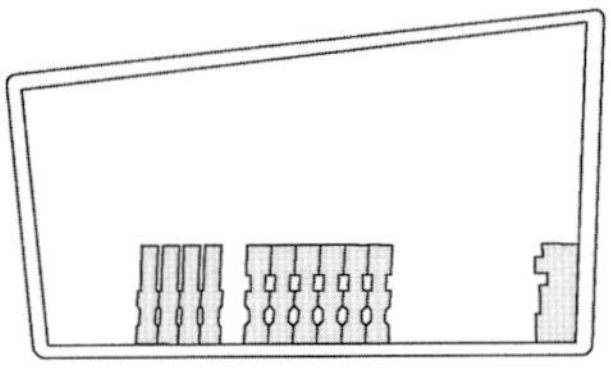

1904
the first subway connecting manhattan and the bronx opens.

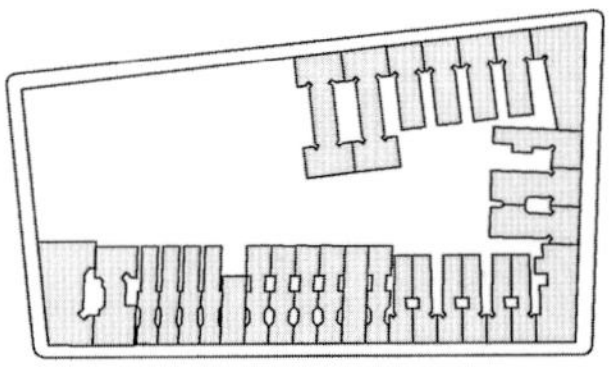

1915
the economy of the Bronx grows as hundreds of thousands of immigrant workers move to the area.

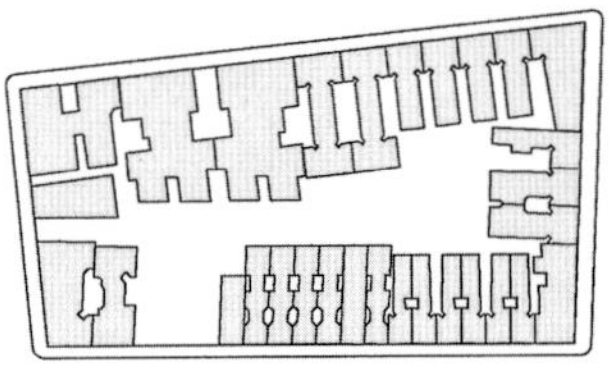

1950
the south bronx population increases as displaced people from manhattan relocate due to slum clearing.

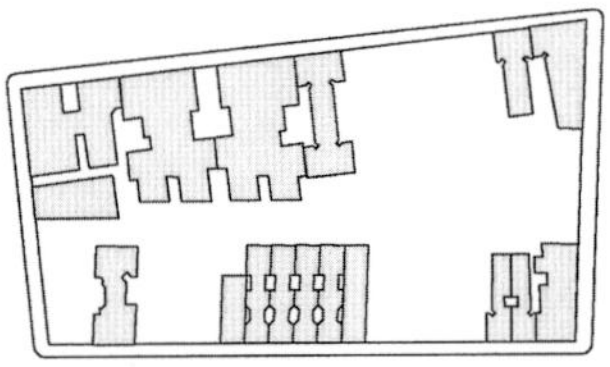

1977
half of all south bronx buildings are abandoned due to withdrawal of city services. the elevated train bypasses stations on route to the north bronx. firehouses and schools are closed. area is plagued by rampant arson and called the worst slum in america by president jimmy carter.

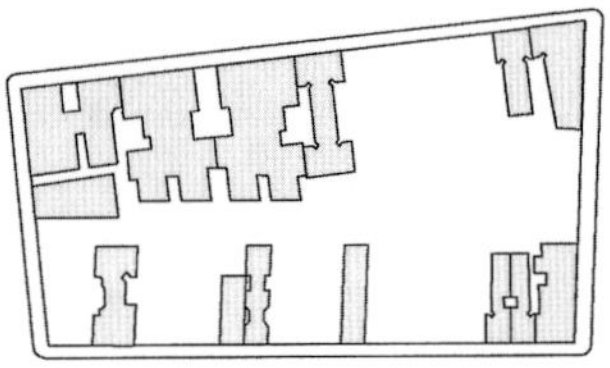

1980
area is designated as an urban renewal zone. substandard structures are removed.

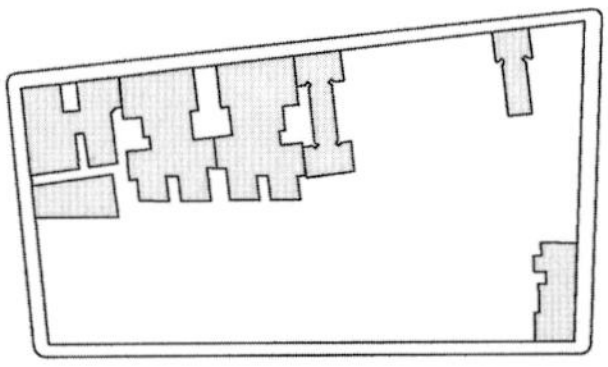

1986
neighborhoods are vacated and bulldozed. industrial warehouses replace housing.

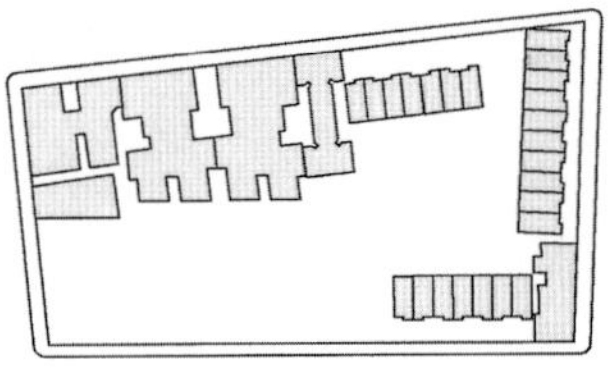

1996
apartment stock begins to be restored. public schools become overcrowded.

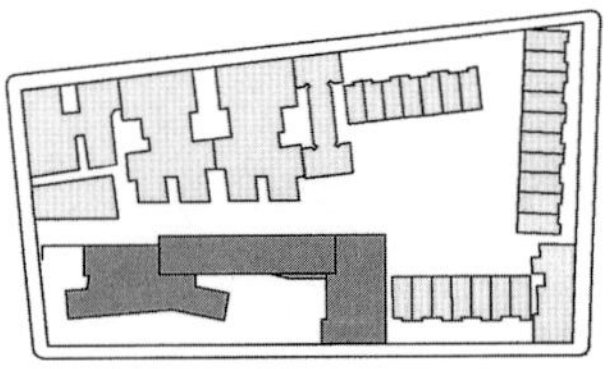

2004
bronx preparatory charter school is built on an urban renewal site, providing an educational alternative for students in the neighborhood.

existing
programmatic needs
baseline red herring
individual identity
maximum outdoor play
community oriented
legibility
campus
pilotis for varied outdoor space
accessibility
centralized common space
integrated solution
sculpted for space and light

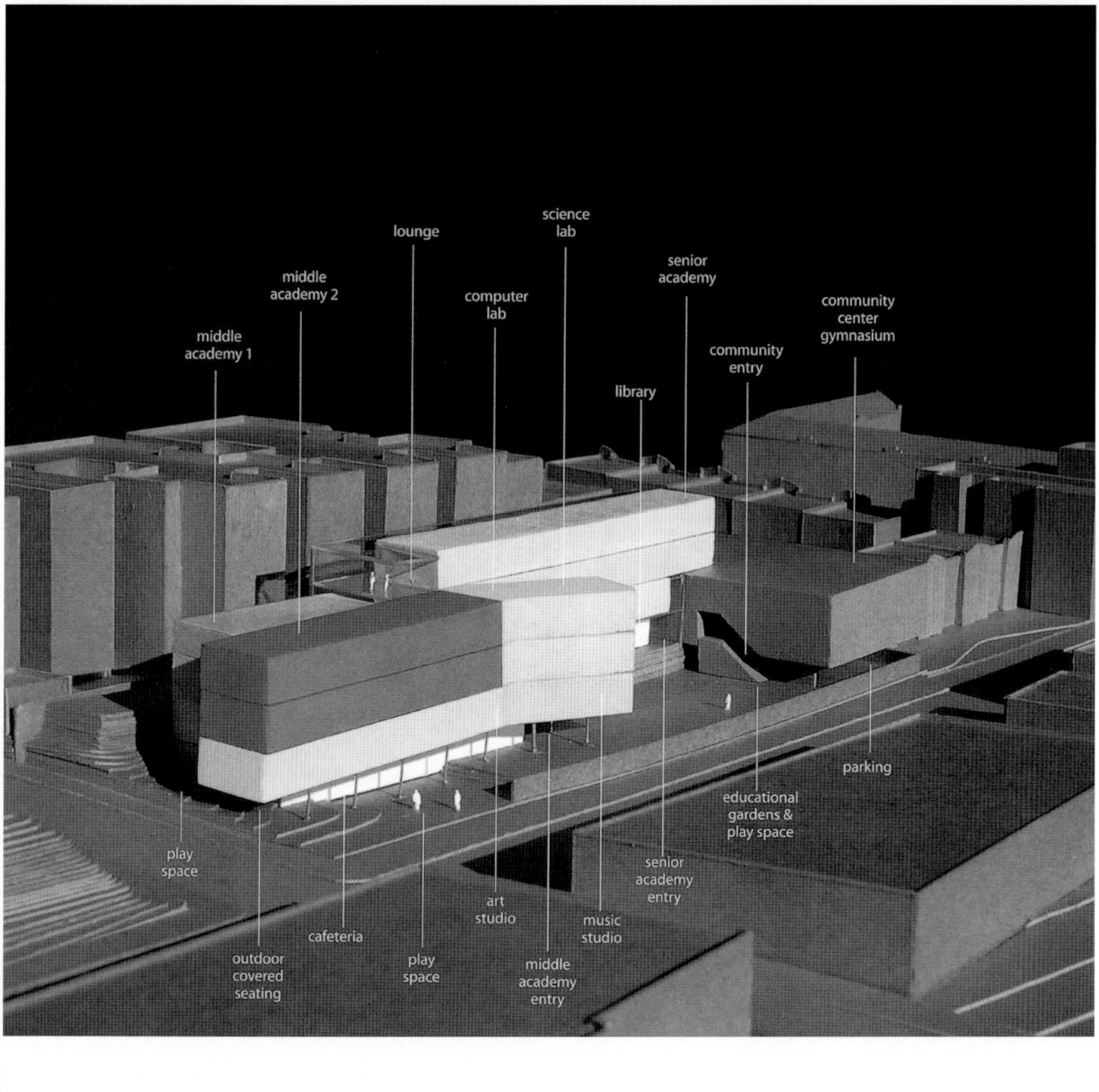
science lab
lounge
senior academy
middle academy 2
computer lab
community center gymnasium
middle academy 1
community entry
library
parking
educational gardens & play space
play space
senior academy entry
art studio
music studio
cafeteria
outdoor covered seating
play space
middle academy entry

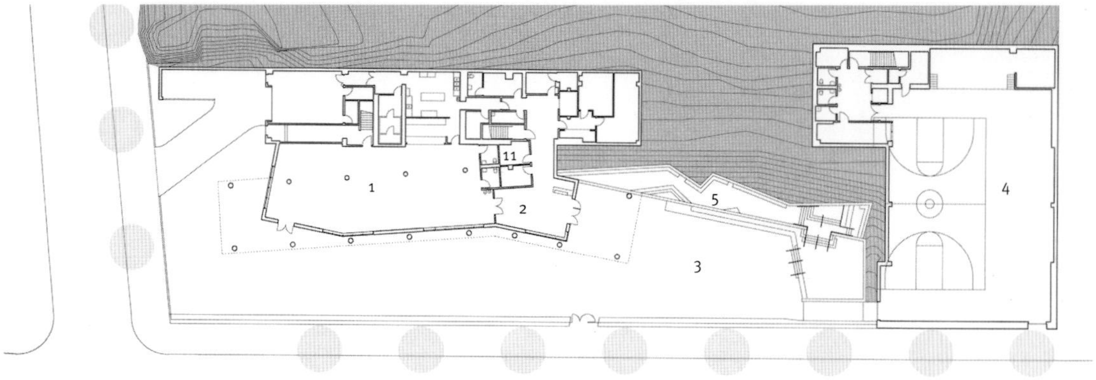

ground floor plan

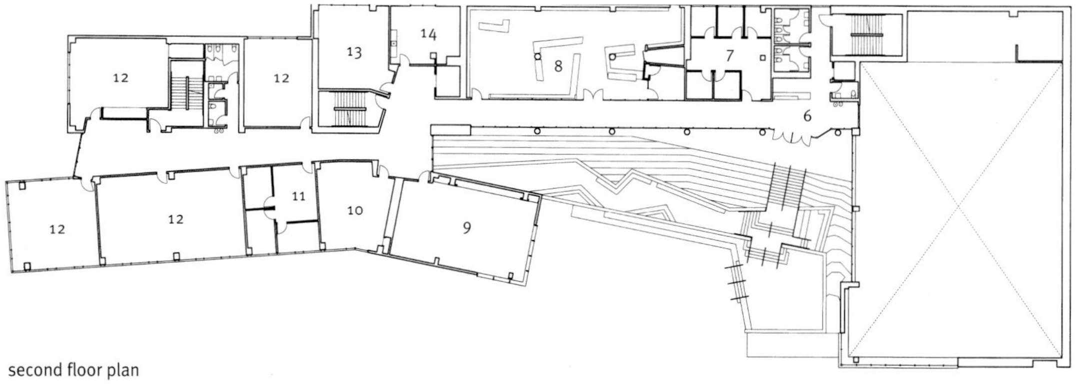

second floor plan

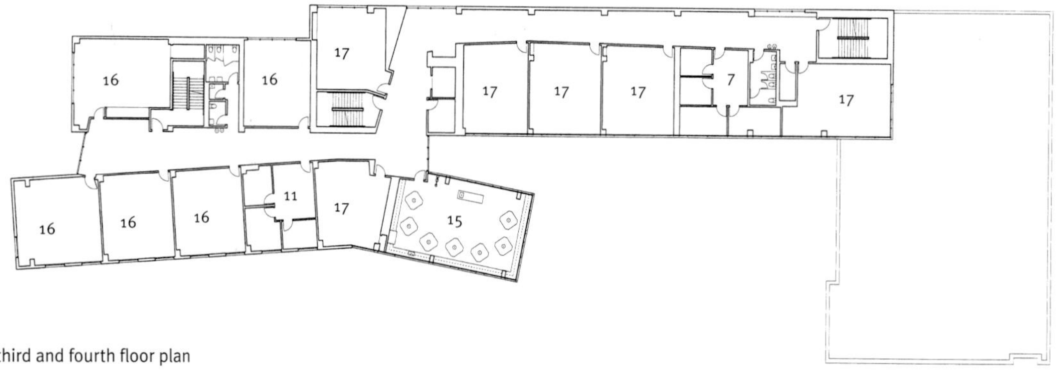

third and fourth floor plan

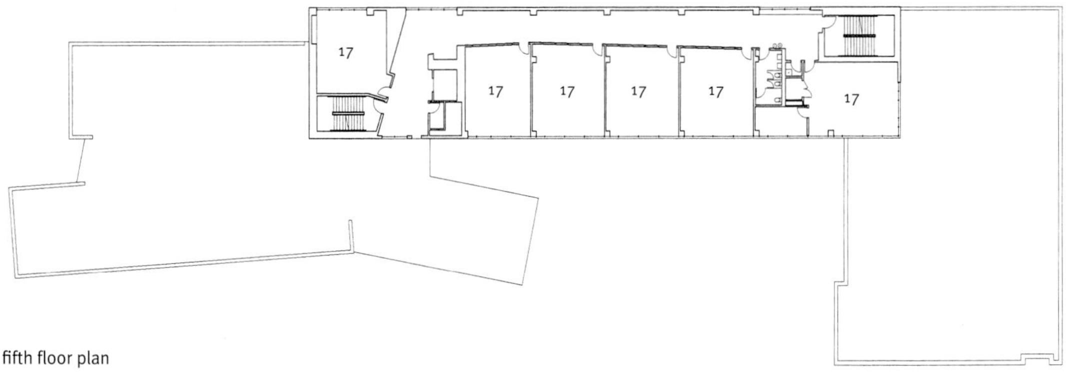

fifth floor plan

street view digital rendering

1 cafeteria
2 entrance to middle school
3 play space
4 gymnasium
5 ramped garden
6 entrance to high school
7 hs offices
8 library
9 music studio
10 art studio
11 middle school office
12 middle school classroom
13 computer lab
14 staff room
15 science lab
16 middle school classroom
17 high school classroom

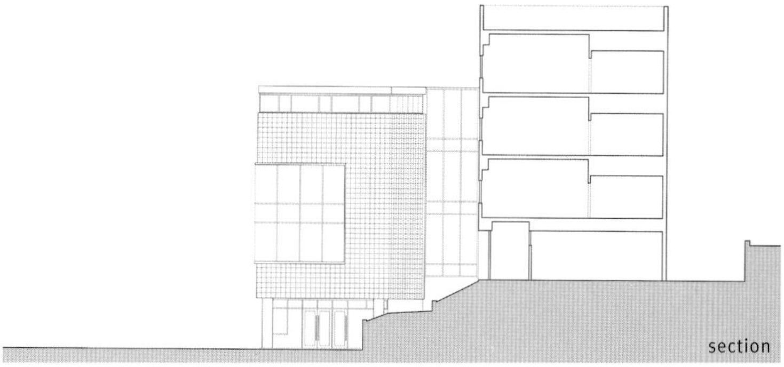

section

street view digital rendering at night

street view digital rendering

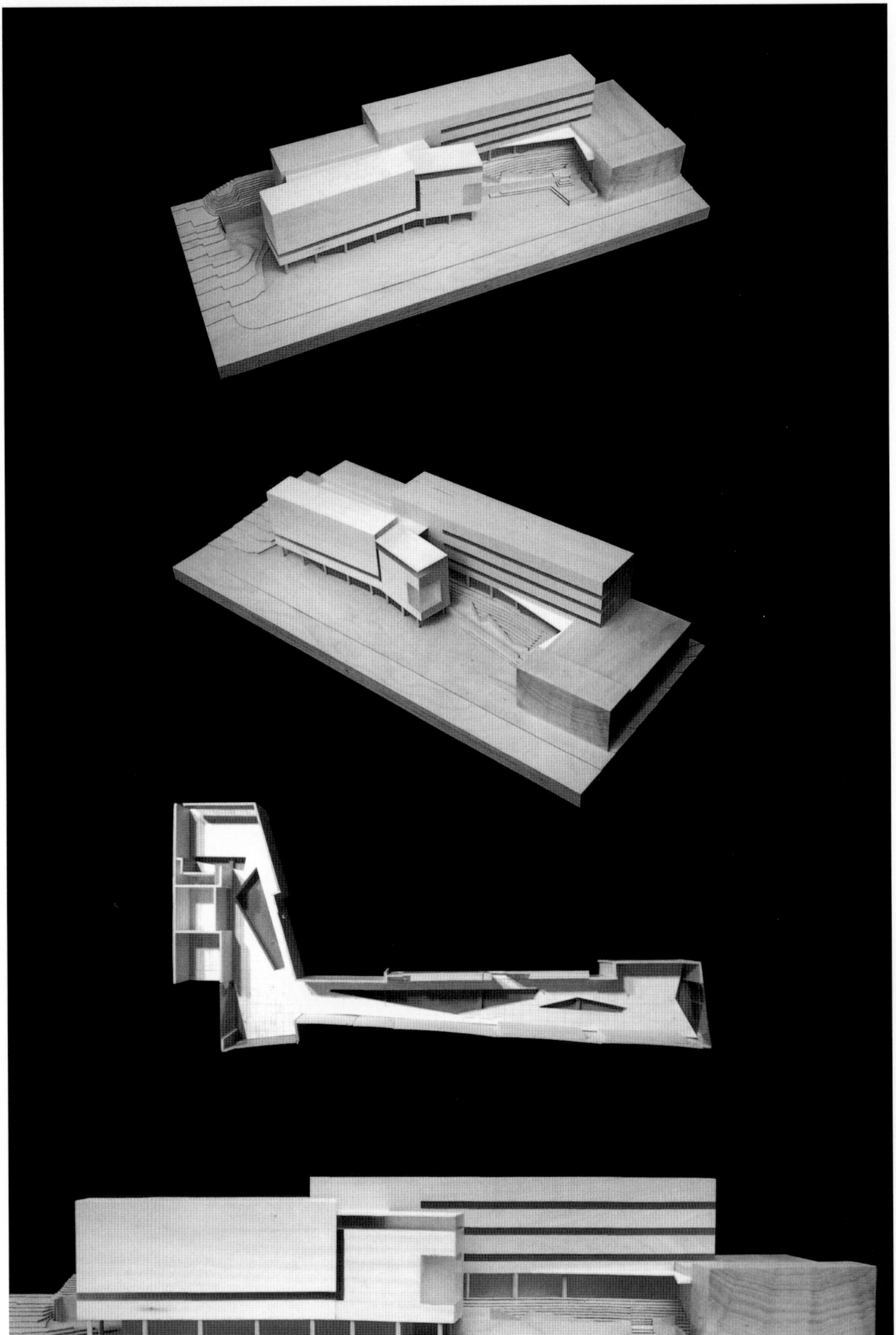

1

2

3

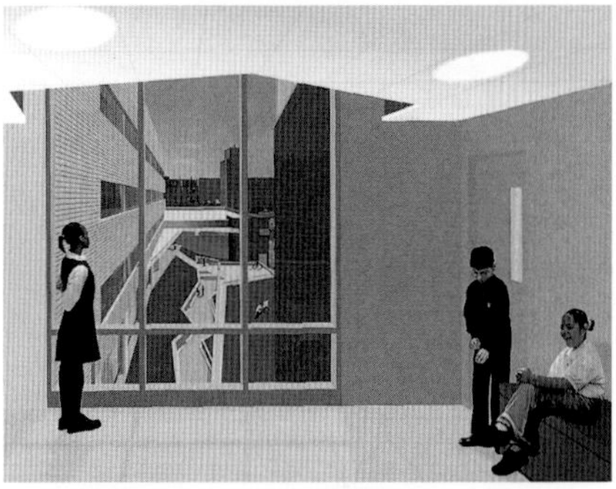
4

5

6

digital renderings

1 cafeteria
2 corridor
3 library
4 third floor lobby
5 typical classroom
6 music room

model views

social services center

New York, New York

Client: Little Sisters of the Assumption Family Health Services
Project Team: Marc Gee, David Mabbott, Christoph Plattner, Frederik Rissom, Elaine Sun

Lot Size: 5,500 sf (511 m²)
Building Size: 21,500 sf (1,997 m²)
Date of Design: 2001
Construction Completed: 2003

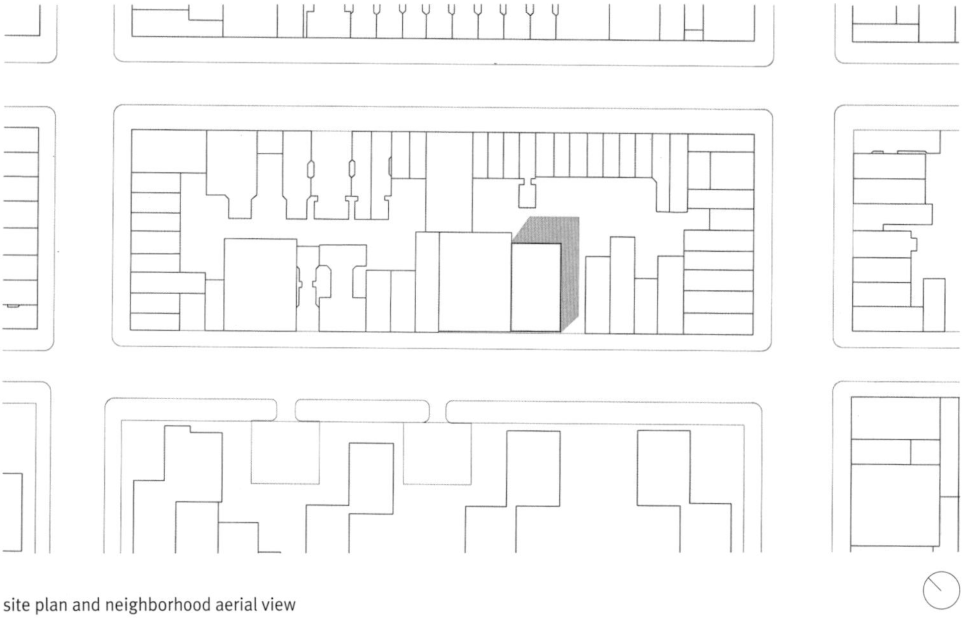

site plan and neighborhood aerial view

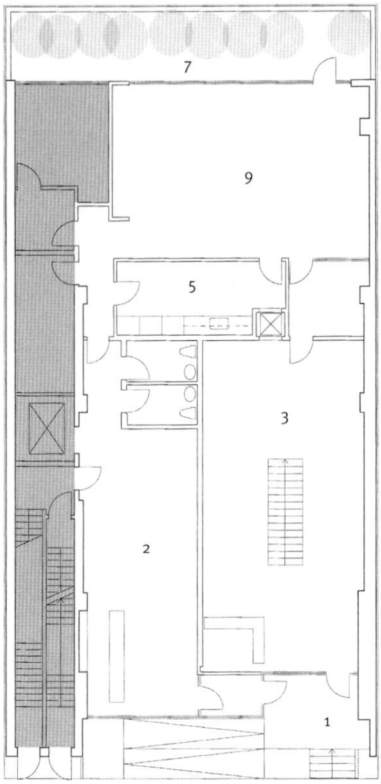

ground floor with partitions

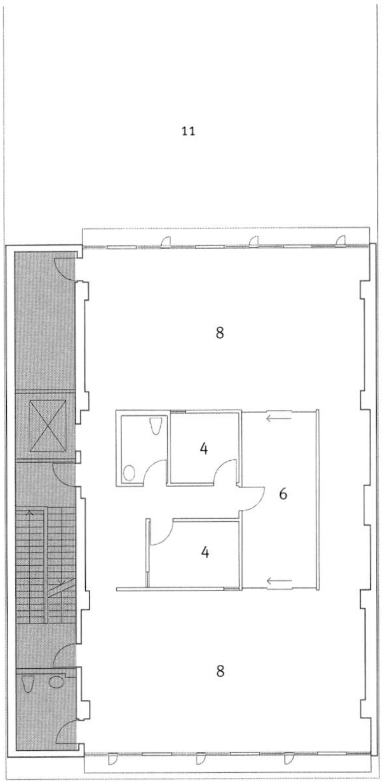

typical floor with partitions

1 entrance
2 lobby
3 thrift store
4 meeting room
5 pantry
6 office space
7 garden
8 office space
9 meeting room
10 storage
11 outdoor space on second floor

façade study

Photomontage of location on street

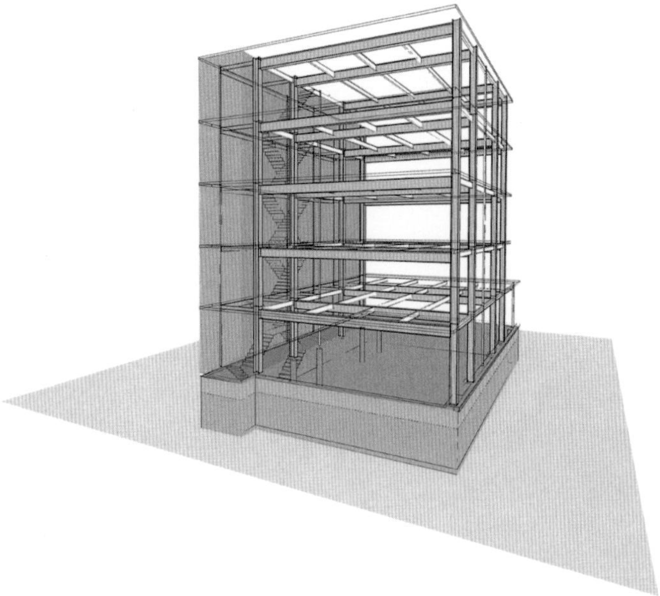

structural diagram & façade studies

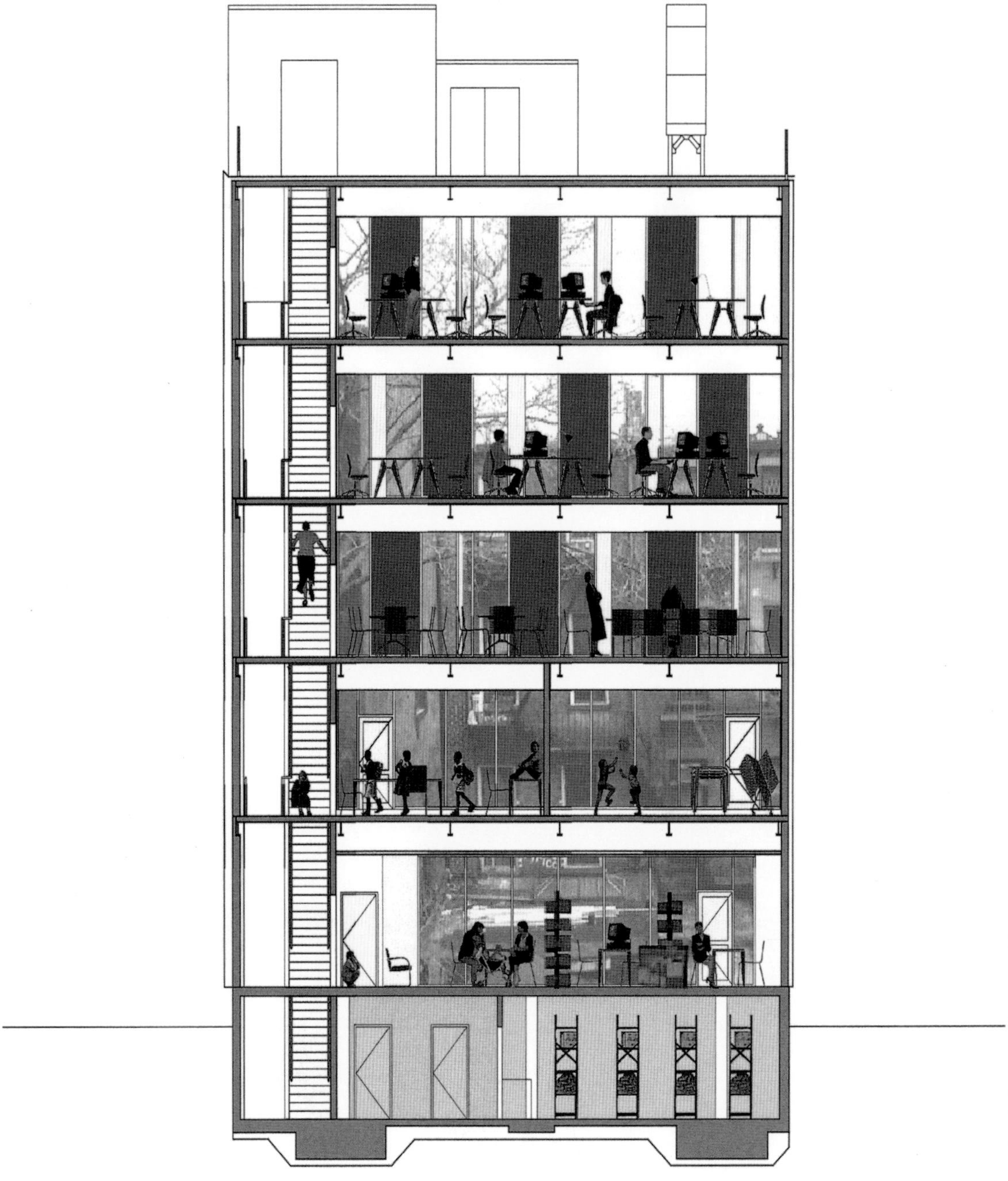

section/interior elevation

construction

Construction Since the construction of a building is the equivalent of a musical performance that makes the score of the composer real, the architect is often the person best suited to oversee the implementation of his designs. In that spirit the construction of the Floating Box House (page 308) is here detailed in photographs which record the process of feedback between design and building that is critical to the realization of what we call architecture.

site

To retain the rural feeling of the native Texas landscape evoked by the live-oak grove and also frame the view of the modern urban skyline in the distance, the house is split into parts that either float above or are buried below the ground. The preservation of the elegance of the site with its unusual combination of city and country determined the form of the house.

01.2000

demolition

After the initial design and construction documents, we oversaw the careful demolition of the existing house and pool, followed by adjustments to the position and dimensions of the new house that could only be made once the site was cleared. These changes, though burdensome at an advanced stage of the design, made it possible to preserve the sensitive nature of the site.

08.2002

xcavation

almost surgical excavation of 7,000 yards rock was necessary to protect the roots the landmarked live oaks. The rock's ability permitted sharp vertical cuts so the use could be nestled close to the trees in a mposition that makes the building look as t had always been there. Excavation costs re reduced by selling the rock for nearby hway construction.

11.2002

drainage/waterproofing

Because the house is partly buried to reduce its bulk and lower energy costs, it required particularly efficient drainage and waterproofing. Since underground repair is costly or impossible, the system was designed with enough redundancy to allow for deterioration over time. Waterproofing the grassed roof demanded micro-supervision of construction to ensure a leak-proof building.

11.2002

10.2002

12.2002

09.2003

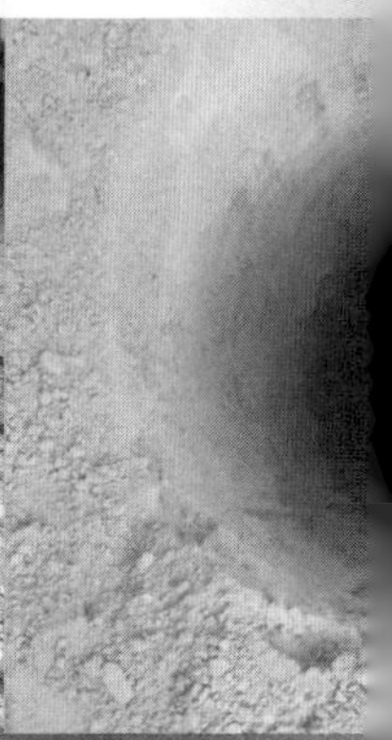

foundation

The buried building involved extensive retaining walls, whose continuous footings had to be poured on undisturbed soil, a condition difficult to preserve on a site with such extensive excavation. Where the soil was poor, pilings were used instead of spread footings.

10.2002

11.2002

12.2002

01.2003

02.2003

concrete

The extensive retaining walls necessitated an unusual amount of reinforced concrete work for a house, but their extent made it possible to use standard steel forms and commercial contractors at reasonable cost. This also made it economical to use concrete for the floor slabs, with the advantage of added stability and soundproofing.

03.2003

05.2003

steel

he floating box, with its 80-foot span, and ne continuous glass wall of the room below equired steel construction. Steel minimized novement and deflection, and permitted risp interior detailing without the cracking aused by normal shrinkage or settling.

04.2003

06.2003

05.2003

07.2003

09.2003

06.2003

ıechanicals

e box appears to "float" because there are
solid walls in the room below, which meant
at all pipes and ducts had to be fitted into
e exterior fins that buttress the floating box
d then routed through carefully predeter-
ned openings in the steel structure.
achieve this, the steel and mechanical
awings were produced and coordinated
house by the architects.

08.2003

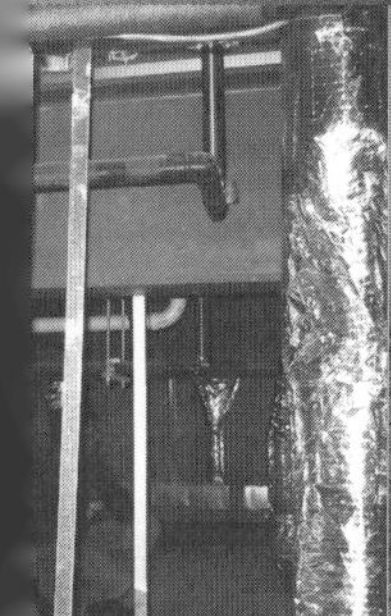

06.2003

07.2003

framing

Metal stud walls increase stability and minimize movement, and also help to prevent mold and rot in the extremely humid climate.

08.2003

09.2003

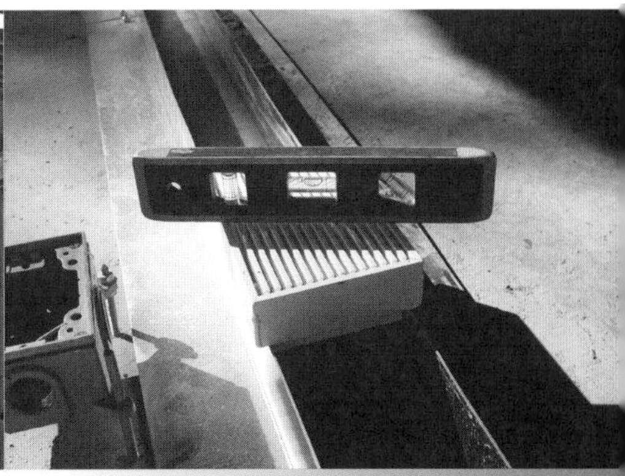

drywall

Gypsum board was installed with two overlapping layers skim-coated for a smooth finish that was as elegant as plaster but far cheaper and easier to maintain.

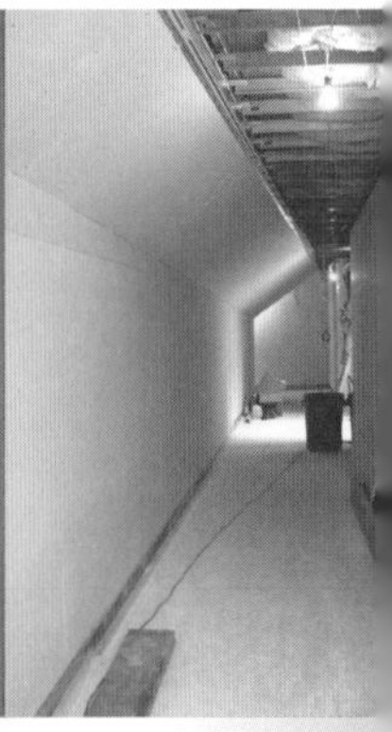

05.2004

06.2004

09.2004

sheathing

Standard sheathing plywood adds to structural stability and also serves as the substrate for the exterior rain screen. A building wrap that acts as a vapor barrier covers the plywood sheathing.

12.2003

rain screens

An exterior rain screen protects the walls from extreme heat, UV light, and moisture. The screen on the floating box is made up of resin-impregnated panels finished with mahogany veneer while glass-bead-blasted stainless steel panels cover the two utility fins. Spaced 5/8" inch from each other, the panels allow air to circulate and keep the walls cool and dry.

05.2004

06.2004

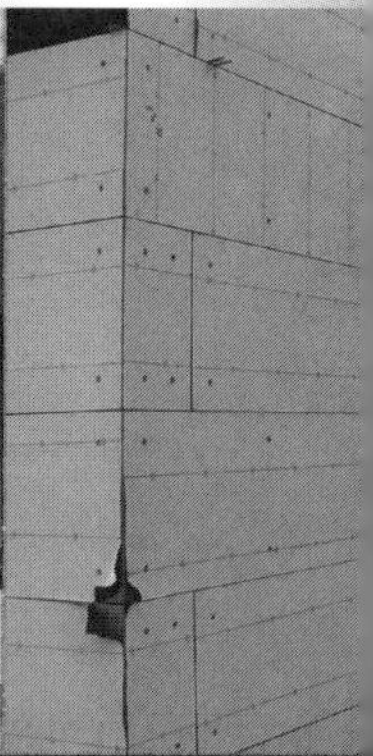

07.2004

12.2004

glass

The box floats because of the absolute transparency of the glass-walled space below, providing an unobstructed view of the city in the distance. To create this effect butt-glazed, lead-free, laminated glass spanned from floor to ceiling with huge, specially fabricated steel sliding doors opening the room to the outside.

02.2004

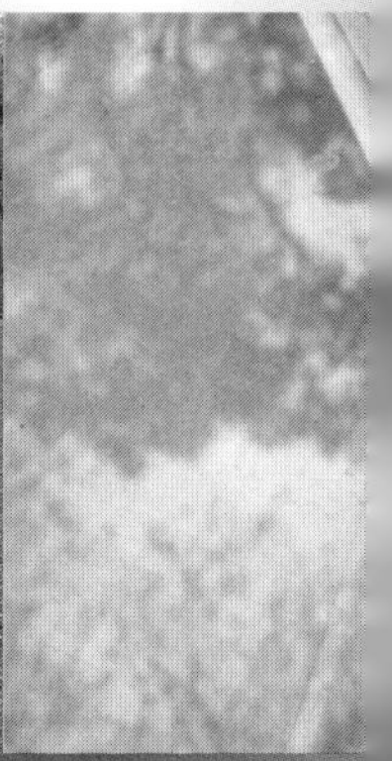

wood frame windows

In contrast to the transparent space between them, the floating box and the spaces partially below grade are meant to read as more solid or opaque. For that reason the windows are set within deep mahogany frames and glazed with insulating glass that reflects the green landscape on the lower level and the dark blue sky in the box above.

12.2004

04.2004

06.2004

07.2004

I directed robert to clean up these feathered edges
at the sloped walls.

06.2004

05.2004

skylights

The green roof is studded with an irregular pattern of square and rectangular skylights set flush with the grass. As one walks among and across the translucent (and at night, glowing) glass, the skylights hint at the private spaces enclosed below the lawn.

08.2003

10.2003

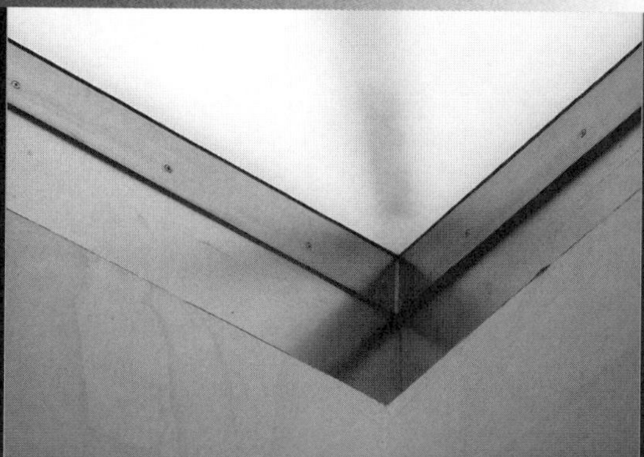

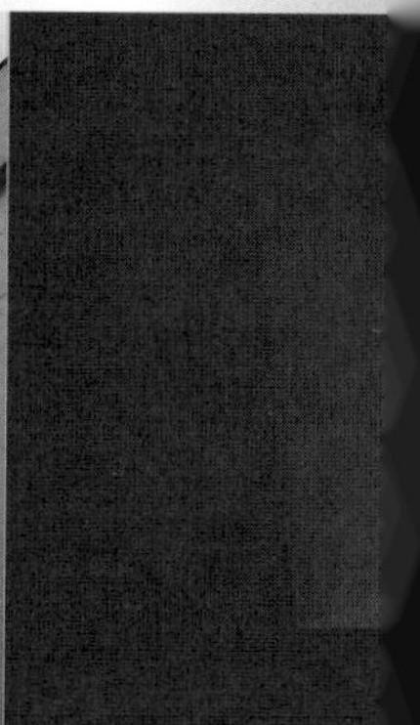

07.2004

09.2004

stairs

The three major horizontal spaces are linked by a soaring ribbon of dark, burnished steel plate that forms an entirely open three-story stair with cantilevered steel-plate risers and a protective veil of light steel rods. Contrary to its appearance of lightness, the prefabricated sections weighed as much as 3,500 pounds each and were assembled with a specially built rigging and then welded in place.

06.2004

08.2004

09.2004

10.2004

11.2004

driveway

To eliminate the automobile from the landscape, the driveway winds through native woods and then takes a steep, curving dive into the underground garage, the curve concealing the driveway from above. Through a trick of grading, the entry hall from the underground garage opens immediately onto the grassy lawn on the other side of house.

12.2002

10.2003

02.2003

11.2004

pool

The pool is located at the far edge of the site, where it drops off so steeply that the distant city becomes the main view. In this way the slash of water marks the boundary between the rural setting and the urban skyline, One side of the pool aligns with the partly underground office, which has a window into the blue light of the water.

04.2003

5'-0"

5'-0"

004

bond wire prevents swimmers
from acting as ground for power

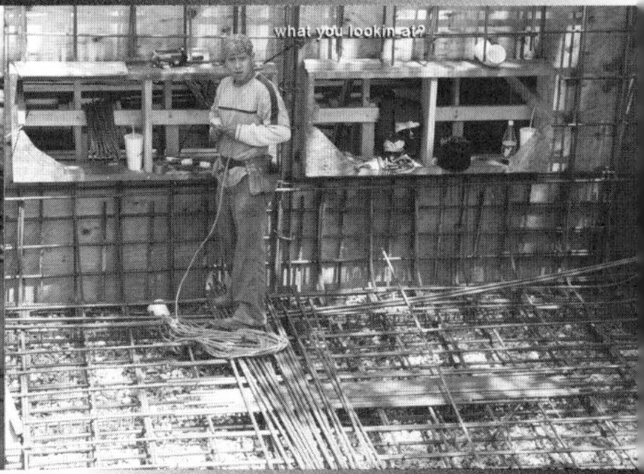
what you lookin at?

04.2004

earth cut

The earth is sculpted, blurring the distinction between the ground plane and the entrance. The deep grassed cut also makes the outdoors immediately accessible on both the lower and upper levels. Its sharp contours are held in place by a steel frame and retaining cups of the sort used for highway embankments. A trench drain at the bottom draws the water away from the house.

12.2003

09.2004

07.2004

06.2005

drawings

Technical drawings (construction documents or working drawings) are critical to the implementation of any design. They are the intermediate stage in which an architect's idea is turned into built form by a complicated, uncoordinated, and not necessarily sympathetic assemblage of trades, craftsmen, and manufacturers.

Today, when buildings are constructed by a large number of often unrelated subcontractors, none of whom is responsible for the whole, technical drawings play an even more important role. For that reason, we produce our own construction documents (including mechanical and structural drawings), and, equally important, we organize them by trade, preparing a separate set of documents that detail the requirements and responsibility of each one.

These drawings also constitute the core of the financial contract between the builder and the client, so that clarity and detail are essential for controlling the project and its costs.

site plan

LOT
LOT 34
PERMANENT 18" CULVERT
MAILBOX. STYLE AND LOCATION PER CITY OF WEST LAKE ORDINANCE
15'-0" FLAT AREA AT ENTRANCE TO DRIVE
PROPERTY LINE
FRONT YARD SETBACK
AREA= 8495 SQFT.
DRIP IRRIGATION FIELD, (SEE WASTE WATER DETAILS)
NO BED IS GREATER THAN 30% SLOPE
R100'-1" WELL SETBACK
WELL
ELECTRIC EASMENT
SEWER TREATMENT SYSTEM (SEE WASTE WATER DETAILS)
MAIN HOUSE PRIMARY SEPTIC TANK (SEE WASTE WATER DETAILS)
BENCH MARK: ASSUMED ELEVATION OF 1001'-0" @ TOP OF IRON ROD
CAPITAL VIEW
940
925

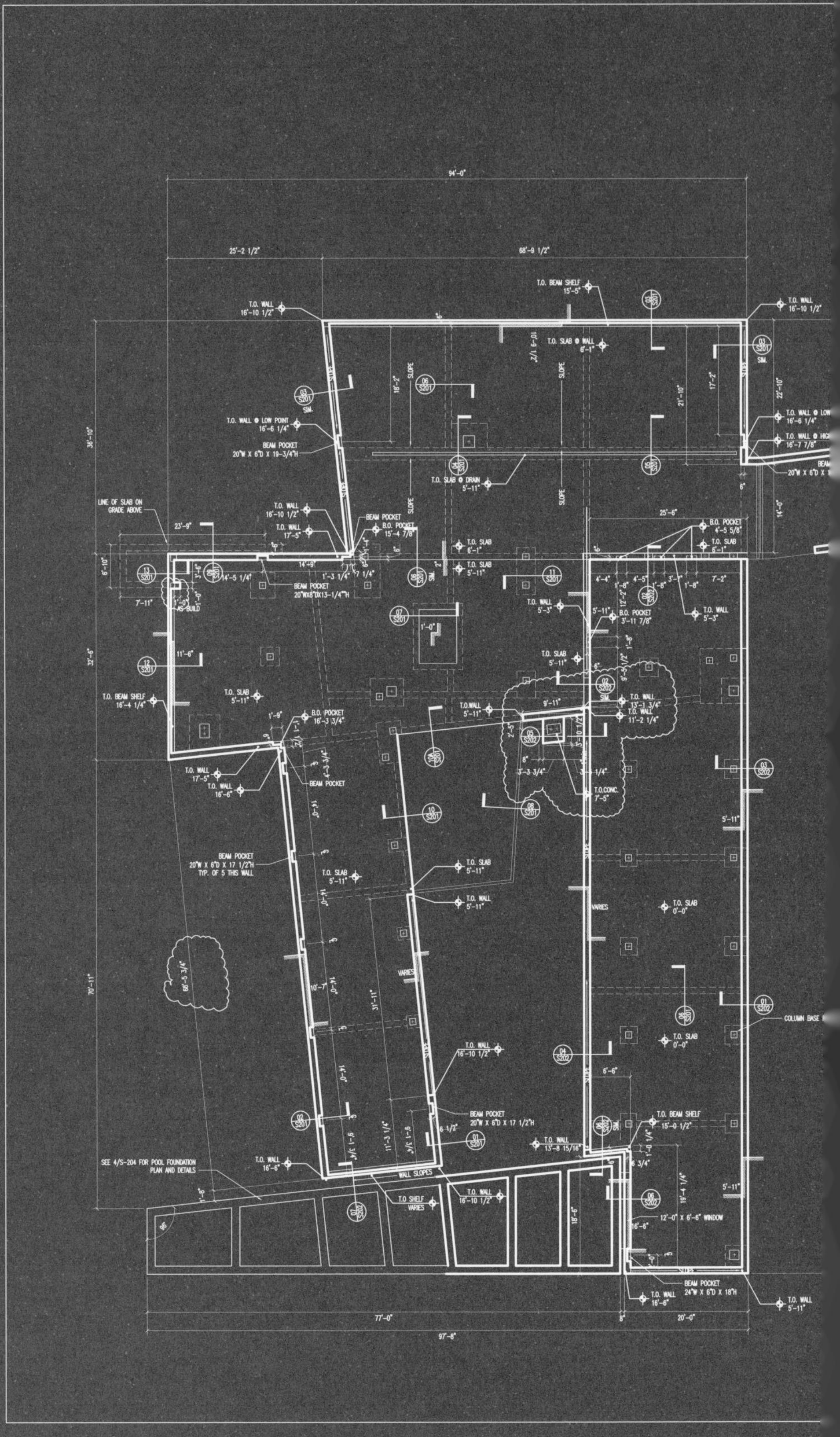

foundation finish
surface plan

NOTES

1. ELEVATION OF 0'-0" IS SET AT THE ASSUMED ELEVATION OF 100'-1" FROM THE SURVEY / SITEPLAN
2. REFER TO DETAILS FOR REINFORCEMENT SPECIFICATION AND SPACING.
3. CONTRACTOR SHALL FORM 5-1/2" x 1-1/2" KEYWAY ON SLAB AS INDICATED & PER DETAILS.
4. DO NOT SCALE FROM DRAWINGS
5. AXON PROVIDED FOR ILLUSTRATION ONLY; WHERE AXON AND PLAN ARE INCONSISTENT, PLAN GOVERNS
6. SLOPE CONCRETE WITHIN 2'-0" RADIUS OF FLOOR DRAINS DOWN TO DRAIN TO ACHIEVE A MIN. DROP FROM SLAB TO DRAIN OF 1/2".
7. SLEEVE DIAMETER IS INSIDE DIMENSION, TYP.

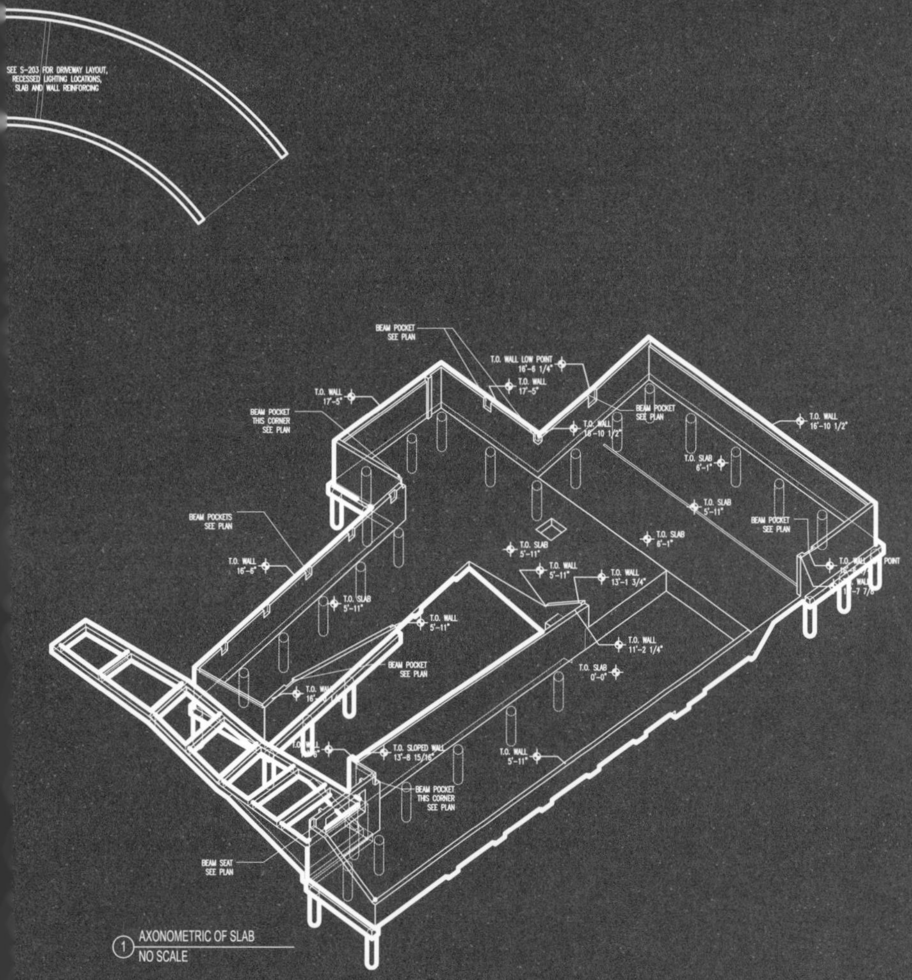

1 AXONOMETRIC OF SLAB
NO SCALE

N/A	07.07.03	FRAMING SET FOR CONSTRUCTION	N/A
N/A	03.31.03	FRAMING SET FOR BID	N/A
N/A	01.03.03	PLUMBING SET FOR CONSTRUCTION	N/A
N/A	12.17.02	WATERPROOFING FOR CONSTRUCTION	N/A
△2	12.05.02	REVISED CONC. FOR CONST.	N/A
△1	12.05.02	REVISED CONC. FOR CONST.	N/A
N/A	11.18.02	CONCRETE FOR CONSTRUCTION	N/A
N/A	11.13.02	WATERPROOFING FOR REVIEW	N/A
N/A	11.01.02	FOUNDATION REVISIONS	N/A
N/A	10.03.02	STEEL SET; FOR BIDDING ONLY	N/A
N/A	09.23.02	CONCRETE REVIEW SET	N/A
N/A	09.18.02	PLUMBING SET; FOR BIDDING ONLY	N/A
N/A	09.12.02	WATERPROOFING; FOR BIDDING ONLY	N/A
N/A	08.27.02	2ND CONC. SET; FOR BIDDING ONLY	N/A
N/A	08.05.02	FILING SET	N/A
Revision #	Date:	Notes:	S.K. #:

CONSTRUCTION

Peter L. Gluck and Partners, Architects
646 West 131st Street @ Twelfth Avenue NY, NY 10027 Tel., 212 690 4950 Fax 212 690 4961

PROJECT NUMBER: 2003
DRAWN BY:
DRAWING SCALE: 1/8" = 1'
DATE: 05.03.02

FOUNDATION FINISH SURFACE PLAN

S-102

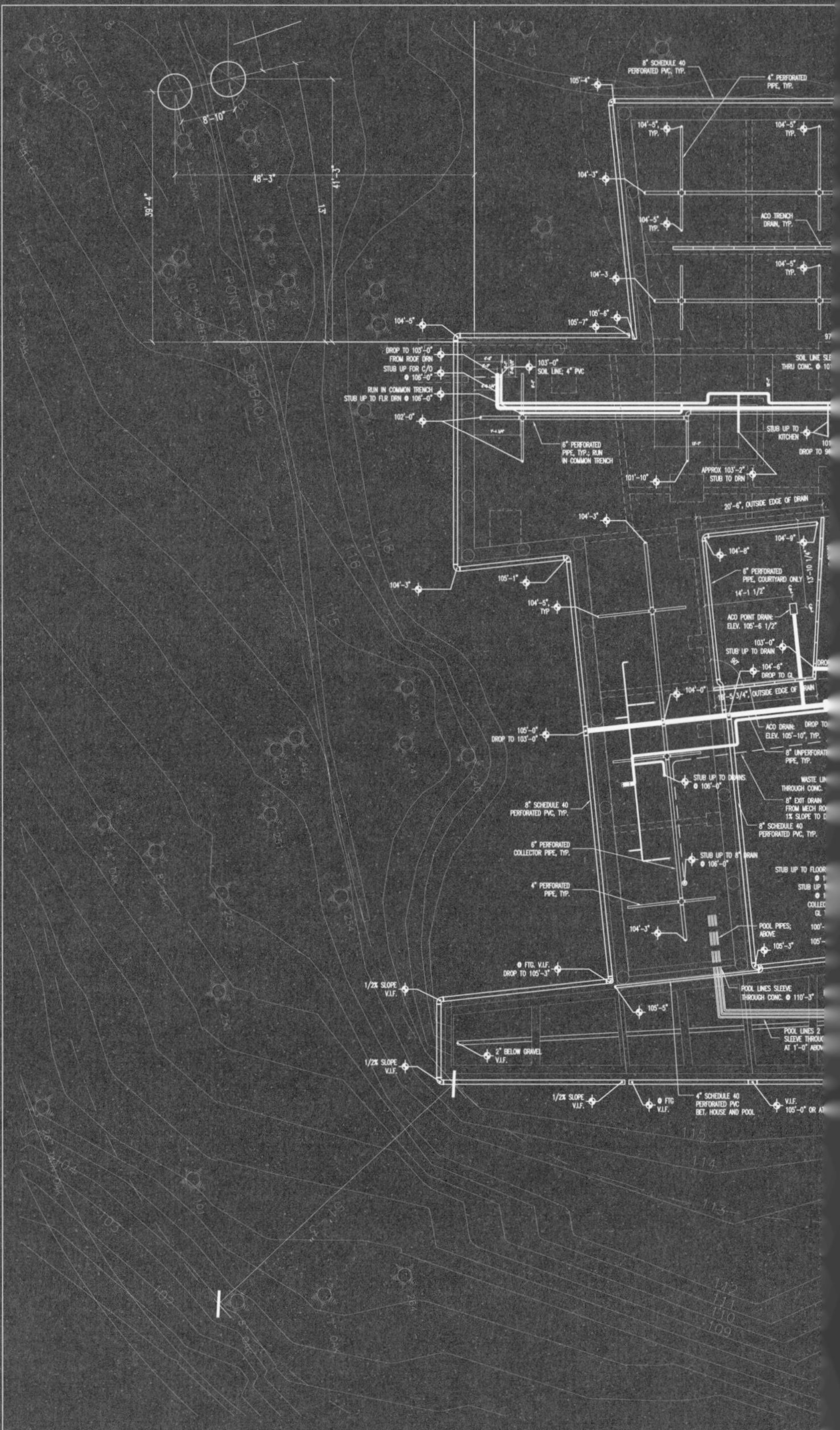

foundation drainage plan

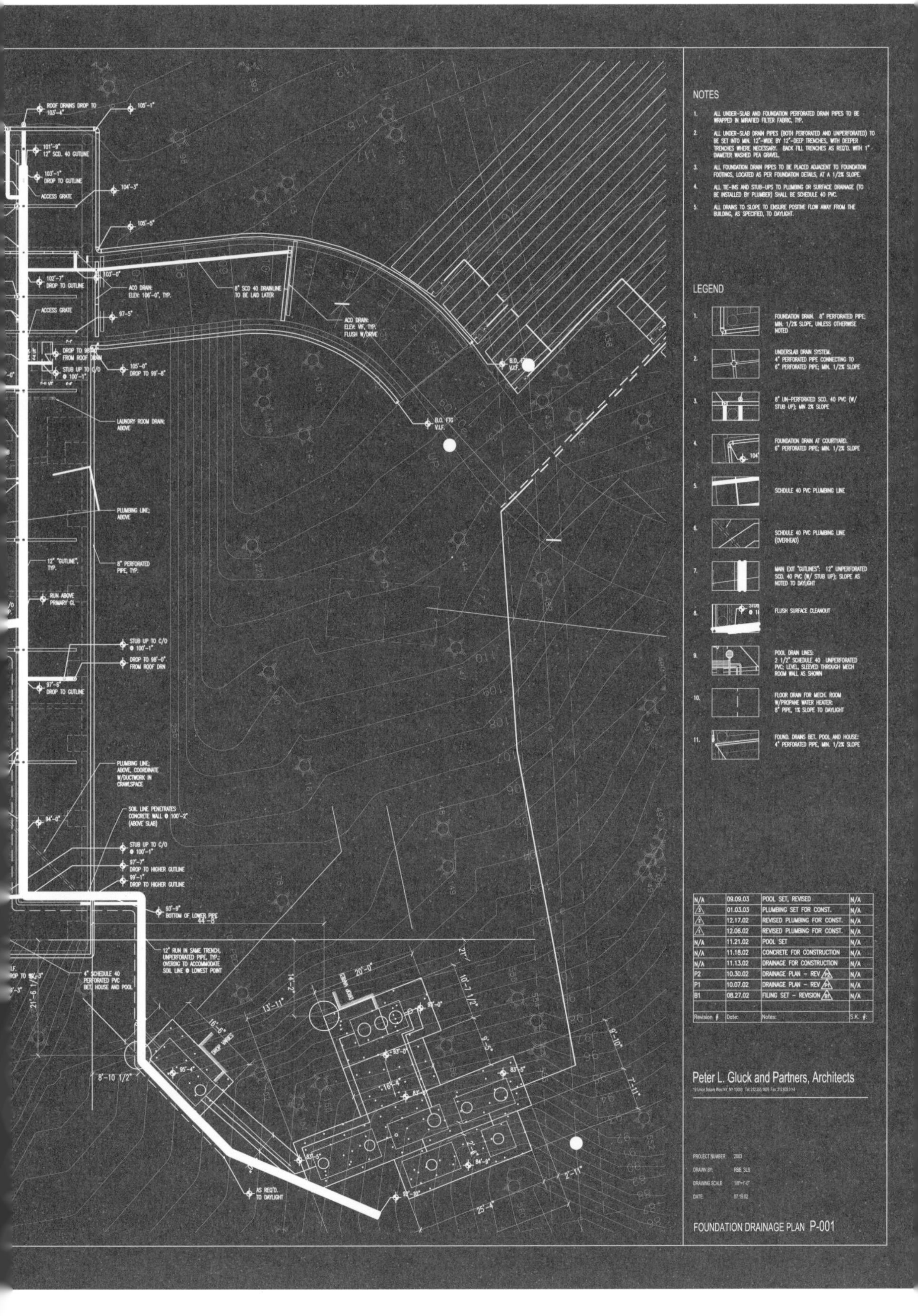
NOTES
1. ALL UNDER-SLAB AND FOUNDATION PERFORATED DRAIN PIPES TO BE WRAPPED IN MIRAFIED FILTER FABRIC, TYP.
2. ALL UNDER-SLAB DRAIN PIPES (BOTH PERFORATED AND UNPERFORATED) TO BE SET INTO MIN. 12"-WIDE BY 12"-DEEP TRENCHES, WITH DEEPER TRENCHES WHERE NECESSARY. BACK FILL TRENCHES AS REQ'D. WITH 1" DIAMETER WASHED PEA GRAVEL.
3. ALL FOUNDATION DRAIN PIPES TO BE PLACED ADJACENT TO FOUNDATION FOOTINGS, LOCATED AS PER FOUNDATION DETAILS, AT A 1/2% SLOPE.
4. ALL TIE-INS AND STUB-UPS TO PLUMBING OR SURFACE DRAINAGE (TO BE INSTALLED BY PLUMBER) SHALL BE SCHEDULE 40 PVC.
5. ALL DRAINS TO SLOPE TO ENSURE POSITIVE FLOW AWAY FROM THE BUILDING, AS SPECIFIED, TO DAYLIGHT.
LEGEND
1. FOUNDATION DRAIN. 8" PERFORATED PIPE; MIN. 1/2% SLOPE, UNLESS OTHERWISE NOTED
2. UNDERSLAB DRAIN SYSTEM. 4" PERFORATED PIPE CONNECTING TO 6" PERFORATED PIPE; MIN. 1/2% SLOPE
3. 8" UN-PERFORATED SCD. 40 PVC (W/ STUB UP); MIN 2% SLOPE
4. FOUNDATION DRAIN AT COURTYARD. 6" PERFORATED PIPE; MIN. 1/2% SLOPE
5. SCHDULE 40 PVC PLUMBING LINE
6. SCHDULE 40 PVC PLUMBING LINE (OVERHEAD)
7. MAIN EXIT "GUTLINES": 12" UNPERFORATED SCD. 40 PVC (W/ STUB UP); SLOPE AS NOTED TO DAYLIGHT
8. FLUSH SURFACE CLEANOUT
9. POOL DRAIN LINES: 2 1/2" SCHEDULE 40 UNPERFORATED PVC; LEVEL, SLEEVED THROUGH MECH ROOM WALL AS SHOWN
10. FLOOR DRAIN FOR MECH. ROOM W/PROPANE WATER HEATER: 8" PIPE, 1% SLOPE TO DAYLIGHT
11. FOUND. DRAINS BET. POOL AND HOUSE: 4" PERFORATED PIPE, MIN. 1/2% SLOPE
N/A 09.09.03 POOL SET, REVISED N/A
3 01.03.03 PLUMBING SET FOR CONST. N/A
2 12.17.02 REVISED PLUMBING FOR CONST. N/A
1 12.06.02 REVISED PLUMBING FOR CONST. N/A
N/A 11.21.02 POOL SET N/A
N/A 11.18.02 CONCRETE FOR CONSTRUCTION N/A
N/A 11.13.02 DRAINAGE FOR CONSTRUCTION N/A
P2 10.30.02 DRAINAGE PLAN – REV P2 N/A
P1 10.07.02 DRAINAGE PLAN – REV P1 N/A
B1 08.27.02 FILING SET – REVISION B1 N/A
Revision # Date: Notes: S.K. #:
Peter L. Gluck and Partners, Architects
19 Union Square West NY, NY 10003 Tel: 212.255.1876 Fax: 212.633.0144
PROJECT NUMBER: 2003
DRAWN BY: RBB, SLS
DRAWING SCALE: 1/8"=1'-0"
DATE: 07.19.02
FOUNDATION DRAINAGE PLAN P-001
ROOF DRAINS DROP TO 103'-4"
105'-1"
101'-9" 12" SCD. 40 GUTLINE
103'-1" DROP TO GUTLINE
ACCESS GRATE
104'-3"
105'-5"
103'-0"
102'-7" DROP TO GUTLINE
ACO DRAIN: ELEV: 106'-0", TYP.
8" SCD 40 DRAINLINE TO BE LAID LATER
ACCESS GRATE
97'-5"
ACO DRAIN: ELEV: VIF, TYP. FLUSH W/DRIVE
105'-0" DROP TO 99'-8"
LAUNDRY ROOM DRAIN; ABOVE
B.O. FTG V.I.F.
PLUMBING LINE; ABOVE
12" "GUTLINE", TYP.
8" PERFORATED PIPE, TYP.
RUN ABOVE PRIMARY CL
STUB UP TO C/O @ 100'-1"
DROP TO 98'-0" FROM ROOF DRN
97'-6" DROP TO GUTLINE
PLUMBING LINE; ABOVE, COORDINATE W/DUCTWORK IN CRAWLSPACE
SOIL LINE PENETRATES CONCRETE WALL @ 100'-2" (ABOVE SLAB)
94'-0"
STUB UP TO C/O @ 100'-1"
97'-7" DROP TO HIGHER GUTLINE
99'-1" DROP TO HIGHER GUTLINE
93'-9" BOTTOM OF LOWER PIPE
12" RUN IN SAME TRENCH, UNPERFORATED PIPE, TYP.; OVERDIG TO ACCOMMODATE SOIL LINE @ LOWEST POINT
4" SCHEDULE 40 PERFORATED PVC BET. HOUSE AND POOL
8'-10 1/2"
AS REQ'D. TO DAYLIGHT
20'-0"
10'-7 1/2"
13'-11"
16'-6"
9'-5"
9'-10"
7'-11"
2'-11"
25'-4"

NOTES

1. TOP OF STEEL ELEVATION VARIES; SEE TOP OF STEEL ELEVATION PLAN THIS SHEET
2. ALL W10x45 JOIST CONNECTIONS TO SUPPORTING BEAMS SHALL BE SIMPLE SHEAR, DOUBLE ANGLE CONNECTIONS. REFER TO DETAIL PAGE S-250 & S-251 FOR TYP. CONNECTION
3. ALL CAMBERS SHOULD LOCATE MAXIMUM CAMBER AT MIDSPAN OF SECTION. WHERE TYPICAL FABRICATION CAMBER EXCEE3DS CAMBER NOTED, DEFER TO NATURAL FABRICATION CAMBER INSTEAD. CAMBERS SHOWN ARE MINIMUM CAMBERS. CAMBER TOLERANCE +/-1/8. HEATING STEEL MEMBERS IN THE FIELD IS NOT AN ACCEPTABLE MEANS OF ACHIEVING CAMBERS.

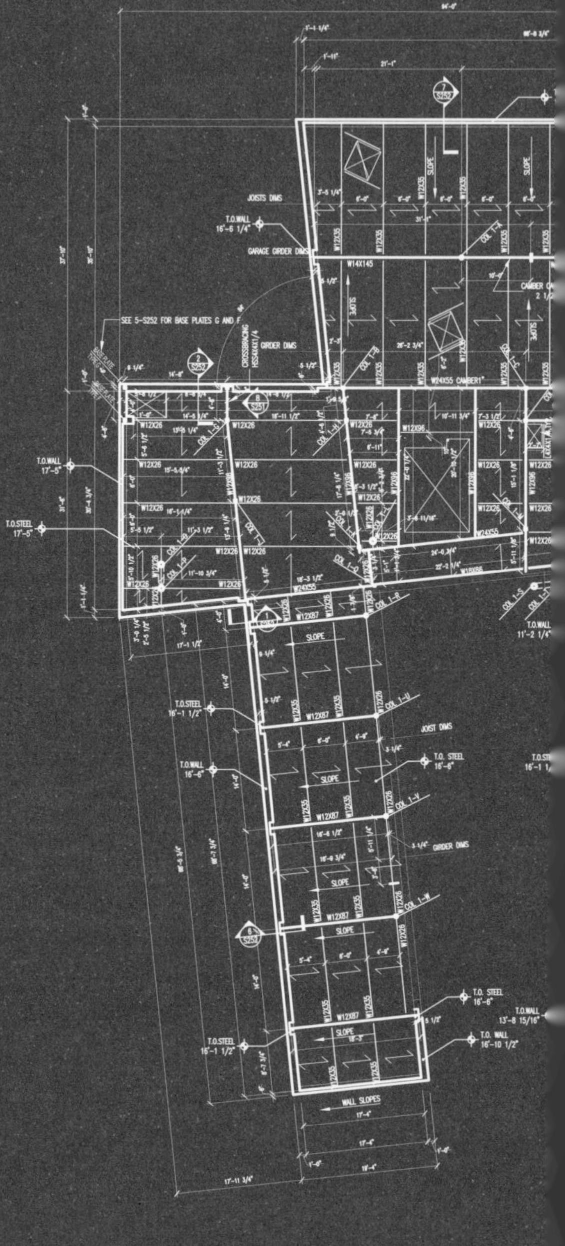

COLUMN SCHEDULE
1ST FL. FRAMING PLAN

TYPE	COLUMN
COL 1-A	12" PIPE COL
COL 1-B	HSS4X4X1/4
COL 1-C	HSS4X4X1/4
COL 1-D	HSS4X4X1/4
COL 1-E	HSS6X6X3/8
COL 1-F	HSS4X4X1/4
COL 1-G	HSS4X4X1/4
COL 1-H	HSS4X4X1/4
COL 1-I	HSS4X4X1/4
COL 1-J	HSS4X4X1/4
COL 1-K	HSS4X4X1/4
COL 1-L	10" PIPE 90'
COL 1-M	HSS4X4X1/4

COLUMN SCHEDULE
1ST FL. FRAMING PLAN

TYPE	COLUMN
COL 1-N	HSS4X4X1/4
COL 1-O	8" PIPE 75'
COL 1-P	8" PIPE 90'
COL 1-Q	HSS3X3X3/8
COL 1-R	6" PIPE COL
COL 1-S	8" PIPE 69'
COL 1-T	8" PIPE 90'
COL 1-U	6" PIPE COL
COL 1-V	6" PIPE COL
COL 1-W	6" PIPE COL

first floor
framing plan

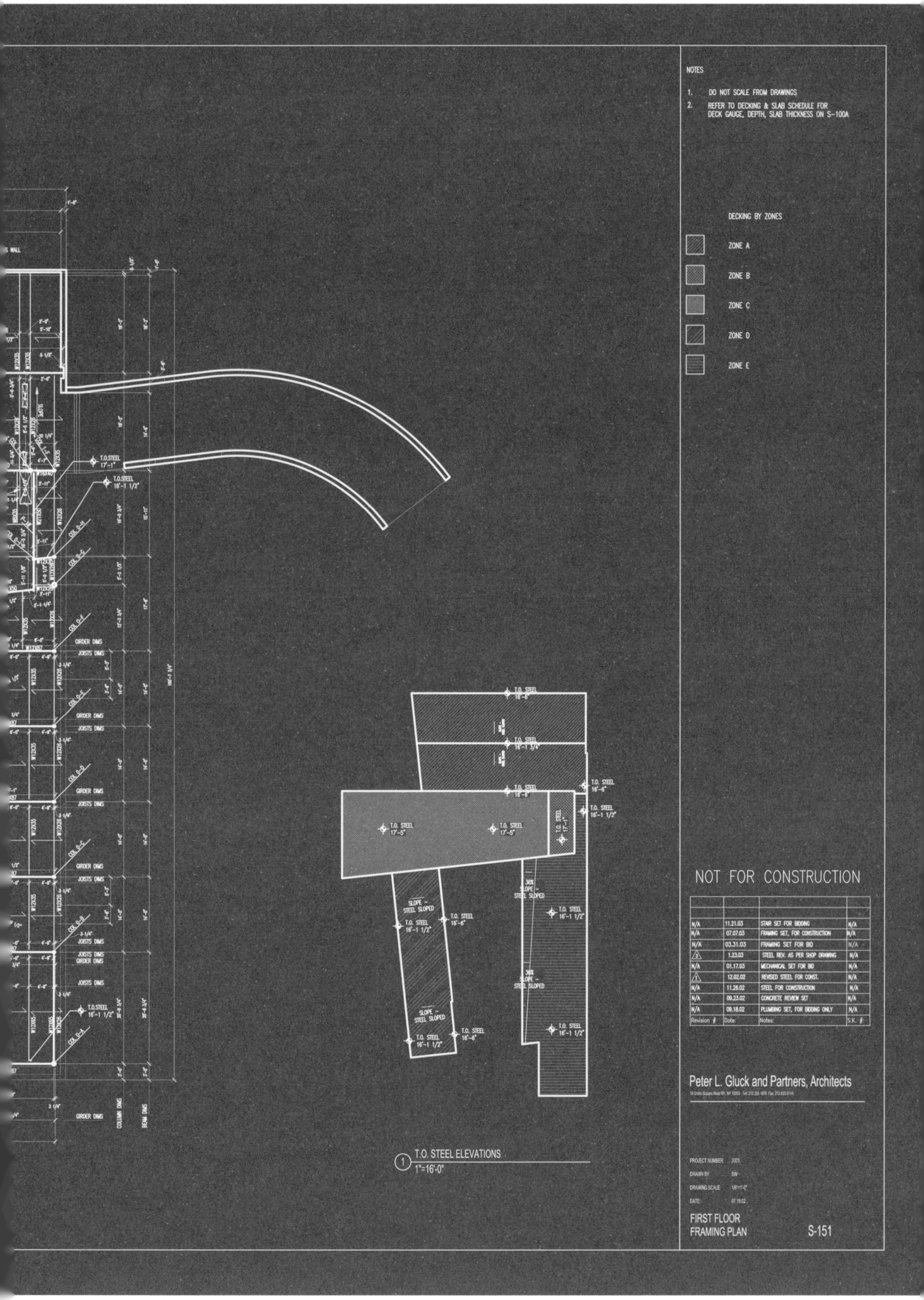
NOTES
1. DO NOT SCALE FROM DRAWINGS
2. REFER TO DECKING & SLAB SCHEDULE FOR DECK GAUGE, DEPTH, SLAB THICKNESS ON S-100A
DECKING BY ZONES
ZONE A
ZONE B
ZONE C
ZONE D
ZONE E
NOT FOR CONSTRUCTION
N/A 11.21.03 STAIR SET FOR BIDDING N/A
N/A 07.07.03 FRAMING SET, FOR CONSTRUCTION N/A
N/A 03.31.03 FRAMING SET FOR BID N/A
3 1.23.03 STEEL REV. AS PER SHOP DRAWING N/A
N/A 01.17.03 MECHANICAL SET FOR BID N/A
1 12.02.02 REVISED STEEL FOR CONST. N/A
N/A 11.26.02 STEEL FOR CONSTRUCTION N/A
N/A 09.23.02 CONCRETE REVIEW SET N/A
N/A 09.18.02 PLUMBING SET, FOR BIDDING ONLY N/A
Revision # Date: Notes: S.K. #:
Peter L. Gluck and Partners, Architects
FIRST FLOOR FRAMING PLAN
S-151
T.O. STEEL ELEVATIONS
1"=16'-0"
GIRDER DIMS
JOISTS DIMS
COLUMN DIMS
BEAM DIMS

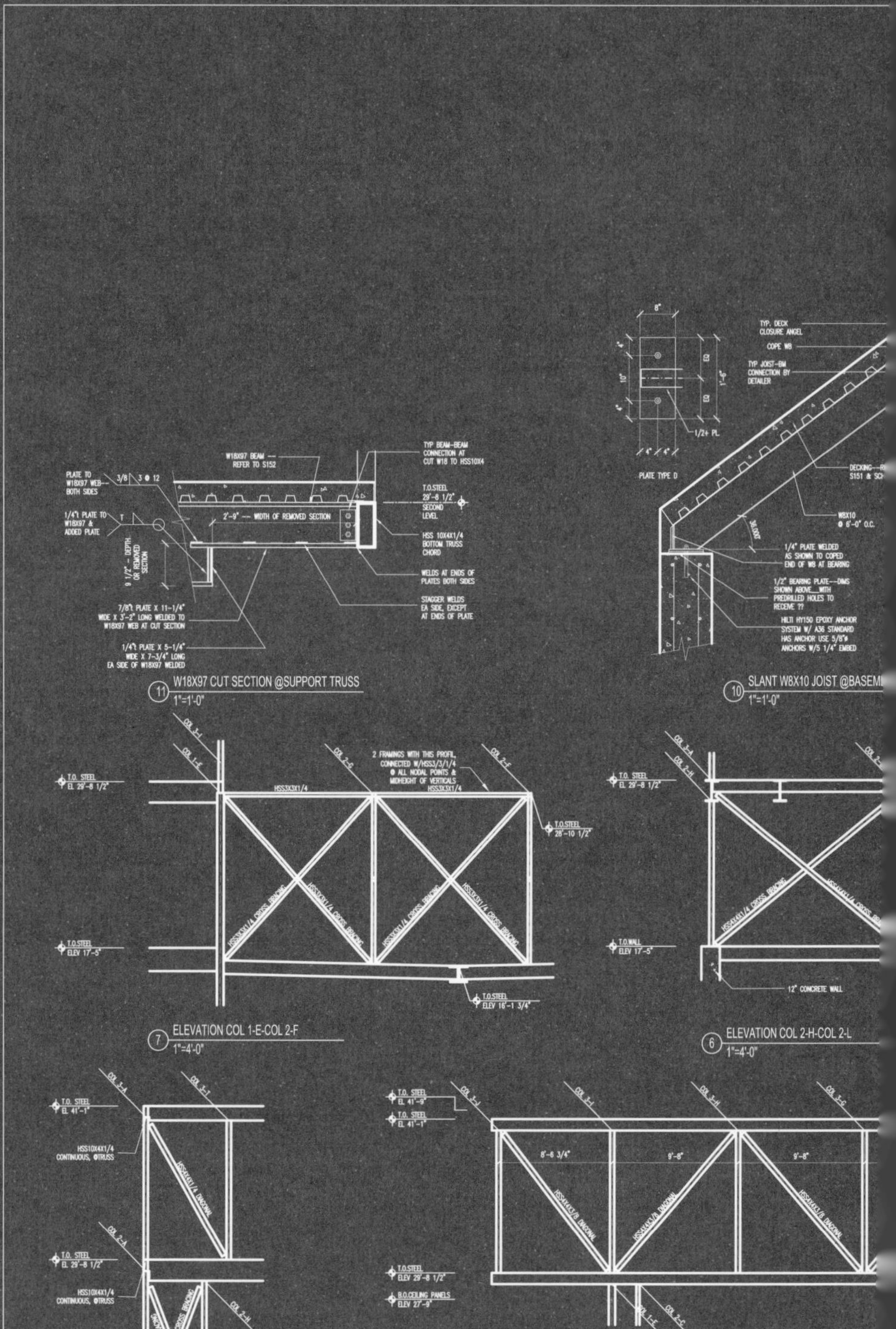

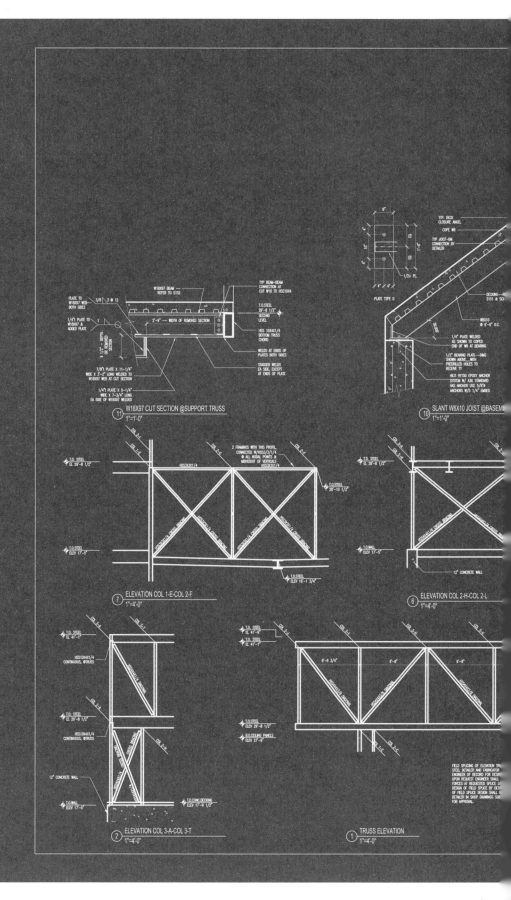

steel details
frame elevations

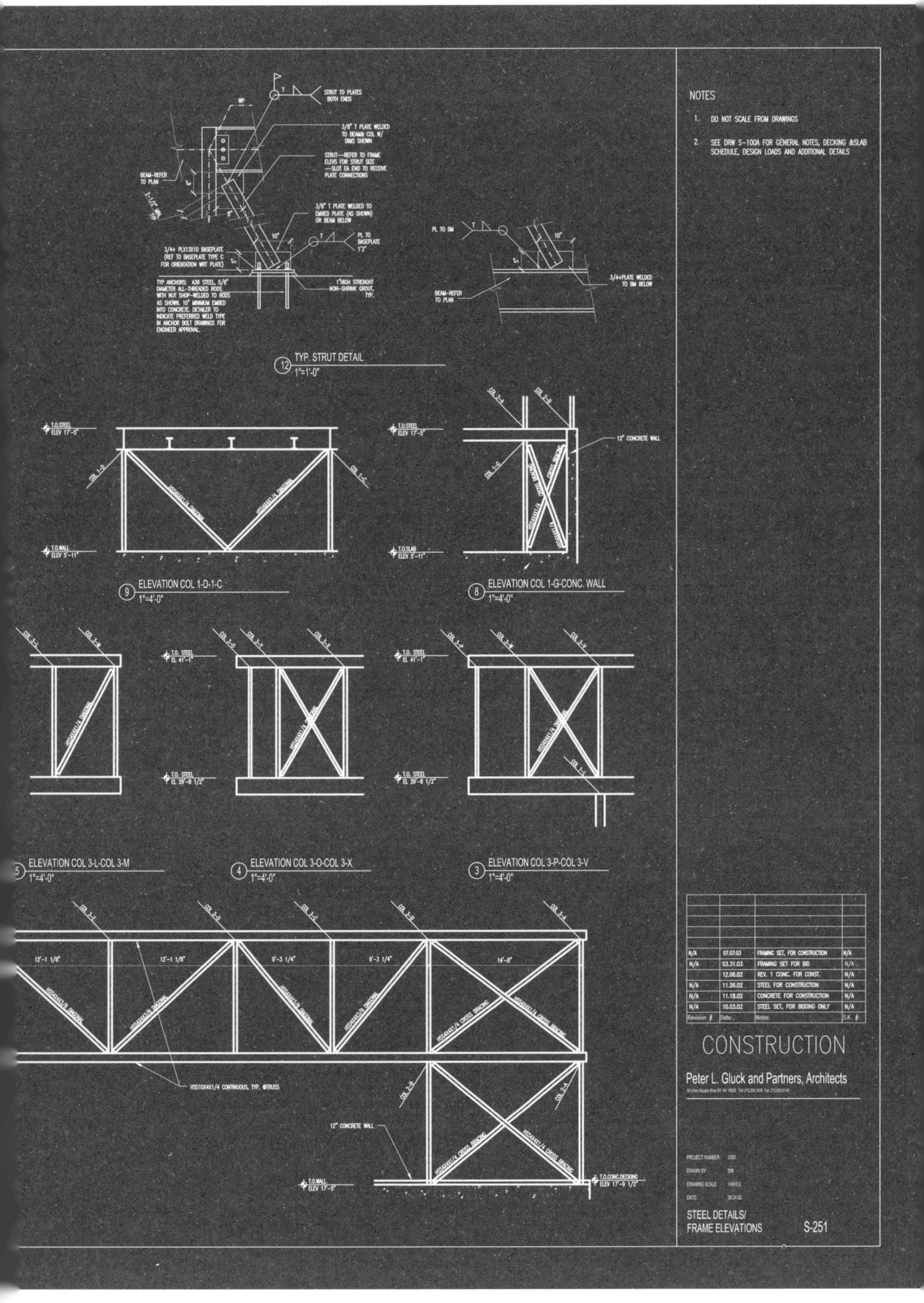
NOTES
1. DO NOT SCALE FROM DRAWINGS
2. SEE DRW S-100A FOR GENERAL NOTES, DECKING &SLAB SCHEDULE, DESIGN LOADS AND ADDITIONAL DETAILS
STRUT TO PLATES BOTH ENDS
3/8" T PLATE WELDED TO BEAM: COL W/ DIMS SHOWN
STRUT—REFER TO FRAME ELEVS FOR STRUT SIZE —SLOT EA END TO RECEIVE PLATE CONNECTIONS
BEAM-REFER TO PLAN
3/8" T PLATE WELDED TO EMBED PLATE (AS SHOWN) OR BEAM BELOW
PL TO BASEPLATE
3/4+ PLX13X10 BASEPLATE (REF TO BASEPLATE TYPE C FOR ORIENTATION WRT PLATE)
TYP ANCHORS: A36 STEEL, 5/8" DIAMETER ALL-THREADED RODS WITH NUT SHOP-WELDED TO RODS AS SHOWN. 10" MINIMUM EMBED INTO CONCRETE. DETAILER TO INDICATE PREFERRED WELD TYPE IN ANCHOR BOLT DRAWINGS FOR ENGINEER APPROVAL.
1" HIGH STRENGHT NON-SHRINK GROUT, TYP.
PL TO BM
3/4+PLATE WELDED TO BM BELOW
BEAM-REFER TO PLAN
12 TYP. STRUT DETAIL 1"=1'-0"
T.O.STEEL ELEV 17'-5"
T.O.WALL ELEV 5'-11"
COL 1-D
COL 1-C
9 ELEVATION COL 1-D-1-C 1"=4'-0"
T.O.STEEL ELEV 17'-5"
T.O.SLAB ELEV 5'-11"
12" CONCRETE WALL
8 ELEVATION COL 1-G-CONC. WALL 1"=4'-0"
T.O. STEEL EL 41'-1"
T.O. STEEL EL 29'-8 1/2"
5 ELEVATION COL 3-L-COL 3-M 1"=4'-0"
4 ELEVATION COL 3-O-COL 3-X 1"=4'-0"
3 ELEVATION COL 3-P-COL 3-V 1"=4'-0"
12'-1 1/8"
12'-1 1/8"
9'-3 1/4"
9'-3 1/4"
14'-8"
HSS10X4X1/4 CONTINUOUS, TYP. @TRUSS
12" CONCRETE WALL
T.O.WALL ELEV 17'-5"
T.O.CONC.DECKING ELEV 17'-9 1/2"
N/A | 07.07.03 | FRAMING SET, FOR CONSTRUCTION | N/A
N/A | 03.31.03 | FRAMING SET FOR BID | N/A
| 12.06.02 | REV. 1 CONC. FOR CONST. | N/A
N/A | 11.26.02 | STEEL FOR CONSTRUCTION | N/A
N/A | 11.18.02 | CONCRETE FOR CONSTRUCTION | N/A
N/A | 10.03.02 | STEEL SET, FOR BIDDING ONLY | N/A
Revision # | Date: | Notes: | S.K. #
CONSTRUCTION
Peter L. Gluck and Partners, Architects
PROJECT NUMBER: 2003
DRAWN BY: SW
DRAWING SCALE: VARIES
DATE: 09.24.02
STEEL DETAILS/ FRAME ELEVATIONS
S-251

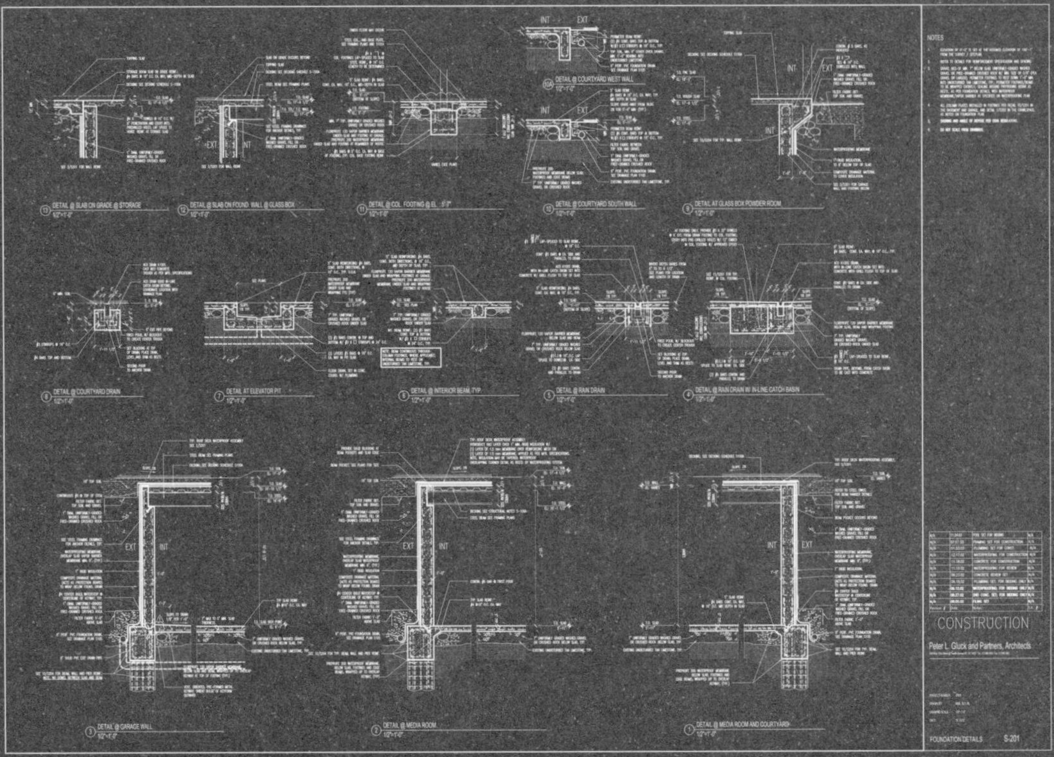

foundation details

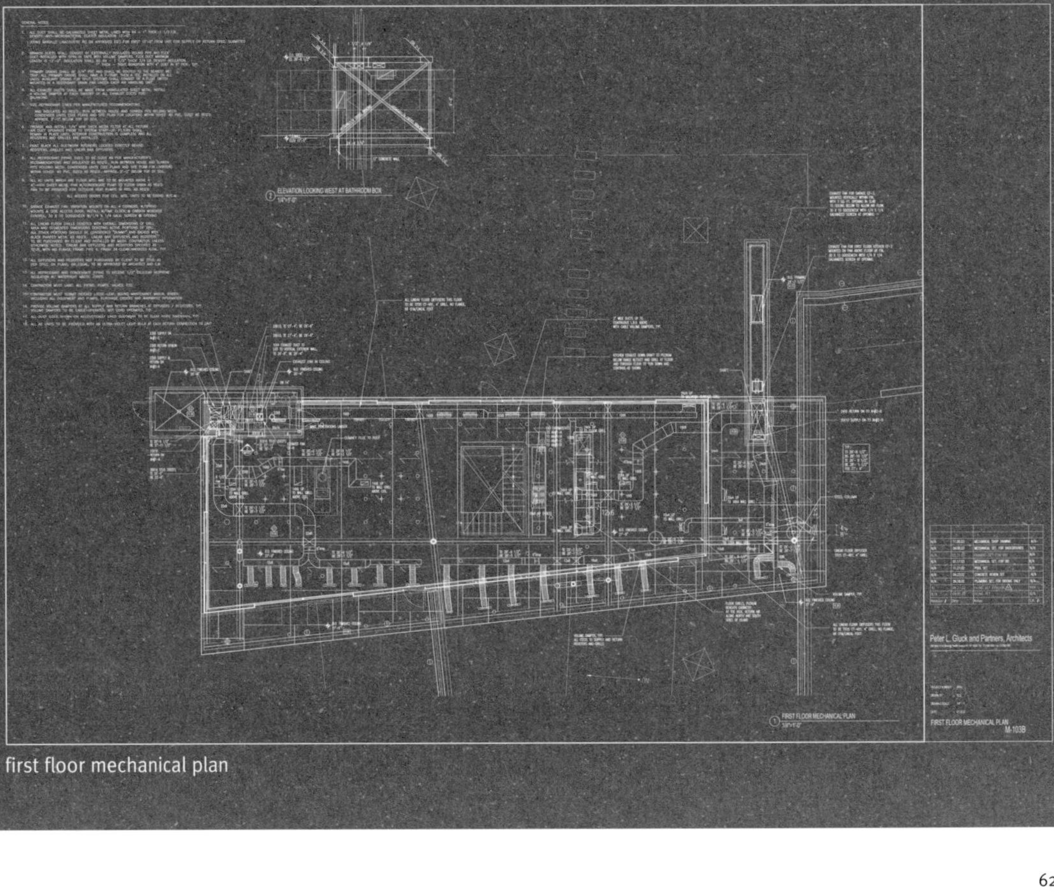

first floor mechanical plan

work in progress

work in progress The early years of the twenty-first century continued the favorable conjuncture that began in the 1990s, producing a global abundance of good architecture, which was richer, more personal, and less formulaic than in some periods in the long history of modernism. No single means of expression or formal vocabulary dominated the profession; the design landscape appeared ecumenical and open-ended; and the appetite and enthusiasm for good architecture continued to grow.

Our current work benefits from the firm's long experience in design and construction and its distinctive methodology for producing buildings from conceptual start to detailed finish. And because the first decade of the century has seen a resurgence of concern with cities and social needs, we are able to resume my early interest in the social effectiveness of architecture in our institutional and commercial projects, many of them in the inner city.

urban development

New York, New York

Project Team: Tom Gluck, David Hecht
Lot Size: 4,050 sf (376 m²)
Building Size: 40,000 sf (3,716 m²)
Date of Design: 2006
Completion date: To be stablished

To renovate and expand an early 20th-century warehouse block for mixed use development, the scheme entirely preserves the original buildings and places the new construction above it, clearly demarcating the old from the new. The new three-story structure takes advantage of the excess capacity of the large columns of the five-story existing building, making the construction extremely efficient and cost-effective.

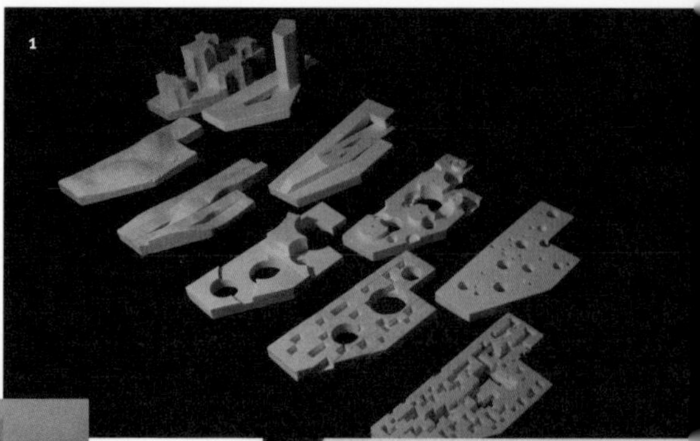
1

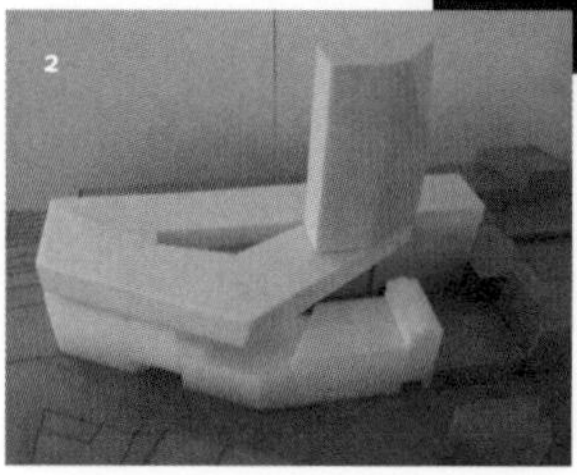
2

3

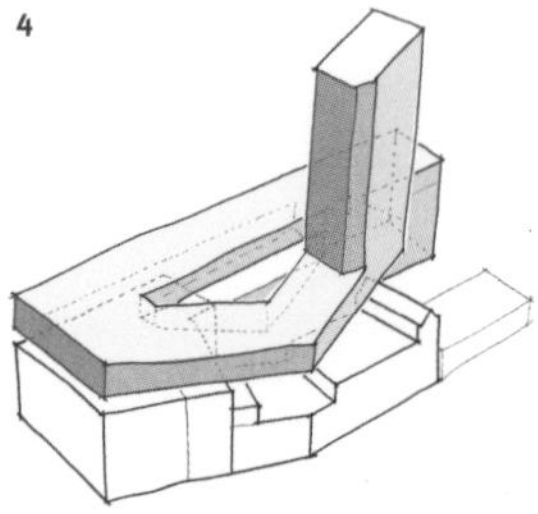
4

5

6

1 study models
2 snake scheme-model
3 street view
4 snake scheme-sketch
5 interior court
6 pancake scheme 1-model
7 tower scheme-sketch
8 study models
9 pancake scheme-sketch
10 entry and façade proposal
11 eroded slab-model
12 study models

7

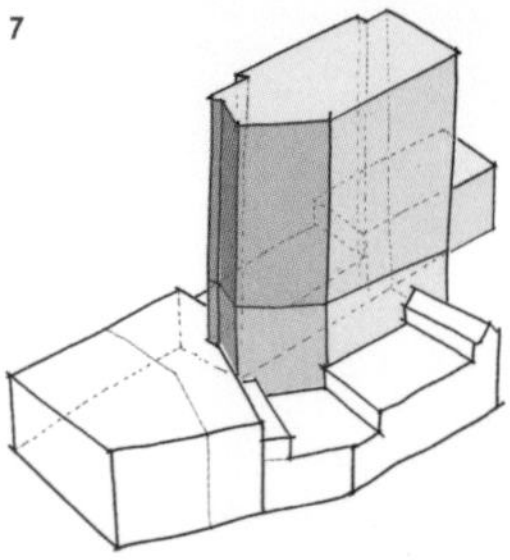

8

9

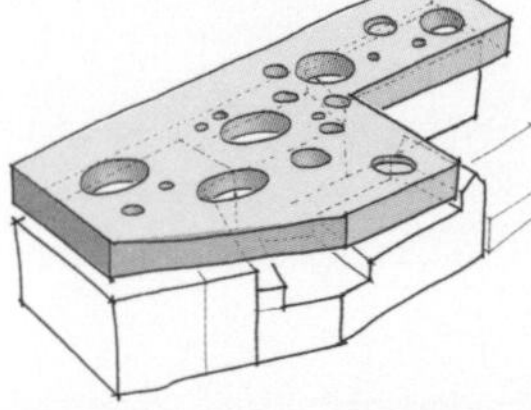

10

12

11

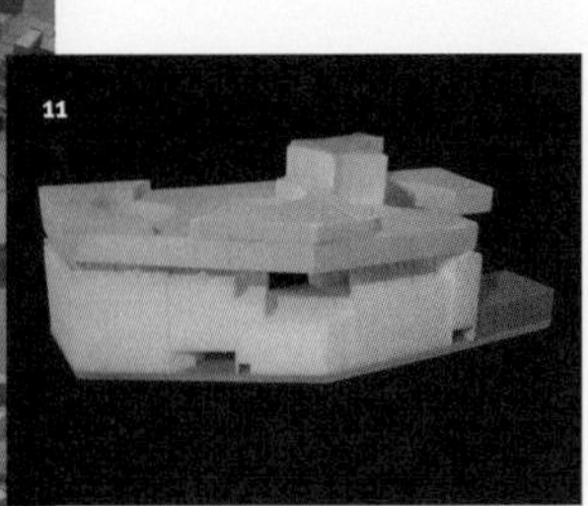

high tech offices

Aspen, Colorado

Project Team: Charlie Kaplan, James Macgillivray, Jill Reinecke, Noah Walker
Lot Size: 9,000 sf (836 m²)
Building Size: 7,000 sf (650 m²)
Date of Design: 2006
Completion Date: 2010

Combining a landmarked frame house and specimen tree on the town's main street with a glass-and-steel office building led to a seemingly disjunctive approach. The landmarks are preserved and enhanced in a park-like precinct, which is wrapped by the irregularly faceted glass skin of the new L-shaped building. The façade clearly declares the contemporaneity of the high-tech occupants within and also strengthens the presence of the old house and tree reflected and refracted in the glass.

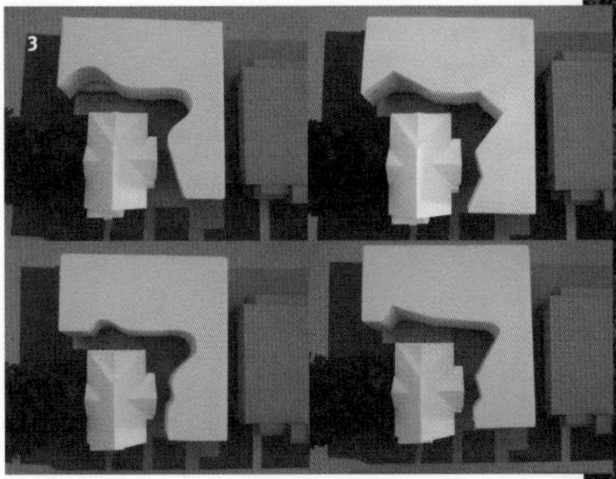

1 aerial collage of site context
2 model view, front elevation
3 massing study models
4 model view
5 model view
6 model view
7 ground level plan
8 second floor plan
9 model view

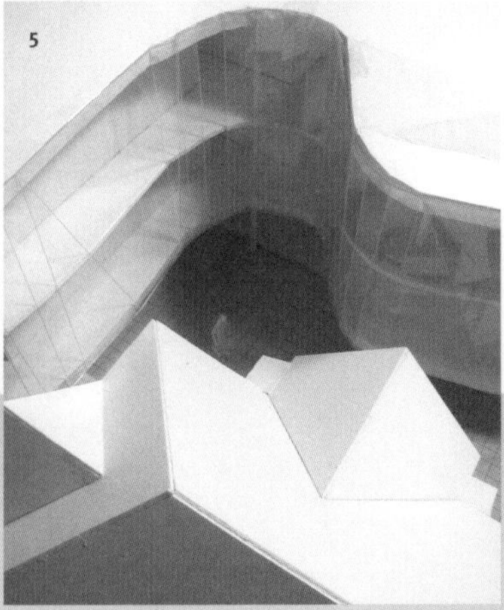
5

6

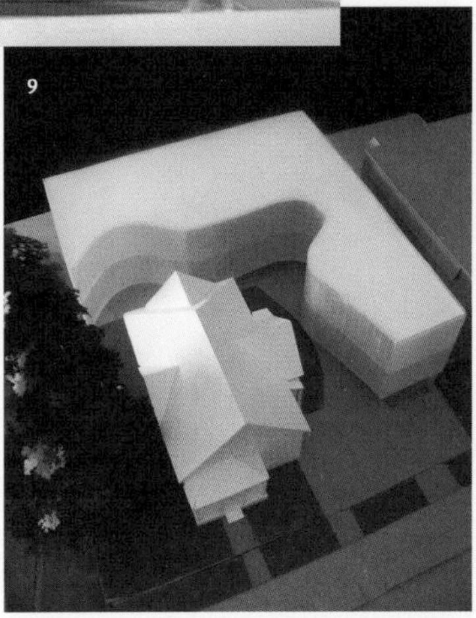
9

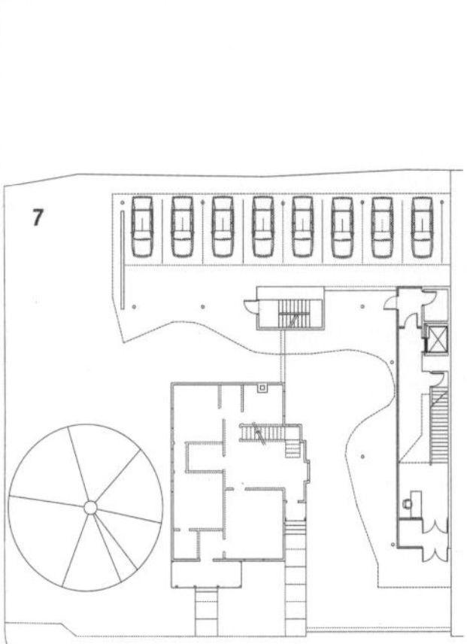
7

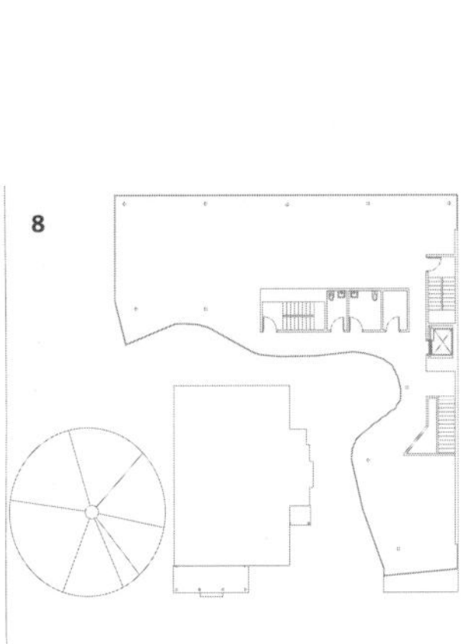
8

community center

Bronx, New York

Project Team:
Frederik Rissom, Elaine Sun
Lot Size: 39,000 sf (3,623 m²)
Building size: 45,000 sf (4,180 m²)
Date of Design: 2001

The Community Center is meant to be both a symbol of inner-city resilience and a magnet for the after-school activities central to the lives of inner-city kids. The 45,000-square-foot building, which serves 5,000 students, entirely fills the odd-shaped site, intentionally creating a strong sculptural presence that can hold its own against the 12-story towers of the massive neighboring housing complex. The pool-roof slopes gradually to the street level, providing a welcoming entrance to the Center and also acting as a roof playground. Industrial materials, warehouse-like construction, and a simple plan allow for spatial and functional complexity at extremely low cost.

1 schematic design option 1
2 site aerial view
3 building axonometric
4 street view
5 short section
6 schematic design option 2
7 rear yard view
8 long section
9 schematic design option 3
10 aerial view
11 gym and pool level
12 community level
13 partial entry plan
14 schematic design option
15 section through pool

1

2

3
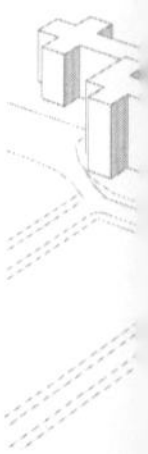

4

5
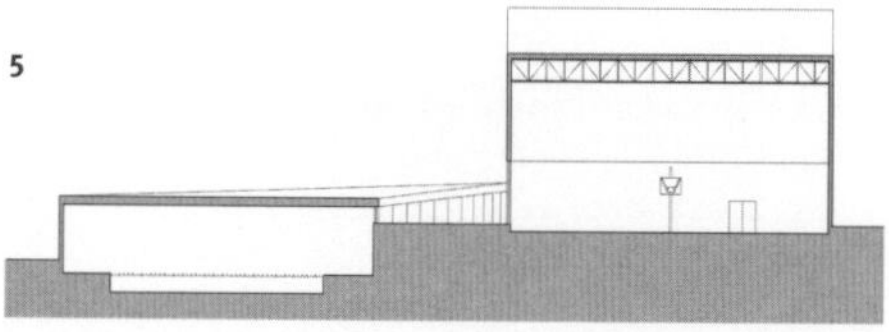

6
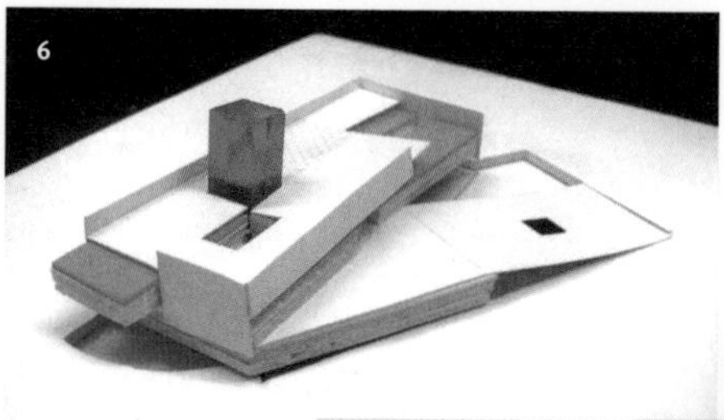

7

8

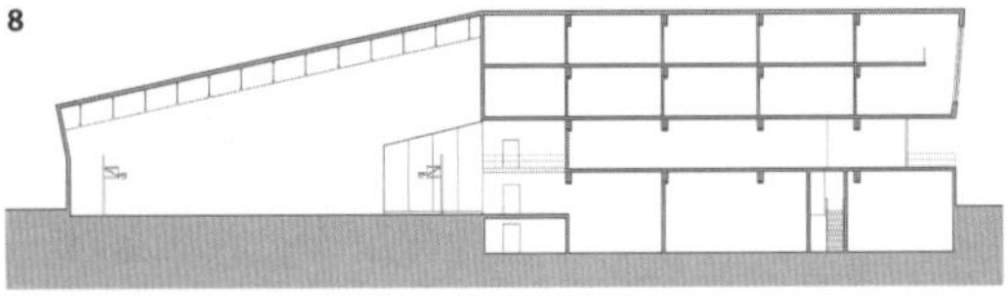

9

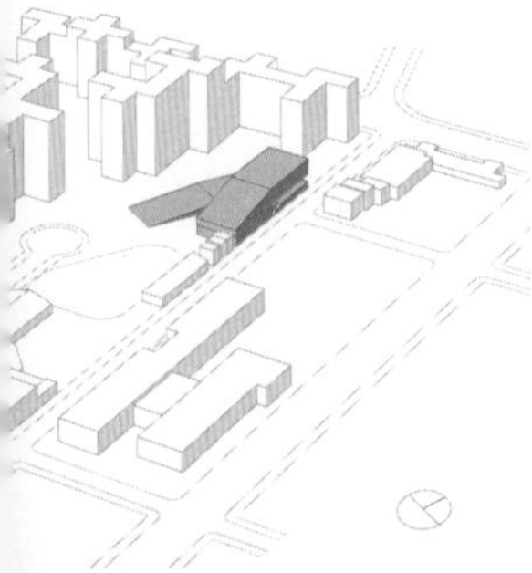

10

11

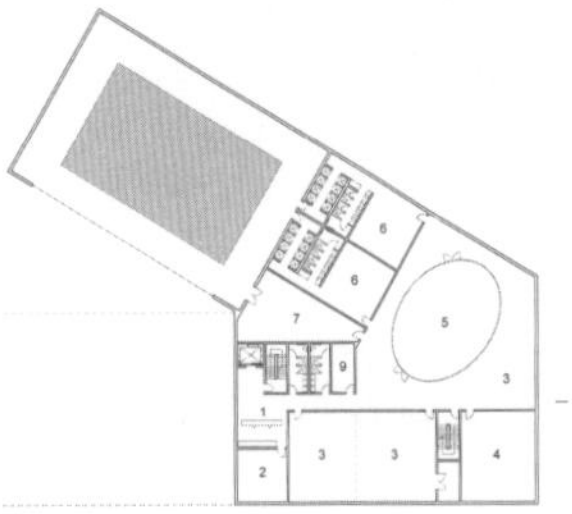

12

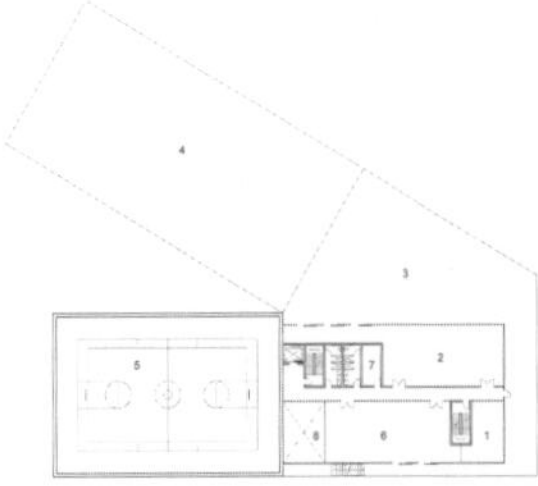

14

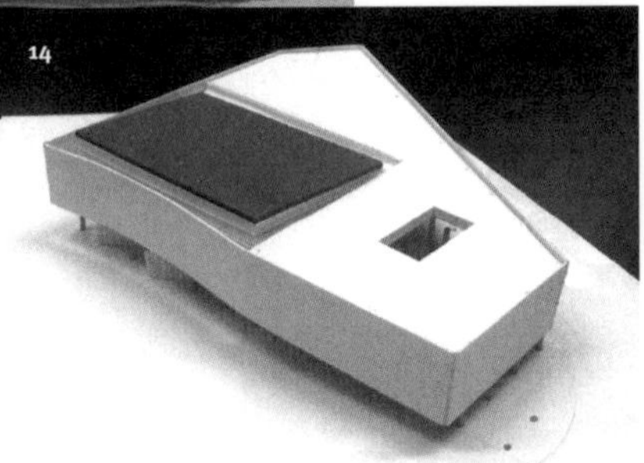

13

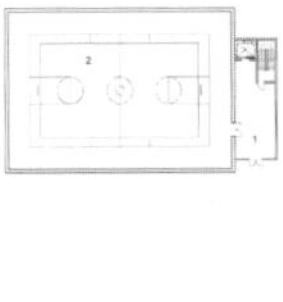

15

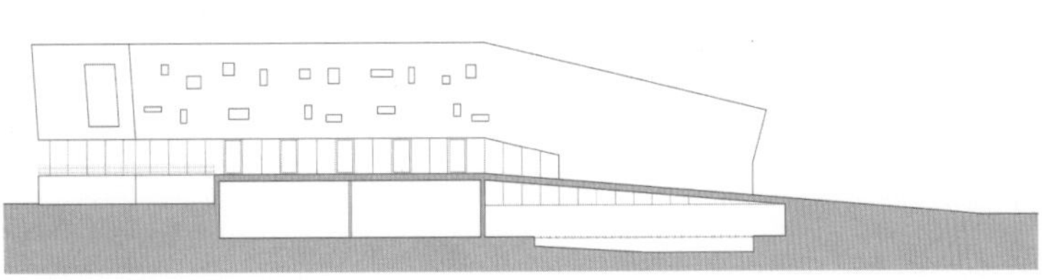

synagogue school

Westchester, New York

Project Team: Peter Guthrie, Peter McMahon, LJ Porter, Dan Silver
Lot Size: 2.6 acres (1 hectare)
Building renovation: 9,800 sf (910 m^2)
Addition: 6,200 sf (576 m^2)
Date of Design: 2000
Completion Date: 2002 first phase, 2010 second phase interiors

To add a new school to an existing synagogue set in a complex of ad hoc buildings in disrepair, we first rationalized the plan to separate the secular school from the sacred sanctuary. Then we preserved the 1960s wooden sanctuary and linked it to a new school building with its own distinctive identity. The horizontal bands of zinc on the façade give the school a strong presence but also play with the scale by disguising the height of the building.

1

2

3
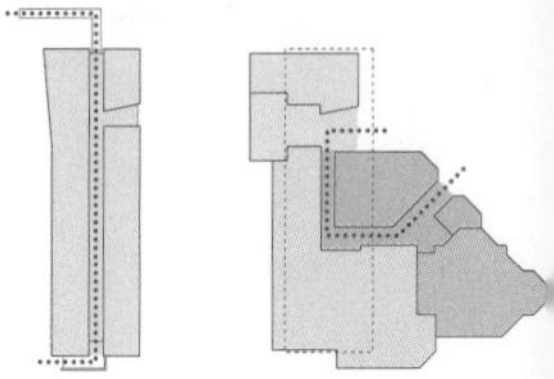

4

5

6

1 section
2 classrooms
3 circulation
4 entry
5 view west
6 bridge
7 entry
8 view east
9 site plan
10 foyer
11 axonometric

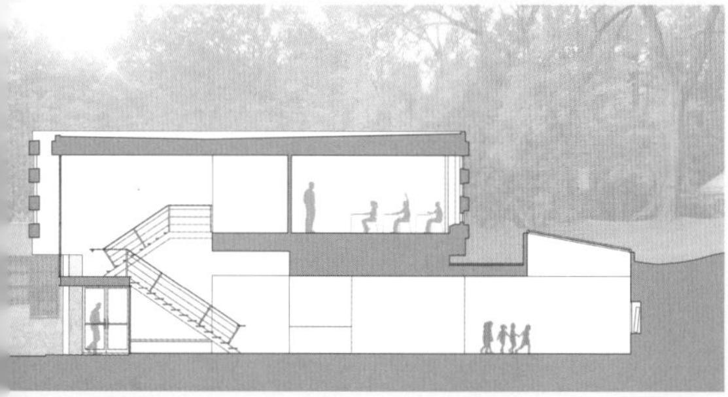

7

8

9

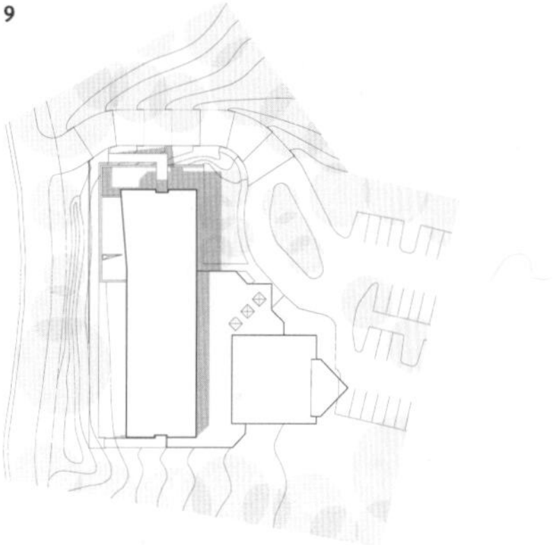

10

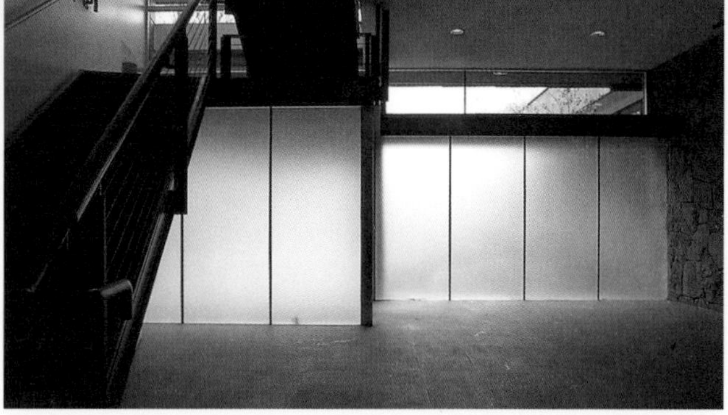

11

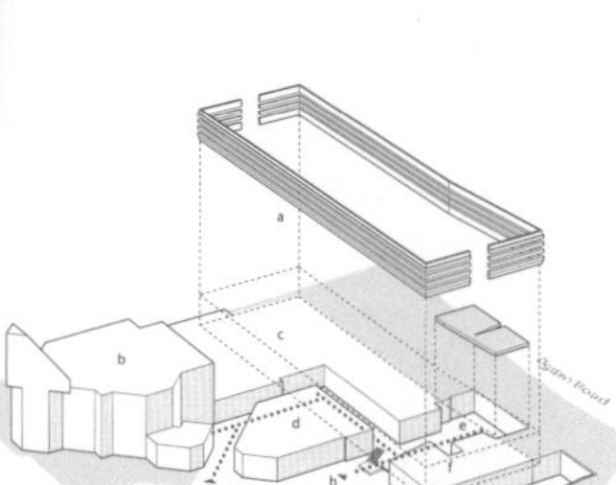

harlem school

East Harlem, New York

Project Team: Kees Brinkman, Kathy Chang, Marc Gee, Bethia Liu, Jill Reinecke, Elaine Sun, Stacie Wong
Lot Size: 10,000 sf (929 m^2)
Building Size: 27,000 sf (2508 m^2)
Date of Design: 2006
Completion expected 2008

The design of the new school reinforces the principles of this grass-roots, community-based organization. Offices and classrooms are integrated to allow for open interaction, with natural light throughout. Light screen panels enliven the front of the building, both screening and also revealing the uses within. The individual panels relate to the spaces within the building, while the pixilated façade as a whole marks a vivid presence in the community.

1

2

2

2

3

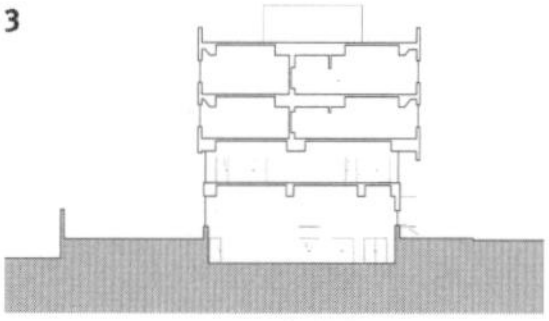

4

5

1 façade study
2 circulation study models
3 section
4 building under construction
5 rear terrace view
6 section
7 façade study models
8 street front view
9 plans
10 massing study with terraced volumes
11 section

6

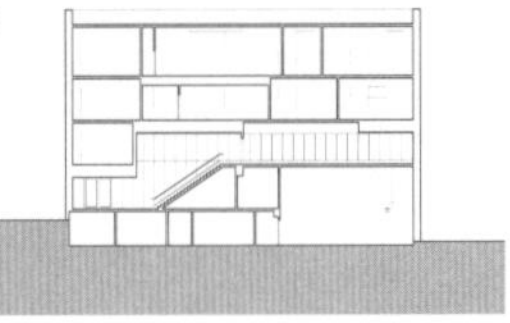

7

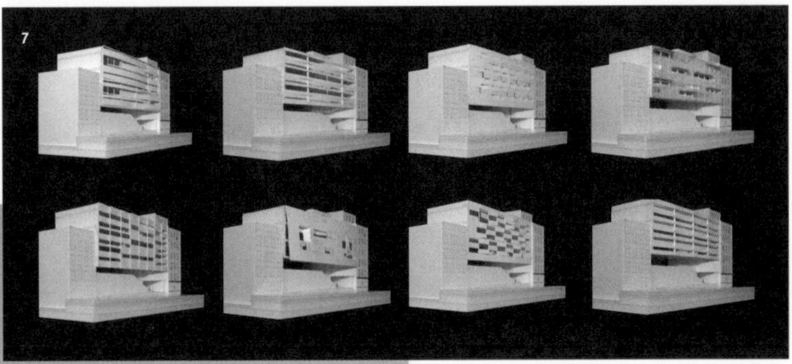

9

10

11

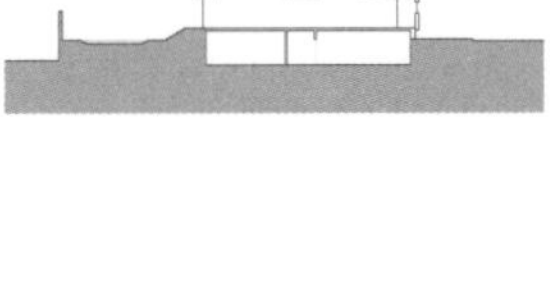

house in historic district

Evanston, Illinois

Project Team: Chaitanya Karnik, Jason Kreuzer, David Mabbott
Lot Size: 16,275 sf (1,512 m^2)
Building Size: 9,000 sf (836 m^2)
Date of Design: 2007
Completion expected 2009

The strict zoning requirements and historic district guidelines in this suburban town weighed as heavily in the design as the program and the site. As a gesture to the town, the street façade was kept narrow and a corner of the lot was left unbuilt to visually link the park on one street to the public beach in front. The L-shaped plan provides stunning lake views through floor-to-ceiling glass on the sides away from the street. Since glass was an issue in the historic guidelines, movable wood louvers modulate the window walls, adding complexity to the façade and also shielding it from strong eastern sunlight.

1 site plan
2 view from lake
3 model
4 elevation north
5 view from park
6 sectional models
7 elevation south
8 model
9 model
10 elevation east
11 view from third floor
12 view from entry
13 sectional models
14 view from street
15 first floor plan
16 second floor plan
17 third floor plan
18 view from third floor
19 view from park
20 view from second floor
21 section
22 view from second floor

1

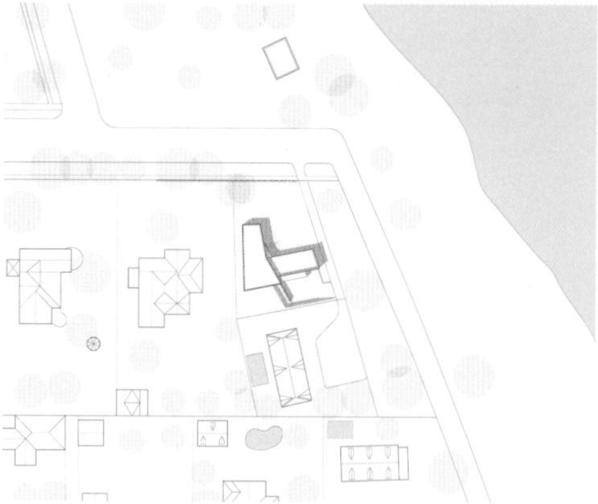

2

3

4

5

6

7

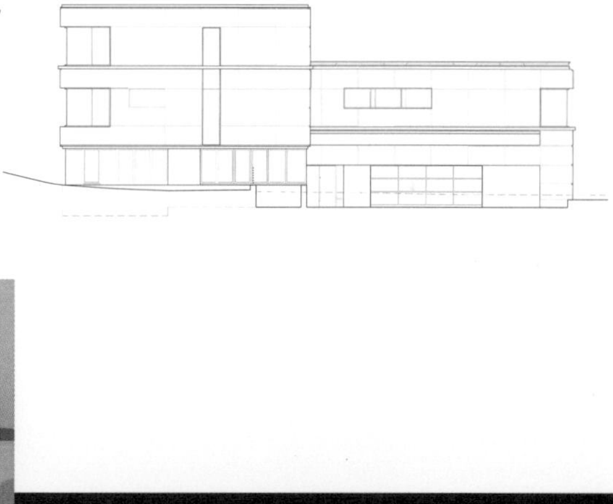

8

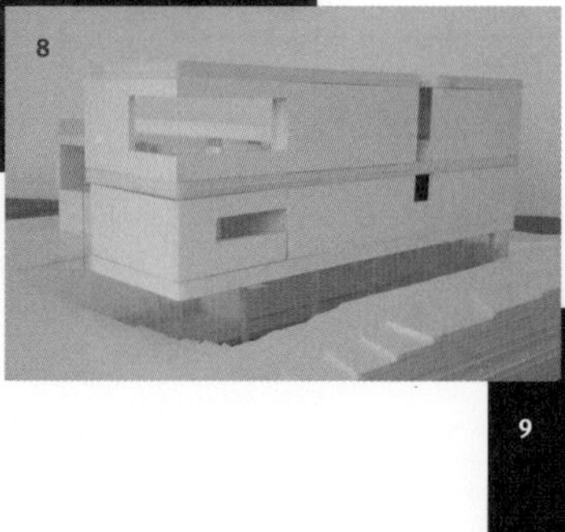

9

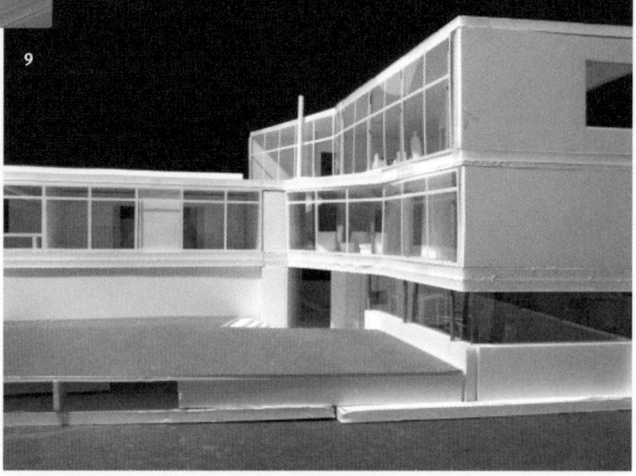

10

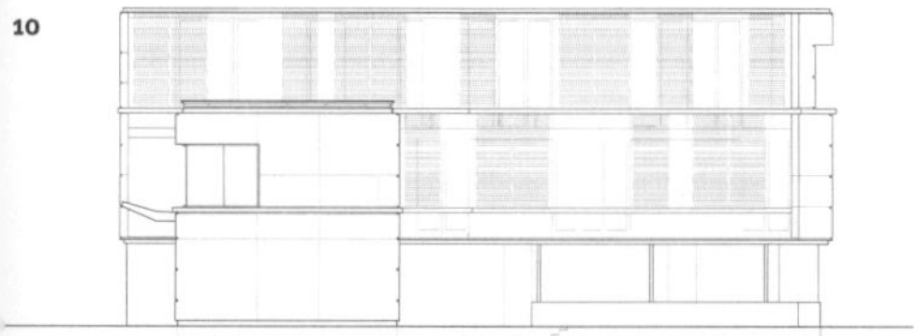

12

11

13

15

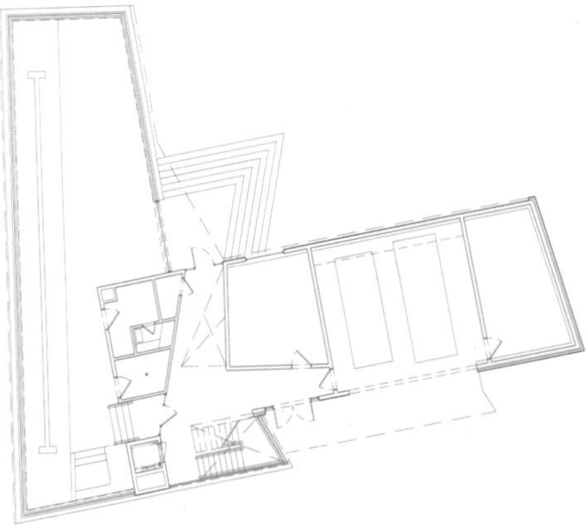

16

19

18

17

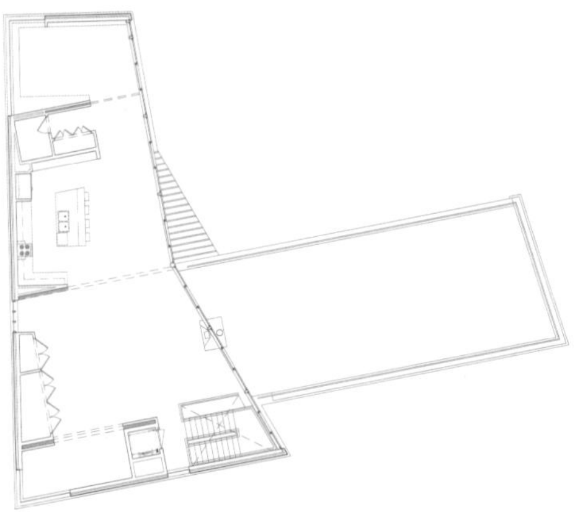

21

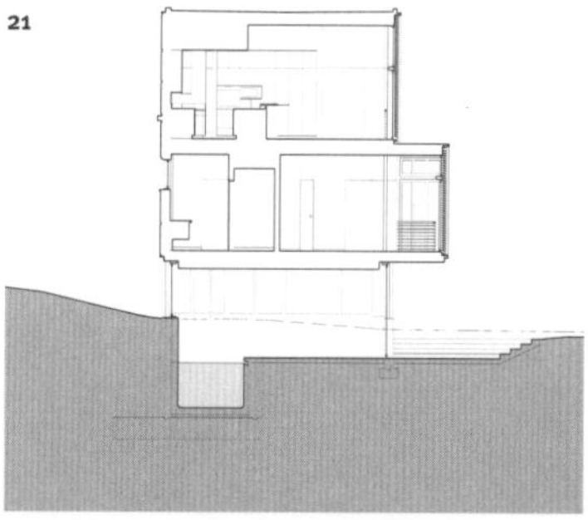

20

22

glass veil house

Chicago, Illinois

Project Team: Jennifer Bloom, Eun Buettner, Marc Gee, Cindy Lordan, LJ Porter, Hiroaki Takimoto
Lot Size: 15,700 sf (1,459 m²)
Building Size: 23,000 sf (2,137 m²)
Date of Design: 2002

The owners of this house imagined a landscaped "oasis" within the urban fabric of Chicago's Near North Side. The street façade is covered with a veil of translucent glass, which is folded into a series of undulating planes proportional to – and continuous with – the façades of the neighboring buildings. By day, the veil reflects trees, sky, and the buildings across the street; by night, it reveals the shadows of activity within the house, adding vitality to the passing street scene. The street façade respects and enhances the urban dynamic while the interior garden provides an oasis of green and privacy within the heart of the city.

1 model
2 elevation
3 view south
4 street to garden filtering
5 section
6 veil sketches
7 view north
8 plan/section sketch
9 location plan and site
10 garden terrace
11 garden terrace
12 night view
13 window panel studies
14 section/perspective
15 garden façade
16 master floor
17 living/garden floor
18 ground floor
19 pool study

1

2

3

4

5

6

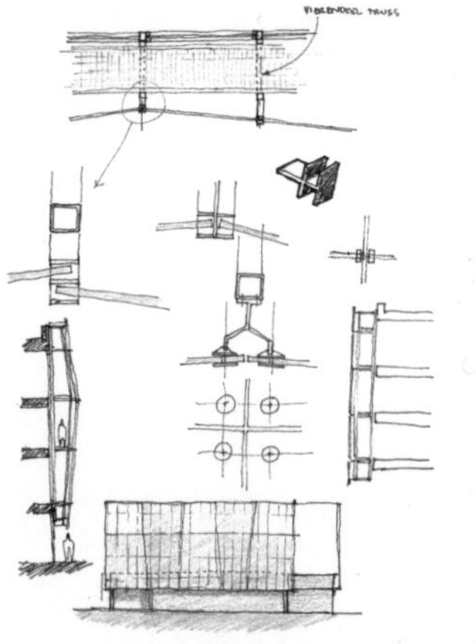

9

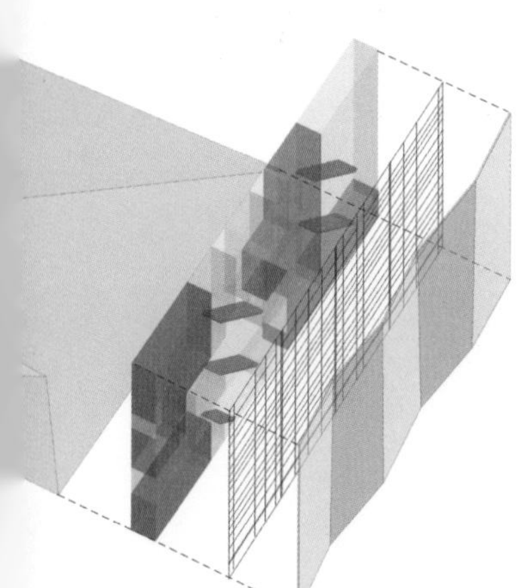

8

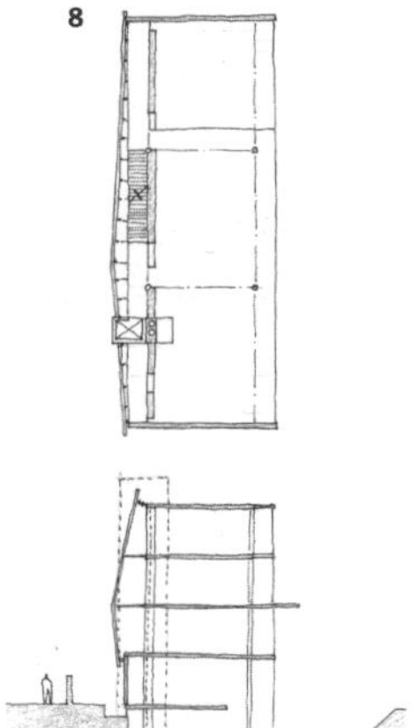

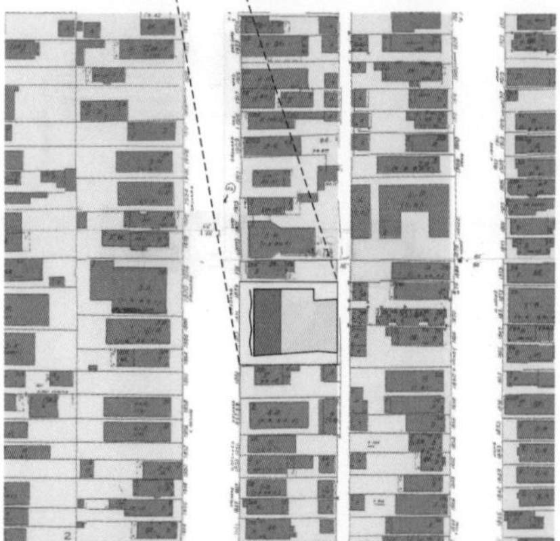

10

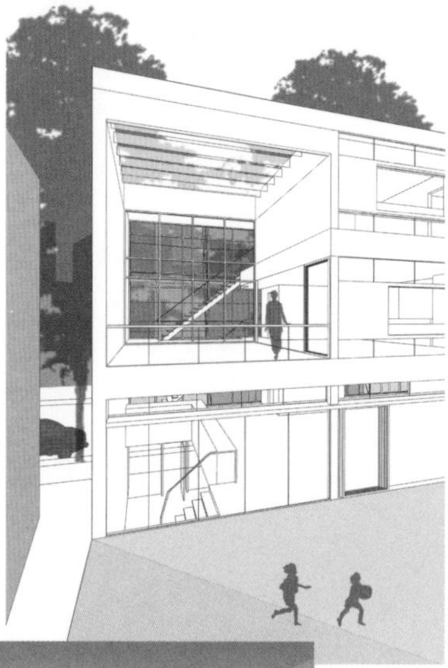

11

12

13

14

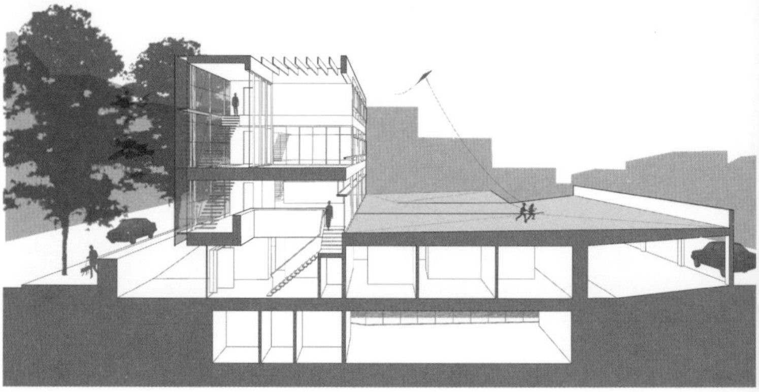

15

16
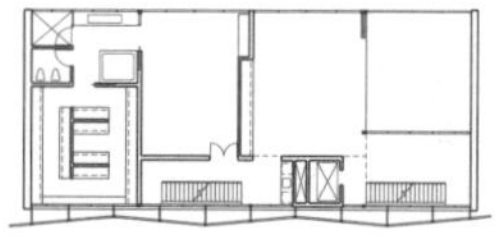

17
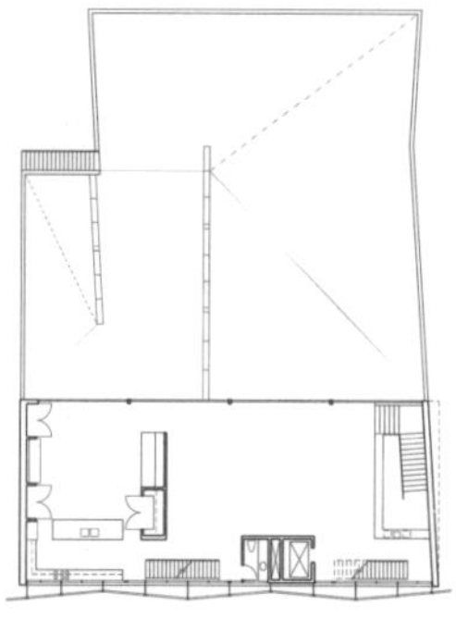

18
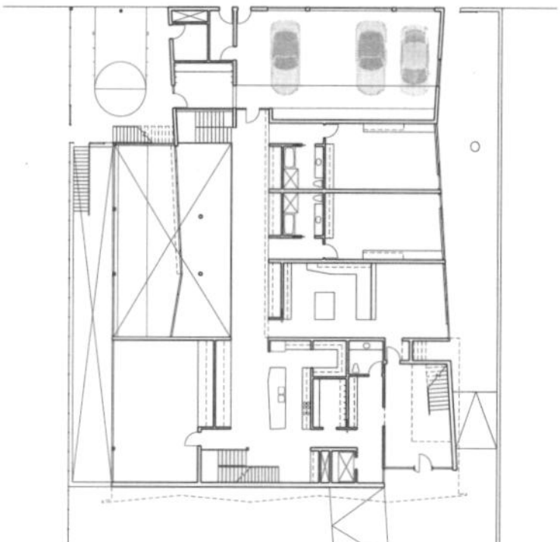

19

house on the bluff

Winnetka, Illinois

Project Team: Shannon Bambenek, Kees Brinkman, Steven Chen, Clay Collier, Cynthia Lordan, Joe Phillip, Christoph Plattner, LJ Porter, Jorge Prado, Leia Price, Jim True, Shuo Wang, Andrea Zaff
Lot Size: 1.6 acres (6,475 m²)
Building Size: 25,700 sf (2,388 m²)
Date of Design: 2004
Completion expected 2008

1

2

3

From the street and from inside, this house appears rather simple and unimposing, but in fact it is a very large house with an extremely complex program. Following the strategy of some of our earlier work, we cut significant parts of the house into the hillside, none of which are visible from the street. From the lake side, the buried spaces appear as irregular horizontal tears in the side of the hill. To take advantage of a spectacular site on a steep bluff, the house consists of a series of experiential spaces, set off from one another in both plan and section, which afford dramatic and ever-changing views of the lake.

4

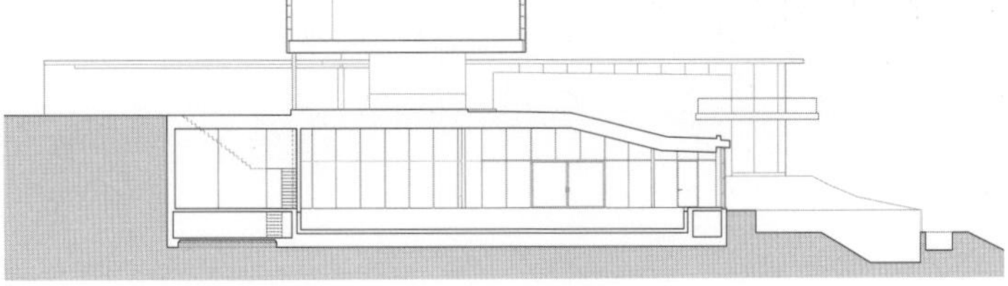

5

1 lakeside view
2 entry view
3 view east
4 section
5 construction
6 lakeside view study
7 foundation
8 model study
9 view north
10 night view
11 living room
12 section looking north
13 section through pool
14 section through basketball court
15 pool wall construction
16 spa/pool
17 spa/gym/service
18 entry view of floating upper floor
19 bedroom
20 third floor hall
21 corner detail of mock up
22 first floor plan
23 second floor plan
24 third floor plan

6

7

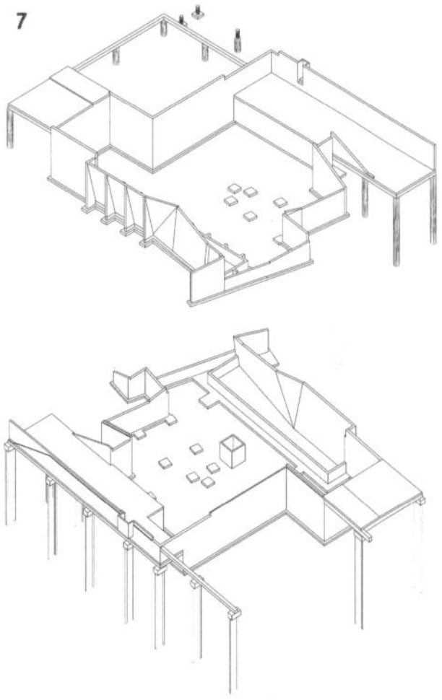

8

9

10

11

12

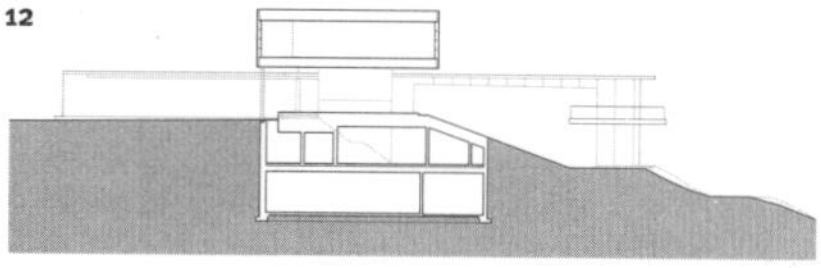

13

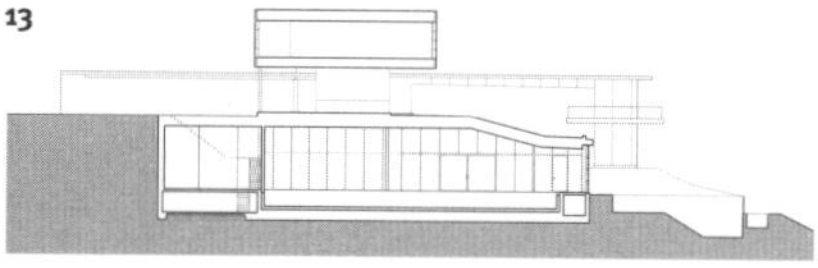

14

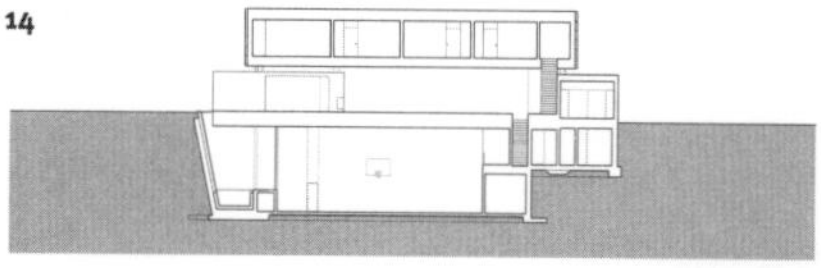

15

16

17

18

19

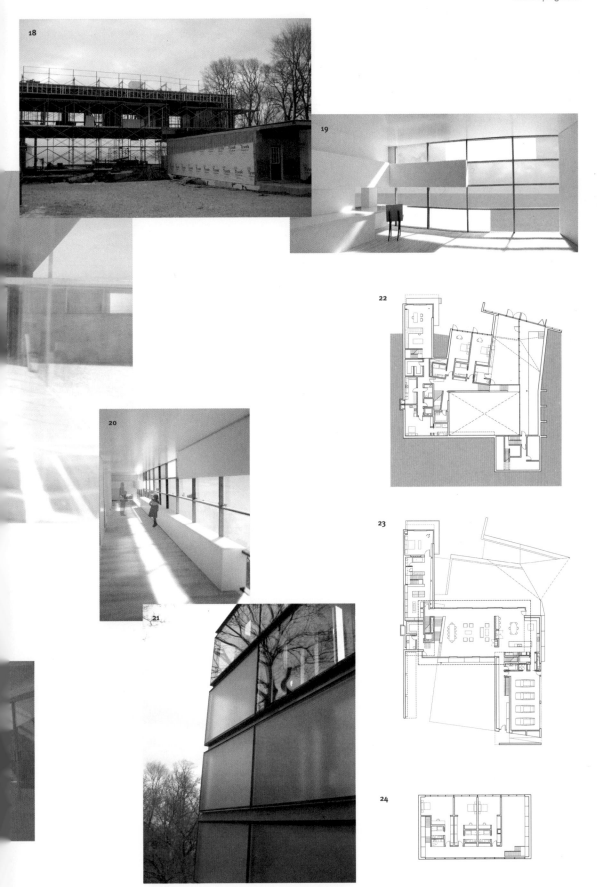

20

21

22

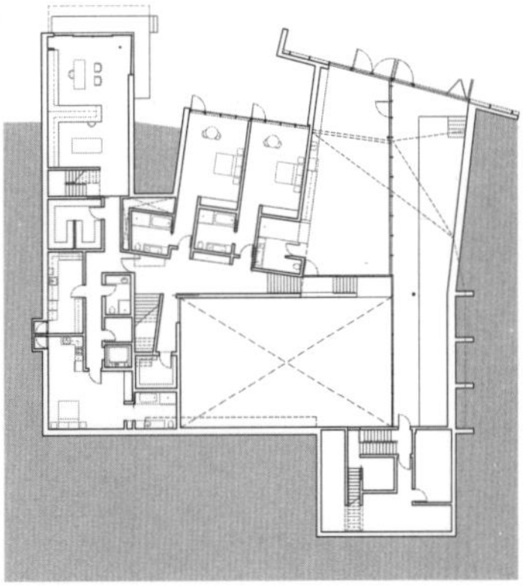

23

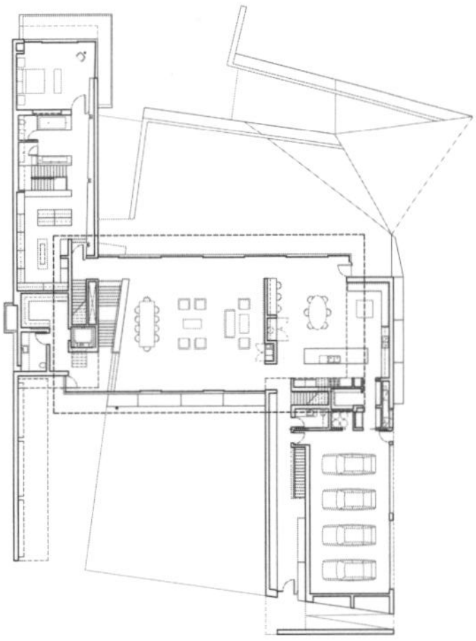

24

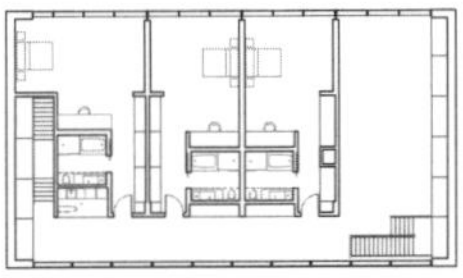

lakeside retreat

Lake George, New York

Project Team: Kees Brinkman, Holly Chacon, Kathy Chang, Steven Chen, Christopher Farnum, Bethia Liu, Adam Manrique, Jorge Prado, Eric Schaefer, Jenny Wu
Lot Size: 924,778 sf (85,914 m2)
Project Size: 39,090 sf (3,631 m2)
Completion expected 2009

A large program is distributed among a series of small buildings set into the sloping landscape, providing a play of levels and terraces that diminishes the built presence and enhances the experience of the lakeside site. Every interior level opens to the ground plane making nature central while the sod-covered roofs and wood-screened glass make the buildings ecologically green as well.

1 compound view from lake
2 site plan
3 model from above
4 aerial model view
5 construction
6 construction
7 pavilion first floor plan
8 pavilion second floor plan
9 main house second floor plan
10 model view from lake
11 façade studies
12 main house section
13 pavilion interior courtyard
14 boat house from lake
15 boat house detail
16 concept sketch
17 roof views
18 house and lake view
19 house view from north
20 boat house view from house

1

2

3

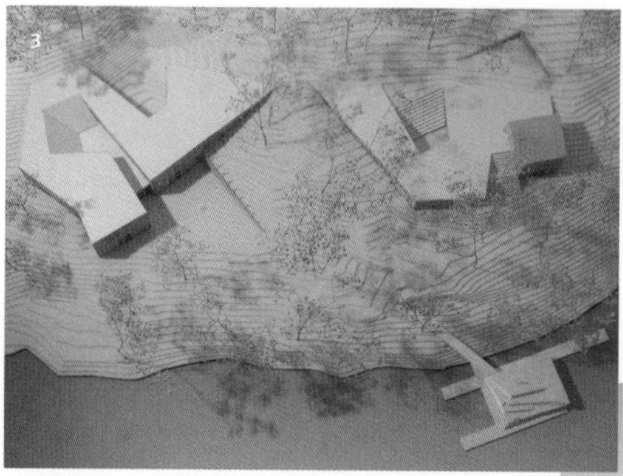

4

5

6

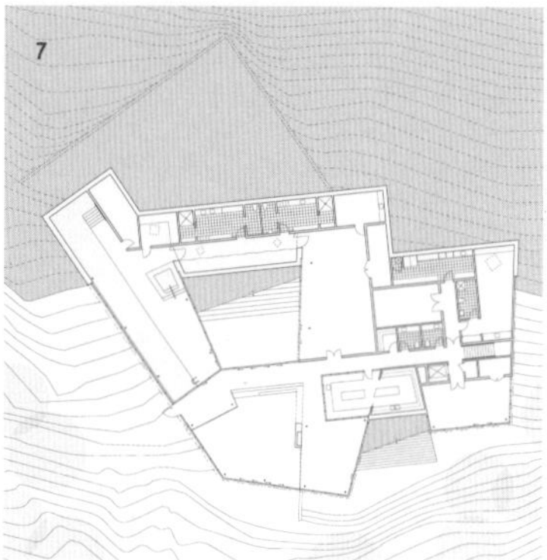

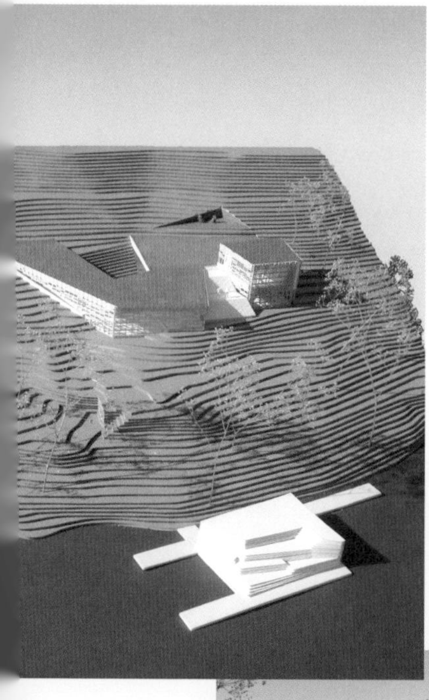

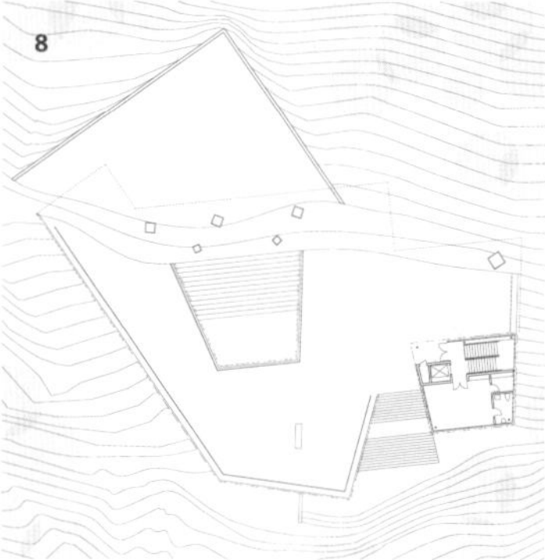

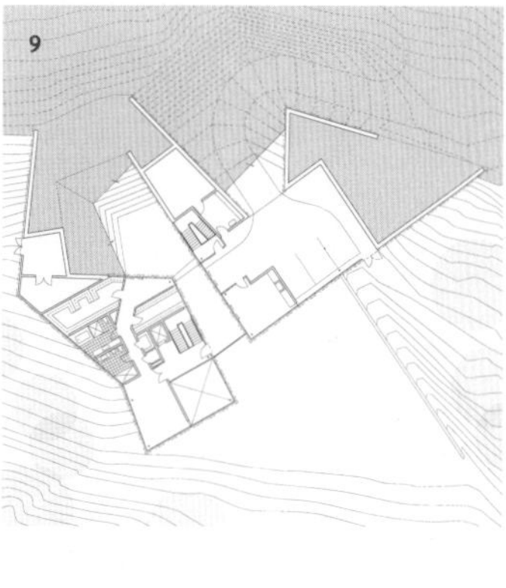

11

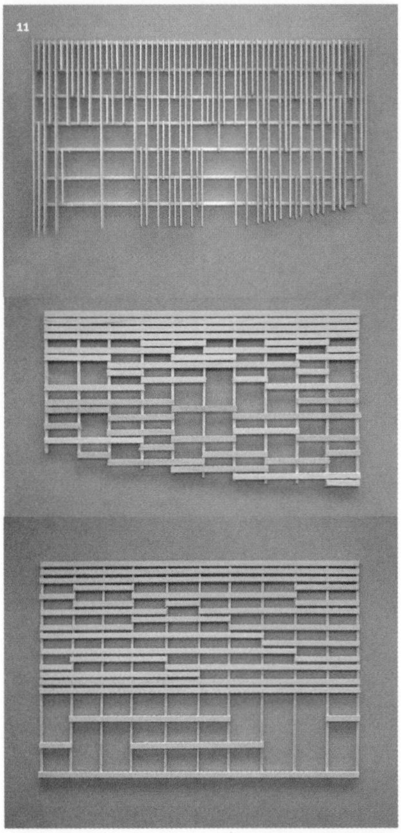

12

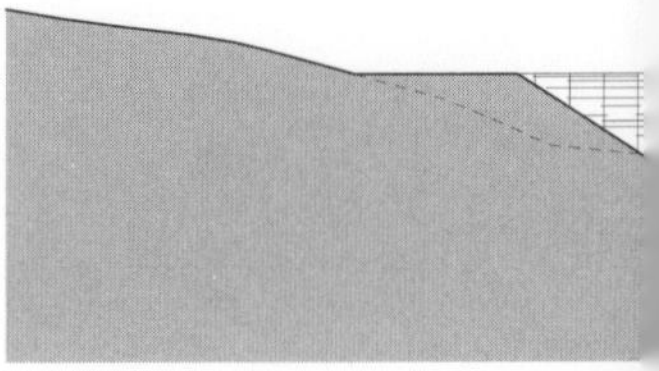

13

14

15

16

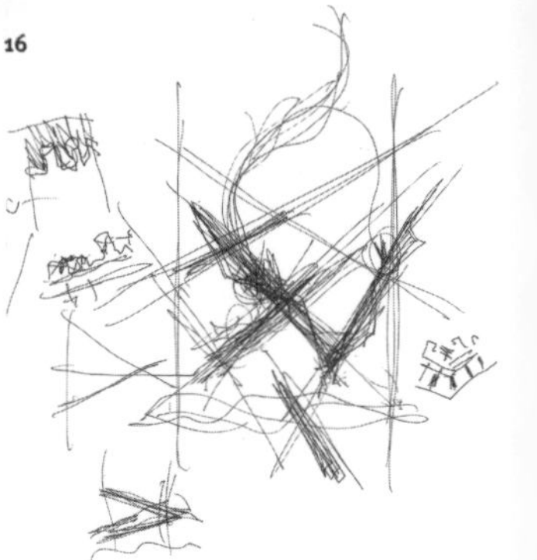

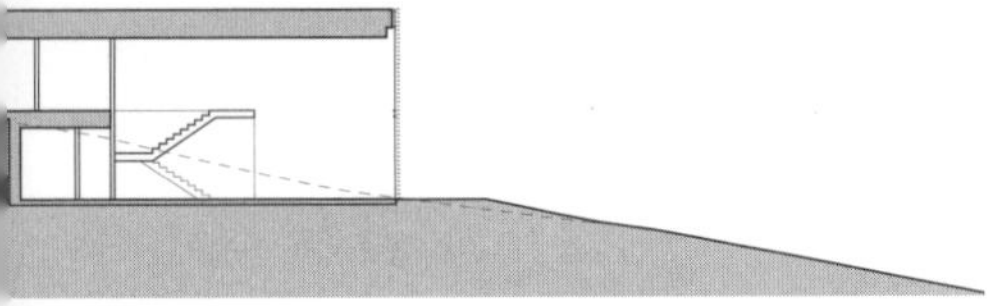

18

19

20

pool pavilion

Lake George, New York

Project Team: Jennifer Bloom, Eun Buettner, Maria Elena Fanna, Charlie Kaplan, Michael Moffitt, Doug Weibel
Lot Size: 8.3 acres (3.4 hectares)
Building Size: 5,260 sf (489 m^2)
Date of Design: 2006
Completion expected 2008

This lap pool, gym, and small office structure is conceived of as a rift in the landscape along the shore of the lake: less of a building than an earth form. The indoor pool has a sod-covered roof that creates a lawn and playing field above. The glass on one long side of the pool faces the lake, and on the other, a protected sunken courtyard. The experience of the pool and its adjoining spaces is as much about being in the landscape as it is about viewing it.

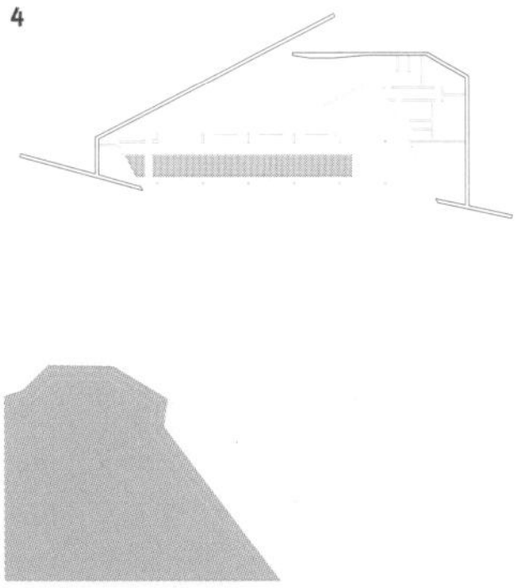

1 view from southeast
2 view from east
3 aerial view from southwest
4 ground floor plan
5 model view from east
6 transverse building section
7 model view from south end
8 pool pavilion from north east
9 construction
10 pool pavilion from east
11 model view from northeast
12 view from south end of pool
13 second floor and roof plan

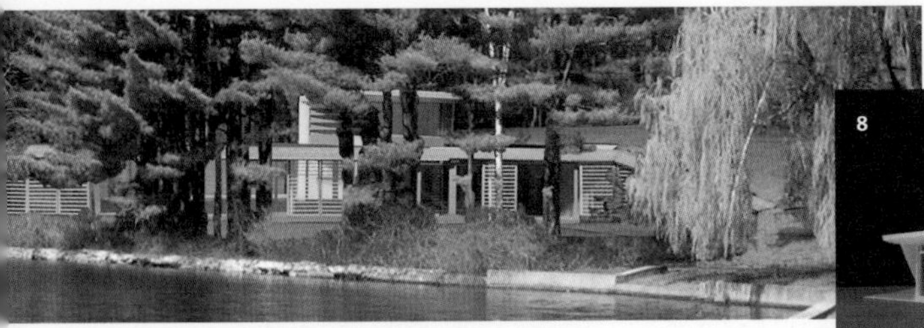

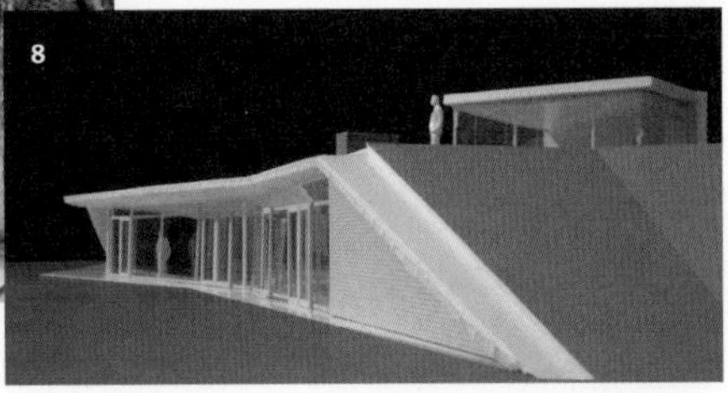

8

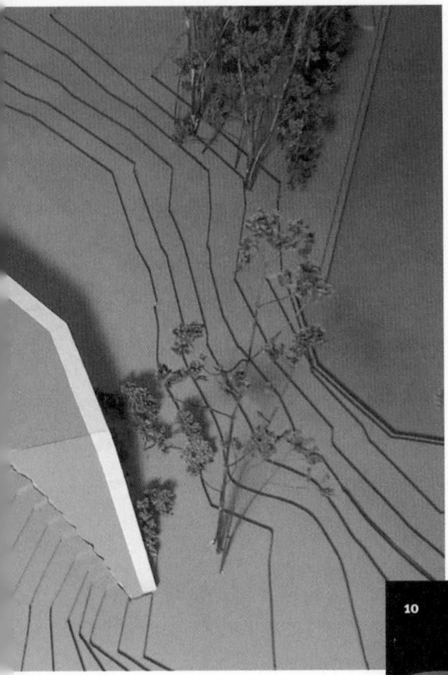

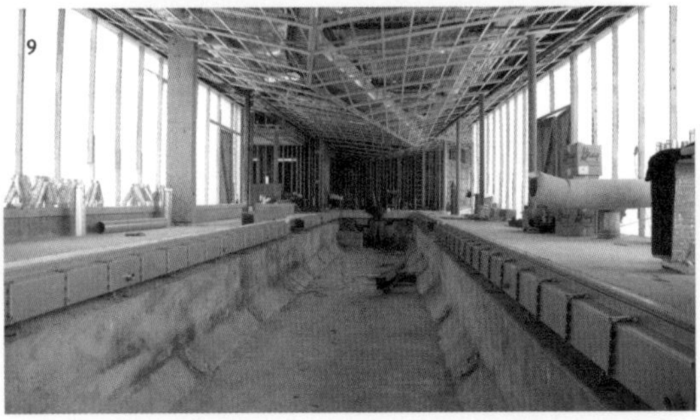

9

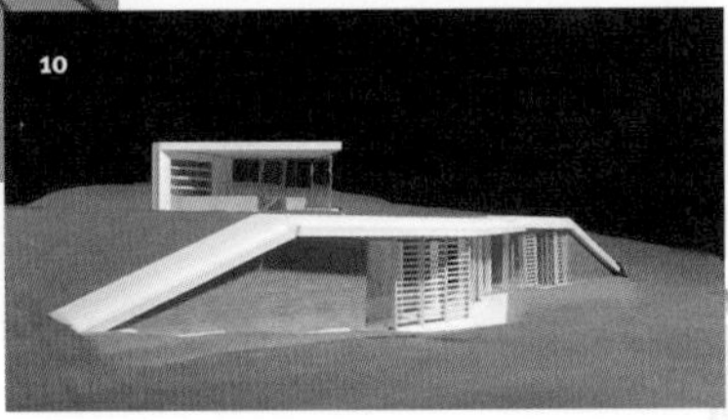

10

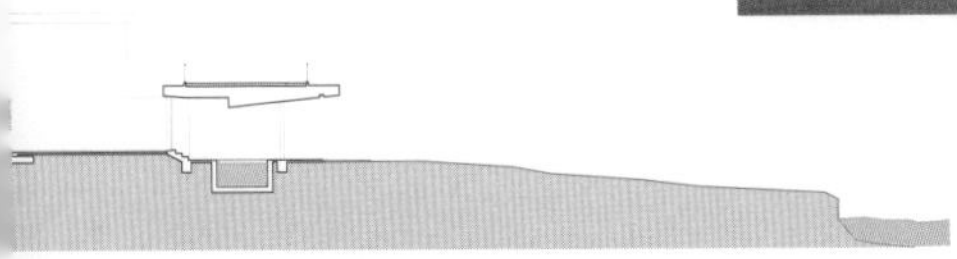

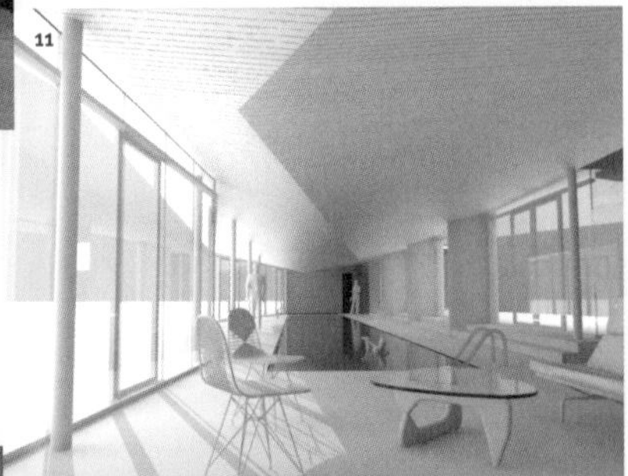

11

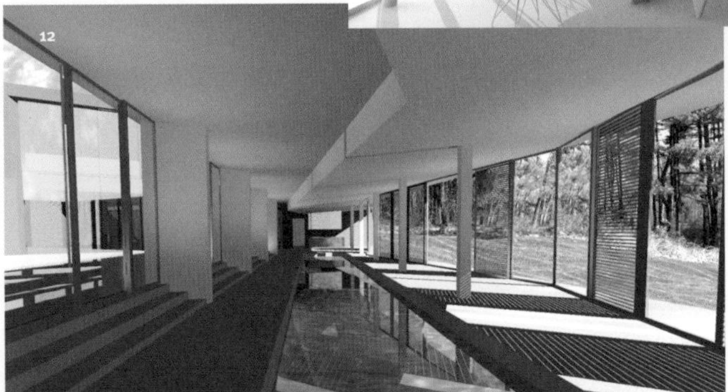

12

13

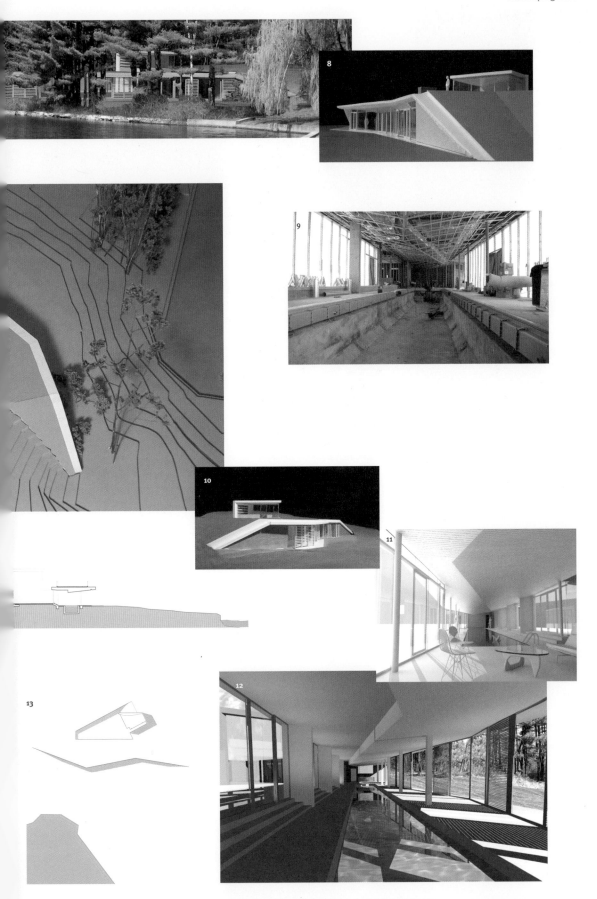

tower house

Ulster County, New York

Project Team:
Tom Gluck, David Hecht
Lot Size: 16 acres (6.5 hectares)
Building Size: 2,000 sf (186 m^2)
Date of Design: 2005
Completion expected 2008

This small vacation house is designed as a stairway to the treetops. Keeping the footprint to a minimum so as not to disturb the wooded site, each of the first three floors has only one small bedroom and bath, with complete privacy. The fourth floor, which contains the living spaces, spreads out from the tower like the surrounding forest canopy, providing views of the lake and mountains in the distance. The glass-enclosed stair highlights the procession from forest floor to treetop aerie, while the dark green enameled exterior camouflages the house by reflecting the surrounding woods, reinforcing the experience of nature that is the centerpiece of the design.

1 view from parking
2 construction sequence
3 view towards entry
4 view towards front
5 living room interior
6 longitudinal section
7 floor plans
8 living room exterior
9 study model
10 cross section
11 view from parking
12 living room
13 view towards entry

1

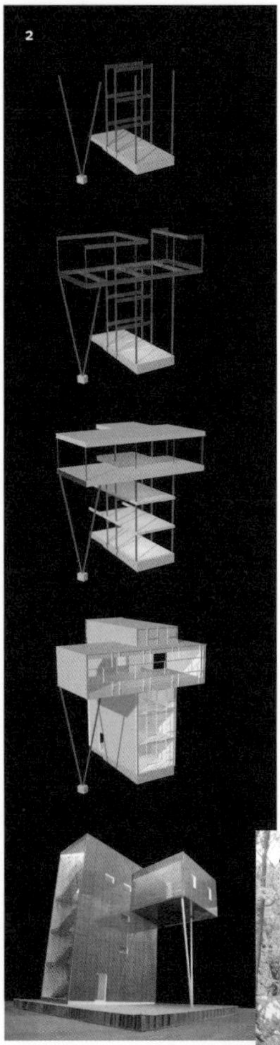

2

3

4

5

6

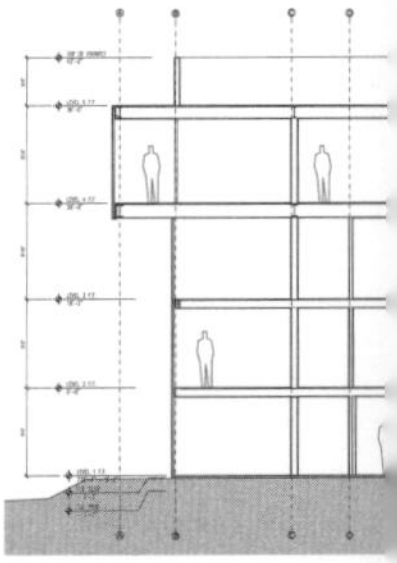

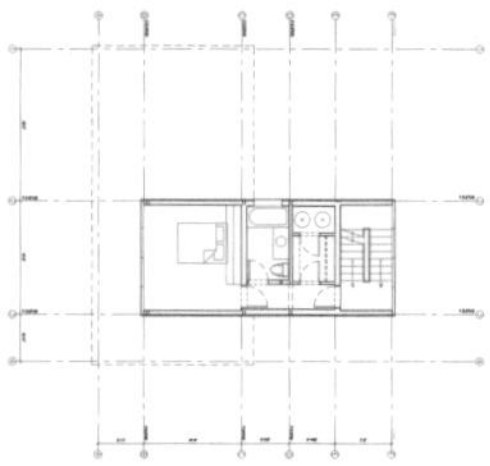

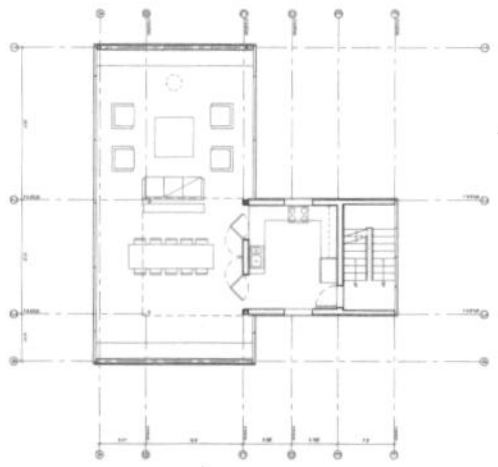

8

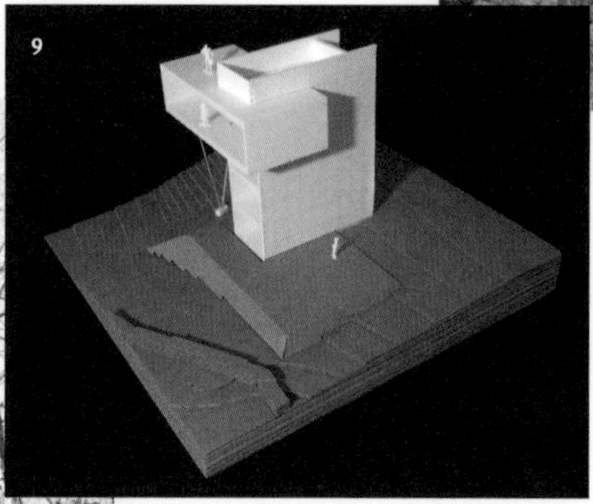

9

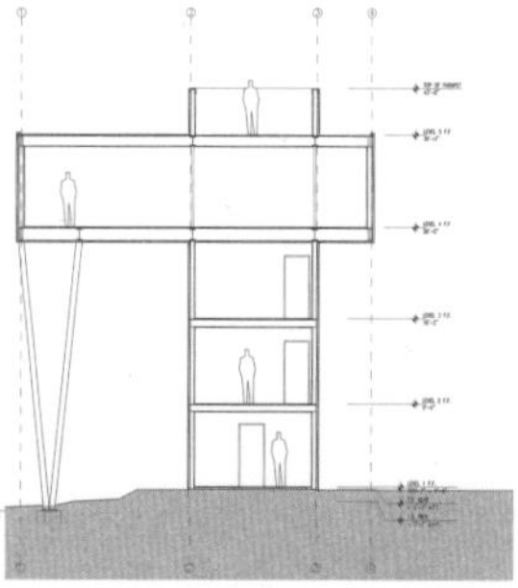

10

11

12

13

urban condo

New York, New York

Project Team: Rafael Herrin-Ferri, David Mabbott, Sam Sassa
Lot Size: 2,000 sf (186 m²)
Building Size: 12,000 sf (1,115 m²)
Date of Design: 2005
Completion expected 2008

Converting a narrow masonry warehouse into condominiums, we removed the original façade with its small, cramped windows and replaced it with an asymmetrically glazed glass wall. The building now has two readings from the street: one of the entire structure with a continuous vertical window wall, which is scaled to the cityscape, and the other, a stacked series of individual condo units appropriate in scale to the residences within.

1 façade model studies
2 exterior rendering
3 interior model view
4 façade view
5 typical apartment plan
6 interior model views
7 building view
8 façade figure/ground studies
9 entry studies

1

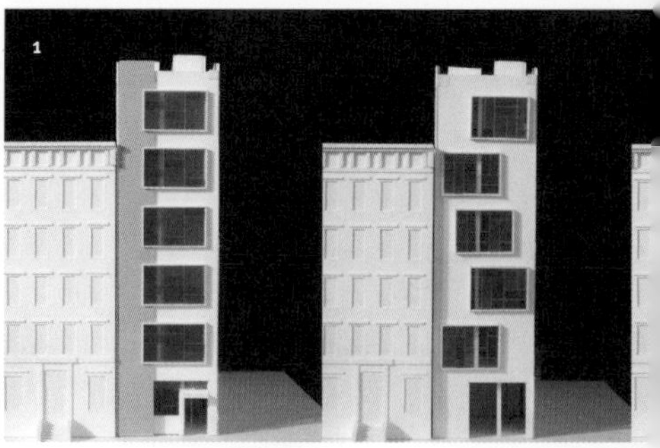

2

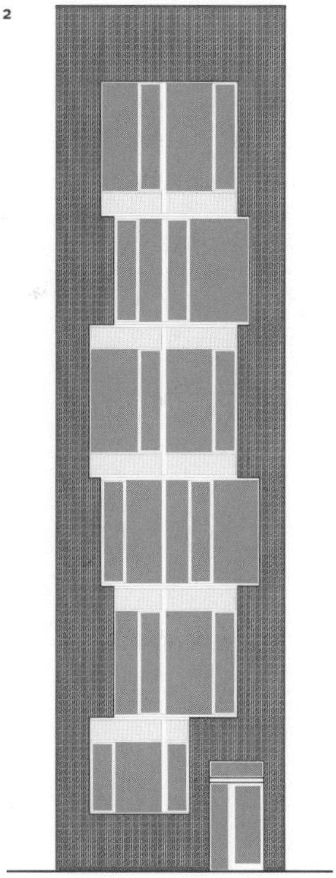

3

4

5

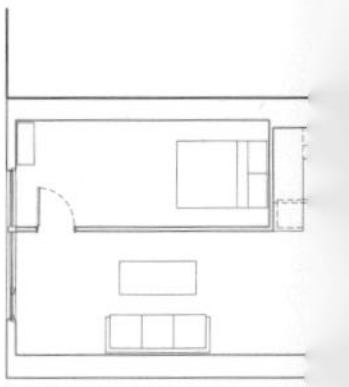

6

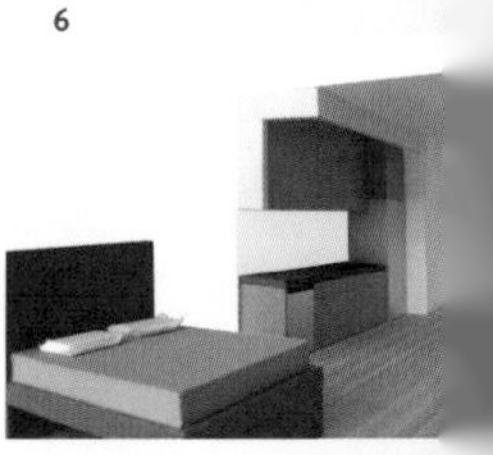

7

8

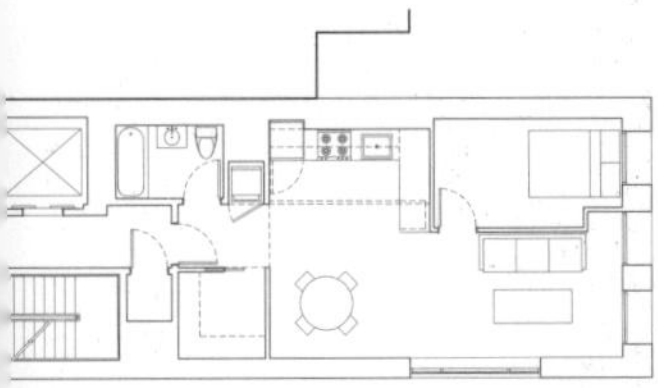

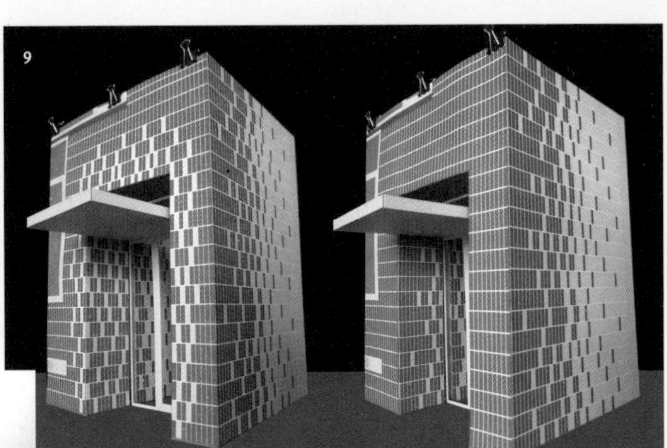

9

urban tower

New York, New York

Project Team: Guido Furlanello,
Tom Gluck, Chaitanaya Karnik,
Jorge Prado
Lot Size: 44,000 sf (4,088 m^2)
Building Size: 500,000 sf (46,452 m^2)
Date of Design: 2005
Completion date TBD

Because every inch counts in Manhattan development, planning the 16-story building for the most efficient use of space was like solving a puzzle whose pieces ranged from fulfilling zoning regulations to maximizing sculptural effect. In an otherwise low-rise area, we consciously created a dialogue in massing and façade with a similarly tall condo across the street to take into account the visibility of the two buildings from many downtown vantage points.

1

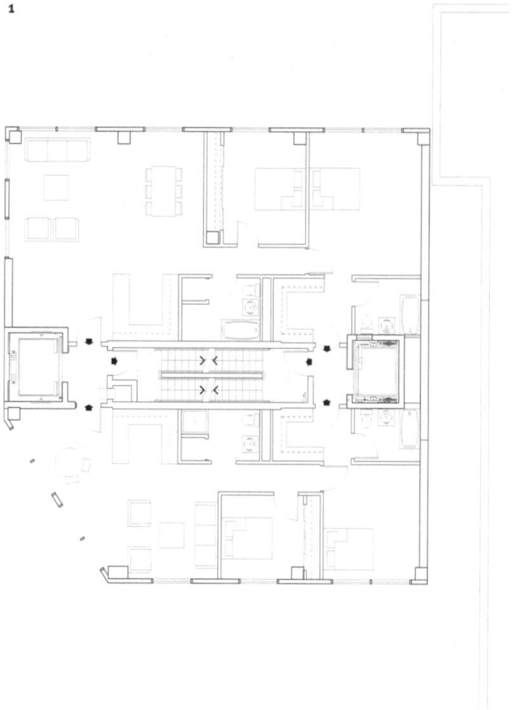

4

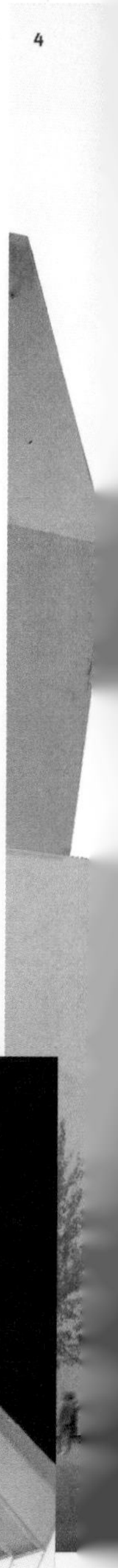

2

3

1 typical unit plan
2 massing model northwest view
3 massing model aerial view
4 renderings
5 study models
6 study model
7 penthouse plan
8 study models

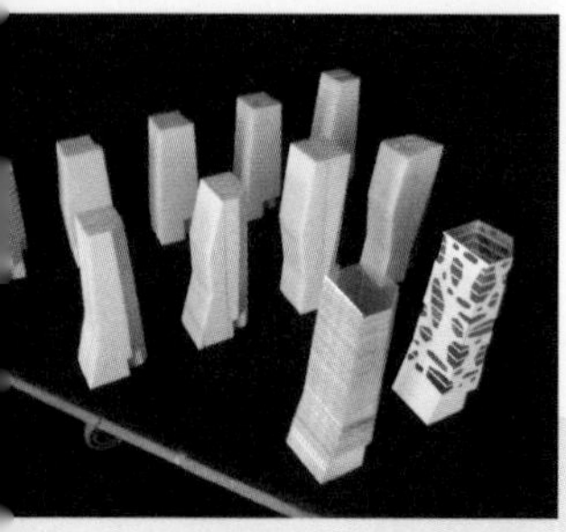

6

7

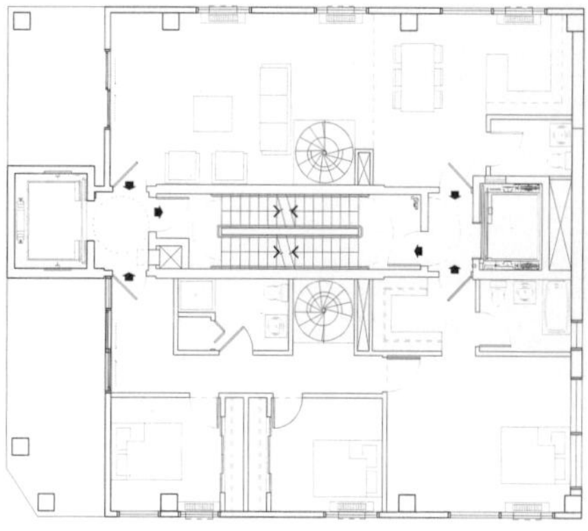

8

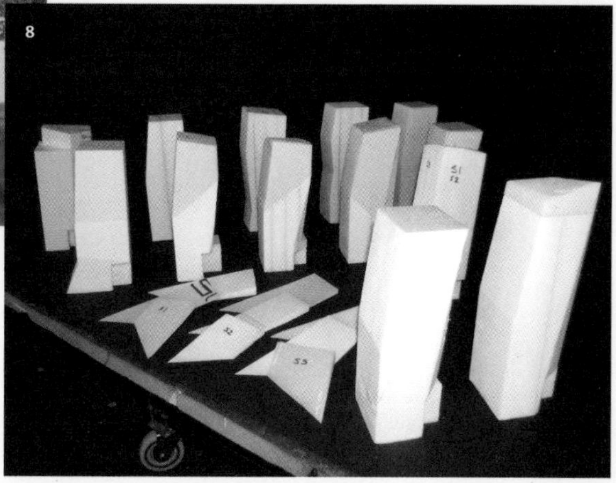

play structure

New York, New York

Project Team: Marc Gee, Katie Winter
Lot Size: 2,400 sf (223 m^2)
Building Size: 2,400 sf (223 m^2)
Date of Design: 2002
Completion Date: 2003 first phase, second phase interiors TBD

Housed in makeshift space next to its parish church, this elementary school had no gymnasium. We used a small adjacent vacant lot owned by the church to create an unconventional year-round play space by enclosing the 35-foot by 80-foot site with a greenhouse-like structure that is sunlit, waterproof, and heated in the winter with infrared panels. The roof over the steel structure is translucent plastic, the walls are sliding fiberglass panels that open to provide natural ventilation, which is facilitated by the slope of the steel truss. For one-fifth the price of a conventional gymnasium and almost no operating costs, the children can now go "outside" to play during recess and yet remain "inside" a gym-like space, which works in all seasons and weather.

1

2

3

4

5

6

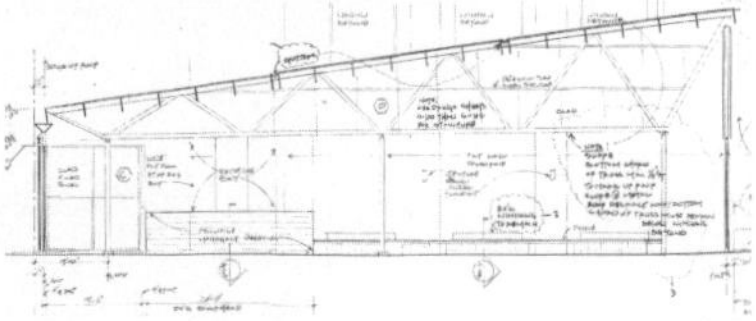

7

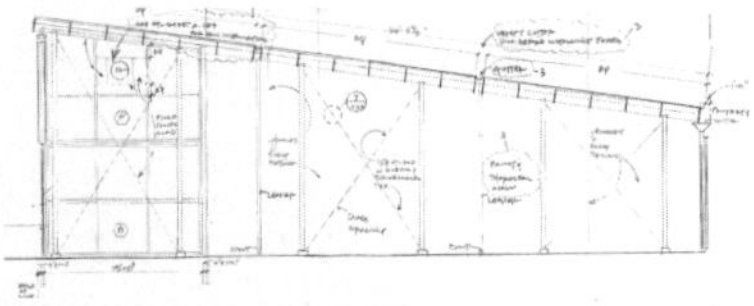

8

1 existing site
2 rear yard view with panels closed
3 view to south
4 view to southeast
5 rear yard view with panels open
6 section to east
7 section to west
8 view to southeast

appendices

firm profile

Located in New York City since 1972, Peter L. Gluck and Partners are known for their integrity of design and sensitivity to the relationship between architectural form and context. Rather than specializing in a particular building type or specific architectural style, the goal is to provide appropriate responses to often difficult and conflicting requirements. The firm has designed buildings throughout the United States, ranging in type from houses, schools, religious buildings, and community centers to hotels, corporate interiors, university buildings, and historic restorations. Many of these projects have won national and international design awards and have been published in architectural journals and books in many countries.

The firm is dedicated to the idea that the architect must take responsibility for the architectural process from conception to construction, assuming oversight of all aspects of design. This commitment led to the establishment of AR/CS (Architectural Construction Services), Inc. in 1992, an integrated system of architectural design and construction management, which provides clients with sophisticated design, quality construction, and unusually low costs in an increasingly difficult building environment. In order to develop these ideas further, Aspen GK, Inc. was established in 1997 as a development partnership, founded to produce both well-designed, high-quality speculative housing and low-cost affordable housing.

Peter Gluck received a Bachelor of Arts from Yale University in 1962 and a Master of Architecture from the Yale School of Art and Architecture in 1965. After designing a series of houses from New York to Newfoundland, he worked in Tokyo designing large projects for a leading Japanese construction consortium. This experience influenced Gluck's later work, both in his knowledge of Japan's traditional aesthetics and of its efficient modern methods of integrated construction and design.

Exhibitions of Gluck's award-winning work have been held in New York, Chicago, Connecticut, and Tokyo. He has taught at Columbia and Yale Schools of Architecture and served on many award selection juries. He has curated museum exhibitions at New York's Museum of Modern Art and the Milano Triennale. In addition to the book *Ten Houses: Peter L. Gluck and Partners* (Rockport, 1997), his work has appeared in many books, newspapers, and journals, including *Architectural Record, Progressive Architecture, Architecture and Urbanism [a + u], Space Design, Japan, Architectural Forum, L'architecture d'aujourdhui, Global Architecture, Architektur.aktuell, Oculus, Interior Design, Industrial Design, Engineering News Record, Artforum, The Columbia Art Review, Architectural Digest, House Beautiful, House and Garden, Wallpaper, Metropolis,* and others.

Recent prizes include multiple AIA awards for the Affordable Housing, the Social Services Center, the Scholar's Library, the Floating Box House, and others.

list of selected projects

Beach House
Westhampton, Long Island, New York
1965

Leisure House
Happy Adventure, Newfoundland
1965

House on the Beach
Sagaponack, Long Island, New York
1966

Model House
Armonk, New York
1966

House on a Lake
Westminster, Vermont
1967

Locus-Bolton Townhouses
Bolton Valley, Vermont
1968

Ardec Housing System
Prefabricated components
1968

Warner Bros.
New York, New York
1978

Waterfront Resort
Key West, Florida
1979

Landscaped Hotel
Ojai, California
1980

Bethesda Fountain Restoration,
Central Park, New York, New York
1980

Cherry Hill Fountain Restoration,
Central Park, New York, New York
1980

Pitch-roof Inversion Farmhouse
Olive Bridge, New York
1980

Medical Center
Napa, California
1981

Two-Sided House
Lincoln, Massachusetts
1982

Arden Homestead, Columbia University
Harriman, New York
1983

Jewelry Store
Soho, New York, New York
1983

Technimetrics Ltd. Warehouse building renovation
and corporate offices
New York, New York
1985

Lloyd's Bank International
New York, New York
1985

Brooklyn Medical Offices
Brooklyn, New York
1985

Pineapple Ltd., Dance studios
New York, New York
1985

Lehrer/McGovern Offices
New York, New York
1985

Uris Hall Addition, Columbia University School of Business
New York, New York
1986

Bloomingdale's
Dallas, Texas
1986

Mies House Addition
Weston, Connecticut
1984-1989

Park Ave Apartment
New York, New York
1986-1989

Yale Club Library
New York, New York
1988

Amev Holding Inc.
World Trade Center, New York, New York
1989

Beldock Levine & Hoffman, Lawyers
New York, New York
1989

Shaare Torah High School
Brooklyn, New York
1989

Hitchcock Presbyterian Church
Scarsdale, New York
1989

Manor House with Music
Mamaroneck, New York
1989

Three-Gable House
Lakeville, Connecticut
1989

Frederick Wildman & Sons, wine-tasting rooms
New York, New York
1992

Usonian House Addition
Pleasantville, New York
1994

Jacobson Partners Offices
New York, New York
1995

Kellner Dileo Offices
New York, New York
1995

Farmhouse with Lap Pool
Worcester, New York
1995

Bridge House
Olive Bridge, New York
1996

Linear House
Millerton, New York
1996

Lake House with Court
Highland Park, Illinois
1997

Corner House
Brooklyn, New York
1998

Cube House
Aspen, Colorado
1998

Community Center
Parkchester, New York
1998

Boat House
Lake George, New York
2001

Glass Veil House
Chicago, Illinois
2001 - design phase

Community Center
Bronx, New York
2001 - design phase

Double House
New Canaan, Connecticut
2002

Synagogue and School Complex
Scarsdale, New York
2002

Zinc House
Aspen, Colorado
2002

Play Structure
New York, New York
2003

Scholar's Library
Olive Bridge, New York
2003

Family Health Services Center
New York, New York
2005

Bar House
Aspen, Colorado
2005

Inverted Outbuilding
Lake George, New York
2005

Burlingame Affordable Housing Competition
Aspen, Colorado
2005

Urban Tower
New York, New York
2005 - design phase, in progress

Charter School
Bronx, New York
2006

Floating Box House
Austin, Texas
2006

Affordable Housing
Aspen, Colorado
2006

Tower House
Ulster County, New York
2006 - design phase, 2008 - completion

Urban Condo
New York, New York
2006 - design phase, 2007 - completion

House on the Bluff
Winnetka, Illinois
2006 - design phase, 2009 - completion

House in Historic District
Evanston, Illinois
2006 - design phase, 2008 - completion

Residential Compound in San Rafael
San Rafael, California
2006 - design phase, 2008 - completion

High Tech Offices
Aspen, Colorado
2006 - design phase, 2008 - completion

Harlem School
East Harlem, New York
2006 - design phase, 2008 - completion

Pool Pavillion
Lake George, New York
2006 - design phase, 2008 - completion

Urban Development
New York, New York
2006 - design phase, in progress

Family Compound on a Lake
Lake George, New York
2007 - design phase, in progress

2007

Zacks, Stephen. "Peter Gluck's Social Work." Metropolis, September.
Giovannini, Joseph. "Above and Beyond." Architectural Digest, October.
von Westersheimb, Kay. "The American New Way." Nuevo Estilo Diseño Arquitectura, No. 88.
Vercelloni, Mateo. "Volume sospesso/Suspended volumes." Interni, August.
Pearson, Clifford A. "Peter Gluck builds an open-and-shut case for inventive design with the Inverted Guest House." Architectural Record, July.
Chan, Yenna. Contemporary Design in Detail: Small Environments." Rockport Publishers.
The AD 100, *Architectural Digest*, January.
Ultimate New York Design, *Loft Publications*.

2006

Trulove, James Grayson. "A Lookout for Learning." *New York Spaces*, November.
Liu, Rowena. "Inverted Guest House, Lake George New York." *IW Magazine*, Vol 52, November.
McCown. "1 of a Kind." *Continental*, November.
"Floating Box House" Texas Architect, September/October.
Sullivan, Thomas D. "Architecture Lessons." *Oculus*, Summer.
Wettstein, Kay. "Neue Modern." *md, mobel interior design*, September.
Trulove, James Grayson. *The New Glass House*. Boston: Bulfinch.
Bell, Jonathan. "Gluck of the Draw." *Wallpaper**, June/July.
Read, Laura. "Affordable Housing Solutions." *Tahoe Quarterly, Mountain Home.*

2005

Beekman, Kimberly. "Mountain Modernism." *Ski Magazine's Mountain Home*, December.
Yee, Roger. "Build This If you Can." *Oculus*, Summer.
Lubell, Sam. "Five Cubes and a Blimp." *Architectural Record*, April.
von Westersheimb, Kay. "House in New Canaan, Connecticut." *Architektur.aktuell*, April.
Bronx Preparatory Charter School. *Real Estate and Construction Review*, vol. 4.
2004 AIA New York Chapter Design Awards. *Oculus*, vol. 67, issue 1, pp. 19-20.

2004

Riera Ojeda, Oscar, and James McCown. *Colors*. Gloucester: Rockport Publishers.
Riera Ojeda, Oscar, and James McCown. *Spaces*. Gloucester: Rockport Publishers.
Guiney, Anne. "AIA-NY Announces 2004 Award Winners," *The Architect's Newspaper*, 19 October.
North Reiss, Gwen. "The New Canaan Continuum." *Connecticut Cottages and Gardens*, October.
Barbanel, Josh. "Charter School Rises in Bronx on Hill of Gifts," *New York Times*, 30 May.
Louie, Elaine. "Currents: Adding Some Color to Make Children's Days Brighter," *New York Times*, 22 April.
Giovannini, Joseph. "On Breaking the Mold." *Architectural Digest*, March.
The AD 100, *Architectural Digest*, January.

2003

Williams, Joe. "Klein's Plan: Build Cheap," *Daily News*, 3 November.
Riera Ojeda, Oscar, ed. *40:Houses*. Gloucester: Rockport Publishers.
Butler, Dana. "Aspen Modern." *Aspen Magazine*, late summer/fall.
Gluck, Peter L. and Bill Stirling. "Tall Versus Sprawl." *Aspen Magazine*, late summer/fall.
Riera Ojeda, Oscar, and Mark Pasnik. *Materials*. Gloucester: Rockport Publishers.
Riera Ojeda, Oscar, and Mark Pasnik. *Elements*. Gloucester: Rockport Publishers.
Eck, Jeremiah. *The Distinctive Home*. Newtown: Taunton Press.
"Great Design." *Architectural Digest*, May.

2002

Brozan, Nadine. "New Building in E. Harlem for Family Health Services," *New York Times*, 28 April.
The AD 100, *Architectural Digest*, January.

2001

Webb, Michael, and Roger Straus III. "Mies van der Rohe, Wolf House." *Modernism Reborn: Mid-Century American Houses*. New York: Universe Publishing.
Grayson Trulove, James, and Il Kim. "House on Lake Michigan." *New American House III*. New York: Watson-Guptill Publications
The AD 100, *Architectural Digest*.

2000

Asensio Cerver, Francisco. *Houses of the World*. Cologne: Konemann.
Pochoda, Elisabeth. "Light Catcher." *House and Garden*, January.
The AD 100, *Architectural Digest*, January.

1999

Chung, Sarah S., "Castle or eyesore?" *Aspen Times Weekly*, 2,3 October.
Iovine, Julie V. "Bridge into the Trees," *New York Times*, 18 February.

1998

Schmertz, Mildred. "North Shore New Wave." *Architectural Digest*, July.
Asensio Cerver, Francisco. *Architects of the World*. New York: Whitney Library of Design.

1997

Riera Ojeda, Oscar, ed. *Ten Houses*. Gloucester: Rockport Publishers, 1997. (monograph).
Riera Ojeda, Oscar. "Mies House Pavilions and Second Addition." *The New American House 2*. New York: Watson-Guptill Publications.

1996

Geran, Monica, "Use of computers at Peter L. Gluck and Partners," *Hyper Realistic*. New York: McGraw Hill
"Tasting room for an importer of fine wines." *Interior Design*, October.
The AD 100, *Architectural Digest*, September.
Goldberger, Paul. "Sleek Geometries in Upstate New York." *Architectural Digest*, June
Hoyt, Charles K. "Record Houses: Annex Supports Varied Pursuits." *Architectural Record*, April.

1994

"Wright Thinking." *Hudson Valley Magazine*. October
Louie, Elaine. "Updating Wright's Ideal," *New York Times*, 5 May.

1993

Larson, Kent. "A Virtual Landmark: Kahn's Unbuilt Synagogue." *Progressive Architecture*, September.

1992
Goldberger, Paul. "Modifying Mies: Peter L. Gluck Rises to the Modernist's Challenge." *Architectural Digest*, February.

1991
"Computer Modeling as a Design Tool." *Progressive Architecture*, October.
The AD 100 Architects, *Architectural Digest*, August.
Dixon, John Morris. "Geometry Meets Tradition." *Progressive Architecture*, April.

1990
"Contemporary Tradition: A Multifaceted Design for a Westchester County Residence." *Architectural Digest*, December.

1986
Kimball, Roger. "Business as More Than Usual: Addition to Uris Hall." *Architectural Record*, April.
"Uris Hall Addition at Columbia University." *Building Stone Magazine*, January/February.

1985
"Pavilion and Pool at Mies van der Rohe House." *Global Architecture Houses* #17, February.
"A New Facade for Modernism." *The Columbia Art Review*, Spring.
"Manhattan job fights tight city site." *Engineering News-Record*, 25 April.
"Reasserting a Beaux-Arts Tradition: An Expansion Plan for Columbia's Business School." *Architectural Record*, February.
"Delafield Estate." *Progressive Architecture*, January.

1984
G., M.F. "High-Tech, High Touch." *Architectural Record*, September.
Sorkin, Michael. "A Masterful Meeting: Architect Peter L. Gluck adds to a Classic House by Mies van der Rohe." *House and Garden*, January.
Yee, Roger. "Technimetrics' Ugly Duckling Lays Golden Eggs." *Corporate Design & Realty*, November/December.
"Return to Grace: Residence, Southern Connecticut." *Progressive Architecture*, April.

1983
Sorkin, Michael. "Architecture: Peter L. Gluck." *Architectural Digest*, October.

1982
Sorkin, Michael. "Architect's House in Ulster County." *Architectural Digest*, December.

1981
Reed, Henry Hope, and Helen Searing. Speaking a New Classicism: *American Architecture Now*. Northhampton: Smith College Museum of Art.
"Trancas Medical Building." *Architectural Record*, April.

1980
"Marriott's Casa Marina Inn." *Architectural Record*, July.

1979
H., C.K. "The Ojai Valley Inn Addition." *Architectural Record*, March.

1978
"Eleven Works of Peter L. Gluck." *Space Design*, Japan, August.

1977
Gluck, Peter L. "Inner Space," *Subways of the World Examined by Cooper-Hewitt Museum*. New York: The Smithsonian Institute.
"Forty Under Forty." *Architecture and Urbanism*, January.
Howell, Betje. "Japan Has Two Faces," *Los Angeles Herald-Examiner*, 17 July.
Seidenbaum, Art. "Japanese Urban Love Feast," *Los Angeles Times*, 29 June.
Degener, Patricia. "The Cultural Complexity of Tokyo's Phenomenal City," *St. Louis Post-Dispatch*, 30 January

1976
Freudenheim, Leslie M. "A case against Baltimore's subway being too clean, sterile," *The Baltimore Sun*. 9 November.
Kelly, Jacques. "Tokyo's Vitality A Tip to Downtown," *The News American*, 21 October.
Patton, Phil. "Shinjuku: The Phenomenal City, Museum of Modern Art." *Artforum*, March.
Hoelterhoff, Manuela. "A Fabulous Artificial City," *Wall Street Journal*, 23 February.
Wiseman, Carter S. "Planning by the People." *Newsweek*, 9 February.
Huxtable, Ada Louise. "Japan Builds the Ultimate Megastructure," *New York Times*, 18 January.

1975
Goldberger, Paul. "Tokyo's Shinjuku: Chaos of Unplanning" *New York Times*, 16 December.

1973
Gluck, Peter L., and Henry Smith. "Shinjuku." *Architecture and Urbanism*, August.

1972
"Peter Gluck, Bookstaver House." *Architecture and Urbanism*, September.
Skurka, Norman. "The best of two worlds." *New York Times Magazine*, 27 August.

1970
"17th Annual Design Review." *Industrial Design*, December.

1969
"Logical Land Use." *The Architectural Forum*, December.
"His Joy is to Build." *House Beautiful*, July.
Guilfoyle, Roger J. "A Standard for Living." *Industrial Design*, March.
"Vacation Houses, Primarily for Skiers, Completed in Vermont," *New York Times*, 19 January.

1968
"Habitations." *l'architecture d'aujourdhui*, February – March.

1967
"Light and Air Houses: Peter Gluck, Architect." *Progressive Architecture*, July

photographic credits

Dan Bibb
Corner House,
Social Services Center

Amy Barkow
Charter School

Henry Bowles
Mies House Addition

Carla Breeze
Farmhouse with Lap Pool

Carlos von Frankenberg
(Julius Shulman Associates)
Hillside Hotel

Wayne Fujii
Mies House Addition

David Glomb
Lake House with Court

Jeff Goldberg (Esto)
House for Music

David Hingston
MoMA Exhibition

Timothy Hursley
Suburban Church

David Macleod Joseph
Corner House (models)

Pablo Mandel
Inverted Outbuilding (model)
Corner House (models),
Double House (models),
Floating Box House (models)

Norman McGrath
Farmhouse Renovation,
Mies House Addition,
Usonian House Addition,
Lake House with Court,
Two-Sided House,
House for Music,
Three-Gable House

Steve Mundinger
Zine House

Barry Rustin
Lake House with Court

Roger Straus III
Mies House Addition

Paul Warchol
Business School Addition,
Mies House Addition,
Farmhouse with Lap Pool,
Linear House,
Bridge House,
Bar House,
Inverted Outbuilding,
Lake House with Court,
Double House,
Corner House,
Social Services Center,
Floating Box House

book credits

historical information:

Charter School Site History,
The Bronx County Historical Society,
Inner City Press Bronx Reporter,
City of New York Department of Housing Preservation and Development,
Bathgate Urban Renewal Project

renderings:

Andrew Deibel (c-2am)
Community Center,
Charter School

David Freeland (c-2am)
Glass Veil House

Leif Halverson (m.o.v.e.)
Floating Box House

book concept:
Oscar Riera Ojeda

graphic desgin, and layout
Oscar Riera Ojeda,
Pablo Mandel,
Ian B. Szymkowiak

editorial assistance:
Agna Brayshaw,
Sandra Ho,
Rosemary Suh

editorial advice:
Carol Gluck
Tom Gluck

Peter Gluck & Partners, Architects
646 W 131st Street
New York, NY 10027
info@gluckpartners.com
www.gluckpartners.com

editor Oscar Riera Ojeda is a publisher and designer based in Philadelphia and New York. Born in Buenos Aires,Argentina in 1966, he moved to the United States in 1990. Since that time, Mr. Riera Ojeda has completed more than one hundred books, working with publishers ORO editions, Birkhäuser, Byggförlaget, The Monacelli Press, Gustavo Gili, Thames & Hudson, Rizzoli, Whitney Library of Design, Taschen, Images, Rockport, and Kliczkowski. Mr. Riera Ojeda is also the creator of several series of architectural books including Architecture in Detail, Art and Architecture, Contemporary World Architects, Ten Houses, The New American Apartment, as well as The New American House.

Oscar Riera Ojeda & Associates
Architecture Art Design
143 South Second Street, Suite 208
Philadelphia, PA 19106-3073
Telephone: 215.238.1333
Facsimile: 215.238.1103
www.oro-associates.com

copyright

ORO *editions*
Gordon Goff & Oscar Riera Ojeda
Publishers

West Coast
PO Box 150338,
San Rafael, CA 94915
Telephone: 415-456-0789

East Coast
143 South 2nd Street, Suite 208
Philadelphia, PA 19106-3039
Telephone: 215-238-1333

www.oroeditions.com
info@oroeditions.com

Library of Congress Catalog
Card Number
ISBN: 978-0-9746800-5-2
Peter Gluck, Architecture: The Modern Impulse

Printed in China by ORO *editions* HK

Distribution
USA:
Distributed Art Publishers, Inc.
155 Sixth Avenue, Second Floor
New York, NY 10013
United States

United Kingdom:
RIBA Bookshops
15 Bonhill Street,
London, EC2P 2EA
UK

Asia:
Page One Publishing Private Ltd.
20 Kaki Bukit View
Kaki Bukit Techpark II
Singapore 415967